Yale Egyptological Studies 9

A Royal Book of Protection of the Saite Period: pBrooklyn 47.218.49

Yale Egyptological Studies

Yale Egyptological Studies 9

A Royal Book of Protection of the Saite Period

pBrooklyn 47.218.49

Paul F. O'Rourke

Yale Egyptological Institute · New Haven, CT

Yale Egyptological Studies 9

ISBN 978-0-9740025-7-6

The drawing of the ear is adapted by Téa Jukyong Beer based on:
Ear, 1539–1075 BC. Wood, 1 × 1/2 × 2 1/5 in (2.5 × 1.2 × 5.7 cm);
Brooklyn Museum, Charles Edwin Wilbour Fund, 37.2041.4E

Library of Congress Cataloging-in-Publication Data

O'Rourke, Paul F. (Egyptologist)
A royal book of protection of the Saite period : pBrooklyn 47.218.49 / Paul F. O'Rourke.
pages cm -- (Yale Egyptological studies ; 9)
In English and Egyptian.
Includes bibliographical references and index.
ISBN 978-0-9740025-7-6 (acid-free paper)
1. Brooklyn Museum of Art. Manuscript. P. Brooklyn 47.218.49. 2. Egyptian language--Papyri, Hieratic. 3. Egyptian language--Papyri, Hieroglyphic. 4. Inscriptions, Egyptian. 5. Protection magic--Egypt--History--Sources. 6. Egypt--Kings and rulers--Protection--History--Sources. 7. Egypt--History--To 332 B.C.--Sources. 8. Egypt--Religious life and customs--Sources. I. Brooklyn Museum of Art. II. Title.
PJ1681.B75O76 2014
893'.1--dc23
2014033247

Typeset in Minion Pro and Warnock Pro,
Transliterations in Transliteration v. 2.0,
Hieroglyphics in JSesh (v. 4.3).

Printed in the United States of America on acid-free paper.

For Barbara

who made this and
so much more
in my life
possible

Contents

List of Plates

List of Tables

Acknowledgments

This book is a reworked version of a dissertation submitted to the Department of Middle Eastern and Islamic Studies of New York University in the academic year 2001–2002. The original translation has been improved upon, the commentary has been considerably expanded, the bibliography has been brought up to date, and much that is here reflects my change in thinking about the original composition of the papyrus. I wish to thank Richard Fazzini, Chairman Emeritus of the Egyptian Department of the Brooklyn Museum and Head of the Brooklyn Mut Expedition, for originally granting me permission to study and publish *pBrooklyn 47.218.49*.

I have many to thank for their eyes and ears during the writing and revisions of this work. In addition to granting permission to publish this papyrus, Richard Fazzini has, for many years now, routinely put at my disposal his encyclopedic knowledge of Egyptian thought, art, and religion, and over that time he taught me how to think about some of the more arcane matters that one routinely encounters in this field of study. I would also like to thank my other colleagues in the Egyptian Department of the Brooklyn Museum: Dr. Edna R. Russmann, Curator Emeritus, Dr. Edward Bleiberg, Curator, Dr. Yekaterina Barbash, Associate Curator, the late Dr. James F. Romano, Curator, and Kathy Zurek-Doule, Curatorial Assistant. They continue to be a supportive family in all of my work and endeavors.

The original study of the Brooklyn papyrus could not have been done without my graduate school advisor, Dr. Ogden Goelet. He was a steadfast source of support and on more than one occasion helped me to ground myself in reality. I would like to thank Dr. Richard Jasnow of Johns Hopkins University for his thoughtful comments on a preliminary draft of my dissertation from which I profited greatly. I also thank Mr. William Hogeland for reading an early draft of this work. His comments and advice were enormously helpful. Dr. Hans Fischer-Elfert read a draft of the book in 2010 and made a number of helpful suggestions and pointed out a few bibliographic items that I had overlooked. I thank Dr. John Coleman Darnell and Dr. Colleen Manassa as well. Both of them read through sections of the text, and their ideas about the reorganization of some of the material were quite useful and have helped improve the overall structure of this work. I thank them also for their suggestions about bibliography. My heartfelt thanks also go to Mary McKercher, Chief Photographer of the Brooklyn Mut Expedition. She not only took the photographs for the plates of this work, but spent many hours photoshopping them, maneuvering misplaced fragments into their proper positions. Her help here has been immeasurable. I benefited greatly from several discussions with Dr. Yeketerina Barbash about some of my readings of the more difficult sections of the papyrus. Dr. Joachim Quack was kind enough to look over my transcription of the difficult seventh column of the papyrus and help confirm some of my readings and make suggestions for improvements on some others. I thank Drs. Barbash and Quack for their help and input. Needless to say, I claim all responsibility for any errors that remain. I thank my former student, Téa Jukyong Beer, Yale Class of 2017, for the line drawing of the ear that appears on the cover and is used as a logo throughout the book. I also thank Susanne Wilhelm, Design and Production Manager at ISD, for her helpful and patient guidance during the transformation of manuscript to book. I thank the William K. and Marilyn M. Simpson Egyptology Endowment Fund of the Department of Near Eastern Languages and Civilizations, Yale University, for making this publication possible.

For their professional, financial and collegial support of my pursuit of an advanced degree, I would like to thank the administration of St. Ann's School in Brooklyn where I served on the faculty from the fall of 1969 until the spring of 2003. My thanks go particularly to the late Stanley Bosworth, Headmaster Emeritus, Linda Kaufman, former Associate Head of School and now Senior Advisor to the Head of School and Archivist, and Risa Pollock, former Director of Finance.

I owe a debt of gratitude to Andrew and Eleanor Beer, Founders of Pierrepont School in Westport, Connecticut, where I currently serve as Head of Languages and Humanities, for their steadfast encouragement and support of my professional career outside of the school. I also thank Nancy Webber, Head of School and Tunde Jackson, Associate Head of School, for the flexible schedule that allows me to happily serve two masters, Pierrepont School and the Brooklyn Museum.

Finally, I would like to thank the members of my family, my late wife Barbara, my daughter Meghan, and my sons Liam and Eamon. My children continue to be my strongest advocates and kindest critics, listening with patience and thought to the ideas and reflections that I have routinely come to share with them. My wife never failed to encourage and humor me in any of my endeavors, especially at those moments when I had reached the threshold of frustration with a project. During the two and one-half years of the illness which eventually claimed her, she did nothing but encourage me to continue with my work. For her love and her support beyond measure, I thank her and dedicate this work to her and to her memory. It is my most profound regret that she did not live to see it in its final, published form.

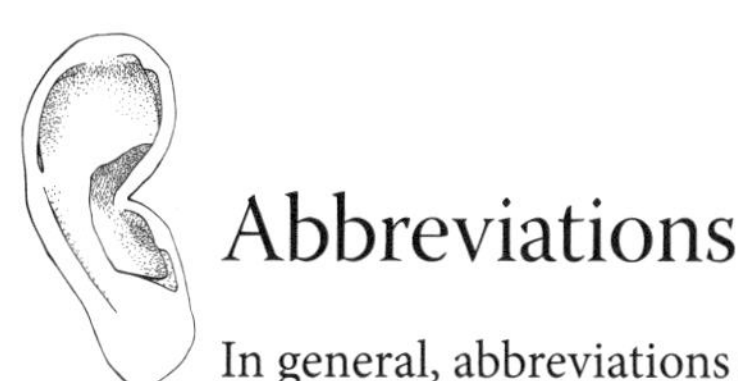

Abbreviations

In general, abbreviations are based on those used in W. Helck and E. Otto, eds., *Lexikon der Ägyptologie*, 7 vols. (Wiesbaden 1975–1989).

JOURNALS AND STANDARD REFERENCE WORKS

AnAe	*Analecta Aegyptiaca*
ADAIK	*Abhandlungen des Deutschen Archäologischen Instituts Kairo*
ÄA	*Ägyptologische Abhandlungen*
ÄAT	*Ägypten und Altes Testament*
ACF	*Annuaire du Collège de France*
Aeg	*Aegyptus. Rivista italiana di egittologica e di papirologia*
ÄF	*Ägyptologische Forschungen*
AoF	*Altorientalische Forschungen*
AH	*Aegyptiaca Helvetica*
ÄIB	*Ägyptische Inschriften aus den königlichen Museen zu Berlin* (Leipzig: J.C. Hinrichs, 1913–1924)
ALex	*Année lexicographique*
AnBib	*Studia Biblica et Orientalia* (Rome: Pontificio Istituto Biblico, 1959)
AnOr	*Analecta Orientalia*
APAW	*Abhandlungen der Preussischen Akademie der Wissenschaften*
ASAE	*Annales du Service des Antiquités de l'Égypte*
BACE	*Bulletin of the Australian Centre for Egyptology*
BdE	*Bibliothèque d'Étude*
BdEC	*Bibliothèque d'Études Coptes*
BIE	*Bulletin de l'Institut d'Égypte*
BIFAO	*Bulletin de l'Institut français d'archéologie orientale*
BMA	*Brooklyn Museum Annual*
BSAK	*Studien zur altägyptischen Kultur. Beihefte*
BSEG	*Bulletin de la Société d'égyptologie de Genève*
BSFE	*Bulletin de la Société française d'égyptologie*
CD	Faulkner, R.O., *A Concise Dictionary of Middle Egyptian* (Oxford: Griffith Institute, 1962)
CdE	*Chronique d'Égypte*
CG	*Catalogue général des antiquités égyptiennes du Musée du Caire*
CLES	*Corpus of Late Egyptian Sculpture*
DAWW	*Denkschrift der kaiserlichen Akademie der Wissenschaften in Wien, philosophisch-historische Klasse*

DG	Gauthier, H., *Dictionnaire géographique,* 7 vols. (Cairo: IFAO, 1925–1932)
DIE	*Discussions in Egyptology*
DLE	Lesko, L., *A Dictionary of Late Egyptian,* 5 vols. (Berkeley, CA: Scribe, 1984–1990)
EG[3]	Gardiner, A.H., *Egyptian Grammar,* 3rd ed. rev. (London: Griffith Institute, 1957)
Enchoria	*Enchoria. Zeitschrift für Demotistik und Koptologie*
ÉPHE	*École practique des hautes études*
EU	*Egyptologische Uitgaven*
FIFAO	*Fouilles de l'Institut français d'archéologie orientale du Caire*
GH	Hannig, R., *Grosses Handwörterbuch Ägyptisch-Deutsch* (Mainz: von Zabern, 2001)
GM	*Göttinger Miszellen*
GOF	*Göttinger Orientforschungen*
HÄB	*Hildesheimer Ägyptologische Beiträge*
HAT	*Handschriften des altägyptischen Totenbuches*
HP	Möller, G., *Hieratische Paläographie,* 3 vols. (Leipzig: J.C. Hinrichs, 1927–36)
HPBM	*Facsimiles of Egyptian Hieratic Papyri in the British Museum*
JARCE	*Journal of the American Research Center in Egypt*
JEA	*Journal of Egyptian Archaeology*
JEH	*Journal of Egyptian History*
JEOL	*Jaarbericht van het Vooraziatisch-Egyptisch Genootschap (Gezelschap) "Ex Oriente Lux"*
JNES	*Journal of Near Eastern Studies*
JSSEA	*Journal of the Society for the Study of Egyptian Antiquities*
KÄT	*Kleine Ägyptische Texte*
Kêmi	*Kêmi. Revue de philologie et d'archéologie égyptiennes et coptes*
LÄ	Helck, W., E. Otto, and W. Westendorf, eds., *Lexikon der Ägyptologie,* 7 vols. (Wiesbaden: Harrassowitz, 1975–1989)
LEG	Černý, J. and S.I. Groll, *A Late Egyptian Grammar,* 3rd updated ed. Studia Pohl. Series Maior 4 (Rome: Biblical Institute, 1984)
LingAeg	*Lingua Aegyptia. Journal of Egyptian Language Studies*
MÄS	*Münchener Ägyptologische Studien*
MAFC	*Mission archéologique française au Caire. Mémoires*
MDAIK	*Mitteilungen des Deutschen Archäologischen Instituts. Abteilung Kairo*
Mélanges Dussaud	*Mélanges syriens offerts à M. Réne Dussaud* (Paris: P. Geuthner, 1939)
Mélanges Michałowski	*Mélanges offerts à Kazimierz Michałowski* (Warsaw: Państwowe Wydawnictwo Naukowe, 1966)
MIFAO	*Mémoires publiés par les membres de l'Institut français d'archéologie orientale du Caire*

MIO	*Mitteilungen des Instituts für Orientforschung*
MRE	*Monographies Reine Élisabeth*
NG	Erman, A., *Neuägyptische Grammatik*, Zweite, völlig umgestaltete Auflage (Leipzig: W. Engelmann, 1933)
OBO	*Orbis biblicus et orientalis*
OIP	*Oriental Institute Publications. The University of Chicago*
OLA	*Orientalia Lovaniensia Analecta*
OLP	*Orientalia Lovaniensia Periodica*
OMRO	*Oudheidkundige Mededelingen uit het Rijksmuseum van Oudheden te Leiden*
Or	*Orientalia: Commentarii periodici Pontificii instituti biblici*
PDM	Betz, H.D., ed., *The Greek Magical Papyri in Translation, Including the Demotic Spells* (Chicago: University of Chicago, 1992)
PGM	K. Preisendanz, *Papyri graecae magicae. Die griechischen Zauberpapyri*, vol. 1 (Leipzig: Teubner, 1928)
PL	P. Wilson, *A Ptolemaic Lexicon*. OLA 78 (Leuven: Peeters, 1997)
PSBA	*Proceedings of the Society of Biblical Archaeology*
RdE	*Revue d'égyptologie*
RIHAO	*Revista del Instituto de Historia Antigua Oriental*
RT	*Recueil des travaux relatifs à la philologie et à l'archéologie égyptiennes et assyriennes*
StudAeg	*Studia Aegyptiaca*
SAGA	*Studien zur Archäologie und Geschichte Altägyptens*
SAK	*Studien zur Altägyptischen Kultur*
SAOC	*Studies in Ancient Oriental Civilization*
SASEA	*Supplements aux Annales du Service du Antiquités de l'Égypte*
SBAW	*Sitzungsberichte der Bayerischen Akademie der Wissenschaften*
SO	*Sources Orientales*
SSR	*Studien zur spätägyptischen Religion*
UGAÄ	*Untersuchungen zur Geschichte und Altertumskunde Ägyptens*
Urk.	*Urkunden des ägyptischen Altertums*
Urk. VI	S. Schott, *Urkunden mythologischen Inhalts*. Erstes Heft. *Bücher und Sprüche gegen den Gott Seth* (Leipzig: J.C. Hinrichs, 1929)
Wörterbuch	Erman, A. and H. Grapow, eds. *Wörterbuch der ägyptischen Sprache*, 7 vols. (Leipzig: J.C. Hinrichs; Berlin: Akademie-Verlag, 1st ed.: 1926–1931; 2nd ed.: 1957)
Wb.	Erman, A. and H. Grapow, eds. *Wörterbuch der ägyptischen Sprache*, 7 vols. (Leipzig: J.C. Hinrichs; Berlin: Akademie-Verlag, 1st ed.: 1926–1931, 2nd ed.: 1957)
WbDN	von Deines, H., H. Grapow, and W. Westendorf, *Wörterbuch der ägyptischen Drogennamen*. Grundriss der Medizin der alten Ägypter 6 (Berlin: Akademie-Verlag, 1959)

WbMT	von Deines, H. and W. Westendorf, *Wörterbuch der medizinischen Texte.* Grundriss der Medizin der alten Ägypter 7/1–2 (Berlin: Akademie-Verlag, 1961)
Wilbour Monographs	*Wilbour Monographs* (Brooklyn)
WZKM	*Wiener Zeitschrift für die Kunde des Morgenlandes*
YES	*Yale Egyptological Studies*
ZÄS	*Zeitschrift für ägyptische Sprache und Altertumskunde*

TEXT PUBLICATIONS AND TERMS

AEMT	Borghouts, J., *Ancient Egyptian Magical Texts.* Nisbada 9 (Leiden: Brill, 1978)
AEO	Gardiner, A.H., *Ancient Egyptian Onomastica,* 2 vols. (London: Oxford University, 1947)
Amduat	Hornung, E., *Das Amduat. Die Schrift des verborgenen Raumes,* ÄA 7 (Wiesbaden: Harrassowitz, 1963)
BD	Book of the Dead (cited by spell number; translations mine)
Book of Caverns	Piankoff, A., "Le livre des Quererts," *BIFAO* 41 (1942): 1–11; *BIFAO* 42 (1944): 13–74; *BIFAO* 43 (1945): 1–90; *BIFAO* 45 (1947): 1–42
CLEM	Caminos, R., *Late Egyptian Miscellanies,* Brown Egyptological Studies 1 (Oxford: Oxford University, 1954)
CT	Coffin Texts (cited by spell number; translations mine)
Dendara	Chassinat, E. and F. Daumas, *Le Temple de Dendara,* 9 vols. (Cairo: IFAO, 1934–1987)
Edfu	Chassinat, E. and Le Marquis de Rochemonteix, *Le Temple d'Edfou,* 14 vols. MAFC, Mémoires 10–11; 20–31 (Cairo: IFAO, 1897–1985)
Esna	Sauneron, S., *Esna,* 8 vols. (Cairo: IFAO, 1959–82)
GLEM	Gardiner, A.H., *Late-Egyptian Miscellanies.* Bibliotheca Aegyptiaca 7 (Brussels: Fondation Égyptologique Reine Élisabeth, 1937)
Gunn, *Studies*	Gunn, B., *Studies in Egyptian Syntax* (Paris: P. Geuthner, 1924)
HO	Gardiner, A.H., and J. Černý, *Hieratic Ostraca* 1 (Oxford: Griffith Institute 1957)
KRI	Kitchen, K., *Ramesside Inscriptions: Historical and Biographical,* 8 vols. (Oxford: Blackwell, 1969–1990)
Litany of Re	Piankoff, A., *The Litany of Re,* Bollingen Series 40, Egyptian Religious Texts and Representations 4 (New York: Bollingen Foundation, 1964)
Livre de la Nuit	Roulin, G., *Le livre de la nuit,* OBO 147/1–2 (Fribourg: Universitätsverlag, 1996)
LJ	Piankoff, A., *Le livre du jour et de la nuit* (*Livre du jour* only) (Cairo: IFAO, 1942)

LJN	Piankoff, A., *Le livre du jour et de la nuit* (Cairo: IFAO, 1942)
LN	Piankoff, A., *Le livre du jour et de la nuit* (*Livre de la nuit* only) (Cairo: IFAO 1942)
Manetho	Waddell, W.G., *Manetho,* Loeb Classical Library 350 (Cambridge: Harvard University, 1980)
MuK	Erman, A., *Zaubersprüche für Mutter und Kind aus dem Papyrus 3027 des Berliner Museums* (Berlin: Verlag der Königlichen Akademie der Wissenschaften, 1901)
Mythes et légendes	Meeks, D., *Mythes et légendes du Delta d'après le papyrus Brooklyn 47.218.84,* MIFAO 125 (Cairo: IFAO, 2006)
n.	note
Oracle Papyrus	Parker, R., *A Saite Oracle Papyrus from Thebes in The Brooklyn Museum [Papyrus Brooklyn 47.218.3],* Brown Egyptological Studies 4 (Providence: Brown University, 1962)
o	ostracon
oGlasgow	McDowell, A.G., *Hieratic Ostraca in the Hunterian Museum, Glasgow* (Oxford: Griffith Institute, 1993)
oNash	Borghouts, J.F., "The Ram as Protector and Prophesier," *RdE* 32 (1980): 33–46
p	papyrus
pAmunhymnus	Zandee, J., *Der Amunhymnus des Papyrus Leiden I 344,* Verso, 3 vols. Collections of the National Museum of Antiquities at Leiden 7 (Leiden: Rijksmuseum van Oudheden, 1992)
pAnastasi 2	Gardiner, A.H., *Late-Egyptian Miscellanies,* Bibliotheca Aegyptiaca 7 (Brussels: Fondation Égyptologique Reine Élisabeth, 1937): pls. 12–20
pBerlin 3038	Wreszinski, W., *Die Medizin der alten Ägypter* 1. *Der grosse medizinische Papyrus des Berliner Museums (Pap. Berl. 3038)* (Leipzig: J.C. Hinrichs, 1909)
pBoulaq 6	Koenig, Y., *Le papyrus Boulaq 6: Transcription, traduction et commentaire,* BdE 87 (Cairo: IFAO, 1981)
pBremner-Rhind	Faulkner, R.O., *The Papyrus Bremner-Rhind (Brit. Mus. No. 10188),* Bibliotheca Aegyptiaca 3 (Brussels: Fondation Égyptologique Reine Élisabeth, 1933)
pBM 9997	Leitz, C., *Magical and Medical Papyri of the New Kingdom,* HPBM 7th ser. (London: British Museum, 1999): 3–21; pls. 1–8
pBM 10042	Leitz, C., *Magical and Medical Papyri of the New Kingdom,* HPBM 7th ser. (London: British Museum, 1999): 31–50; pls. 12–25
pBM 10059	Leitz, C., *Magical and Medical Papyri of the New Kingdom,* HPBM 7th ser. (London: British Museum, 1999): 51–84; pls. 26–46
pBM 10081	Schott, S., "Drei Sprüche gegen Feinde," *ZÄS* 65 (1930): 35–42

pBM 10209	Haikal, F.M.H., *Two Funerary Papyri of Nesmin I–II,* Bibliotheca Aegyptiaca 14 and 15 (Brussels: Fondation Égyptologique Reine Elisabeth, 1970–72)
pBM 10288	Caminos, R., "Another Hieratic Manuscript from the Library of Pwerem Son of Kiki (Pap. B.M. 10288)," *JEA* 58 (1972): 205–24
pBM 10309	Leitz, C., *Magical and Medical Papyri of the New Kingdom,* HPBM 7th ser. (London: British Museum, 1999): 24–30; pls. 9–11
pBM 10474	Lange, H.O., *Das Weisheitsbuch des Amenemope aus dem Papyrus 10474 des British Museum* (Copenhagen: Andr. Fred. Høst, 1925)
pBM 10683	see *pChester Beatty III*
pBrooklyn 47.218.2	unpublished
pBrooklyn 47.218.48+85	see *pOphiologie*
pBrooklyn 47.218.50	see *pConfirmation*
pBrooklyn 47.218.84	see *Mythes et légendes*
pBrooklyn 47.218.87	unpublished
pBrooklyn 47.218.135	see *pBrooklyn Wisdom*
pBrooklyn 47.218.138	see *pProphylaxie*
pBrooklyn 47.218.156	see *pIllustré*
pBrooklyn Wisdom	Jasnow, R., *A Late Period Wisdom Text (P. Brooklyn 47.218.135),* SAOC 52 (Chicago: University of Chicago, 1992)
pBudapest 51.1960	Kákosy, L., "Fragmente eines unpublizierten magischen Textes in Budapest," *ZÄS* 117 (1990: 140–157 and Taf. VI–VII)
pBudapest 51.1961	Kákosy, L., "Ein magischer Papyrus des Kunsthistorischen Museums in Budapest," *Acta Antiqua Academiae Scientiarum Hungaricae* 19: 3–4 (1979): 159–77
pCairo 58027	Pries, A.H., *Das nächtliche Stundenritual zum Schutz des Königs und verwandte Kompositionen. Der Papyrus Kairo 58027 und die Textvarianten in den Geburtshäusern von Dendara und Edfu,* SAGA 27 (Heidelberg: Heidelberger Orientverlag, 2009)
pCairo 86637	Bakir, A., *The Cairo Calendar No. 86637* (Cairo: General Organisation for Govt. Print. Offices, 1937)
pChester Beatty 1	Gardiner, A.H., *The Library of A. Chester Beatty. Description of a Hieratic Papyrus with a Mythological Story, Love Songs, and other Miscellaneous Texts,* The Chester Beatty Papyri, No. 1 (London: Priv. print. by J. Johnson at the Oxford University Press and pub. by E. Walker, limited, 1931)
pChester Beatty 2–19	Gardiner, A.H., *The Chester Beatty Gift,* HPBM 3rd ser., 2 vols (London: British Museum, 1935)
pConfirmation	Goyon, J.-C., *Confirmation du pouvoir royal au nouvel an [Brooklyn Museum Papyrus 47.218.50],* BdE 52 (Cairo: IFAO, 1972) and Wilbour Monographs 7 (Brooklyn: Brooklyn Museum, 1974)

pDeM 36	Sauneron, S., "Le rhume d'Anynakhté," *Kêmi* 20 (1970): 7–18
pDeM 37	Koenig, Y., "Un revenant inconvenant? (Papyrus Deir el-Médineh 37)," *BIFAO* 79 (1979): 103–19
pDeM 40	Koenig, Y., "Les effrois de Keniherkhepeshef (Papyrus Deir el-Médineh 40)," *RdE* 33 (1981): 29–37
pEbers	Wrezinski, W., *Die Medizin der alten Ägypter* 3. *Der Papyrus Ebers* (Leipzig: J.C. Hinrichs, 1913)
pEdwin Smith	Breasted, J.H., *The Edwin Smith Surgical Papyrus,* OIP 3–4 (Chicago: University of Chicago, 1930)
pGeneva MAH 15274	Massart, A., "The Egyptian Geneva Papyrus MAH 15274," *MDAIK* 15 (1957): 172–85
pHearst	Wreszinski, W., *Die Medizin der alten Ägypter* 2. *Der Papyrus Hearst* (Leipzig: J.C. Hinrichs, 1912)
pIllustré	Sauneron, S., *Le papyrus magique illustré Brooklyn [Brooklyn Museum 47.218.156],* Wilbour Monographs 3 (Brooklyn: The Brooklyn Museum, 1970)
pJumilhac	Vandier, J., *Le papyrus Jumilhac* (Paris: Centre National de la Recherche Scientifique, 1962)
pKölner	Kurth, D., H.-J. Thissen, and M. Weber, *Kölner ägyptische Papyri (p. Köln. ägypt.)* (Opladen: Westdeutscher Verlag, 1980)
pLeiden I 343+345	Massart, A., *The Leiden Magical Papyri I 343 + I 345,* OMRO 34 (Supplement) (Leiden: Brill, 1954)
pLeiden I 344	see *pAmunhymnus*
pLeiden I 346	Bommas, M., *Die Mythisierung der Zeit. Die beiden Bücher über die altägyptischen Schalttage des magischen pLeiden I 346,* GO (IV Reihe: Ägypten) 37 (Wiesbaden: Harrassowitz, 1999)
pLeiden I 347	Massy, A., *Le Papyrus de Leiden I 347* (Ghent: H. Engelcke, 1885)
pLeiden I 348	Borghouts, J.F., *The Magical Texts of Papyrus Leiden I 348,* OMRO 51 (Leiden: Brill, 1971)
pLeiden I 349	Buck, A. de and B. Stricker, "Teksten tegen Schorpioenen naar Pap. I 349," *OMRO* 21 (1940): 53–62
pLeiden I 350	Zandee, J., *De Hymnen aan Amun van Papyrus Leiden I 350,* OMRO 28 (Leiden: Brill, 1947)
pLeiden I 358	Klasens, A., "An Amuletic Papyrus of the 25th Dynasty," *OMRO* 56 (1975): 20–28
pLille 139	see *pVandier*
pLouvre I 3079	Goyon, J.-C., "Le cérémonial de glorification d'Osiris du papyrus du Louvre I 3079 (colonnes 110 à 112)," *BIFAO* 65 (1965): 89–156
pLouvre 3176	Barguet, P., *Le papyrus N. 3176(S) du Musée du Louvre,* BdE 37 (Cairo: IFAO, 1962)
pLouvre E3229	Johnson, J.H., "Louvre E3229: A Demotic Magical Text," *Enchoria* 7 (1977): 55–102

pLouvre 3233	Goyon, J.-C., "Un phylactère tardif: Le papyrus 3233 A et B du Musée du Louvre," *BIFAO* 77 (1977): 45–54
pLouvre 3279	Goyon, J.-C., *Le papyrus du Louvre N. 3279*, BdE 42 (Cairo: IFAO, 1966)
pLouvre E 3661	Ledrain, E., "Le papyrus de Luynes," *RT* 1 (1870): 89–95
pLuynes	see *pLouvre E 3661*
pOphiologie	Sauneron, S., *Un traité égyptien d'Ophiologie*, Bibliothèque générale 11 (Cairo: IFAO, 1989)
pProphylaxie	Goyon, J.-C., *Le recueil de prophylaxie contre les aggressions des animaux venimeux du Musée de Brooklyn Papyrus Wilbour 47.218.138*, SSR 5 (Wiesbaden: Harrassowitz, 2012)
pRamesseum	Gardiner, A.H., *The Ramesseum Papyri* (Oxford: Griffith Institute, 1955)
pRylands	Griffith, F.L., *Catalogue of the Demotic Papyri in the John Rylands Library, Manchester, with Facsimiles and Complete Translations* (Manchester: Manchester University, 1909)
pSallier 2	Helck, W., *Der Text des 'Nilhymnus,'* KÄT (Wiesbaden: Harrassowitz, 1972)
pSalt 825	Derchain, P., *Le papyrus Salt 825 (B.M. 10051), rituel pour la conservation de la vie en Égypte* (Brussels: Palais des académies, 1965)
pTurin 1983	Edwards, I.E.S., *Oracular Amuletic Decrees of the Late New Kingdom*, HPBM 4th ser., 2 vols. (London: British Museum, 1960)
pTurin 54050 and 54051	Roccati, A., *Magica Taurinensia. Il grande papiro magico di Torino e i suoi duplicati*, AnOr 56 (Rome: Gregorian and Biblical Press, 2011) (citation by page and line number)
pTurin 54003	Roccati, A., *Papiro Ieratico N. 54003. Estratti magici e rituali del Primo Medio Regno*, Catalogo del Museo egizio di Torino, Seria prima: Monumenti e testi 2 (Turin: Edizioni d'arte F.lli Posso, 1970)
pVandier	Posener, G., *Le Papyrus Vandier*, Bibliothèque générale 7 (Cairo: IFAO, 1985)
pVatican 19a	Suys, P., "Le papyrus magique du Vatican," *Or* 3 (1934): 63–87
pVienna 8426	Flessa, N., *"(Gott) schütze das Fleisch des Pharao:" Untersuchungen zum magischen Handbuch pWien AEG 8426*, Corpus Papyrorum Raineri 27 (Munich: K.G. Sauer, 2006)
PT	Pyramid Texts (cited by spell number; translations mine)
Ramesseum Papyri	Barns, J., *Five Ramesseum Papyri* (Oxford: Griffith Institute, 1956)
rt.	Recto
Sign-list	"List of Hieroglyphic Signs," in Gardiner, A.H., *Egyptian Grammar*, 3rd ed. rev. (London: Griffith Institute, 1957): 438–548

SocBehague	Klasens, A., *A Magical Statue Base (Socle Behague) in the Museum of Antiquities at Leiden*, OMRO 33 (Leiden, 1952)
Sonnenlitanei	Hornung, E., *Das Buch des Anbetung des Re im Westen,* 2 vols. AH 2 (Geneva: Editions de Belles-Lettres, 1975)
Studien Westendorf	Junge, F., ed., *Studien zu Sprache und Religion Ägyptens. Zu Ehren von Wolfhart Westendorf überreicht von seinen Freunden and Schülern,* 2 vols. (Göttingen: Hubert & Co., 1984)
Tebtunis	Tait, W.J., *Papyri from Tebtunis in Egyptian and Greek,* Egypt Exploration Society: Texts from Excavations 3 (London: Egypt Exploration Society, 1977)
vo.	Verso

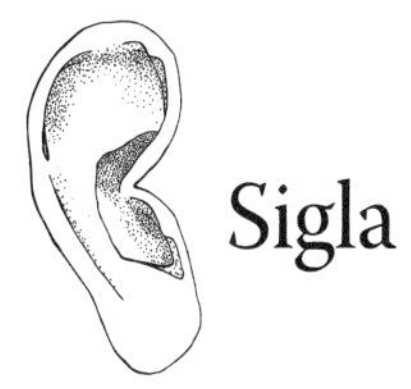

Sigla

The diacritical signs used in the transliteration and translation are given as follows.

…	used in the Transliteration to mark a lacuna in the text
<signs>	used in the Transliteration to mark a sign or signs due to scribal error
{signs}	used in the Transliteration to mark a sign or signs due to a scribal error that was corrected in antiquity
<u>signs</u>	underlining used in the Transliteration to indicate text written in red
[…]	used in the Translation to mark a lacuna in the hieratic text
[words]	used in the Translation to mark the restored reading of a lacuna
(words)	used in the Translation to improve the English reading of the text
words	italics used in the Translation to indicate text written in red

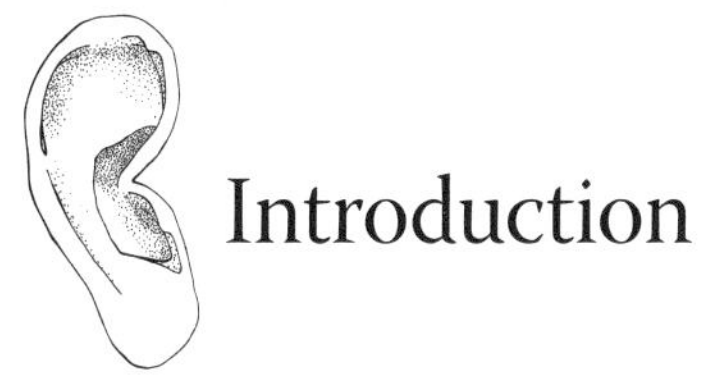

Introduction

*p*BROOKLYN *47.218.49* was acquired by Charles Edwin Wilbour during his sojourns in Egypt between 1881 and 1896.[1] The papyrus came to the museum in 1947,[2] still rolled, as part of a bequest from the estate of Wilbour's daughter, Ms. Theodora Wilbour. That gift consisted of approximately 158 papyri in varying states of preservation.[3] In the winter of 1966–67, the papyrus was unrolled and mounted under glass by Serge Sauneron, along with a number of other papyri from the 1947 bequest.[4] No records giving a description of the unrolling or placing of the fragments exist.[5] Though mentioned in passing in publications of other papyri in the collection of Brooklyn Museum, the papyrus has never been systematically studied.[6]

DESCRIPTION OF THE PAPYRUS

The accession records of the Egyptian collection describe *pBrooklyn 47.218.49* as follows:

Roll of papyrus. Inscribed in Hieratic in red and black. Relatively small hand.
Text unidentified.
Period: [not given]
Measurements: Height, 24 cm.
Provenance: Unknown. Container marked "4·LA".
Bequest of Miss Theodora Wilbour from the collection of her father,
Charles Edwin Wilbour.
Condition. Fair. Tightly rolled. Portions of about ten outer layers lost. Interior fragile but roll can certainly be opened. Only a few loose fragments.

1 On the provenance of the papyrus, see pp. 17ff. below.

2 At that time, the official name of the museum was The Brooklyn Museum.

3 The number 158 represents the number of individual accession numbers assigned to the lots of papyri that form this part of the museum's holdings. It should be noted that many of these lots consist of fragments that belong to a single papyrus. See O'Rourke, "Charles Edwin Wilbour and the Provenance of His Papyri," in V. Lepper, ed., *Essays on Elephantine*; idem, *The Papyri in the Egyptian Collection of the Brooklyn Museum* (forthcoming).

4 Sauneron, *BMA* 8 (1966–67): 98–102; Sauneron, *BMA* 10 (1968–69): 109–13.

5 See pp. 4–5 below concerning the (mis)placement of the fragments of *pBrooklyn 47.218.49*.

6 Sauneron, *Le papyrus magique illustré,* p.17 (henceforth, *pIllustré*); Sauneron, *Un traité égyptien d'Ophiologie,* pp. 114, 119, 125, 132 (henceforth, *pOphiologie*).

During his stay in Brooklyn in 1952–53, George Posener undertook a preliminary survey of the papyri acquired in 1947. The notes he made during his study describe pBrooklyn 47.218.49 simply as "a badly damaged papyrus roll." No previous transcriptions of the papyrus, whole or in part, are known to exist.

pBrooklyn 47.218.49 was manufactured by attaching a number of sheets together with a slight overlap.[7] There are fourteen extant fragmentary or complete sheets; the complete sheets show a slight variation in width, ranging from approximately 18.5 cm to 20.5 cm. The overlap between sheets is 0.3 cm. Due to damage at the top and bottom of the roll, the height of the papyrus now varies, as well, between 19.5 cm and 21.2 cm.[8] The margins between columns are approximately 1 cm where such distances can be determined.[9] Each of the completely preserved columns of text averages slightly over 19 cm in width and approximately 20 cm in height. The scribe left ample space between each line, allowing for the addition of supralinear signs.[10] The papyrus now exhibits a range of colors from light tan to dark brown. The damage to the papyrus and the occurrence of numerous rubrics in the darker portions of the papyrus have both made the reading of a number of signs in those places difficult.

The papyrus presently consists of twelve fragments of varying dimensions. When Sauneron unrolled the papyrus and placed it under glass, he assigned each fragment a number. In some cases, however, his assigned number represents one or two columns of text, while in others it represents a fragment that has only a portion of text from one or two columns. I have reassigned numbers to the fragments and the columns for the sake of uniformity and clarity.[11]

---

7 See Černý, *Paper & Books,* pp. 9ff. for an overview of the traditional methods used for constructing a papyrus roll.

8 Černý, *Paper & Books,* pp. 16–17, gives no discussion of the physical characteristics of papyrus rolls manufactured later than the Ramesside Period; he notes, however, that sheets with heights ranging from 18 cm to 21.5 cm are already common in the New Kingdom. For the sake of comparison with the other published Brooklyn papyri from the Late Period, the height of *pBrooklyn 47.218.48+.85* (*pOphiologie*) is c. 27 cm; that of *pBrooklyn 47.218.84* (*Mythes et légendes*) is 16.5 cm; that of *pBrooklyn 47.218.135* (*pBrooklyn Wisdom*) ranges from 17.5 to 20 cm; that of *pBrooklyn 47.218.50* (*pConfirmation*) ranges from 22–25 cm; that of *pBrooklyn 47.218.156* (*pIllustré*) differs from the others radically, being only 12.5 cm in height.

9 See Černy, *Paper & Books,* pp. 20–21 for a discussion of the more common scribal practice of disregarding joins when writing columns of hieratic. A number of the other Brooklyn papyri of the 1947 gift were written in that manner, e.g., *pBrooklyn 47.218.84* (*Mythes et légendes*) and *pBrooklyn 47.218.48+85* (*pOphiologie*). Cf., however, *pBrooklyn 47.218.50* (*pConfirmation*) and *pBrooklyn 47.218.138* (*pProphylaxie*), both of which show the use of sheet joins as margins. In the present papyrus, there are a few instances where, at the end of a line, the scribe has written a sign that crosses the join.

10 For the supralinear signs in *pBrooklyn 47.218.49,* see p. 23ff. below.

11 The individual fragments of the papyrus now have Arabic numerals whose sequence is 1–12. The individual columns are labeled x + 1, etc. from beginning to end, given the likelihood that the first extant column is not the original first column of the papyrus. x + 14 represents the last column of the papyrus.

The first eight fragments[12] are the result of damage to the outer layers of the papyrus while still rolled. That damage has caused a substantial loss of text from the columns to which these fragments belong. Additional loss has occurred at the top and the bottom of some fragments as well. It has not always been possible to determine exactly how much text has been lost. The fragments numbered Nine through Twelve were made at the time the papyrus was unrolled. To accommodate the placement of the papyrus between sheets of glass, the papyrus was cut at the end of every second column. The dimensions of each of the fragments are given as follows:

Fragment One: max. height: 18.5 cm; max. width: 7.8 cm.
Fragment Two: max. height: 18.5 cm; max. width: 7.5 cm.
Fragment Three: max. height: 19.5 cm; max. width: 7.4 cm.
Fragment Four: max. height: 19.8 cm; max. width: 7.4 cm.
Fragment Five: max. height: 20.0 cm; max. width: 7.4 cm.
Fragment Six: max. height: 20.5 cm; max. width: 7.5 cm.
Fragment Seven: max. height: 20.0 cm; max. width: 7.0 cm.[13]
Fragment Eight: max. height: 19.5 cm; max. width: 4.6 cm.
Fragment Nine: max. height: 21.2 cm; width 40.0 cm.[14]
Fragment Ten: max. height: 20.7 cm; width: 37.8 cm.
Fragment Eleven: max. height: 21.1 cm; width: 37.8 cm.
Fragment Twelve: max. height: 21.1 cm; width: 49.0 cm.[15]

In its present state, with the fragments placed in what is assumed to be their correct position, the papyrus measures 221.2 cm in length. If the partially preserved column on the right edge of Fragment One is the original first column of text of the papyrus, the overall length of the original document would have been slightly in excess of 240 cm, including the lacunae between the first eight fragments and the four fragments belonging to the end of the papyrus.[16]

Fourteen fully extant or incomplete columns of text can be identified at present. Fragments One through Eight from the damaged part of the papyrus collectively show text from five partially preserved columns. Fragment Nine has two columns marred by five extensive vertical lacunae extending from the top of the papyrus. Only the bottom

12 Labeled Fragment One through Fragment Eight.

13 There are several small fragments mounted with this piece that have not been placed.

14 There are additional fragments mounted with this section that have not been placed. It is still unclear whether these small pieces belong to Fragment Nine or Fragment Eight.

15 There are, in addition, five fragments of varying small sizes belonging to Fragment Twelve that were not placed when the papyrus was unrolled, cut, and placed under glass. A note in Sauneron's handwriting taped to the glass reads: "P. 15 [sic] les fragments ne sont pas remis en ordre."

16 A number of small fragments have been located that at first seemed to belong to what is now labeled column x + 1. A careful examination showed, however, that they did have the same line spacing as that column.

seven lines of these columns are complete.[17] Both Fragments Ten and Eleven contain two complete columns. Fragment Twelve comprises two complete columns and a third column that is damaged at its left edge. In that third column, all of the lines are fragmentary, due to the damage at the end of the papyrus. Nonetheless, it can be seen clearly that the eighth and final line of text of this column ends approximately halfway across the page, indicating that it is the final column of the papyrus.

Thus, the extant text of fourteen columns is distributed among the fragments as follows:

Fragment One: the end portion Column x + 1[18] and the beginning of Column x + 2.
Fragment Two: the middle portion of Column x + 2.
Fragment Three: a few signs from the first five lines of the end of Column x + 2 and the beginning of Column x + 3.
Fragment Four: the middle portion of Column x + 3.
Fragment Five: the beginning of Column x + 4, the initial signs of each line now missing.
Fragment Six: the middle portion of Column x + 4.
Fragment Seven: the beginning of Column x + 5.
Fragment Eight: the middle portion of Column x + 5.
Fragment Nine: the end portion of Column x + 5, Column x + 6 and Column x + 7.
Fragment Ten: Columns x + 8 and x + 9.
Fragment Eleven: Columns x + 10 and x + 11.
Fragment Twelve: Columns x + 12, x + 13, and x + 14.

A number of errors unfortunately occurred when the papyrus was unrolled. First, Fragments Seven, Eight, and Nine, the three fragments that have the remains of Column x + 5, became separated at the time of the unrolling. Fragments Seven and Eight, which form the right edge and center part of Column x + 5, respectively, were put under one sheet of glass but without consideration given to their correct relative placement. Fragment Nine, which contains the left edge of Column x + 5 and the extant portions of Columns x + 6 and x + 7, was placed under a different sheet of glass. Thus, it became necessary to reposition these three fragments relative to one another in order to reconstruct what remains of Column x + 5. An assumed width of 19 cm (the average width of each of the complete columns) and the use of several uniform damage marks as guides have allowed a provisional though reasonably accurate placement of these fragments.

Secondly, the placement and the numbering of two other fragments were misconstrued after the papyrus had been cut. Fragment Ten, which actually preserves Columns x + 8 and x + 9, was accidentally placed directly after Fragment Eight; its columns were incorrectly numbered x + 7 and x + 8. Fragment Nine, which actually preserves the left

17 For the number of lines in each column, see the discussion below.

18 As was stated above, there is no way of knowing whether this is the original first column of the text; thus, it has been labeled Column x + 1.

edge of Column x + 5 and Columns x + 6 and x + 7, was then placed after Fragment Ten; its columns were incorrectly numbered x + 9 and x + 10. The damage patterns of the papyrus, however, and a study of the text of these fragments indicated that the text at the right of Fragment Nine continues the text of Fragments Seven and Eight and that these three fragmentary pieces of text belong to a single column.[19]

The scribe did not use a uniform number of lines for each column.[20] Given the absence of an overall fixed number of lines per column and the damage that occurs at the top and bottom of the papyrus, the original number of lines in some of the damaged columns cannot be determined with any certainty. The number of extant lines in the undamaged columns fluctuates, for the most part, between 18 and 19. The number of lines per column is given as follows:

Column x + 1: 22 lines.[21]
Column x + 2: 18 lines.
Column x + 3: 17 lines.
Column x + 4: 18 lines.
Column x + 5: 18 lines.
Column x + 6: 19 lines.
Column x + 7: 19 lines.
Column x + 8: 19 lines.
Column x + 9: 18 lines.
Column x + 10: 19 lines.
Column x + 11: 19 lines.
Column x + 12: 19 lines.
Column x + 13: 19 lines.
Column x + 14: 7 fragmentary lines and 1 partial though complete line.

19 Careful study showed that the text at the end of line 14 of the column located at the right hand edge of the fragment originally numbered nine continued into line 15 of the column located at the left edge of the original fragment seven. The same also holds true for the the end of line 16 of the column located at the right edge of the original fragment nine and the beginning of line 17 of the original fragment seven.

20 Overall, the papyrus does not have the crowded appearance of other Late Period texts. *pBrooklyn 47.218.48+85* (*pOphiologie*) is 27 cm in height and has twenty-seven lines of text per column; the scribe of that papyrus wrote the lines of text rather close together and left sizable upper and lower margins, giving the text a somewhat compressed look. Other Brooklyn papyri have more judicious spacing and show the addition of supralinear strokes as well, e.g., *pBrooklyn 47.218.84* (*Mythes et légendes*).

21 The handwriting in this column is considerably smaller than that of the rest of the text but appears to be that of the same scribe.

SCRIPT AND DATE

Although the handwriting of this papyrus is generally similar to that found in Late Period hieratic papyri, the hand and the overall appearance do not compare easily with those of other published Late Period papyri. It does not have the neat and somewhat uniform appearance seen in papyri that have been dated in past publications to the fourth century BC or to the early Ptolemaic Period.[22] The scribe of *pBrooklyn 49.218.49* has a somewhat idiosyncratic hand: the vertical signs are fairly narrow, and the horizontal signs show a somewhat flattened appearance. Many of the signs seem made in an almost cursory manner, and often two or more signs, typically written with only some similarity in Late Period hieratic, have an identical appearance in the Brooklyn papyrus.[23] Only a few ligatures are encountered.

The difficulty in dating Late Period hieratic papyri on paleographic grounds is well-known. It has even been implied that attempts to do so are exercises in futility.[24] Recent studies, however, show that differences in hieratic administrative script can be found as early as the later Ramesside Period and that by the Third Intermediate Period at the latest we can see the emergence of Lower and Upper Egyptian variants.[25] It has also been established that what is called late hieratic/late cursive hieratic begins its development into "abnormal hieratic" as early as the Twenty-first Dynasty.[26] As more hieratic texts and texts showing the transition from hieratic to demotic are published, it becomes clear that many of the changes in the writing of normal hieratic that scholars have dated to the end of the Third Intermediate Period and later actually took place much earlier.[27] An increase in the publication of hieratic texts from the Third Intermediate and Late Periods, moreover, is beginning to improve the prospects for the establishment of more narrowly defined date ranges for hieratic texts from these times.[28] Additionally, the com-

22 The dates offered for many of these texts have now been revised. See the discussion below.

23 See Table 4 below.

24 See, for example, Caminos, *JEA* 58 (1972): 206, where he remarks that the individual signs within a single document can be favorably compared with those from a broad chronological range; see also Winand, *RdE* 46 (1995): 188–89 and nn. 9–10.

25 See, for example, Depauw, *Demotic Studies,* p. 22 and bibliography cited there.

26 Malinine, *BdE* 64 (1973), pp. 31–35, esp. pp. 31–32; Vittmann, *LÄ* 4 (1982): cols. 748–50 for a list of texts published by 1982; see Depauw, *Demotic Studies,* pp. 22, 28, and 70–71 on questions about the transcription and transliteration of texts so designated, as well as those termed "early demotic;" on the latter, also Vleeming, *CdE* 56 (1981): 31–47.

27 An illustrative example: Posener, *pVandier,* p. 11, n. 21, states that the sign 𓂋 (Sign-list F21) was generally written with one tick before the reign of Darius I and with two afterwards. Cf., however, Munro, *HÄT* 1 (1995), p. 6, fig. 3, Nr. 158/159, where the sign 𓂋 is found written once with one and once with two ticks in the writing of the verb *sḏm*, illustrating that such changes in writing were taking place as early as Dynasty Eighteen.

28 Verhoeven, *BdE* 127 (1999), pp. 255–65, has argued successfully that the paleography of Saite Period Books of the Dead can be used profitably to date other religious and secular texts; see further Verhoeven, *Untersuchungen,* pp. 276ff. The hieratic papyri from these periods now being published are, for the most part, Books of the Dead. That genre has numerous

parative study of the paleography of a number of Third Intermediate and Late Period texts undertaken by Verhoeven now offers a valuable tool for the study of these texts.[29]

At present, there are only a few hieratic papyri that can be dated without question to the Twenty-sixth Dynasty. The Brooklyn Oracle Papyrus, prepared in Thebes, dates unequivocally to 651 BC.[30] The handwriting of the scribe who prepared the main section of the papyrus is quite distinct and bears no resemblance whatsoever to that of *pBrooklyn 47.218.49*.[31] The Book of the Dead of Nespasefy is dated to the reign of Psamtik I on prosopographical grounds.[32] Additionally, the Book of the Dead of Iahtesnakht has been dated, quite convincingly, to the middle of the Twenty-sixth Dynasty, around 600 BC, based on a paleographical comparison with BD Nespasefy.[33]

Verhoeven used the paleography of these latter two texts as the touchstone for a re-examination of a number of Late Period papyri that had been provisionally dated in earlier publications. Six of those that she studied had been assigned dates ranging from the Twenty-second Dynasty to the Ptolemaic Period.

CONVENTIONAL DATES ASSIGNED IN OLDER LITERATURE

pSalt 825 (pBM 10090 + 10051): date range of Psamtik I–Alexander[34]
pBM 10474 (Amenemope): both Dynasty 22[35] and Dynasty 26[36]
pBrooklyn 47.218.48+.85 (*pOphiologie*): Dynasty 30–beginning of the Ptolemaic Period[37]
pBrooklyn 47.218.50 (*pConfirmation*): end of the 5th century–beginning of the 4th century BC[38]

---

hieratic exemplars from the Third Intermediate Period and the pre-Ptolemaic Late Period, but many of these remain unpublished. See, for example, the catalogue in Wüthrich, *SAT* 16, pp. 170–244, where she lists 219 Third Intermediate Period and Late Period Books of the Dead, 179 of which are written in hieratic or both hieratic and hieroglyphs; 128 texts of that corpus, i.e., 72%, are still unpublished.

29 Verhoeven, *Untersuchungen*, passim, but esp. pp. 276ff. on the (re-)dating of a number of papyri from the Late Period, three of which are in Brooklyn.

30 See Parker, *Oracle Papyrus*, p. x.

31 The Oracle Papyrus is actually a compilation of different hands. In addition to the main text in the hand of the scribe who drew up the document, there are fifty witness entries, all individually written and signed. Of those entries, seventeen are written in "normal" hieratic, twenty-seven in abnormal hieratic, and six in what appears to be a mixture of the two. See Parker, *Oracle Papyrus*, p. 14.

32 Verhoeven, *HÄT* 5, p. 70; Vittmann, *Priester und Beamte*, pp. 66–91; Bierbrier, *BiOr* 36 (1979): 307ff.; Kitchen, *TIP*[3], p. 563ff.; § 481ff.

33 Verhoeven, *Tb des Iatesnacht*, pp. 3–12; Verhoeven, *Untersuchungen*, p. 72; see also Munro, *HAT* 12 (2011) pp. 4–5 for two Books of the Dead that are dated to the reign of Amasis based on genealogy.

34 Derchain, *pSalt 825*, pp. 119–27.

35 Herbin, *BIFAO* 82 (1982): 239, 280.

36 Shirun-Grumach, *LÄ* 3 (1979): col. 971.

37 Sauneron, *pOphiologie*, p. xi.

38 Goyon, *pConfirmation*, p. 8.

Table 1 Signs in *pBrooklyn 47.218.49* most closely resembling those of *pBDNespasefy* and *pBDIahtesnakht.*

Gardiner Verhoeven	**Hieroglyph**	**pBrooklyn 47.218.49**	**Tb Nespasefy**	**Tb Iahtesnakht**
A1				
A2a				
A5				
A24				
D1				
D2c				
D4				
D35a				
D41				
E23				
F8				
F21				
F31				
G1				
G17d				
M2				
M3				
N41/2				
T28				
U36				
V4				
V15				
W11				
Y5				
Z6				
Aa2				
Ag9				

pBrooklyn 47.218.135 (*pBrooklyn Wisdom*): 4th century BC[39] and 5th–4th century BC[40]
pLille 139 (*pVandier*): a range from Dynasty 26 to Dynasty 30, with a preference for a dating on the earlier side of that range[41]

Using the paleography of the two Saite Period Books of the Dead that she had published, Verhoeven was able to demonstrate that these texts could not only be redated, but all dated within a narrower time frame. She placed all of them firmly in the Saite Period and several in the reign of Psamtik I.

NEW DATES ASSIGNED BY VERHOEVEN

pSalt 825 (pBM 10090 + 10051): Dynasty 26, reign of Psamtik I[42]
pBM 10474 (*Amenemope*): Dynasty 26, reign of Psamtik I[43]
pBrooklyn 47.218.48+.85 (*pOphiologie*): second half of Dynasty 26[44]
pBrooklyn 47.218.50 (*pConfirmation*): beginning to early 6th century BC[45]
pBrooklyn 47.218.135 (*pBrooklyn Wisdom*): end of Dynasty 26[46]
pLille 139 (*pVandier*): 625–575 BC[47]

It seems, therefore, that a comparison of the paleography of *pBrooklyn 47.218.49* with that of the two Saite Books of the Dead would be a profitable venture (Table 1).

One can see that the handwritings of these three papyri compare favorably, and that there is more than just a general resemblance in the paleography. Thus, assigning a date in the Twenty-sixth Dynasty to *pBrooklyn 47.218.49* seems more than reasonable.

Such a date for *pBrooklyn 47.218.49* would set it firmly among the other Late Period Brooklyn papyri mentioned above that are now dated to the Saite Period.[48] Given the narrow time frame for the production of all of the Late Period Brooklyn papyri published to date, one must address the question of their possible relationship. At present, only the following can be said with certainty. A comparison of the hands of the papyri redated by Verhoeven with that of *pBrooklyn 47.218.49* makes it clear that these texts are certainly not

39 Jasnow, *pBrooklyn Wisdom*, p. 7.

40 Winand, *CdE* 73 (1998): 42.

41 Posener, *pVandier*, p. 11.

42 Verhoeven, *Untersuchungen*, pp. 280–89, esp. p. 287.

43 Ibid., pp. 290–303, esp. p. 301; note that Black, "The Instruction of Amenemope: A Critical Edition and Commentary—Prolegomenon and Prologue" (Ph.D. dissertation, University of Wisconsin–Madison, 2002) gives a later date of late Dynasty 26–early Dynasty 27.

44 Ibid., pp. 304–7, esp. p. 306.

45 Ibid., pp. 308–18, esp. p. 318.

46 Ibid., pp. 319–28, esp. p. 325.

47 Ibid., pp. 329–37, esp. p. 336.

48 For these texts and their dates, see the discussion at pp. 7ff. above.

Table 2 Unusually Shaped Signs.

Gardiner Verhoeven	Hieroglyph	pBrooklyn 47.218.49
D4		
Aa27		

Table 3 Pointed Signs in *pBrooklyn 47.218.49*.

Gardiner Verhoeven	Hieroglyph	pBrooklyn 47.218.49
Aa27		
A2		
F31		
M2		

Table 4 Signs made similarly in *pBrooklyn 47.218.49*.

Gardiner Verhoeven	Hieroglyph	pBrooklyn 47.218.49
A2		
G7		
D37		
D40		
A2		
Aa27		

the work of a single scribe.[49] But the fact that several of these papyri share a small number of words known only to them establishes at least one connection between some of them.[50] Secondly, a number of the published and unpublished Brooklyn papyri mention the protection of the king as one, if not the main, focus.[51] On the other hand, the date range now offered for these papyri still remains between 85 and 130 years. We presently know

49 That does not rule out that the Brooklyn papyri were produced in one scribal school or House of Writing.

50 See, for example, Sauneron, *pIllustré*, pp. 7ff.

51 See pp. 29ff. below.

of no archive of such a length from Late Period Egypt with which to make a meaningful comparison.[52] Until further determination can be made on the possible provenance(s) of these texts, it seems best to state that whether or not the Brooklyn Late Period papyri once formed a single collection of texts or part thereof remains open to question.[53]

In addition to paleography, two pieces of internal evidence can be offered as additional criteria for a more certain dating of the Brooklyn papyrus.

In *pBrooklyn 47.218.49*, the name : *psmṯk* (Psamtik) is encountered twenty-four times, always written in a cartouche. It alternates with the term : *pr-ꜥꜣ*, "pharaoh," written nineteen times but only once in a cartouche. The occurrence of the name provides a *terminus post quem* for the composition of the papyrus, namely the beginning of the second third of the seventh century BC when the reign of the first king named Psamtik began.

If we assume that the text was prepared during the reign of one of the three kings named Psamtik, the date for its composition would be limited to a range from the first half of the seventh century BC to the end of the third quarter of the sixth century BC, when the reign of the ephemeral Psamtik III ended. Thus, the date would be restricted to some point in their reigns, whose range covers 139 years.[54]

Table 5 Date Ranges for Psamtik I–III.[55]

King	Accession	Latest Date
Psamtik I	664 BC	610 BC
Psamtik II	595 BC	589 BC
Psamtik III	526 BC	526 BC

In its twenty-four occurrences in the text, the name Psamtik is consistently written . The writing with high *ś* is attested as a spelling of the *nomen* of all three kings named Psamtik.[56] When preparing the text, the scribe may have been instructed to use the *nomen* of the king rather than his *praenomen*. The *praenomen*

52 On ancient Egyptian archives, see Quirke in Loprieno, ed., *Ancient Egyptian Literature*, pp. 379–401.

53 On possible provenance, see pp. 17ff below.

54 Note that this time span conforms well to that now proposed for the other Late Period papyri in Brooklyn.

55 The list of pharaohs named Psamtik given here does not include the three Libyan dynasts so-named. The first two of these, called Psamtik IV and V to indicate their chronological order, lived during the First Persian Period and are called "kings of the Libyans" by the Classical historians Thucydides and Philochoros. The third dynast, Psamtik VI, lived in the period immediately following and was called king of Egypt by Diodorus. The Egyptian evidence supporting their position as kings of Egypt is extremely scanty and problematic. See Spalinger, *LÄ* 4 (1982): cols. 1173–76 for a discussion of these rulers; also, Pestman, in Thissen and Zauzich, eds., *Grammata Demotika*, pp. 145–55. I thank Richard Jasnow for this reference. See also the discussion and references in Vleeming, *Gooseherds of Hou*, pp. 3–4. See as well Quack, *JEH* 4 (2011): 228–46.

56 Von Beckerath, *MÄS* 20, pp. 274–76. In early demotic texts, the writing of the name Psamtik occurs regularly as , referring to both Psamtik I and Psamtik II. See Griffith, *Demotic Papyri in the John Rylands Library*, vol. 2, pl. 1–15, for numerous examples of the

was specifically a royal name, chosen at the time of accession; it often reflected political considerations of the moment. The *nomen* was the name given at birth and was considered the ultimate indicator of an individual's identity and existence.[57] If the Brooklyn text was prepared for the personal protection of a king, the presence of his birth name would have been important. Thus, the writing of the name Psamtik in the Brooklyn papyrus not only confirms a Saite Period date but may point to a more specific dating as well.

As the contents of the papyrus indicate that it is a book of protection,[58] the presence of the name Psamtik and the title *pr-ꜥꜣ* suggest that it is a royal book of protection. Though such texts are known, most focus on generalized protection of the king at the time of the New Year.[59] Such texts employ only the title *pr-ꜥꜣ*, never the name of a specific king, suggesting that, though royal, they were generic.[60]

This brings us to a second piece of evidence, namely that certain passages in the Brooklyn papyrus have a number of close parallels in texts from Crypt B' of the Temple of the goddess Nekhbet at Elkab. That structure and its texts date unquestionably to the reign of Psamtik I.[61] The Crypt B' texts are known in Egypt only at Elkab before the Ptolemaic Period; then parallels can be found in the temples at Edfu, Dendera, and Philae. The texts in question comprise seven short spells with vignettes, all designed for the protection of Psamtik I against dangerous powers associated with Sakhmet and the evils connected with the coming of the New Year.[62] Each spell consists of a series of epithets addressed to a deity who is seen as potentially malevolent, followed by an appeal to that deity to save the Pharaoh from dangers that are enumerated.[63]

Given that the structure of these spells is similar to that of several spells in the Brooklyn text, most notably Spell E, a comparison of the Elkab texts and the parallels found in *pBrooklyn 47.218.49* seems warranted and appears as follows.

---

identical writing of the names of Psamtik I and II. The preference for such a writing may be due to the highly ligatured nature of early demotic. For numerous examples of monumental inscriptions showing writings of the name Psamtik with both high and low *s*, see now Perdu, *Recueil des inscriptions saïtes,* passim.

57 Spieser, *Les noms du Pharaon,* pp. 11ff., esp. p. 12, and nn. 65–67. In the Late Period, there is a common substitution of the word *kꜣ* for *rn*; see Bickel, *La cosmogonie égyptienne,* p. 36 and n. 16.

58 On genre types, see the discussion at pp. 29ff. below.

59 See the discussion below and the list of texts given at pp. 29ff. and nn. 143–49 below.

60 Goyon, *BIFAO* 74 (1974): 75–83, offers a short list of these texts. It should be noted that most of the texts he gives form sections of significantly larger works that would not fall under the rubric "Book of Protection;" see the remarks of Sauneron, *pIllustré,* p. 17, as well as the discussion at pp. 29ff. below. See also Flessa, *Corpus Papyrorum Raineri XXVII*, pp. 35–36.

61 See Capart, *CdE* 15 (1940): 21–29. The texts have both the *praenomen* and the *nomen* of Psamtik I, the latter showing spellings with both low *s* and high *ś*. These texts were later usurped by Amasis.

62 Capart's interpretation of these texts has been challenged by Sauneron, *JNES* 19 (1960): 269–87.

63 On the dangers enumerated in the Brooklyn papyrus, see the discussion at pp. 26ff. below.

Elkab I:

mi nḥm=k nṯr nfr nb tꜣ.wy psmṯk m-ꜥ ḫꜣy.w nw sḫm.t[64]

"Come! May you save the perfect god, the Lord of the Two Lands, Psamtik from the *ḫꜣy.w*-demons of Sakhmet."

pBrooklyn: There is no exact parallel referring to the "*ḫꜣy.w*-demons of Sakhmet," but references to evils associated with Sakhmet and to saving or protecting Psamtik from such occur routinely in the Brooklyn text.

Elkab II:

nḥm=tn nṯr nfr psmṯk m-ꜥ šꜥd [nb…][65]

"May you save the perfect god Psamtik from [any] slaughter…"

pBrooklyn x + 10: 2–3:

nn irr=f šꜥd=f im=f

"He (i.e., the agent of evil) shall not make his slaughter in him (i.e., Psamtik)."

Elkab III:

nḥm=k nṯr nfr wꜣḥ ib Rꜥ sꜣ Rꜥ pzmṯk m-ꜥ dḥr nb m rnp.t tn[66]

"May you save the perfect god *Wah-ib-re,* son of Re, Psamtik from any bitterness in this year."

pBrooklyn x + 4: 15–16:

[nḥm]=tn sw m-ꜥ ḥsb sw m-ꜥ i[ꜣd.t] n rnp.t tn m-ꜥ ḏꜣḏꜣ nb m-ꜥ šmm [nb m-ꜥ] ḥsb nb pr m rꜣ n nṯr nty ḥwi […] tꜣ ḏr=f

"May you save him from doom (?), him from the epi[demic] of this year, from every great fiendish being, from every fever, [from] every doom (?) that comes forth from the mouth of the god who floods […] the entire land."[67]

pBrooklyn x + 10: 3–4:

nn irr=f dḥr ḥꜣ.ty=f

"He (i.e., the agent of evil) will not make his (i.e., Psamtik's) heart bitter."

pBrooklyn x + 3: 5:

[…]*=sn dḥr=f r ib*[*.sn*]…

"…they (i.e., tutelary deities)…his (i.e., the agent of evil) bitterness against [their] hearts."

64 Capart, *CdE* 15 (1940): 22. On the word *ḫꜣy.w,* see Ritner, in Kousoulis, *Ancient Egyptian Demonology,* OLA 175 (2011), pp. 3–24.

65 Capart, *CdE* 15 (1940): 23.

66 Capart, *CdE* 15 (1940): 23.

67 On the restorations to this text and its inherent problems, see the commentary to Spell E below.

Elkab IV:

nḥm=k s3 Rʿ pzmṯk [m-ʿ ḫry(.w)=k mki sw m-ʿ šʿy=k n nsr=k ntf s3 sḫm.t m rnp.t tn ḥr=s is ḫnsw s3 b3st.t ḥr nb 3w-ib][68]

"May you save the son of Re, Psamtik, [from your enemies. Protect him from your slaughter (and) your flame. He is the son of Sakhmet in this year of which she is master. Lo, Khonsu, son of Bastet, Horus, Lord of Joy.]"

pBrooklyn: no exact parallel, although the phrase *i3d.t n rnp.t tn* that is found in the Brooklyn text at x + 4: 15 has close associations with Sakhmet.

Elkab V:

nḥm=tn pr-ʿ3 m-ʿ ḫry.w[69]

"May you save the Pharaoh from the enemies."

pBrooklyn x + 3: 15–16:

mi nḥm=k [pr-ʿ3 m-ʿ] mwt mwt.t ḥm.wt-r3

"Come! May you save [the Pharaoh from] a dead male, a dead female and so on."

pBrooklyn x + 3: 17–18:

mi nḥm=k [pr-ʿ3] m-ʿ ḫft…

"Come! May you save [the Pharaoh] from the enemy…"[70]

pBrooklyn x + 4: 5–6:

mi [nḥm] psmṯk m-ʿ ḫft=f mi nḥm[=k….] m-ʿ 3d sw m sm3y.w […]

"Come! Save Psamtik from his enemy like [you] saved […] from the Furious One, him from the Accomplices ..."

pBrooklyn x + 4: 6:

nḥm mwt mwt.t ḫft ḫft.t n [psmṯk]

"Drive off the dead male, the dead female, the male enemy, the female enemy of [Psamtik]."

Elkab VI:

mi nḥm pr-ʿ3[71]

"Come! Save the Pharaoh."

68 The full hieroglyphic text given here is restored from the more complete versions found at Philae and Dendera. The brackets show what is absent in the damaged section of the Elkab text.

69 Capart, *CdE* 15 (1940): 24–25.

70 The text in brackets represents the conjectured restoration of the Brooklyn text.

71 Capart, *CdE* 15 (1940): 25.

pBrooklyn: no exact parallel to this generalized statement, since in the Brooklyn text the verb *nḥm* is always followed by a prepositional phrase introduced by *m-ꜥ* or *m,* specifying the evil against which the king needs protection.

ELKAB VII:
sẖr sby m ḥꜣt wiꜣ rꜥ nḥm[=k] pr-ꜥꜣ m-ꜥ[...][72]
"Make the rebel fall from the prow of the barque of Re. May [you] save the Pharaoh from [...]"

pBrooklyn x + 3: 4–5:
sẖr=sn sw ḥr [...]
"May they (i.e., tutelary deities) make him (i.e., the agent of evil) fall upon [...]"

The texts from Elkab focus on protecting the king from a variety of dangers, apparently those associated with the New Year.[73] As in the texts of the Brooklyn papyrus, the king, when named, is called Psamtik. Given the unequivocal connection between Psamtik I and the Elkab texts and the evident parallels between these texts and those of the Brooklyn papyrus, the evidence from Elkab lends strong support for a date of the composition of the Brooklyn text in the reign of Psamtik I.

The sole use of the *nomen* Psamtik with no references to a *praenomen* may offer evidence that the papyrus was prepared for Psamtik I, since this name would have a clear and single point of reference, given that there was only one king so named known at that time.[74]

One could argue that the Brooklyn papyrus postdates the Saite Period and that the sections in which the name Psamtik appears are copies of texts that had been prepared in the Twenty-sixth Dynasty.[75] The presence of the word *pr-ꜥꜣ* in other sections of the text would mark them as texts copied from other earlier or later sources. In this case, the scribe of the Brooklyn papyrus faithfully copied whatever text exemplars he was using to create his compilation. So the possibility of a date in the fourth century BC cannot be dismissed. The interest in magical traditions was very strong during that time period which witnessed, for example, the production of the Metternich Stele and many of the so-called

72 Capart, *CdE* 15 (1940): 25–26.

73 Thus, they belong to a well-known genre, for which see the discussion below under the heading "Contents." See Sauneron, *JNES* 19 (1960): 269–87, for a useful discussion of the roles and purposes that texts like those from the Elkab crypt were intended to have. See also de Meulenaere, *CdE* 44 (1969): 13–21. For the goddess(es) associated with these dangers, see Darnell, *SAK* 22 (1995): 47–95; idem, *SAK* 24 (1997): 35–48.

74 In the Elkab texts, the *nomen* Psamtik occurs five times, only once accompanied by his *praenomen wꜣḥ-ib-rꜥ*. The term *pr-ꜥꜣ* occurs twice. On the use of the *nomen* in protection texts, see also the discussion above and n. 57.

75 Some spells refer to the object of protection as Psamtik, some as *pr-ꜥꜣ,* some have both used interchangeably, while a few simply use *s,* "a man." None of the spells has the phrase *mn ms mnt,* "so-and-so, born of so-and-so," commonly encountered in magical and medical texts.

"magical statues," a number of which have a known provenance in the Delta.[76] In the Greek magical texts from later periods,[77] a king named Psammetikhos[78] is encountered who is called a magician.[79] Although there is no specific supporting evidence, it is possible that Psamtik I, the king known by the name Psammetikhos in the Greek historical traditions, had by the fourth century BC gained such stature in the eyes of the Egyptian priests as well. Should that be the case, one can understand the impetus to leave or make use of the name of Psamtik, a powerful magician, in such spells when they were being prepared. But it must be kept in mind that the fourth-century BC commemoration of a king named Psamtik reputed to be a powerful practitioner of magic may be based on the fact that it was during the reign of Psamtik I that a number of compilation texts, many of which fall under the rubric "magical,"[80] seem to have been drawn up.[81] In addition, major objections to such a dating are also offered by the revised dates of the other Brooklyn papyri, all of which are now dated to the Saite Period, as well as the parallels found in the Elkab texts dating to the reign of Psamtik I. Thus, the notion of a date for the papyrus in the fourth century BC is credibly weakened by a lack of tangible evidence and seems rather firmly stuck in the realm of conjecture. All of the above taken into consideration, it seems quite valid to assign the date for this papyrus to the reign of Psamtik I.

---

76 At least three from Athribis: Cairo JE 46341 (Djed-Hor), for which see Vernus, *Athribis,* No. 160, p. 193; and No. 300, pp. 322–23: date Philip Arrhidaeus. Chicago OI 9379, for which see B. van de Walle, *JNES* 31 (1972): 68–83: dating to Dynasty 30, according to *CLES*. Florence 1788/1011, for which see Vernus, *Athribis,* No. 147, pp. 181–82; and Kákosy, *Egyptian Healing Statues in Three Museums in Italy,* pp. 109–17: date given as D. 30. Two from Tell Basta: Cairo JE 87083, unpublished; dating to the reign of Nectanebo II, for which see Habachi, *ASAE* 42 (1943): 369–407: "found beside the temple of Mahes to NW of Hall of *nḫt-ḥr-ḥb* at Tell Basta." Cairo JE 41677, for which see *PM* IV, p. 33; G. Daressy, *ASAE* 11 (1911): 187–91: date given as Nect. II. Furthermore, New York MMA 1989.281.201, Munich ÄS 2824, and Paris Louvre E. 10777, all healing statues, have stylistic affinities that suggest a date in this period or possibly earlier. See Josephson, O'Rourke, and Fazzini, *MDAIK* 61 (2005): 219–41, pls. 37–41.

77 For these texts, see Betz, ed., *The Greek Magical Papyri in Translation;* Meyer and Smith, eds., *Ancient Christian Magic.*

78 The Greek historical tradition seems to have differentiated the three kings named Psamtik through the spelling of their names. In Africanus, the name of Psamtik I was given as Psammetikhos; that of Psamtik II as Psammuthis; and Psamtik III was called Psammecherites. Eusebius states that Psamtik II was also called Psammetikhos; Psamtik III does not appear in his list for Dynasty XXVI. See Waddell, *Manetho,* pp. 168–73.

79 See, for example, *PGM* IV, pp. 154–55, where Psamtik is referred to as ὁ σοφιστής : "the wise man;" for the association of this word with magic, see Betz, *Greek Magical Papyri,* p. 60, n. 44.

80 On the terms "magic" and "magical," see pp. 31ff. below.

81 Note that it was also during the Saite Period that the texts of the Book of the Dead corpus were given their later and more finalized form. Many of the Brooklyn papyri conform to the heading "compilation text."

PROVENANCE

There is no information in the departmental records about the provenance of any of the Late Period papyri belonging to the 1947 bequest, nor has an examination of the Wilbour Notebooks yielded anything about their acquisition. For the Brooklyn papyri published by Sauneron and Goyon, both editors suggested a northern provenance.[82] Focusing solely on internal textual references to gods and rituals associated with Heliopolis and Memphis, they argued, albeit very hypothetically, that those papyri belonged to a temple library in the Memphite-Heliopolitan region. In his publication of the Brooklyn Delta papyrus, D. Meeks stated that the papyrus "appartient à un lot acquis au Caire...."[83]

As noted above, the present collection of spells has close associations with a sequence of texts found at Elkab dating to the reign of Psamtik I. That single connection, however, does not provide strong enough evidence to assume a provenance at that site in southern Egypt. The contents of the papyrus, concerned with the protection of the king, may indicate that it was intended for actual use in ritual.[84] Given that it is a compilation of texts, it may have been a reference work used for the performance of certain rituals or an exemplar used for the production of amuletic texts by a type of Egyptian healer known as, *sꜣ.w*.[85]

Eight of the eighteen lots of Old Kingdom papyrus fragments belonging to the 1947 bequest have an established provenance of Elephantine Island. Notes with eight of these groups in Wilbour's own hand state that he acquired them at Elephantine in February of 1896. In addition, working together with Joachim F. Quack on the unpublished Brooklyn Late Period papyri during the summer of 2012 and the spring of 2013, we discovered an additional 21 fragments that belong to the Brooklyn Illustrated magical papyrus published by Sauneron. Of greater significance was the discovery by Quack of two additional fragments in the collection of the Berlin Museum that belong to the same papyrus and may actually join with the newly discovered fragments in Brooklyn. The Berlin material has an established provenance, Elephantine, as it comes from the Rubensohn excavations that were undertaken beginning in 1906. At this point in the course of our research, it seems that a provenance of Elephantine for at least some of the other Late Period Brooklyn papyri is now a distinct possibility.[86]

---

82 See Sauneron, *pIllustré*, pp. viii–x; Goyon, *pConfirmation*, pp. 13–16. Cf., however, S. Quirke's review of Sauneron's *pOphiologie* and Jasnow's *pBrooklyn Wisdom* in *JEA* 83 (1997): 243–45.

83 *Meeks, Mythes et légendes*, p. 1, a remark apparently based on Sauneron, *pIllustré*, p. ix, n. 8.

84 See Flessa, *Corpus Papyrorum Raineri XXVII*, p. 107, who states that such a compilation "was never intended to be recited coherently."

85 See Hannig, *GHW*, 655a: "Zauberer, Amulettmacher."

86 Three articles discussing the new discoveries and the history of the provenance of the Wilbour papyri will appear in the near future in V. Leper, ed., *Essays on Elephantine*. The three articles are: O'Rourke, "Charles Edwin Wilbour and the Provenance of his Papyri;" O'Rourke and Quack, "New Fragments of the Late Hieratic Illustrated Magical Papyrus at the Brooklyn Museum (pBrooklyn 47.218.156) and Related Fragments at Berlin;" and O'Rourke, "The Old Kingdom Papyri from Elephantine Island in the Brooklyn Museum." On the importance of

GRAMMAR

The language of *pBrooklyn 47.218.49* is essentially the Middle Egyptian one routinely encounters in religious texts from the Late Period; in only one section does it exhibit any features of Late Egyptian grammar. Given the conservative nature of religious texts, the tendency to employ the classical language of Middle Egyptian is not surprising.[87] A sampling of the grammatical forms found in the papyrus is given as follows.[88]

PRONOUNS

a. The suffix pronouns are regularly employed for both possession and as suffix pronoun subjects in *sḏm=f* and *sḏm.n=f* constructions.

1. 1st person singular : x + 8: 1–3.
2. 2nd person singular masculine : x + 8: 12; x + 10: 6–7; 10; 13.
3. 2nd person feminine : x + 13: 11.
4. 3rd person singular masculine : x + 2: 6; 7; 8; x + 4: 9; x + 10: 1; 3–4.
5. 3rd person singular feminine : x + 13: 12; written : x + 13: 12–13; written : x + 8: 12.
6. 2nd person plural : x + 6: 13; 16; 19.
7. 3rd person plural is commonly : x + 1: 19; x + 3: 3; 7. The Late Egyptian form is found at x + 11: 6; 14.

b. The impersonal pronoun subject *tw* occurs at x + 6: 15; x + 10: 11; x + 13: 11 (possibly).[89]

c. The dependent pronouns

1. 2nd person singular pronoun written *tw*: x + 13: 15 (2×)

Elephantine as a findspot for demotic papyri, see also Hoffmann and Quack, *Anthologie der demotischen Literatur,* pp. 230 and 361 n. [a]; Quack, *Einführung in die altägyptische Literaturgeschichte* 3 (2009), pp. 230 and 261.

87 On the development of the vernacular used in religious texts in the transitional period between New Egyptian and Demotic, see Vernus, *RdE* 45 (1994): 153–208; see also Lustman, *Étude grammaticale du papyrus du Bremner-Rhind,* passim, esp. pp. 335ff. for the specific features of Middle Egyptian that appear in that papyrus and give it its "late" character; also Jansen-Winkeln, *WZKM* 85 (1995): 85–115 on the development of Late Egyptian and its ties with Middle Egyptian, and 103–5 on the use of each in texts of the Third Intermediate and Late Periods.

88 The list of examples given here is by no means exhaustive. It is intended to give the reader an overall appreciation of the grammar and language of the text as typically that of classical Middle Egyptian. The grammatical terminology used is generally that found in Allen, *Middle Egyptian.* For the emphatic *sḏm.n=f* form, which Allen does not mention in his work, see Polotsky, *RdE* 11 (1957): 109–17; also, idem, *The Israel Academy of Sciences and Humanities* 2, No. 5 (1965), pp. 1–25, esp. 16ff.

89 See the discussion at notes F and I (x + 13: 11) below.

2. 3rd person singular masculine *sw*: x + 4: 6; x + 8: 3; x + 12: 19
3. 3rd person plural pronoun *st*: x + 11: 11

d. The independent pronoun in nominal sentences
1. *ink*: x + 7: 15; x + 8: 2; 3.
2. *ntf*: x + 2: 16; x + 12: 19; x + 13: 1; 7.

DEMONSTRATIVES

a. The demonstrative adjectives *pn* and *tn* are used regularly. The later form *pwy* is found at x + 3: 2; x + 5: 7; x + 13: 15. The demonstrative forms with prothetic *yod*, *i.ptn*, *i.pn*, and *i.pw* are found at x + 2: 8; x + 9: 3 and x + 13:1; and x + 9: 16, respectively.[90] None of the later demonstrative series , , and : *pꜣ.y*, *tꜣ.y*, and *nꜣ.y* are employed.

ARTICLES

a. The definite article series , , and : *pꜣ*, *tꜣ* and *nꜣ*: x + 9: 13; 15; 17. There are no occurrences of the demonstrative and possessive adjectives derived from them. Both : *pꜣ* and : *tꜣ* are used as vocative markers at x + 10: 12; x + 13: 17.

PREPOSITIONS

a. No Late Egyptian prepositions such as *i.ir*, *i.ir-ḥr*, or *r-bꜣw* occur.

b. Middle Egyptian prepositions
1. : *m* "in, from, etc.:" x + 2: 9; x + 12: 16; x + 13: 1.
2. : *m-ꜥ* "from:" x + 4: 5; 15; 18.
3. : *m-bꜣḥ* "in the presence of:" x + 7: 8.
4. : *m-m* "together with:" x + 6: 13.
5. : *m-ḥꜣt* "in front of; before:" x + 9: 14.
6. : *m-ẖnw* "within:" x + 2: 11; x + 13: 4.
7. : *m-ḫt* "after; accompanying:" x + 4: 7; x + 11: 10; x + 12: 2; x + 13: 13.
8. : *m-ḏr* "after:" x + 11: 1; 17.
9. : *mi* "like; likewise:" x + 4: 5; x + 10: 14; x + 11: 3; 7.
10. : *r* "at; against:" x + 2: 6; x + 12: 16-17; 19.
11. : *r-ḫft-ḥr* "before; in front of:" x + 7: 9; 16; x + 9: 17 (written *ḫft-ḥr n*).
12. : *ḥnꜥ* "and; together with:" x + 7: 9; x + 12: 11.
13. : *ḥr* "upon:" x + 4: 9; x + 5: 4; 10; x + 12: 11.
14. : *ḫft* "as; while; when:" x + 4: 13; x + 5: 3; 12; x + 9: 14; 16; x + 10: 9; x + 12: 10.
15. : *ẖr* "under; in possession of:" x + 5: 12; x + 7: 9; x + 12: 12; 17.

90 These forms are supposedly found in archaic, formal, or archaizing texts, for which see Borghouts, *EU* 24.1, p. 88, § 20.a.2.

GENITIVE MARKER

a. The masculine form 𓈖 *n* occurs at x + 2: 10; 11; x + 7: 11; 15; x + 8: 5.

b. The feminine form 𓈖𓏏 *n.t* is found at x + 2: 7; x + 5: 12; x + 7: 3 (following a masculine noun); x + 9: 14; x + 13: 3.

c. The "plural" writing 𓏌 *nw* appears at x + 4: 15; x + 13: 3.

VERB FORMS

a. *sḏm=f* forms appear regularly and are the most common verb form employed in the text: x + 3: 3; x + 4: 2; 10; 17; x + 6: 12; x + 8: 1; x + 9: 14; x + 11: 3. In many cases, it is difficult to distinguish between the employment of the *sḏm=f* prospective and the *sḏm=f* subjunctive. x + 10: 2–6 appears to contain a long string of *sḏm=f* forms, all negated with *nn* and probably best translated as prospectives.

b. *sḏm=f* passive: x + 13: 11.

c. *iw sḏm=f:* x + 3: 11; x + 8: 12; x + 10: 15.

d. *sḏm.n=f* forms[91] are found in a number of places: x + 2: 7; 13; 14; 15; x + 5: 9; x + 7: 14; x + 13: 6.

e. *iw sḏm.n=f:* x + 3: 11; x + 8: 2; 3; 14; x + 10: 9–10.

f. *iw sḏm.n.tw=f:* x + 3: 11.

g. *sḏm.k3=f:* x + 3: 13.

h. The passive form *rḫ.tw=f* appears at x + 6: 4.

i. *ḏd.tw r3 pn* is found at x + 7: 9.

j. One example of a Late Egyptian relative form occurs at x + 10: 13 (*i.irr=k*).

k. Participles appear frequently in the text: x + 2: 6; x + 4: 8; x + 5: 3; x + 6: 4; 7; 10; x + 7: 7–8; x + 8: 9; x + 9: 6; 13. No distinction in the writings of the imperfective and perfective participles was found, except for the verbs *iri* and *rdi*.

---

91 In the lacunae-ridden sections of the first third of the papyrus, it is difficult to differentiate between a true *sḏm.n=f* form and an imperative + dative construction. I have listed only identifiable *sḏm.n=f* forms here. On the emphatic use of the *sḏm.n=f* form, see n. 88 above.

l. Examples of imperatives can be found at x + 2: 7; x + 3: 15; x + 4: 5; x + 7: 4; 8; x + 13: 7.

m. The verb *iri* shows three spellings: [hieroglyphs], [hieroglyphs], and [hieroglyph]. [hieroglyphs] *irr* is used in the writing of the imperfective participle and [hieroglyph] *ir* for the writing of the perfective participle. In finite verb forms, [hieroglyph] *ir* is used consistently in the writing of *sḏm.n=f* forms: x + 2: 13; 14; x + 8: 14; x + 13: 5–6. The form [hieroglyphs] *irr* is used for the non-prospective *sḏm=f* form: x + 4: 9 and twice for the prospective (indicative) *sḏm=f*: x + 10: 2 and 4. The two writings of [hieroglyphs] for the prospective occur in a series of negative injunctions, each introduced by *nn*. There, the verb *iri* is also twice written [hieroglyphs], to be read *ir* (x + 10: 3 and 4) and once as [hieroglyph], *ir* (x + 10: 4) in parallel clauses that also require the prospective. There seems to be no discernible difference in the employment of these different writings in that section of the text. All three writings are found in sentences that have adverbial adjuncts, but there seems little or nothing that contextually indicates that [hieroglyphs] represents an emphatic form as opposed to [hieroglyphs] and [hieroglyph]. There also seems to be no difference contextually that would require the indicative form [hieroglyphs] or the subjunctive forms [hieroglyphs] or [hieroglyph]. It is worth noting again that the scribe here is likely copying a text, not composing it. The infinitive is written as [hieroglyphs] in x + 9: 6. The writing [hieroglyphs] in x + 10: 2 occurs as a writing of the perfective passive participle.

n. The verb *rdi* shows a variety of writings. [hieroglyphs] *rdi* with the sign [hieroglyph] occurs commonly in the writing of the *sḏm.n=f* form: x + 2: 14; x + 8: 2 (3×); x + 13: 6. The writing [hieroglyph] *di* is used for the prospective: x + 7: 7; x + 8: 3. The writing [hieroglyphs] *didi* appears to have been employed at x + 7: 7–8 for both the imperfective active and imperfective passive participles. The writing [hieroglyphs] is found at x + 12: 10, occuring in the damaged beginning of a line. The writing there appears to be *iw nꜣ.w nṯr.w nb.w r di.t…*; thus, we have the future construction noun + *r* + infinitive. See n. EJ (x + 12: 10) below.

Negation

a. [hieroglyphs] *nn* appears regularly in the text in both non-verbal sentences and *sḏm=f* constructions: x + 1: 12; x + 2: 8; x + 4: 2; 3; x + 6: 4; x + 8: 3; 16; x + 10: 2–5; x + 11: 14. It is found once in a *sḏm.n=f* construction x + 10: 1.

b. [hieroglyphs] *tm* appears occasionally in the text: x + 3: 12; x + 12: 14.

c. [hieroglyph] *bn* occurs once in the text at x + 10: 13, in a passage that seems to show other Late Egyptian grammatical features. See note AJ (x + 10: 13) below.

d. The negative imperative verb *m* is written as [hieroglyph] at x + 12: 19; x + 13: 7; the writing [hieroglyphs] *imi* is found at x + 12: 16 without an expressed subject.

e. The negative subjunctive construction [hieroglyphs] *im=f sḏm* is found at x + 13: 16.

f. The negative noun clause marker [hieroglyphs] *iw.ty* appears at x + 5: 16.

COPULA

The copula with *pw* occurs at x + 7: 18-19, and at x + 10: 18 in an apparent gloss.

The general absence in the papyrus of Late Egyptian forms and syntax[92] and the absence of examples of the phonetic exchange of the letters *g, k,* and *ḳ,* found in some Late Period texts, should come as no surprise. The reason for such a conservative use of language and syntax may be due to the notion that "older is better," an idea that one routinely encounters in religious and medical texts. Certain spells or remedies are said, for example, to have proven themselves "effective millions of times."[93] It may be that the premium placed on the "archaic" was one of the principal driving forces behind the persistence of the Middle Egyptian idiom in religious texts into very late times.[94] That said, we cannot overlook the fact that *pBrooklyn 47.218.49* is a compilation of individual texts, some of which may have been much than older than the time when the papyrus was drawn up; thus, their actual vernacular is true Middle Egyptian.

VOCABULARY AND ORTHOGRAPHY

In general, the vocabulary of *pBrooklyn 47.218.49* is well-known and documented in the lexica. There are a number of words that exhibit the peculiar spellings commonly found in texts that the *Wörterbuch* characterizes as "spät." Additionally, there are a number of words not found in any of the available lexical tools.[95] Most of these words can be found in the publications of other individual papyri that postdate the appearance of the standard reference works. Only a few words or spellings seem known only from *pBrooklyn 47.218.49*. They are

w-r-ʿ: note BF (x + 7, 11)
wr.t (?): note AH (x + 10: 11)
ni(ꜣ): note G (x + 12: 17)
ḫ-n-r-m: note EA (x + 12: 5)

All words discussed in the Text Notes to the spell in which they appear can be found in the Index of Words Discussed at the end of this work.

---

92 The few Late Egyptian forms occuring in the text are discussed in the notes.

93 A coda commonly found in such texts. See, for example, *pEdwin Smith,* 22^{10}; *pEbers,* 2^{1}; 2^{6}; 30^{17}; coda of a text at the beginning of the supplementary spells of the Book of the Dead Leiden T 31: see Allen, *SAOC* 37 (1974), p. 216; BD 190.

94 See Manassa, *Late Egyptian Underworld* 1, p. 477 and n. 243 for a short discussion of later texts that claim to be derived from earlier sources; also Jansen-Winkeln, *WZKM* 85 (1995): 85–115.

95 These would include the *Wörterbuch*, the *Wörterbuch der medizinischen Texte,* Faulkner's *Concise Dictionary,* the three extant volumes of Meeks, *Année Lexicographique,* and Hannig, *Grosses Handwörterbuch.*

SCRIBAL ERRORS, ADDITIONS, AND SUPRALINEAR SIGNS

There are only a few scribal errors in the text. A number of supralinear signs do occur in the text as well. Some have been added to assist the reading of a sign above which they appear; others seem to be signs that were inadvertently omitted but added afterwards above the line where they should have been written. The hand that wrote the supralinear signs appears to be identical to that of the scribe who prepared the text. Additions and corrections are given as follows:

a. The sign at x + 2: 3 to indicate that the signs written below should actually be read .

b. The signs at x + 3: 10 to clarify the reading of the hieratic sign in the word *s3ḥ.w:* "vicinity."

c. The sign at x + 3: 13 to give the full writing of *rwi:* "depart."

d. The signs at x + 7: 11, possibly an inadvertent omission before the signs of the word *rd.wy:* "feet."

e. The addition of at x + 12: 11, where the scribe inadvertently omitted the word *sš:* "writing" and added it later.

f. The addition of at x + 13: 5 to give the full writing of *ˁmˁ.t:* "*ˁmˁ.t*-woman."

g. In several places the scribe who drew up the text, or perhaps another scribe, has crossed out a word or syntactic unit in red. See, for example, x + 8: 2 (the deletion of) and x + 10: 10 (the deletion of). In both places, the deletion of the sign(s) resulted in a more correct grammatical reading.

THE CONTENTS OF P. BROOKLYN 47.218.49

pBrooklyn 47.218.49 is a collection of spells, most of which are concerned with the protection of the king; the focal point of protection, in most cases, is the ear. There are seventeen extant individual spells[96] that vary greatly in length and in the scope of their address. The heading and coda for each is given as follows.

96 An individual spell is defined as one that originally had an introductory heading and a coda.

	Heading	Coda
Spell A	Lost	Lost but traces of rubrics
Spell B	Lost	[hieroglyphs]
Spell C	[hieroglyphs]	Lost
Spell D	Lost	[hieroglyphs]
Spell E	[hieroglyphs]	Lost
Spell F	[hieroglyphs]	[hieroglyphs]
Spell G	[hieroglyphs]	[hieroglyphs] (this coda is extremely long and has several further instructions within it)
Spell H	[hieroglyphs]	[hieroglyphs]
Spell I	[hieroglyphs]	[hieroglyphs]
Spell J	[hieroglyphs]	[hieroglyphs]
Spell K	[hieroglyphs]	[hieroglyphs]
Spell L	[hieroglyphs]	None
Spell M	[hieroglyphs]	None
Spell N	[hieroglyphs]	[hieroglyphs]
Spell O	[hieroglyphs]	[hieroglyphs]
Spell P	[hieroglyphs]	[hieroglyphs] (partly restored)
Spell Q	Too fragmentary to serve any illustrative purpose here.[97]	

97 The word [hieroglyphs] occurs on a single fragment; the group [hieroglyphs] (sic) on another. The coda headings [hieroglyphs] and [hieroglyphs] are found on two fragments as well. Thus, the fragments called Spell Q are quite possibly the remains of at least two different spells.

One should note that there are several types of headings: one group shows : *ky r3* qualified by a prepositional phrase detailing the category of the spell.[98] Spell L, for example, is designated as : *ky r3 n šn.t hh,* "Another spell for recitation (against) heat." Spell N claims to be something of a composite: : *kt.ḫt r3.w nw k3p msḏr dr hh rwi mwt mwt.t m msḏr,* "Other spells for fumigating the ear and driving away heat and turning away a dead male, dead female from the ear." Spell O is : *ky r3 n dr hh m msḏr,* "Another spell for driving away heat from the ear." A second group comprises spells with the heading : *ky r3* immediately followed by the text of the spell itself. The spells of this group should perhaps be understood as codicils to the preceding spell or group of spells. In such cases, the heading *ky r3* would be best understood as "another version" or "variant." Note that only spell G has the different heading : "book" in place of : "utterance."[99] Given the extended headings of Spells G, L, N, and O, we have evidence indicating that the Brooklyn papyrus was a deliberately compiled group of texts, drawn up by consulting whatever material may have been available pertaining to the protection of the ear and gathering it all into a single document. There are a number of other papyri from the 1947 bequest that exhibit this feature. Each of them is dedicated to a single *topos,* and an examination of the headings of the individual spells shows that they too appear to have been drawn from a number of different sources.[100]

Where extant, the coda for each spell is introduced by *ḏd mdw ḥr,* "To be recited over…;" *ḏd mdw sp-4,* "To be recited four times;" and twice *ḏd.tw r3 pn,* "One should recite this spell…." A number of these codae are followed by a list of "pharmacological ingredients" over which the spell is to be recited, along with instructions for their application. In some spells, however, the "prescription" consists simply of an instruction for the recitation of the spell. Note that three spells have no prescriptions but simply the instruction "recite."[101]

As stated above, the texts of *pBrooklyn 47.218.49* are concerned with the protection of the king, invariably called pharaoh or Psamtik;[102] the specific locus of protection, when mentioned, is the ear. The word *msḏr* is the most commonly encountered, showing three

98 The word *ky* is written , , and .

99 This heading is more fully discussed below.

100 For example, *pBrooklyn 47.218.75+.86* (unpublished), a text for treating ailments of the back and buttocks; *pBrooklyn 47.218.87* (O'Rourke, forthcoming), a text that deals with the protection of the mouth; *pBrooklyn 47.218.2* (Guermeur and O'Rourke, forthcoming) concerns itself with pre-natal and postparturition disorders and with crying children.

101 Spells F, K, and N, for which see below.

102 *pCairo 58027,* for example, is specifically dedicated to the protection of the Pharaoh during the twelve hours of the night; see now Pries, *SAGA* 27 (2009); *pBrooklyn 47.218.156,* another apotropaic text dedicated to warding off a wide array of demonic forces, regularly identifies Pharaoh as the one (potentially) threatened; see Sauneron, *pIllustré,* 1^2; 2^4; 4^2; 4^6; 4^8; 4^9; 5^4; also *pBrooklyn 47.218.138,* for which see now Goyon, *pProphylaxie.*

different writings: [hieroglyphs] (40×); [hieroglyphs] (4×); [hieroglyphs] (1×). The word ꜥnḫ.wy occurs as well in the writing [hieroglyphs] (3×). An additional writing [hieroglyphs] (4×) is found, probably to be read *ꜥnḫ.wy.*[103]

For the most part, the content of each spell consists of a series of statements made to inimical forces that have entered or that threaten to enter[104] the ear of Pharaoh, ostensibly to inflict pain or damage. A number of the spells extend their point of reference from the ear to other parts of the anatomy, such as the head, the temple, the heart, the limbs, or the body in general.[105] These diverse anatomical parts form a list of bodily regions to which the assailing forces are denied access or from which they are to be driven. These physical areas are to be seen as extensions of the ear, the anatomical location of primary concern.[106]

The inimical forces enumerated are those commonly encountered in Egyptian religious and apotropaic texts.[107] Malevolent powers called [hieroglyphs] *ḫft,* "enemy," [hieroglyphs] *mwt,* "dead male,"[108] [hieroglyphs] *ḏ3,* "male adversary," and the like are catalogued in lists, some long, some abbreviated; these beings are commonly found in pairs male and female as well.[109] In the longer lists in the Brooklyn papyrus, one encounters, for example, [hieroglyphs] *ḫft pft mwt mwt.t ḏ3y ḏ3y.t ḥm.wt-r3.w,* "enemy, fiend, dead male, dead female, male adversary, female adversary, et al."[110]

In a number of the lists in *pBrooklyn 47.218.49,* we find the term [hieroglyphs] *hh,* in some places as one of the malevolent beings coming against the ear, in others as an element

103 The writing [hieroglyphs] with *.t* is found only in Spells C, D, and E and is the only writing of the word "ear" in those spells, except for a single instance of the word *ꜥnḫ.wy* in Spell E. In all of the other spells, the different writings seem to have been used interchangeably, even within a given spell. The writing [hieroglyphs] is undoubtedly *ꜥnḫ.wy,* as that word occurs only as a dual form. But note that the *Wörterbuch* does not give this writing as an abbreviated writing of *ꜥnḫ.wy.*

104 Some of the texts of the papyrus indicate the presence of the inimical forces in the ear; others have an apotopaic function, warding off the forces that threaten to enter the ear. For the former, see, for example, Spell N; for the latter, see, for example, Spells C, D, G.

105 Examples can be found in the text at x + 2: 8; x + 8: 5; x + 9: 3; x + 10: 3-5; x + 12: 4; x + 13: 1.

106 They are not to be thought of as interchangeable entities, however, as Brunner-Traut, *Frühformen des Erkennens,* p. 72, has implied.

107 See Lucarelli, *SAT* 11 (2006), pp. 203–12.

108 Not "the dead" generically, but those who did not attain the state of becoming an *3ḫ* or who failed at judgment in the netherworld, i.e., "the damned." See n. 109, following.

109 See Lucarelli, *EU* 23, pp. 232ff. for a discussion of the crossover of "the dead" between the realms of the dead and the living; idem, *SAT* 11 (2006), pp. 203–12; Zandee, *Death as an Enemy,* 198ff.; 217ff.; also Walker, *BACE* 4 (1993): 86ff.; Meeks, *SO* 8 (1971), passim, on the various types of demons encountered and their respective spheres of influence, and esp. 191–92. Sauneron, *JNES* 19 (1960): 282–83 describes such beings as divinities who have the power to inflict evil or to withhold it; they are regularly seen as the emissaries of Sakhmet. A good, basic study of the Egyptian fear of the dead is still that of Posener, *MDAIK* 16 (1958): 252–70; see also Spiegelberg, *ZÄS* 65 (1930): 121; Koenig, *pBoulaq 6,* p. 49, n. d with references; Frankfurter, *Evil Incarnate,* pp. 13–30 offers a good general discussion of the demonic in antiquity and how such hostile powers were viewed and dealt with.

110 E.g., x + 10: 12; 17; x + 11: 15; 18; for the translations given for these words, see the discussion of these terms in the text notes below.

that the inimical forces intend to make in the ear. The word *hh* appears 32 times in the papyrus, showing five different writings: (1×);[111] (3×);[112] (20×);[113] (4×);[114] (4×).[115] The *Wb.* gives a word *hh.yt* with the meaning "eine Krankheit des Gehörsinnes oder des Ohres,"[116] citing its occurrence in the medical text *pBerlin 3038*.[117] Hannig offers "Ohrensausen; Unempfindlichkeit" for the same spelling.[118] The presence of the determinative (Sign-list F21) in *hh.yt* is evidently what prompted the translation "Taubheit."[119] A somewhat similarly written word is found in a passage in *pRam III B* 17, where the editor has offered the translation "hoarse,"[120] since the word is found there in connection with the throat, not the ear.[121] It occurs also in *pAnastasi* 5, written .[122] Caminos gives the translation "deafen," citing the Berlin papyrus.[123]

The heading of the Berlin text is *k3p n dr hh.yt nt ˁḳ m rw.t,* "Fumigation (text) for dispelling *hh.yt* that enters from the outside."[124] The subsequent spell in that papyrus is a variant with the heading *kt nt sḥri mwt m msḏr,* "Variant for driving away a dead male from the ear."[125] The occurrence of the negative term *mwt* in the variant suggests a negative meaning for its parallel *hh.yt* as well, but little more. In the three passages in which the word is found, only in *pBerlin 3038* does the translation "deafness" for seem specifically appropriate. Such a translation seems based solely on the fact that the word is found in connection with the ear. In the Ramesseum and Anastasi texts, the meaning "deafness" works only metaphorically at best. In the Brooklyn papyrus, all writings of the word *hh* but one have the determinative (Sign-list Z6); the contexts in which appears indicate that the aspect of this word is unquestionably negative. The variety of contexts in which the word *hh* is found in its variant spellings suggests

---

111 x + 8: 2.

112 x + 8: 3; 5; 19.

113 x + 8: 10; 11; x + 9: 2; 5; 6; 8; x + 10: 2; 6; 17; x + 11: 9; 16 (2×): 19; x + 12: 6; 12; 16 (2×); 18; x + 13: 9; x + 14: 7.

114 x + 10: 12; x + 12: 3; 7; x + 13: 17.

115 x + 10: 12; x + 12: 3; 7; x + 13: 17.

116 *Wb.* II, 502[11].

117 *pBerlin* 3038, 6[10] (*Bln* 70).

118 Hannig, *GH,* 498a.

119 e.g., Westendorf, *Handbuch* I, p. 59.

120 Barns, *Five Ramesseum Papyri,* p. 22, n. 17.

121 : *n ir ẖẖ=k hwh.yw,* "thy throat has not become hoarse," trans. Barns. A preferable translation may be "soreness;" see the discussion below.

122 Gardiner, *LEM,* p. 65, l. 9; Caminos, *CLEM,* p. 250.

123 : *hh.yw ibw m3ˁ=k,* "pleasures have deafened your hearing," trans. Caminos.

124 See n. 117.

125 *pBerlin* 3038, 6[11] (*Bln* 71).

that perhaps a more generalized meaning than "deafness" should be considered. The rendering "Unempfindlichkeit" given by Hannig draws attention.[126]

The similarly written word *hh* is of interest here.[127] It is encountered in Egyptian texts as one of the more potent weapons in the cosmic arsenal. It is used of the fiery power of the uraeus on the brow of Re.[128] In certain Ramesside Period battle reliefs, the word appears in the accompanying text, not as a term for conflagration, but as a metaphor for the king and his army, especially to denote the supreme power of the king.[129] In texts, it is also found as a weapon used by the forces inimical to cosmic order, and, in turn, by the gods who strive to repel them.[130] Conversely, it can refer to the benevolent heat of the sun.[131] It is also used of the fiery blast of the Eye of Horus.[132] What is relevant as well is its occurrence in *pEbers* in the phrase *hh n pḥ.yt,* "heat of the anus."[133] Taking all of the above into consideration, the only objections to establishing a connection between the writings *hh* and *hh* seem to be that does not show a writing with , nor do the lexica give (Sign-list Z6) as one of its determinatives. All the same, neither of these objections seems insurmountable.[134]

For the Egyptians, pain due to earache or to inflammation of the ear could easily be associated with fire or even understood to be caused by some kind of inner, corporeal fire. In this light, one may see that in the Brooklyn text "heat in the ear" is a threat that one must be protected from or cured of. Note that most of the spells of this papyrus have the goal of not (only) curing the one suffering from ailments of the ears, but protecting him (as well); the one protected might even be one prone to suffering from "heat in the ear."

At this juncture, a thorny question arises: is the Brooklyn papyrus an apotropaic text or one whose main goal was "therapeutic intervention?[135] On the one hand, the contents of most of its texts appear to be apotropaic in nature. On the other, the lists of

126 See n. 118 above.

127 *Wb.* II, 501^{15}–502^{8}, and Hannig, *GH,* 497b: "Gluthauch;" note that Hannig also gives a meaning: "[med] Hitze (*als Krankheitserscheinung*)."

128 For example, *pBM 10042,* 1^{5} and 5^{7}, for which see Leitz, *HPBM* 7, p. 31, Section B and p. 37, Section H.

129 Hasel, *Domination and Resistance,* pp. 28, 40, 84–85, and 248.

130 Zandee, *Death as an Enemy,* pp. 137–38.

131 *pAmunhymnus,* vs. 2, pp. 467–70.

132 *pBremner-Rhind,* 30^{23} and 31^{13}; for a discussion of the goddess(es) of the Eye of Horus and the Eye of Re, see Darnell, *SAK* 24 (1997): 35–48.

133 *pEbers,* 100^{16} (*Eb* 855f).

134 In Late Egyptian writing, one routinely encounters a superfluous *t* in the writing of a masculine grammatical form. The sign (Sign-list Z6) is actually an abbreviated writing of (Sign-list A14). In Late Period writings, the sign seems to have become something of a universal negative marker. Given the negative meaning that the word *hh* largely has in Egyptian texts, the exchange of for (Sign-list Q7) seems logical.

135 See Ritner, *Oxford Encyclopedia of Ancient Egypt* 2, p. 353, for the term, used there in a discussion of ancient Egyptian medicine.

pharmacological ingredients forming a prescription that are found at the conclusion of at least nine of its seventeen texts suggest the presence of what appears to be a form of intervention.[136] We should keep in mind, however, that the Egyptians may have regarded apotropaic practice as a serious form of intervention; such practices may have been the only instances of what we call "preventive" medicine known to them.[137] The difficulty in answering such a question about text genre may be laid to rest by recalling that the Brooklyn papyrus is a compilation of different texts; as such, one may encounter difficulty trying to assign it to a single textual genre.[138]

The inimical forces mentioned in the texts of the papyrus are not to be seen as the disease itself but rather as agents that bring or cause the disease.[139] They are not mere personifications but beings that play an active role in the struggle between the ordered cosmos and the forces of chaos that threaten from without. The Egyptians viewed the body as a microcosm of the ordered universe that was constantly under threat. Forces that lay outside of that structured realm, as well as the malignant aspects of forces within it, posed constant threats, particularly at dangerous times like night or the epagomenal days that preceded the New Year.[140]

If *pBrooklyn 47.218.49* was made for the protection of the king, it belongs to a genre found both on papyri and monumental inscriptions, one that spans a long period of time.[141] Many of these texts are found as short excerpts in longer texts that cannot them-

136 These lists are found at the end of Spells B, C, D, F, G, H, N, O, and P.

137 The papyri that have traditionally been designated as "medical" do seem to show forms of "therapeutic intervention" in their approaches to certain problems and conditions; see n. 135 above. Basic hygiene in ancient Egypt was extremely poor; see Filer, *Oxford Encyclopedia of Ancient Egypt* 2, pp. 133–36. See also Assmann, in Schäfer and Kippenberg, *Envisioning Magic,* p. 8; and Gyóry, in Kousoulis, *OLA* 175 (2011), pp. 151–66.

138 There are other papyri and individual texts that have apotropaic content and the presence of pharmacological lists. See, for example, *pCairo 58027* (night ritual for the protection of the king). *pBrooklyn 47.218.2* (Guermeur and O'Rourke, forthcoming) comprises texts that deal with pre-natal and post-parturition disorders. Some of the texts are clearly apotropaic in nature; their content is deeply rooted in the mythological. Other texts are simple prescription texts that simply give lists of ingredients and an instruction for the application of the prescription. The final section of the papyrus deals with children who cry in the night; there, the content is again largely mythological.

139 See the remarks of Sauneron, *Kêmi* 20 (1970), p. 15.

140 See Sauneron, *JNES* 19 (1960): 282–83, where these forces are described as divine beings who have the power to inflict evil or to withhold it; they are regularly seen as the emissaries of Sakhmet; also Walker, *BACE* 4 (1993) 86ff.; Lucarelli, *EU* 23, pp. 232ff.

141 The texts in the abbreviated list found in Goyon, *BIFAO* 74 (1974): 75–83, range from the Second Intermediate Period to the Roman Period. See the remarks of Sauneron, *pIllustré,* p. 17; also Goyon, *BdE* 141 (2006), passim, but esp. pp. 125–34.

selves technically be called protection texts.[142] But there also exist a number of lengthy texts whose apparent sole purpose is the protection of the king.

1. *pBrooklyn 47.218.49:* protection of the king with focus on the ears.[143]
2. the assemblage of texts of Crypt B' at Elkab.[144]
3. *pCairo 58027:* protection of the king during the twelve hours of night.[145]
4. *pVienna 8426:* an assemblage of texts largely for the protection of the king against the evils of the year.[146]
5. *pBrooklyn 47.218.156:* protection of the king against a number of inimical beings.[147]
6. *pBrooklyn 47.218.87:* protection of the king with focus on the area of the mouth.[148]
7. an assemblage of texts found on the architraves of the Edfu Temple: protection of the king against the dangers that occur at the change to the New Year.[149]

Putting *pBrooklyn 47.218.49* aside for the moment, it is worth noting that all of the other texts are clearly generic in their focus on the protection of the king, as they employ the term *pr-ꜥꜣ* and do not use the name of a specific king. Does the presence of the name Psamtik in the Brooklyn text preclude its use as a generic text? Not necessarily, if we note that the term *pr-ꜥꜣ* appears almost as often as the name Psamtik.[150] The presence of the name may simply point to the time when the text was drawn up or compiled.[151] Perhaps

142 See, for example, the short texts found at the end of the medical book *pEdwin Smith* at 18^{19}; 18^{14-15}; 19^{9}; 19^{10-11}. These texts are all protection texts against the dangers of the *iꜣd.t (n) rnp.t*, "pestilence of the year," and against the destructive breath of the emissaries of *ḏs-ḥr* and Sakhmet. See Goyon, *BIFAO* 74 (1974): 77, citations 1–4. See also *pChester Beatty 8*, vs. 10^{8-9}; *pChester Beatty 9*, rt. 17^{4}; and *pLeiden I 346*, 2^{4}; 2^{6}; 2^{7}; and 2^{11}.

143 The present study, dating to the reign of Psamtik I.

144 See above at pp. 12ff.

145 For a recent publication of *pCairo 58027*, see Pries, *SAGA* 27; it is dated to the late Ptolemaic–early Roman Periods and employs only the title *pr-ꜥꜣ*.

146 *pVienna 8426* is now published, for which see Flessa, *Corpus Papyrorum Raineri 27;* it is dated to the second half of the first century–first half of the second century AD. Susanne Töpfer of Heidelberg University is currently preparing *pCarlsberg 646 vs* for publication, a parallel to the Vienna papyrus; it also dates to the Roman Period, 2nd century AD.

147 Sauneron, *pIllustré;* dated to the fourth century BC by Sauneron, a date that perhaps should be revised based on criteria used in the Late Period hieratic study by Verhoeven. See the discussion above.

148 Publication forthcoming; dated to the Saite Period.

149 Goyon, *BdE* 141 (2006); dated to the Ptolemaic Period.

150 See p. 11 above.

151 Note that the name of Apries is present in *pBrooklyn 47.218.135* (*pBrooklyn Wisdom*) at column x + 1: 14 and was used by the editor as the *terminus post quem* from which to date the papyrus. See the discussion above.

the scribe used the name Psamtik, as well as the title *pr-ꜥ3,* to give further potency to the spells of the text. Even if the papyrus was originally reserved for the use of Psamtik, as a comprehensive compilation it retained the potential for more universal application. We must reserve judgment for the moment, however, as there are a number of texts included in *pBrooklyn 47.218.49* in which neither the name Psamtik nor the title *pr-ꜥ3* is found.[152]

A further note on modern terminology: texts like those contained in *pBrooklyn 47.218.49* have been described over the last century by a number of terms, such as "magical,"[153] "magico-medical,"[154] or "magico-religious"[155] — designations that continue to be used, almost interchangeably. Such terms are helpful only in the limited way in that they indicate the contents of a given text. Terms like "magico-medical" and "magico-religious," moreover, have the unfortunate problem of making a text so described sound like a hybrid, which it certainly is not.[156]

It has long been established that the power of the spoken word was understood by the Egyptians to be of pre-eminent effectiveness.[157] It is worth noting that the framing of each spell with *ky r3* and *ḏd mdw ḥr,* common in texts of this genre, emphasizes that much — if not all — of the effectiveness of a spell lies in its "oral application." Nine of the seventeen spells of the Brooklyn papyrus conclude, however, with a list of pharmacological ingredients. We should caution that a text of this type, which concludes with a "pharmaceutical" prescription, is not one that works through the double power of magic and medicine.[158] The instructions in the coda are to recite the text "over" the prescription. Thus, it is this oral recitation that gives the prescription its power. Similarly, we find in a number of these papyri instructions for the recitation of the text over a thread that is to be tied in seven knots and applied to the victim's neck. Such a text is not a "pure magical" text.[159] In such texts, like those of the Brooklyn papyrus, the effectiveness of the treatment lies in the empowerment that the thread or a list of pharmacological ingredients has just received from the text "recited over" it. Furthermore, texts whose instructions are simply given as *ḏd mdw ḥr,* "to be recited…," were quite possibly to be

---

152 See, for examples, Spells J and K.

153 Gardiner, *HPBM,* 3rd ser., p. 50: describing the texts of verso of *pChester Beatty 5;* p. 55: describing the recto and verso of *pChester Beatty 7;* Flessa, *Corpus Papyrorum Raineri XXVII,* uses the phrase "magisches Handbuch" in the title of his publication of *pVienna 8426,* another book of protection for the pharaoh listed above.

154 Gardiner, *HPBM,* 3rd ser., p. 125; describing *pChester Beatty 15.*

155 Gardiner, *HPBM,* 3rd ser., p. 66; describing the recto and some of the texts on the verso of *pChester Beatty 8.*

156 See Ritner, *SAOC* 54 (1992), passim, but especially pp. 4–28, where he fully discusses the problems of terminology in attempting to define the term "magic" and its range of applicability.

157 See the remarks of Assmann, *Death and Salvation,* pp. 237–38 and 243–47.

158 Westendorf's "Zaubertexte mit medizinischer Anwendung verknüpft," for which see Westendorf, *Handbuch* 1, p. 82.

159 For such a text, see, for example, *pEbers,* 95^{7-14} (*Eb* 811); Westendorf, *Handbuch* 1, p. 527; also Ritner, *SAOC* 54 (1992), pp. 142–44, nn. 638–39; on the concept of a "pure magical text," see Westendorf's category "Reine Zaubertexte" in idem, *Handbuch* 1, p. 92.

recited over the patient. The effectiveness of a text of this type, I stress again, lies in its "oral application."

Spells like the ones in the present papyrus often involve the replay of an event in a cosmic drama.[160] In a number of Egyptian texts, for example, we encounter the child Horus who has been stung by a scorpion after he was left alone by his mother.[161] In other texts, the afflicted one is identified as Horus,[162] or sometimes as Re, and the role of protector is played by Isis,[163] another deity,[164] or a number of deities.[165] In these texts, the cosmic drama is reenacted, but its desired outcome is already known. In this way, the one treated is "cured" or "protected," and the hostile forces are rendered impotent, at least for the moment.

A number of spells in *pBrooklyn 47.218.49* show variations on this theme. The diseased or threatened part of the body, the ear for the most part in this papyrus, becomes the cosmic location where the struggle between the forces of order and chaos takes place. The prescription of Spell J (x + 8: 11–15), for example, states that the text of the spell is "to be recited over an image of Horus (and) an image of Seth drawn upon the ear of a man." Thus, the mythological struggle between Horus and Seth is considered to be taking place at or in the ear. Since the outcome of that battle is already known, the recitation of the text (hopefully) predicts and brings about the successful cure or protection of the patient. Spell I (x + 8: 6–11) has an image of the barque of Re in its prescription. In this text, the attempt to cure or protect the ear was possibly associated with the daily journey of the sun and, specifically, the sun god's triumph over his enemies.[166] As stated above, the process of establishing a cure or protection from the disease is twofold: the agents responsible for the disease are destroyed, dispelled, or neutralized through the act of ritual utterance; the anatomical part of the body that is currently threatened or diseased is treated with a physical remedy or amulet, now fully charged through the act of oral recitation.

SUMMARY

As for the Brooklyn papyrus as a whole, a few observations can be made. The seventeen individual spells of *pBrooklyn 47.218.49* vary in length and, at first glance, do not seem to have an evident overall organization.[167] In a number of individual texts, the scribe used the name Psamtik and the term *pr-ꜥꜣ,* often interchangeably within a given spell. Based

160 The technical term for such a text is *historiola,* for which see Ritner, *SAOC* 54, p. 76 and n. 338.

161 Examples of such texts can be found in *pBM 10059,* 10^{8}–11^{4}, for which see Leitz, *HPBM* 7, pp. 72–73 (Incantations 34–36) and pls. 35–36; Klasens, *Socle Behague,* p. 68. These texts address both scorpion bites and burns.

162 For example, *pBM 9997,* 4^{3} and 4^{6}, for which see Leitz, *HPBM* 7, p. 10 and pl 4.

163 For example, *pBM 10059,* $8^{5ff.}$, for which see Leitz, *HPBM* 7, p. 66 and pl. 33.

164 Anubis, for example, in *pBM 10059,* 9^{7-8} and 9^{14}, for which see Leitz, *HPBM* 7, pp. 68–69 and pl. 34.

165 Examples can be found in *pChester Beatty 5,* 4^{1}; also below in Spell N, x + 9: 8–x + 10: 2.

166 See note P (x + 8: 15) below.

167 See the remarks in the Commentary to each spell below.

on the presence of this name and title, the papyrus appears to have a provenance that is royal; hence, the word "Royal" in the title of the present work.

The word compilation has been used throughout this discussion to describe the Brooklyn papyrus. The internal evidence used to reach such a conclusion is not extensive, but what there is seems to carry weight. The inconsistent use of the name Psamtik in the papyrus — it is found in some spells but not in others — suggests that the Brooklyn papyrus was not an original individual text. We would expect to find greater consistency in the use of terminology in such a document. The inconsistent use of the term *pr-ꜥꜣ* speaks to that matter as well. These patterns seem to indicate that the scribe who prepared this papyrus was copying, not composing. Secondly, the writings of the word *msḏr* show a great variation in this papyrus, as noted above. Spells C, D, and E show only a single writing of *msḏr:* , excluding the one writing of *ꜥnḫ.wy* in Spell E; nowhere else in the papyrus is such a spelling found. This evidence strongly suggests that the origin of these three texts was an exemplar different from the other one(s) the scribe used. The fact that these three spells appear sequentially seems then to be no accident and offers further support for seeing the Brooklyn papyrus as a compilation. The lengthy Spell N offers some evidence as well. It exhibits several Late Egyptian grammatical forms; no other text in the papyrus does so. Additionally, the lengthy address at the beginning of the spell has parallels in several of the Chester Beatty papyri, texts that are dated to the New Kingdom. It is quite probable that the exemplar used for Spell N was of a New Kingdom date as well.

With all of this in mind, we can offer three suggestions regarding the original purpose of the papyrus. First, there is the possibility that a king named Psamtik[168] was prone to ear disorders, and that the text was created specifically for him to maximize his protection against such ailments. Following such an interpretation, we should see this text not so much as a royal book of protection, but as a book of protection for an individual who happens, in this case, to be pharaoh.[169] What mitigates against this view is the presence of texts that make no mention of his name or the term *pr-ꜥꜣ*;[170] furthermore, the evidence outlined above indicates that this papyrus is a compilation drawn from several or even more exemplars. We do know of other papyri from the genre of protection texts that were prepared for single individuals;[171] none of them are as extensive as the Brooklyn papyrus, and none of them have any royal associations.[172]

168 For the king so named, see the discussion above.

169 See the discussion above.

170 See, for example, Texts G, J, and K. The highly fragmentary individual texts have not been considered here.

171 See, for example, Koenig, *RdE* 33 (1981): 29–37 (*pDeM* 40, made for the use of a man named Keniherkhepeshef); Sauneron, *Kêmi* 20 (1970): 7–18, (*pDeM* 36, prepared for the use of an individual named Anynakht).

172 For protection texts with royal associations, see the texts cited at nn. 143–49 above.

Second, the text was intended for the protection of the ears of the king,[173] here Psamtik, during times of danger, like the time of the approach of the New Year. Such an interpretation would argue for the existence of other papyri whose purpose may also have been the protection of different parts of the king's body. The presence in the Brooklyn collection of a fragmentary papyrus whose focal point is the protection of the mouth of the king lends some support to such a view.[174] A number of texts in the Brooklyn papyrus, but not all, fit this description.[175]

A third interpretation is that the Brooklyn papyrus was an intentional compilation of what may have been all known texts that were intended for the protection of the ears. In the place of the more commonly encountered identification *mn ms n mn.t,* "so and so, born of so and so" or *s/st,* "man/woman,"[176] the scribe used the name Psamtik. It is quite possible that the name Psamtik and the term *pr-ꜥꜣ* were used to give valence to the papyrus as a whole, to mark it as *the* exemplar on which all future copies of even shorter texts that have to do with the protection of the ear should be based. The presence of the title *pr-ꜥꜣ* may also serve to indicate that these texts were prepared under the aegis of the king or palace, thus working along the lines of a royal *imprimatur.*[177] Such an interpretation may explain the presence of the title *pr-ꜥꜣ* found in the fragmentary Late Period medical and protection texts in Brooklyn whose primary focus appears to be women's health and protection. That said, we can still argue that the papyrus as a whole is a protection text drawn up for the king, with the specific locus of protection being (largely) the ears. The presence of the texts that do not employ the name Psamtik or the title *pr-ꜥꜣ* may be explained as follows. Their inclusion gave the papyrus as a whole an increased efficacy, because they made the collection of texts that much more comprehensive. Finally, it may

---

173 As noted above, however, not all of the texts seem to have clear connections with the ear. But see the Commentary following the Text Notes for each spell.

174 *pBrooklyn 47.218.87* (O'Rourke, forthcoming); see n. 148 above. Although *pIllustré* was seemingly intended to guard the king against snake and scorpion bites, note that the coda to each of the two texts in this papyrus states: "Words to be recited over this image [which is in writing] [and drawn upon] a new roll of papyrus [and placed at the neck of] a woman or child" and "Words to be recited over this image which is in writing on a new roll of papyrus (and) placed at the neck of a man," respectively. Clearly, both of these texts are "generic." Another fragment group, a subset of *pBrooklyn 47.218.4,* was intended to protect the "belly (*ẖ.t*) of *pr-ꜥꜣ*."

175 If this conjecture is valid, then it is likely that all Egyptian temples had a set of such texts. But see further below.

176 It seems defensible to suggest that the one reciting such a generic text would insert the name of the patient during the act of recitation. See Flessa, *Corpus Papyrorum Reineri 27,* pp. 35–36.

177 See Quack, in Schaper, *Die Textualisierung der Religion,* pp. 29ff., for how this idea may have informed the creation of the Saite Recension of the Book of the Dead. Most of the papyri in Brooklyn whose focus is women's health and protection are very fragmentary. The fragments are currently being catalogued with the goal of grouping them into their proper lots and placing them under glass.

simply be the case that we should see *pBrooklyn 47.218.49* as fulfilling all of these roles. As a comprehensive and royal copy that was to be seen as the exemplar *par excellence,* it possessed formidable power as a resource to be drawn upon.

As discussed above, there are a number of papyri in the Brooklyn collection that also bear the marks of the activity of compilation. Several of them are now dated with greater certainty to the beginning of Dynasty Twenty-six, as is *pBrooklyn 47.218.49*. This activity may have a recognizable kin in the so-called Saite Recension, the total reorganization of the text corpus of the Book of the Dead that took place during this time. Thus, there seems to be growing evidence that in the Saite Period there was a conscious and deliberate movement to "reorganize and (re)codify knowledge."[178] This subject needs further consideration and study before anything more can be stated. However this process unfolded, it was certainly an involved and complex one.[179]

Beyond these observations and suggestions, little more can be said at present. We sincerely hope that further investigation and study of the texts in the Brooklyn collection will bring forward additional evidence that may allow us to speak more specifically about the nature and function of a text like *pBrooklyn 47.218.49* and its place in the Egyptian textual tradition.

---

178 Munro, in Taylor, *Journey Through the Afterlife,* p. 58, suggests that the initial steps of the reworking of the Book of the Dead "must have taken place during the 25th Dynasty, leading to the copying of monuments and documents of the past, a characteristic of the general archaism of this time." Cf., however, Quack, in Schaper, *Die Textualisierung der Religion,* p. 30: "Selbst dann kann man sich den Prozess schon rein nur in der Zeit eines zentral durchorganisierten Staaates vorstellen, und von daher ist es auch plausibel, dass ein solcher Schritt etwa in die Saitenzeit fällt, nicht etwa in die politisch fragmentierte Dritte Zwischenzeit." What seems to be going on in the Saite Period is not so much the activity of copying, but that of compilation and reorganization, activities that seem to have little, if anything, to do with the archaizing tradition. See O'Rourke in *Égypte, Afrique & Orient* 71 (2013): 33–40.

179 See Quack, in Schaper, *Die Textualisierung der Religion,* pp. 11–34, on the complexity of Egyptian funerary traditions and for a good discussion on what informed the creation and production of the Saite Recension.

Spell A — Translation with Commentary

COLUMN X + 1: 1–19 (P. BROOKLYN 47.218.49)

TRANSLITERATION

COLUMN X + 1

1. … *m tp*
2. … *[ꜣ]ḫ.w*
3. … *psd*
4. … *[psm]ṯk ꜥ.w.s.*
5. … *[ps]mṯk*
6. … *[d]p ḥn*
7. … *=f mn*
8. … *ꜣḫ.w*
9. … *w=f r*
10. … *ỉb…*
11. … *b mw*
12. … *nn ḏꜣ[…]*
13. … *n rꜥ ỉrr*
14. … *kꜣ ḥr*
15. … *ỉr.w […]*
16. … *[s]w rꜥ smꜣ*
17. … *wḏꜣ.t ṯz*
18. … *.t pr*
19. … *=sn r*

TRANSLATION

1. […c. 17 cm…] in the head[A]
2. […c. 17 cm…] blessed dead[B]
3. […c. 17 cm…] spine[C]
4. […c. 16 cm…][D] [Psam]tik,[E] l.p.h.
5. […c. 17 cm…][F] [Psa]mtik
6. […c. 17 cm…] [De]p[G] *ḥn*
7. […c. 17 cm…] his(?)[H] *mn*

8. […c. 17 cm…] spells[I]
9. […c. 18 cm…] his … towards[J]
10. […c. 18 cm…] *ib*…[K]
11. […c. 18 cm…] water[L]
12. […c. 17 cm…] without *ḏ3*…[M]
13. […c. 17 cm…the barque (?)] of Re who does[N]
14. [Maat…c. 17 cm…] bull upon[O]
15. […c. 17 cm…] forms[P] […]
16. […c. 17 cm…] of Re *sm3*[Q]
17. […c. 17 cm…] Wadjet raise (?)…[R]
18. […c. 17 cm…][S] going forth
19. […c. 17 cm…] their […] towards

TEXT NOTES

A. (x + 1: 1) The writing of the sign appears slightly different elsewhere in the papyrus.

B. (x + 1: 2) The traces before appear to suit .

C. (x + 1: 3) , *psd*, “spine” (*Wb.* I 556, 1–9, citing writings with the determinative).

D. (x + 1: 4) Before the name Psamtik, possibly restore one of the following: *m ii r msḏr n*] *Psmṯk*, “Do not come against the ear of Psamtik l.p.h.;” or *irr hh m msḏr n*] *Psmṯk*, “…who make heat in the ear of Psamtik l.p.h.” Compare, for example, x + 2: 7 and x + 8: 10 where each of these phrases occurs, respectively.

E. (x + 1: 4) This is the first of twenty-four occurrences of the name Psamtik in the extant portions of the text; it interchanges with *pr-ʿ3*, which occurs nineteen times.

F. (x + 1: 5) For the restoration of the end of this lacuna, see x + 1: 4, n. D. above.

G. (x + 1: 6) The restored reading *dp* is based on the traces and the sign ⊗ (Sign-list O 49).

H. (x + 1: 7) probably represents the suffix pronoun =*f* following a word, now lost, written with the knife-determinative (Sign-list T30).

I. (x + 1: 8) Beyond its meaning “blessed dead,” commonly encountered in funerary texts, the word *3ḫ.w* can mean “protection” or “spells,” although *r3*, “spell,” is the commonly employed term in this text. The word *3ḫ.w* can also be found in protection texts, in lists of malevolent beings.

J. (x + 1: 9) [hieroglyphs] are written clearly enough here, but their relationship is uncertain. Elsewhere the scribe writes the suffix pronoun [hieroglyph] above the horizontal signs that follow, possibly due to his eye for economy of space. See x + 2: 6, n. C, below.

K. (x + 1: 10) [hieroglyphs] [...], *ib*-, possibly the beginning of [hieroglyphs] *ibr.t*, which is also found at x + 3: 14, for which see x + 3: 14, n. YY below.

L. (x + 1: 11) The writing [hieroglyphs] is either *m-ꜥ mw* or simply *mw*, as [hieroglyphs] is a Late Period writing of *mw*, "water" (*Wb.* II, 50, 7–9). The sign which precedes this group may be [hieroglyph] *b* (Sign-list D58).

M. (x + 1: 12) [hieroglyphs] is possibly the beginning of the word [hieroglyphs] *ḏꜣ*, "male adversary," or [hieroglyphs] *ḏꜣ.t*, "female adversary," as both occur frequently in this text. Note, however, that the phrase *nn ḏꜣ* does not appear anywhere else in the papyrus.

N. (x + 1: 13) Before [hieroglyphs] *n Rꜥ*, the restoration of *wiꜣ*, "barque," seems possible. The following word *irr* could then refer to the activity of the deity or being belonging to "the barque of Re." The phrase *irr mꜣꜥ.t* would be a possible restoration.

O. (x + 1: 14) The traces before [hieroglyphs] *ḥr* seem to be [hieroglyphs] *kꜣ*, but the meaning of this group remains elusive. The word [hieroglyphs] could be the beginning of a prepositional phrase or a verbal construction.

P. (x + 1: 15) The determinative [hieroglyph] (Sign-list A53) commonly appears with the nouns [hieroglyphs] *ḫpr.w*, "manifestation" or "form" (*Wb.* III 265, 20–266, 17); [hieroglyphs] *ir.w*, "form" (*Wb.* I 113, 8–114, 7); and [hieroglyphs] *twt*, "image" (*Wb.* V 255, 8–256, 20). Only the first two terms occur later in the text.

Q. (x + 1: 16) [hieroglyphs] *smꜣ*, "vereinigen" (*Wb.* III 446, 3–447, 13).

R. (x + 1: 17) The sign after [hieroglyph] is clearly [hieroglyph], but I can make little sense of the two, possibly three, signs that follow.

S. (x + 1: 18) The signs that precede [hieroglyphs] *pr* seem to be [hieroglyphs].

COMMENTARY

The lacunae in this column of the papyrus are considerable and preclude restoration. It remains unclear whether this column is the original first column of the papyrus. The title *pr-ꜥꜣ* does not occur, but the name Psamtik appears twice, parallels for which are found in a number of spells in the papyrus. Little else can be added.

Spell B — Translation with Commentary

COLUMNS X + 1: 20–X + 2: 6 (P. BROOKLYN 47.218.49)

TRANSLITERATION

20. … *sꜣ.w n*
21. … *msḏr wnmi n*
22. … *[inḏ] ḥr=tn*

COLUMN X + 2

1. … *ḥr n* …
2. … *rꜥ i irr* …
3. *ṯz…=f n* … *[ḥr] n gif m ṯꜣrw* … *r*
4. *.w wbꜣ rꜣ* … *n mḥ.t rn n wsir iw ḏd[=k]* … *=f sw*
5. *ḏd mdw ḥr smꜣ* …*y.wt ḥs šꜣi wꜣḏ 20* … *.ty*
6. *di r msḏr*

TRANSLATION

20. […c. 17 cm…] *protections* (?) *for*[A]
21. […c. 17 cm…] the right ear[B] of[C]
22. […c. 17 cm…] hail to[D] you

COLUMN X + 2

1. […9 cm…] face of (?)[E] […9 cm…]
2. […8.5 cm…] Re.[F] O one who makes[G] […9 cm…][H]
3. raise (?) […7 cm…] face of an ape[I] in Sile[J] […4.5 cm…][K]
4. sack(?)[L] opening[M] the mouth […4.5 cm…] of a *mḥ.t*-bowl[N] the name of Osiris while [you] say[O] […4.5 cm…] he … him…[P]
5. *Words to be recited over* […4 cm…][Q] [plant-name],[R] fresh[S] excrement of a swine,[T] 20 […4 cm…] (and)
6. placed at the ear.[U]

TEXT NOTES

A. (x + 1: 20) The rubrics are somewhat faint here, but the signs at the end of the line seem to be [hieroglyphs] *s3.w n* "…protections for…." The rubric and the word *s3* indicate the beginning or end of a spell, as rubrics are used in this text only to indicate spell headings and codas. Given the extensive lacunae and the varying length of spells in this papyrus, it is impossible to tell exactly how many spells were originally written at the beginning of the text.

B. (x + 1: 21) Only here is the word [hieroglyphs] *msḏr*, "ear," qualified as "right" or "left." *pEbers*, 100[3] (*Eb* 854f) states that the right ear is that through which the "breath of life" enters, the left through which the "breath of death" enters. See also Ritner, *SAOC* 54 (1992), p. 89, n. 425, for further references. In Egyptian religious texts, "right" is generally associated with good and "left" with evil; see Borghouts, *pLeiden I 348*, pp. 70–71, n. 106. At x + 8: 13 below, fire is said to come forth on the left side of Isis and of Nephthys; also, at x + 8: 18 there is a reference to branding or burning on the left side.

C. (x + 1: 21) The group [hieroglyphs] is a writing of *wnmi* followed by the preposition *n*.

D. (x + 1: 22) The traces of what appears to be [hieroglyph] suggest [hieroglyphs] *inḏ* before [hieroglyphs] *ḥr*. The addition of the sign [hieroglyph] (Sign-list G7) to the group [hieroglyphs] indicates that deities are invoked in the phrase *inḏ-ḥr*, "Hail to you…" See x + 6: 16 below and *pChester Beatty 1*, 2[1] for further examples.

E. (x + 2: 1) The damage to the upper portion of the papyrus has left only the signs [hieroglyphs] *ḥr n*, "face of," at the center of this line and is too extensive to allow a determination of whether this is the first line of the column or not.

F. (x + 2: 2) The traces of the sign ☉ preceding the determinative [hieroglyph] possibly indicate a writing of [hieroglyphs] *rꜥ*, "Re," or [hieroglyphs] *wsir*, "Osiris."

G. (x + 2: 2) [hieroglyphs] is the writing of the vocative indicator *i* routinely encountered in this papyrus. Note the dotted writing of the sign [hieroglyph] (Sign-list A2).

H. (x + 2: 2) The scant traces seen at the bottom of the break at the end of the line point to a restoration of [hieroglyphs] *tp*, "head."

I. (x + 2: 3) [hieroglyphs] *gif*, "Affe; Meerkatze" (*Wb.* V, 158 12–16; "Grüne Meerkatze [*Cercopithecus aethiops*])," Hannig *GH*, p. 896a. For parallels to the phrase *ḥr gif*, "face of an ape," see Kákosy, *ZÄS* 117 (1990), where *pBudapest 51.1960*, Col. A, l. 9 has *iw=f ḥr gif* […]; also *pBM 10042*, 9[4] for *p3 nty im=f m ḥr n gif*, "…the one who is in it [the shrine] with the face of an ape…;" *BD* 136A: *sḳdi=i im=f m gif*…, "I will sail in it with/as the ape…."

J. (x + 2: 3) The hieratic as written presents difficulties. The reading of each of the first three signs is clear, though their relationship is not. Given that the phoneme *mꜣ-* is generally written in Egyptian with the sign , one possible solution is to understand the first sign as the preposition *m* governing whatever word follows. The *Wörterbuch,* however, gives no word with the spelling *ꜣṯꜣ*, nor does it give any word written *ꜣṯ* in which the sign (Sign-list G47) is to be read as *t*. The solution lies in the supralinear sign , used as a gloss in Greek and Demotic magical texts and some hieratic texts as well. Thissen, *Religion und Philosophie im alten Ägypten,* pp. 299–300, discusses the various readings and meanings that have been assigned to it, namely *hꜣ*, "O," *ii tw*, "Welcome," or *iꜣw*, "Greetings." Here the sign is apparently used to draw attention to an inversion of signs. The text should read *m ṯꜣrw*. The word is probably *ṯꜣrw*, Hannig, *GH* 1405a: "Sile (al-Qantara)," or possibly Hannig, *GH* 949a: *ṯꜣr.t*, "ship's-cabin." I thank Dr. Hans Fischer-Elfert for pointing out the correct order of the hieratic signs here.

K. (x + 2: 3) The traces at the end of the line suit . See x + 2: 4, n. L following.

L. (x + 2: 4) The sign (Sign-list V19) is the determinative of the last word written in the preceding line; taken with the sign *r* at the end of the preceding line, a possible restoration is *ẖꜣr*, "sack" (Hannig, *GH* 631a).

M. (x + 2: 4) The sign is written with the phonetic complements and and is followed by , the whole group reading *wbꜣ rꜣ*, "opening the mouth." It is unlikely, however, that this phrase refers to the well-known ritual of the Opening of the Mouth. It seems more likely that it refers to the patient or of one of the inimical beings assailing him.

N. (x + 2: 4) *mḥ.t*, "Schale, Napf" (*Wb.* II 126, 12–15), occurs again in this papyrus at x + 12: 11. The *mḥ.t*-vase played an important role in medical and protection texts; see, for example, *pEbers* at 4^{6} (*Eb* 13); 18^{1} (*Eb* 57); 53^{7} (*Eb* 308); and 93^{16} (*Eb* 788); and *pLeiden I 348,* rt. 13^{2} and vs. 11^{8}. Spells were written on the vase, thus empowering any liquid poured into it. The liquid was then drunk by the patient as a curative. For this practice, see Borghouts, *pLeiden I 348,* p. 132, n. 304, and p. 173, n. 420, and the general discussion on "swallowing" by Ritner, *SAOC* 54 (1992), pp. 102–10. Both authors discuss a vase in Cairo (CG 18490) with a *cippus* carved directly onto its side that is inscribed with the so-called B-text of the Metternich Stela, a standard protection text. It should be noted that the Cairo vase is also inscribed with the name of Psamtik I. See also Derchain, *pSalt 825,* p. 20*, fig. 19a, which has the inscription *ṯꜣ n ḥḏ ḥr r mḥ.t*, "a head of garlic (drawn?) upon a *mḥ.t*-dish," written above a circle with a cryptographic inscription. The *mḥ.t*-bowl is also mentioned in the heading of *BD* 167 as the object on which the original text of that spell was found. See Wüthrich, *SAT* 16, p. 7, n. 31.

O. (x + 2: 4) The traces after *iw* suggest *ḏd*, "to say."

P. (x + 2: 4) The traces at the end of the line suit . The first sign is probably the suffix pronoun subject of a verb now lost, and the word *sw* is the object.

Q. (x + 2: 5) The rubric at the beginning of the line marks the end of the spell and the beginning of its prescription and directives. The common practice of the scribe of this papyrus was to write only the first few words of the coda in red. The prescription then continues in black ink. The rubricized heading of the next spell, *ky r3*, can be seen in line x + 2: 6. I have no suggestions for the restoration of the word beginning .

R. (x + 2: 5) represent the final signs of a word indicating the name of a plant. A possible restoration is *git* or *gi.w* (Germer, *Heilpflanzen*, pp. 145–48). It occurs at x + 5: 6 below. Other possibilities include *š3w.yt* (ibid., p. 125), a yet to be identified plant; *sbtt.yt* (ibid., p. 114), another unidentified plant; *s3.yt* (ibid., pp. 107–8), yet another unknown plant; and finally *ḫ3s.yt* (ibid., pp. 98–100), whose identification as *Bryonia dioica* Germer calls into question.

S. (x + 2: 5) The signs *w3ḏ*, "new; fresh," following *š3i* give *ḥs š3i w3ḏ*, "fresh excrement of a swine."

T. (x + 2: 5) *ḥs*, "excrement," is a common ingredient in the prescriptions of medical texts. Written thus, it occurs also at x + 13: 18: *ḥs* [*m*]*iw ḥs msḥ ḥs* […], "… excrement of a cat, excrement of a crocodile (?), excrement of …." It is invariably qualified by the name of a specific animal. Here, we have *ḥs š3i*, "excrement of a swine," an ingredient that is found in *pBerlin 3038*, 6^{4} (*Bln* 64) in conjunction with *ḥs ʿ3*, "excrement of an ass;" the term occurs as well in *pEbers*, 83^{4} (*Eb* 663) and *pTurin 1993*, vs. 7^{6}–10^{1}; *pBrooklyn 47.218.2*, x + 6^{7}; x + 6^{12} (Guermeur and O'Rourke, forthcoming). *ḥs š3iw* may occur at *pLeiden I 343+345*, rt. 1^{3} and vs. 2^{9}, where the damaged phrase *š3i ḥnʿ ḥs*, "…] of pigs (and) feces of [pigs (?)…" appears. The ingredient *ḥs mi3*, "excrement of a cat" is also used in a prescription in *pLeiden I 348*, rt. 1^{4}. The occurrence of pigs in medical and protection texts likely stems from their Sethian nature. The employment of such ingredients is typical of the Egyptian *topos* of "reversal," in which the powers and elements associated with the forces of disorder are used against them. On the connections between pigs and the god Seth, see te Velde, *Studia Aegyptiaca* 14 (1992): 571–78; idem, *Seth, God of Confusion*, p. 22; Yoyotte, *ÉPHE* V^e 89 (1980–81): 52; Sauneron, *pIllustré*, 4^{1} and pp. 7–8, who discusses the positive and negative associations of pork; also Manassa, *The Late Egyptian Underworld* 1, pp. 112–13 and references given there.

U. (x + 2: 6) The traces at the beginning of the next line suggest *di r*, "placed at." The prescription likely concluded with *di r msḏr*, "…place(d) at the ear," an instruction commonly encountered at the end of spells in this text. See, for example, x + 5: 11; x + 8: 6; and x + 13: 10 below.

COMMENTARY

The lacunae are extensive, leaving the spell very fragmentary. The spell contains one allusion to Re and one to Osiris and concludes with a fragmentary prescription. Little can be stated positively about its contents and purpose, other than that the mythological references found in the body of the text and the list of pharmacological ingredients concluding the spell have parallels in a number of other spells in the papyrus. The [hieroglyphs] *mḥ.t*-bowl mentioned in line x + 2: 4 does have a specific parallel in line x + 12: 11 below. As noted above, this object is commonly found in medical and protection texts.

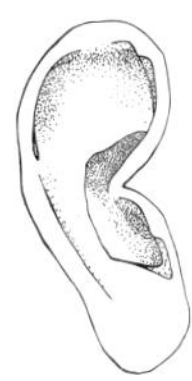

Spell C — Translation with Commentary

COLUMN X + 2: 6–18 (P. BROOKLYN 47.218.49)

TRANSLITERATION

6. *ky rꜣ ḥꜣ=k … [bw.w]t ḏd=f nb r msḏr n pr ꜥꜣ … rk*
7. *m ꞽꞽ r msḏr=f sḏm [mdw.wt nw rꜥ m] ꜣḫ.t ꞽꜣb.t.t n.t pt ḏd.n=f …*
8. *m rꜥ pn nn ḫsf=tw m [msḏr=f pn m mꜣꜥ=f pn] m ꞽb=f pn m ꜥ.wt=f nb.t i.ptn ḥr [ntt ntf ꞽn-*
9. *-m pr m ḥꜥ.w [n wsꞽr ꜥb].wy ꞽm=f n ḫnty-ḫm [šnꞽ]*
10. *ḥr.w n tp[=f m ḥr sꜣ ꜣs].t ꞽw ꜥnḫ.wy=f m-ẖnw wḏ[ꜣ.t sḏm]*
11. *mdw.wt n rꜥ rꜥ nb m-ẖnw [ꜣḫ.t ꞽꜣb.t.t n.t pt] ꞽ<w> ḫft pft mwt mwt.t ḏꜣ ḏꜣ[.t ḥm.wt-rꜣ ꞽrr]*
12. *[mḥr]=f tn r pr-ꜥꜣ mḥ m snf [bꜥbꜥ] m dš[r.t]=f gs m ṯr n [ꜥmꜥ.t*
13. *ꞽr[.n]=f ꜥb.t=f r pr-ꜥꜣ … [ḏd=f] sb n=f m ḳs[.w=f] wnm=f m tbn=f wšꜥ[=f m ḥ]ꜥ.w=*
14. *=f ꞽr.n=f bw.t n rꜥ rdꞽ.[n=f ꜣtf] m tp-ꜥ nrꞽ.n=f nṯr.w ꞽm.y.[w ꞽꜣt]=s-*
15. *n dgy n=f nṯr.w [tp-ꜥ.wy=s]n mꜣꜣ=sn sw ḫtꞽ ḥm sn …*
16. *ꞽrr.w=f m hꜣ ḥr=f m [ꞽꞽ r=f] ntf ḥr sꜣ ꜣs.t sꜣ ḥꜣ sꜣ ꞽꞽ sꜣ [ḏd mdw ḥr] snf*
17. *n [msḏr n] dꜣgy.t … bnw tp n nry … snwḫ …ḥr*
18. ………………………

TRANSLATION

6. … *Another spell.*[A] Back, you […4 cm… abom]inations (?),[B] everything that he says[C] against the ear of Pharaoh[D] […4.5 cm…]
7. Do not[E] come against his ear. Hear [the words of Re in][F] the eastern horizon of heaven![G] He has said[H] [You shall not … him. He is Ptah][I]
8. on this day. One shall not make war in[J] [this ear of his, in this temple of his, in this][K] heart of his, in all these limbs of his, [because to him belongs the skin][L]
9. that comes forth from the body of [Osiris. The horns][M] on him are those of[N] Khenty-Khem.[O] [The hair of][P]
10. the top of his head [belongs to Horus, son of Isis.][Q] His ears are within the S[ound Eye.[R] Hear the][S]

11. words of Re every day[T] with[in the eastern horizon of heaven!][U] O[V] enemy,[W] fiend,[X] dead male, dead female,[Y] male adversary, female advers[ary, and so on who make][Z]
12. [this sickness][AA] of his against the Pharaoh, filled with [blood, immersed][BB] in his red-blood,[CC] smeared[DD] with the red (blood)[EE] of[FF] [an *amat*-woman].[GG]
13. He has done his enmity[HH] against Pharaoh [...] [He says that][II] he who has come to him in his bones,[JJ] he who feeds on his head,[KK] [he who chews on his body],[LL]
14. [he has done][MM] the abomination of Re.[NN] He has put on [the *atef*-crown][OO] from before (?).[PP] He has terrorized[QQ] the gods who [are in their mounds][RR]
15. [...].[SS] The gods [who were their predecessors][TT] hide[UU] from (?) him when they see him. Fall back! With[draw! Pass by!],[VV]
16. (O) one whose nature is evil (?).[WW] Do not assail[XX] him! Do not [come against him!] He is[YY] Horus, son of Isis. A protection behind a protection, there comes a protection![ZZ] [*Words to be recited over*] *the blood*[AB]
17. [of the ear of] a bat[AC] [...] of a *bnw*-plant,[AD] the head of a vulture[AE] [...] brought to a boil[AF] with [...][AG]
18. ....

TEXT NOTES

A. (x + 2: 6) The writing *k(y) r3*, "Another spell," is a commonly encountered abbreviation of the heading of a new text. For the various headings of the spells in this papyrus, see the discussion at pp. 24ff. above. The suggested restorations given in the notes to this spell are based on the largely parallel text of Spell O found below.

B. (x + 2: 6) At the end of the lacuna, I have tentatively restored the word *bw.wt*, "abominations; taboos" (*Wb.* I 453, 7–454, 7), as the presence of the sign (Sign-list K2) suggests. The sign below it that seems to be (Sign-list G37) is written slightly differently elsewhere in the writing of *bw.t* in the papyrus. It may in fact be the sign ; in addition, the oblique stroke at the end of the word is hard to explain. The lacuna does not help matters either.

C. (x + 2: 6) In the group *dd=f nb*, "everything he says," the writing of above the sign rather than below the group may be due to this scribe's eye for economy of space.

D. (x + 2: 6) The hieratic traces at the edge of this fragment better suit the reading of *pr-ʿ3*, "Pharaoh," than of *psmṯk*, "Psamtik."

E. (x + 2: 7) I have taken the sign *m* as the negative imperative, as the parallels in the less damaged texts of the papyrus suggest. The traces at the end of the preceding line of the particle *rk* also support such a reading. The idea of inimical forces coming against the ear of the Pharaoh occurs repeatedly throughout the texts of this papyrus.

F. (x + 2: 7) Beginning here, the text occupying the rest of column x + 2 has parallels in Spell O (x + 12: 16–x + 13: 9) below. Where the texts differ is discussed in the Text Notes for each spell. The discussion of the phrases and clauses of the text restored here is largely to be found in the Text Notes for Spell O. Where appropriate, the reader will be directed to the notes for that section of the text. The restoration *sḏm mdw.wt nw Rꜥ m ꜣḫ.t iꜣb.t.t n.t pt*, "Hear the words of Re in the eastern horizon of heaven," is based on the parallels at x + 12: 19 and x + 13: 3 and the available space. For a discussion of the phrase *sḏm mdw.wt*, see note S (x + 12: 19) below.

G. (x + 2: 7) The parallel text at x + 12: 19 continues with the phrase *rꜥ nb*, "every day."

H. (x + 2: 7) The parallel text does not have the phrase *ḏd.n=f*. This phrase is either an imperative, translated as "Say to him…," or a *sḏm.n=f* form, as taken here, introducing what Re has said.

I. (x + 2: 7) The lacuna at the end of this line contains the beginning of an address by Re. A possible restoration at the end of the line is *ntf ptḥ*, "he is Ptah," based on the parallel found at x + 12: 19. The hieratic sign at the beginning of the next line, however, appears to be a writing of . Unfortunately, the verb employed in the parallel is missing as well, and the two versions of the spell clearly differ at this point. Nonetheless, the context requires some phrase like ["One shall not come against him. He is Ptah] on this day." See the discussions at notes T and U (x + 12: 19) below.

J. (x + 2: 8) The text here has *nn ḫsf*, while the parallel at x + 12: 19 has *nn sḫm*. *sḫm* means "prevail over; gain power," but the idea of not gaining power is what is warranted here; therefore, read *ḫsf* in its meaning "jemd. bekriegen" (*Wb.* III, 335, 19).

K. (x + 2: 8) After *nn ḫsf=tw m*, I have restored [*msḏr=f pn m mꜣꜥ=f*] *m ib=f pn*, "in [this ear of his, in this temple of his, in] this heart of his," based on the parallel at x + 12: 19–x + 13: 1 and the available space. In this text, the word *ib* is often listed in conjunction with the word *ḥꜣ.ty*. *ib* usually appears first, followed either immediately or somewhat later by the term *ḥꜣ.ty*. In the past, a majority of scholars have seen little, if any, difference between the two terms *ib* and *ḥꜣ.ty* as used in the medical and religious literature. Gardiner, *AEO* II, pp. 250*–52*, concluded that there was no difference, as does *WbMT*, pp. 40–42. See further Malaise, *MRE* 4 (1978), p. 9, n. 3, who stated that these terms ultimately represented our concept of "bosom" as it appears in Victorian literature.

More recent discussions of these terms, however, have attempted to draw a clear distinction between them. See Smith, *Mortuary Texts,* p. 68; Bardinet, *Les texts médicaux,* pp. 68–81; Assmann, *Death and Salvation,* pp. 28–31; Fabian, *BSAK* 3 (1988): 249ff; Borghouts, *EU* 24.1, pp. 451b and 466a; Walker, *Ancient Egyptian Anatomical Terminology,* pp. 147–86; Hollis, *Two Brothers,* pp. 131–42, esp. pp. 141–42.

L. (x + 2: 8) The restoration of the text at the end of the line is hampered somewhat by damage in the parallel passage at x + 13: 1 as well. The partial reconstruction of *ḥr-*[*ntt ntf i*]*nm*, "be[cause to him belongs the sk]in," or possibly "because he is the…," adopted here is based on the parallel that continues at the beginning of x + 13: 2 and the signs at the beginning of x + 2: 9. See the discussion at note X (x + 13: 1).

M. (x + 2: 9) The present passage differs from that of the parallel. The text here has *pr m ḥꜥ.w* […], "that comes forth from the body […];" the parallel text at x + 13: 1–2 has *pr m Wsir*, "that comes forth from Osiris." There is room to restore *n Wsir ꜥb.w* after *pr m ḥꜥ.w*, "…that comes forth from the body [of Osiris, the hor]ns…," a restoration that would follow the general sense if not the exact wording of the parallel. See the discussion at note X (x + 13: 1).

N. (x + 2: 9) The text has *n*, as does its parallel at x + 13: 2; thus, the translation "those of…" seems warranted.

O. (x + 2: 9) Read here, based on the parallel at x + 13: 2. is a writing of *ḫm*, "Letopolis," replacing the earlier writing . In Late Period texts, is also found as a writing of the word *sḫm*, "sanctuary;" see, for example, Goyon, *BIFAO* 75 (1975): 393, l. 6. See also Meeks, *Mythes et légendes,* p. 51, n. 34, on the relationship between the two preceding words. See the discussion below at note Y (x + 13: 2).

P. (x + 2: 9) At the end of the lacuna, restore *šni*, "hair" (*Wb.* IV 499, 9–501, 3). Note that the parallel at x + 13: 2 requires 3 cm to write this group of signs, while the lacuna here is 3.5 cm.

Q. (x + 2: 10) After *ḥr n tp* restore [*=f m ḥr sꜣ ꜣs.t*], the whole yielding "…the hair of the top of [his] head [namely (that) of Horus, son of Isis."], following the parallel at x + 13: 2. The space available here equals that of the parallel.

R. (x + 2: 10) The restoration of *wḏꜣ.t* is possible after *m ḫnw*, based on the traces and the parallel at x + 13: 2–3; it should be noted, however, that at x + 13: 2 *wḏꜣ.t* is written without the sign . The writing *m-ḫnw* for seems to occur early; according to Koenig, *pBoulaq 6,* p. 42, n.e, the writing of for *ḫnw* is already the characteristic orthography by Dynasty 21.

S. (x + 2: 10–11) At the end of this line and the beginning of the next, restore [hieroglyphs] *sḏm mdw.wt n rʿ*, "Hear the words of Re…," following the parallel at x + 13: 3 and the space available. See note F (x + 2: 7) above and note S (x + 12: 19) below.

T. (x + 2: 11) The text at x + 13: 3 does not include the phrase *rʿ nb*, "every day," yet the parallel at x + 12: 19 does. The god Re repeats his warnings daily because the cosmic battle must be fought each morning.

U. (x + 2: 11) The restoration here should probably be [hieroglyphs] *m-ẖnw ꜣḫ.t iꜣb.t.t n.t pt*, "…within the eastern horizon of heaven." The parallel at x + 13: 3 simply has *m*, while the traces here seem to indicate *m ẖnw*.

V. (x + 2: 11) The text has [hieroglyphs], most likely an error for [hieroglyphs] *i*, the vocative marker and the writing found in the parallel at x + 13: 3. For a similar direct address to disease-demons following the imperative *sḏm mdw.wt*, see *pLeiden I 343+345*, rt. 11[8–10] (= vs. 172). Both of those passages are somewhat lacuna-ridden, but the word [hieroglyphs] clearly follows *kꜣ sḏm=k nꜣ n mdw* in the verso text.

W. (x + 2: 11) On the identity of the beings in this list, see the discussion above in the Introduction, pp. 26ff.

X. (x + 2: 11) The word [hieroglyphs] *pft* is usually translated in lists of this sort as "fiend." Citing a number of texts from the New Kingdom and later, Borghouts, *pLeiden I 348*, p. 54, n. 50, has suggested that *pft* was originally nothing other than the demonstrative pronoun. Further evidence for his interpretation, not cited by him, is supplied by the Middle Kingdom text *pRamesseum C*, vs. II[8–9] where the term [hieroglyphs] *ḫft*, "enemy," is followed directly by [hieroglyphs] written without any determinative. The same text has [hieroglyphs] *pft* at vs. I[7], making Borghouts' interpretation quite certain, even for texts dating to earlier than the New Kingdom. Koenig, *RdE* 33 (1981): 30, n. b., states that the writing *pft* seems to be the feminine equivalent of *ḫft*, a remark repeated in his *pBoulaq 6*, p. 49 (c). He bases his remarks on an observation already made by Gardiner, *pChesterBeatty 2–9*, 1, p. 125, n. 2. Koenig does not note, however, any distinction between *pf* and *pft*. Goyon, *Cérémonial*, p. 113, n. 38, states that *pf(y)* is simply a euphemism for Seth, used in order to avoid pronouncing his name. For this interpretation, see also Vittmann, *ZÄS* 111 (1984): 167, n. v.

Y. (x + 2: 11) Malevolent beings called *mwt mwt.t*, "dead males, dead females," are encountered as agents of evil as early as the Execration Texts and the Coffin Texts; they are not simply "the dead" but more properly those who failed to pass judgment; they seem to be transient beings, excluded from the realms of the blessed dead but not those of the living. Several variants of *CT* 23 have *mwt mwt.t* where the others have the more generic *ḫft ḫft.t*, "male enemies, female enemies;" see also Breasted, *pEdwin Smith*, vol. 2, pp. 470 and 472. See also p. 26 and nn. 107–109 above.

Z. (x + 2: 11) At the end of this line, restore *ḏꜣ[.t ḥm.wt-rꜣ irr]* following the parallel at x + 13: 4. The phrase *ḥm.wt rꜣ* is common in medical and protection texts. Originally, the term seems to have meant "skill of the mouth" or more simply "spells." *MuK,* 2[6], provides a good example of the latter meaning where the heading of a spell is written . Its meaning "and so on" has been discussed a number of times, notably by Gardiner, *JEA* 38 (1952): 26, n. 2; idem, *pRamesseum,* p. 10, n. 4; Borghouts, *pLeiden I 348,* p. 55, n. 51; and Ritner, *SAOC* 54 (1992), p. 43, n. 195.

AA. (x + 2: 12) In the small lacuna at the beginning of the line, restore *mḥr=f tn*, "this sickness of his," following the parallel at x + 13: 4. The same phrase is used as an epithet of a disease-demon at *pLeiden I 348,* rt. 6[4–5].

BB. (x + 2: 12) Based on the traces, the conjectured restoration for the lacuna is *snf bꜥbꜥ*, following the parallel text at x + 13: 4. Note, however, that the parallel has in place of . See the discussion at note DD (x + 13: 4) below.

CC. (x + 2: 12) The lacuna here offers enough space for after , thus yielding *dšr.t*, "das Blut" (*Wb.* V 491, 10–13). See *CT* 75 for an allusion to a malevolent being: *ir mḥr=s n nsw.t n ḥry-ib dšr.w=s*, "…who makes her sickness, namely the fire of the one who is in her redness/red blood…."

DD. (x + 2: 12) *gs*, "salben" (*Wb.* V 201, 12–202, 13). The word occurs a number of times in this papyrus as a technical term for the application of certain prescriptions. The present context requires a less technical meaning and perhaps one that is more graphic; hence, the translation "smear" seems preferable.

EE. (x + 2: 12) *ṯr n: ṯr* is "das Rote als Bez. für das Blut" (*Wb.* V 386, 13, giving only the transliteration *ṯr*, as does Hannig, *GH* 959a). The word appears in Massart, *pLeiden I 343+345,* vs. 23, in a context that indicates that the agent carrying the disease is firmly entrenched in the patient. *WbDN,* pp. 566–67 cites the spelling *ṯrw*, giving it as a mineral of some sort. Cf., however, Wilson, *PL,* p. 1169, who gives the meaning "blood, gore" for the noun *ṯr.* She states that *ṯr* "may be connected to the mineral *ṯrw* (q.v.) and is older than this term." In the Edfu temple, the term occurs in passages that deal with the slaying of Seth, in which his adversaries claim that "they will crunch the flesh and drink down the blood (*ṯr*) of Seth." See Wilson, *PL,* p. 1169, for the citations for these texts.

FF. (x + 2: 12) The parallel has after the word *ṯr;* here, the text shows with the single sign *n* below the plural strokes. The sign *t* of the parallel is superfluous, as the feminine form of the genitive marker is not required there.

GG. (x + 2: 13) After restore at the end of the line and the beginning of the next. It may be that the sign (Sign-list D52) was omitted in the original writing, as it was only added as a supralinear sign in the parallel below. The parallel at x + 13: 5 has [hieroglyphs] *gs m ṯr n ꜥmꜥ.t*, "…smeared with the blood of an *amat*-woman." The restoration given here must be seen as provisional, as the two parallel texts display a number of variants in this section. It should be noted that the 5.5 cm required to fit *ṯr n*(*t*) *ꜥmꜥ.t* do exist at the end of x + 2: 12 and the beginning of x + 2: 13.

HH. (x + 2: 13) The text here continues with [hieroglyphs], just like the parallel below at x + 13: 5. The present passage has *iw ir.n=f ꜥb.t=f r pr-ꜥꜣ*, "he has done his enmity against Pharaoh," but the parallel reading at x + 13: 5 has the preposition *m* after *ir.n=f*. In addition, *ꜥb.t* is followed by the noun *nṯr.w*, not with *=f* as it is here. Thus, the parallel seems to read "…he has acted as an enemy of the gods…." or "he has done the enmity of the gods," with the preposition *m* acting as an object marker. The word [hieroglyphs] *ꜥb.t* (*Wb.* I 174, 13–19) has a range of meanings that, for the most part, focus on impurity. It is written with the [hieroglyph] determinative also in *pCairo 58027* 2[3], 3[1]; in *pKölner 3547*, 1[4], it is transcribed [hieroglyphs], and the editor offers the translation "Unheil," for which see Kurth et al., *pKölner*, pl. 1, l. 4 and p. 21; Koenig, *RdE* 33 (1981): 34, translates the word in a passage from *pTurin 54050*, 22, 3 as "impureté," for which he gives his explanation at p. 33, n. g; see idem, *pBoulaq 6*, rt. 52 and p. 54, n. d., where it is again translated as "impureté" as the context there demands; Edwards, *HPBM* 4, p. 14, n. 12, gives the translation "sickness;" see finally Verhoeven and Derchain, *La déesse Libyque*, p. 31, n. g (citing Germond, *AH* 9, p. 396). For recent and relevant discussions, see Quack, in Bender, Takács and Appleyard, eds., *Studies in Afroasiatic Linguistics* 14, pp. 167–74, 174A, esp. p. 170 with note 19; idem, in Freval and Nihan, eds., *Purity and the Forming of Religious Traditions*, Dynamics in the History of Religion 3, pp. 115–58, esp. p. 138.

The word clearly has negative associations in the present passage, yet "impurity" seems too limiting. Given the context, "enmity" or "danger" comes closer to the desired meaning. For *ꜥb.w* denoting "enmity" or "to act as an enemy," see Sauneron, *pIllustré*, 2[5]; 2[6] (where the word is also written with the determinative [hieroglyph]) and p. 22, n. r. Note, however, that in that text at 5[7] the word *ꜥb.w* is translated as "horn," the explanation for which is given at p. 27, n. hh; there it is written without the determinative [hieroglyph]. Two passages from the Dendera temple offer some support for the meaning "horn" for this term. In both, Isis addresses the king: *di=i n=k iꜥr.t=t* (sic) *m ḥꜣ.t=k ḥr wḏ ꜥb=s r ḫft.yw=k*, "I give to you your (?) uraeus on your forehead while ordering its horn/enmity against your enemies;" and *di=i ꜥb=t* (sic) *bin r ḫft.yw nb.w…*, "I give your horn/enmity of evil against all the enemies of…." For those texts, see *Dendara* I, 151[9], and VIII, 56[2–3], respectively. Another possible parallel may be found in a prayer to Amun on a Dynasty Twenty-two Theban statue (CG 42208). Having asked the god Amun to protect his daughter from those who may try to seize her inheritance, the owner then says to the god: *kꜣ ꜥḥꜣ=k r ꜥḥꜣ r=sn m-ḫt wd=k šsr=k sḏb=k r=sn r sh ꜥnḫ=sn n sfḫ ꜥb=k im=w n ḏt*, "Then you shall fight in order to fight against them afterwards. You shall send your arrows, your evil against them, to destroy their lives without loosening your horn/enmity from them forever." For this text, see Jansen-Winckeln, *ÄAT* 8 1–2, p. 455, ll. 16–17, and p. 48, where he translates the word *ꜥb* as "Horn." A further problem in the present passage is the apparent mixture of *sḏm=f* and *sḏm.n=f* forms. The lacunae in these fragmentary columns make it difficult to establish the relationship between clauses. See note PP (x + 2: 14) below.

II. (x + 2: 13) At the end of the lacuna, the verb phrase *ḏd=f* that occurs in the parallel can be restored. Such a restoration requires less than 2 cm.

JJ. (x + 2: 13) The present passage has the verbal group *sb n=f*, either a participle with a dative or a *sḏm.n=f* form. The parallel at x + 13: 5 has a different verb *sẖd=f* written as a *sḏm=f* form. The two verbs have roughly equivalent meanings. See note HH (x + 13: 5).

KK. (x + 2: 13) *tbn*, "head" (*Wb.* V 261, 12–14).

LL. (x + 2: 13) The restoration of *wšꜥ=f m ḥꜥ.w=f*, "he who chews on his body…" is based on the parallel at x + 13: 5, the traces at the beginning and end of the lacuna, and the sign at the beginning of x + 2: 14. See note II (x + 13: 5) below.

MM. (x + 2: 14) At the beginning of the line, the traces show …]=*f ir.n=f*.

NN. (x + 2: 14) The word *bw.t* occurs commonly in religious texts embodying the idea of "taboo" or "abomination," with the implication of religious or ritual impurity; see Frandsen, *BSAK* 3 (1988): 151–58; also *pEdwin Smith*, 18^{17} and 20^{9}, where the patient claims that he is an "abomination," and vol. 2, p. 479, where it is stated that "the protection consists in becoming something abhorred which the spirits dare not approach." See Lucarelli, *SAT* 11 (2006), pp. 210ff., for a discussion of this type of inversion.

As already noted, there is a general difficulty in the present passage in determining how the various phrases and clauses fit together and to whom the pronoun subjects refer. It is unclear whether the phrase [*ir.n=f*] *bw.t n Rꜥ*, "he has done the abomination of Re" refers to what precedes or to what follows. If it continues the preceding idea, then this section of the text states that whoever violates the body of the Pharaoh "has done the abomination of Re" by such an action. Alternatively, there could be a shift in the subject; in that case, it would be the Pharaoh who does the "abomination of Re" in order to ward off the evil spirits. See note OO (x + 2: 14), following.

OO. (x + 2: 14) The traces clearly indicate the writing of , the determinative of the word *ꜣtf*, "*atef*-crown," the word that is found in the parallel below. The meaning of this sentence is obscure. If the subject of *rdi.n=f* is different from that of *ir.n=f bw.t n Rꜥ*, we should understand that the abomination of Re in the present passage refers to the act of assailing the Pharaoh; then, it is quite likely that the pronoun

=*f* in the phrase *rdi.n=f* refers to the Pharaoh, who attempts to dispel the inimical forces through the reenactment of a mythological incident, in which Re put on the *atef*-crown to strike fear into the hearts of the gods. See the discussion in the Commentary to Spell O below.

PP. (x + 2: 14) The parallel text at x + 13: 6 differs somewhat from the text given here. The present passage has the group *tp-ꜥ*, an adverbial phrase meaning "formerly" or "from before." The parallel passage has *r tp=f*, "towards" or "at his head." Either is a scribal error for , or we are dealing with two different ideas. The number of minor differences in signs and phrases in the two texts simply indicates two versions of the same spell, as the notion of a specific and fixed archetype seems unknown to the Egyptians. See Quack, *Die Lehre des Ani,* p. 17–18, on the "open" nature of Egyptian textual traditions.

QQ. (x + 2: 14) The restoration of , "…he has terrorized…," is based on the parallel and the traces. I have chosen to reading *nri.n=f* as a *sḏm.n=f* form, with the following phrase *nṯr.w im.y.w iꜣt=sn*, "the gods who are in their mounds," as its object. In the parallel at x + 13: 6, the verb *nri* is written as a *sḏm=f* form.

RR. (x + 2: 14) Restore *im.y.[w iꜣt=s]n*, "who are in their mounds," at the end of the line, following the reading at x + 13: 6 below. See the discussion at note KK (x + 13: 6).

SS. (x + 2: 15) The group at the beginning of the line completes the writing of the suffix pronoun =*sn*, whose initial sign is the last sign of the preceding line. This restoration fits the traces and the parallel at x + 13: 6.

TT. (x + 2: 15) Restoring the group *tp-ꜥ.wy=sn*, "who were their predecessors," following the parallel at x + 13: 6–7 and fitting the space required.

UU. (x + 2: 15) *dgi*, "hide" (*Wb.* V 496, 8–14, with [Sign-list A4] or [Sign-list A5] as a determinative). Here the word has the former determinative; the writing at x + 13: 6 shows the latter. This verb follows a series of *sḏm.n=f* forms. Although *dgi* is followed by *n=f*, it does not appear to be a *sḏm.n=f* form here. Given the sense required by the context of the present passage, *dgi* apparently indicates a gesture of deference that is required on the part of the terrorized gods. See notes NN and OO (x + 2: 14) above.

VV. (x + 2: 15) Restore *ẖti ḥm sni*, "Fall back! Withdraw! Pass by…," following the parallel at x + 13: 7. These imperatives, of course, are addressed to the malevolent beings that assail or attempt to assail the Pharaoh. *pLeiden I 348,* rt. 66, provides a useful parallel: *ẖti ḥm n ꜣt ir.t=f*, "Fall back! Withdraw! Because of the striking power of the fiery eye of his!" addressed to a group of malevolent beings. *Socle Behague* M, 60 a 2 similarly has *ẖti ḥm ḥꜣ*, "Fall back! Withdraw! Back!"

WW. (x + 2: 16) The traces here apparently show [hieroglyphs] and the parallel below has [hieroglyphs]. The [hieroglyph] of the parallel can been seen as the last sign of the preceding line. The word seems to be a writing of *ir.w*, given at *Wb.* I 114, 14 as "Bez. für böses Wesen," as that is the only writing of an *iri*-based word that has both the initial *yod* and the determinative [hieroglyph]. There is the possibility that what appear to be the signs [hieroglyph] and [hieroglyph] may actually be a writing of the sign [hieroglyph] (Sign-list Z6), at least here. The writing in the parallel below is quite clearly [hieroglyphs]. The reading [hieroglyphs], thus, seems to mean "…his evil nature/character…." The alternative reading [hieroglyphs] is itself rather odd, but the sign [hieroglyph] could be read as an ideogram for "evil" or even "death," used here as a determinative, indicating that the activity of the verb *iri* is to be understood as evil or hostile. Should there be a miswriting here and we actually have the determinative [hieroglyph], then see Massart, *pLeiden I 343+345*, vs. 8[11] and p. 69, n. 23, for the occurrence and discussion of the term [hieroglyphs] *ẖr.y*; there it is translated as "who are dead," based on the reading of the sign [hieroglyph] as an ideogram or at least a determinative. The verb [hieroglyphs] *ii* is sometimes written with the determinative [hieroglyph] to mark the coming or approach of a being who has evil intentions; the same verb is also written with the determinative [hieroglyph] in the term [hieroglyphs] *ii.t*, lit. "what will come," i.e., bad future events. See, for example, Koenig, *pBoulaq 6*, rt. 3[9] and p. 41, n. b.; Drioton, *Mélanges Dussaud*, pp. 495–506; and Morenz, *Mélanges Dussaud*, pp. 139–50, all of whom discuss the use of such determinatives. See the discussion at note NN (x + 13: 7) below.

XX. (x + 2: 16) The verb [hieroglyphs] *h3i* often has negative associations and is equivalent to "assault" or "assail." See Koenig, *pBoulaq 6*, rt. 3[9], who cites such a meaning for *h3y* in *pChester Beatty* 6, rt. 2[2-9]; *pLeiden I 348*, vs. 2[1]; and *pTurin 54050*, 23, 9.

YY. (x + 2: 16) The phrase [hieroglyphs] *ntf ḥr s3 3s.t*, "He is Horus, son of Isis," provides an example of the nominal constructions commonly following an address to inimical forces to explain why they will fail or have already failed in their attacks. See x + 12: 19 below, where a similar statement occurs: *ntf Ptḥ n hrw pn*, "He is Ptah of this day," associated there with the one assailed by the forces of evil. For further parallels to this usage, see, for example, Sauneron, *pIllustré*, 4[2].

ZZ. (x + 2: 16) [hieroglyphs] *s3 ḥ3 s3 ii s3* (*Wb.* III 414, 14–15) occurs commonly in medical and protection texts; see, for example, *pHearst*, 14[10] (H 215); *pLeiden I 347*, 12[8]; *pBM 10042*, 7[12]; 11[1]; *MuK*, 9[6]; and *pLeiden I 346*, 3[12]. Massart, *pGeneva MAH 15274*, has a variant in *s3 ḥr s3*, "A protection of Horus is a protection!" Borghouts, *AEMT*, p. 48 (No. 77) translates the phrase *s3 ḥ3 s3 ii s3* as "Protection behind protection, protection has arrived!"

AB. (x + 2: 16) The restoration of [hieroglyphs] *dd mdw.w ḥr snf n*, "Words to be recited over the blood of…," is based on the parallel at x + 13: 8 and the traces here. The presence of the rubric indicates the beginning of the coda of this spell, although the damage to the papyrus here and at the top of the next column makes unclear where the coda ends. The rubric ends with the signs [hieroglyphs], but the prescription and the directions for its application continue. Such a writing of the coda occurs often in this papyrus, with only the first few words rubricized to indicate the beginning of the prescription proper.

AC. (x + 2: 17) The lacuna at the beginning of the line has been restored as [hieroglyphs] *n msḏr n*, following x + 13: 8 below. [hieroglyphs], *d3gy.t*, is "belegt *Med.* offizinell verwendet. Vgl. *d3gy* 'Fledermaus' und *dgy.t*" (*Wb.* V 478, 4). *WbDN*, p. 572 gives the writing [hieroglyphs], citing *pEbers*, 63[13] (*Eb* 424) and 63[18] (*Eb* 426), as well as the writing [hieroglyphs], citing *pEbers*, 76[8–9] (*Eb* 596). See finally Barns, *Five Ramesseum Papyri*, p. 18, n.15, where the blood of the *d3gy.t*-mouse is offered as a remedy against an ingrown eyelash.

AD. (x + 2: 17) The restoration of the lacuna is difficult due to the very fragmentary nature of this line; in addition, the parallel at x + 13: 8 is damaged as well. Read [hieroglyphs] based on the traces of the final signs of [hieroglyphs] *bnw*. Given the occurrence of this word in a prescription, it must refer to the *bnw*-plant, for which see Germer, *Arzneimittelpflanzen*, p. 38. In Egyptian texts, the *bnw*-bird, when encountered, refers usually not to a real bird but to a mythological creature associated with the creation of the cosmos or found in the Netherworld; see, for example, Germond and Livet, *Egyptian Bestiary*, pp. 166–69. That reading does not fit well in a prescription, despite the fact that the text here comprises a list of parts of birds.

AE. (x + 2: 17) The group [hieroglyphs] *tp n* seems to mean "head of." Note, however, that the sign *tp* lacks the oblique stroke that normally follows it. The traces after the group [hieroglyphs] do seem to fit the upper part of the hieratic sign [hieroglyph] (Sign-list G14), the determinative of [hieroglyphs] *nr.t*, "vulture;" see Verhoeven, *Untersuchungen*, pp. 136–37, No. 193 (Sign-list G14). *WbDN*, p. 304 gives *snf n nr.t*, "in einem Salbmittel (*gs*) neben *snf n mni.t; snf n smn; snf n mn.t*," citing *pEbers*, 88[22] (*Eb* 737). One other possibility is that the group *nr*… is the beginning of a writing of *nrw*, "ibex," the fat of which animal is a common ingredient in recipes; see, for example, *pHearst*, 8[14] (*H* 114) and 8[16] (*H* 118); 12[13] (*H* 185); 15[5] (*H* 227); *pEbers*, 52[12] (*Eb* 298) and 52[14] (*Eb* 299); *pBM 10059*, 6[2–3]; and *pEdwin Smith*, 16[11]. Nevertheless, the traces here better support the reading as given. It should be noted that this phrase is omitted in the parallel at x + 13: 8–9.

AF. (x + 2: 17) In the lacuna, restore [hieroglyphs] *snwḫ*, "boiled," following the traces here and the parallel at x + 13: 9. The practice of boiling the ingredients of a prescription to make a topical application occurs commonly in these texts. *pLeiden I 348*, rt. 9[7], also uses the word *snwḫ* as the technical term for boiling ingredients; see further *pEbers*, 49[1] (*Eb* 262) and 65[12–13] (*Eb* 454–55).

AG. (x + 2: 17) It is possible that the lengthy prescription of the parallel found at x + 13: 9–10 continued here. Such a restoration would require slightly more than one and one-half lines, meaning that the present text would continue from line 17 to line 18, traces of which can be seen, and then either to a lost line 19 of the present column or to line 1 of Column x + 3. In any case, that last line of the prescription would continue up to the now missing rubric that begins the next spell. One problem with such a restoration, however, is the apparent presence of *ḥr* at the end of line 17, which could be construed as the beginning of the phrase [*ḥr*] *ʿḏ ʿnḫ*, "over the fat of a goat," a restoration that would not follow the parallel at x + 13: 9–10 exactly. Against such an objection, it should be noted that the two passages have shown a number of variations throughout.

COMMENTARY

Spell C (x + 2: 6–18) is basically a parallel to a spell found later in the papyrus, the better preserved Spell O (x + 12: 16–x + 13: 10) below. For an overall discussion of the contents of this spell, see the Commentary at Spell O.

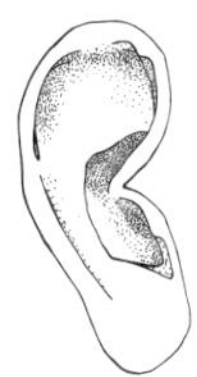

Spell D — Translation with Commentary

COLUMN X + 3: 1–14 (P. BROOKLYN 47.218.49)

TRANSLITERATION

1. *n … wḏꜥ mdw.t … šn …*
2. *n=i … n b … =f pwy n [tm] ii [r msḏr n pr-ꜥꜣ] …*
3. *ib=sn ꜣw mꜣꜣ=sn … =sn nṯr.w rwi=s[n sw m msḏr n pr-ꜥꜣ i]*
4. *mwt mwt.t ẖr=s[n] … rmṯ rwi=sn [sw m msḏr n pr-ꜥꜣ]*
5. *ẖr=sn sw ḥr … =sn dḥr=f r ib=sn …*
6. *bw.t=sn wdi … .=f rḏw.w stt=f fnd … [ẖ]*
7. *nm n ir.wy n rḏw.w … =f ib=sn r ẖft pft mwt m[wt.t ḏꜣ ḏꜣ-*
8. *–.t ḥm.wt-rꜣ r iw n=f r ꜥḥꜥ … r iw n=f r ꜥḥꜥ m ḥs=f i [mwt nb*
9. *mwt.t nb.t ḏꜣ ḏꜣ.t ḥm.wt-rꜣ [nty r]wi m msḏr n pr-ꜥꜣ tm …*
10. *=f m sꜣẖ=k n pr-ꜥꜣ iw nḥm … nb=s iw=s ip n=f ẖr.wy r …*
11. *ꜥ.wy=s[n] iw smꜣ.n=f ḥnꜥ smꜣ[y.wt] iw pnꜥ[.tw]=f ḥr wnn-nfr mꜣꜥ-ẖrw is m …*
12. *rk ẖft pft mwt mwt.t ḏꜣ ḏꜣ[.t irr] ḏw is r pr-ꜥꜣ ir tm=k rw[i m]*
13. *msḏr n pr-ꜥꜣ rwi.kꜣ.tw=k …st=s ẖr.wy … r ꜥḥꜥ=sn [ḏd mdw]*
14. *ḥr mḥi sfṯ ibr ḥḏr … nḏ šnꜥꜥ m ẖt wꜥ.t sẖꜣk m ḥbs di r [msḏr]*

TRANSLATION

1. … pass judgment …[A]
2. I have (?)[B] […2 cm…] of the Evil One[C] […3.5 cm] this his … to not come against [the ear of Pharaoh][D]
3. their[E] hearts are joyful. They see […3 cm…] they […] the gods. May they turn [him (?)[F] back[G] from the ear of Pharaoh. O (?)][H]
4. dead male, dead female. May they make [him (?)] fall[I] […3 cm…] men. May they turn back [him (?)[J] from the ear of Pharaoh][K]
5. May they[L] overthrow him[M] upon (?)[N] […3 cm… May they…] his bitterness[O] against their hearts […3 cm…][P]
6. their abominations. [May they][Q] place (?)[R] […4 cm …his…] effluxes, his mucus, nose[S] […3 cm…]
7. smelling …(?)[T] effluxes […3 cm he …][U] their hearts against the enemy, the fiend, dead male, dead female, [male adversary, female adversary][V]

8. and so on to come for him [W] in order to stand [X] [...2.5 cm...] to come for him in order to stand in front of him.[Y] [O every dead male][Z]
9. every dead female, male adversary, female adversary and so on [who turns back][AA] from the ear of Pharaoh, [... not ...][BB]
10. his [...][CC] when you come [DD] for Pharaoh. [She (?)] saves [EE] [...2 cm...] her lord.[FF] She establishes for him the soundness of[GG] the testicles [HH] [...2 cm...]
11. their two arms (?).[II] He is united with his [confederates.][JJ] He is overthrown on account of[KK] Wennefer,[LL] justified. [...2 cm...]
12. indeed [MM] the enemy, the fiend, dead male, dead female, male [adversary, female adversary who does][NN] evil, indeed,[OO] against the Pharaoh. If you do not [turn back from][PP]
13. the ear of the Pharaoh, then [you] shall be turned back [QQ] ... its place,[RR] possessing (?)[SS] [...][TT] against their multitude.[UU] [*Words to be recited*][VV]
14. *over flax,*[WW] *sft-oil,*[XX] *laudanum,*[YY] *ḥḏr.t,*[ZZ] [...1.5 cm...] *ground finely* [AB] *together* [AC] *(and) filtered through cloth* [AD] *(and) placed at* [*the ear*].[AE]

TEXT NOTES

A. (x + 3: 1) This is the first line of the column, as the blank papyrus above the few signs of this line shows.

B. (x + 3: 2) The group *n=i* may be signs of a *sḏm.n=f* form that would be the final word of x + 3: 1 or a prepositional phrase. It is unclear to whom =*i*, "I/me," refers.

C. (x + 3: 2) *b*, "Evil One" (*Wb.* I 410, 9), is used indiscriminately as a designation of the archetypal enemy of the sun-god or Osiris, namely Apophis and Seth, respectively. See Derchain, *RdE* 9 (1952): 25, n. 6; and Vernus, *Or* 48 (1979): 179, n.12. The same word is found again at x + 8: 17 and at x + 13: 13 and 14.

D. (x + 3: 2) Restore most likely *tm ii r msḏr pr-ꜥꜣ*, "...to not come against the ear of the Pharaoh...," a commonly encountered phrase in this text.

E. (x + 3: 3) The suffix pronoun =*sn*, "they," occurs as the subject of a number of *sḏm=f* forms in this spell. It seems to refer to beings in alliance with the pharaoh, not to the inimical forces. Note that the following Spell E has gods acting as agents of protection for the pharaoh as well. That spell also contains an appeal to "any male, any female, any commoner, any of the Sun-people" to stand behind Psamtik in order to protect and save him. It is possible that the lacunae at the beginning of this spell contained a similar address or description of such a group. Note that the structure of the present spell is that of a third person narrative, while Spell E is a second person address.

F. (x + 3: 3) [hieroglyphs] *rwi*, "leave; turn back" (*Wb.* II 406, 2–407, 4). The presence of *sw* as the direct object of [*s*]*ḫr* in ll. 4–5 suggests a transitive meaning for *rwi* here and in the following line. The direct object of *rwi*, likely the pronoun *sw* in both cases, appeared in the now lost section of text. Additionally, there is suitable room in this line for the restoration *sw m msḏr n pr-ʿ3*, "…him from the ear of Pharaoh." *WbMT* 525 gives the transitive meaning "entfernen vom Heilmittel, das die Krankheit entfernt," citing *pEbers*, 88[21] (*Eb* 763). For *rwi* used transitively with a pronoun object referring to a malevolent being, see Sauneron, *Kemi* 20 (1970): 7–18, esp. n. s. Massart, *pLeiden I 343+345*, rt. 4[5], has *rwi=k tw*, "Remove yourself!" *pConfirmation*, 1[18] offers a transitive use of this verb; see further *pCairo 58027*, x + 3[3]; also Černý, *BIFAO* 35 (1935): 50. For an intransitive use in a protection text, see Massart, *pGeneva MAH 15274*, rt. 4[8]: *rwi=k r-ḥ3t* and the translation "Keep away from…!"

G. (x + 3: 3) On the restoration of the direct object pronoun *sw*, see the preceding note F (x + 3: 3).

H. (x + 3: 3) After the restoration of *rwi=sn* [*sw m msḏr pr-ʿ3…*], "May they turn [him back from the ear of the Pharaoh]," a vocative marker seems needed in light of what appears to be a list of malevolent beings at the beginning of x + 3: 4.

I. (x + 3: 4) We are faced with two possible readings of the word [hieroglyphs]. It could be the noun "…verächtliche Bez. für Feind" (*Wb.* III 321, 7–322, 1). If so, it is the only occurrence of the word in the lists of malevolent beings in this papyrus. The scant traces at the beginning of the lacuna show [hieroglyph], possibly the first sign of the pronoun [hieroglyphs] *sn*. If so, [hieroglyphs] could be the verb *ḫr*, "fall," one that also has the transitive meanings "fällen, niederwerfen" (*Wb.* III 321, 3–5). The pronoun [hieroglyphs] would be the subject of a verb, the phrase paralleling the numerous other transitive, prospective *sḏm=f* forms.

J. (x + 3: 4) On the verb [hieroglyphs] *rwi*, see note F (x + 3: 3) above.

K. (x + 3: 4) Possibly restore [hieroglyphs] *sw m msḏr n pr-ʿ3*, "…him from the ear of the Pharaoh."

L. (x + 3: 5) The pronoun =*sn*, the subject of the verb *ḫr*, apparently refers to the forces fighting on behalf of Pharaoh and the direct object pronoun *sw* to one of the forces of chaos. See note E (x + 3: 3) above.

M. (x + 3: 5) For the antecedent of the pronoun *sw*, see notes F (x + 3: 3) and L (x + 3: 5) above.

N. (x + 3: 5) The sign [hieroglyph] is visible, but there are no traces of what follows.

O. (x + 3: 5) *dḥr(.t)*, "Bitternis" (*Wb.* V 483, 5–10). Citing numerous occurrences of the word, *WbMT,* p. 988 gives a meaning "Name einer dämonischen Krankheit." The word has a generally negative connotation. See, for example, Goyon, *pConfirmation,* 2[6]: *ỉhy sḫm.t Bst.t nḥm=k pr-ʿ3 m-ʿ ʿbw m-ʿ dḥr(.t) nšni nb ḏw n rnp.t,* "O Sakhmet, Bastet, may you save Pharaoh from danger, from bitterness, from every evil raging of the year!" and also p. 90, n. 55, with references; Borghouts, *pLeiden I 348,* rt. 3[5], offers the meaning "sickness;" Piankoff, *Le "cœur,"* p. 100, cites the phrase *dḥr(.t) ḥ3.ty* and translates it as "craintif," yet later at p. 123 gives the translation "amer de cœur." *pEbers,* 100[18–20] (*Eb* 855h) states that *dḥr(.t)* is a disease that can affect various parts of the body and that it enters through the heart; Breasted, *pEdwin Smith,* vol. 2, p. 475, translates it as "sickness," citing the passage in *pEbers.* It appears as well in *pEbers,* 41[20] (*Eb* 205). For further examples, see *pRamesseum 3* B., 2[5]; and *pTurin 1983* T.1, vs. 81–82. For the term *dḥr(.t)* used as a potentially hostile power in the possession of the gods, see *pHearst,* 14[8] (*H* 215): *ḏd=tn n nṯr.w nty ỉs dḥr(.t) ḥr ỉb=sn,* "…you speak to the gods in whose hearts there is indeed *dḥr(.t).*" The word is used in a similar sense in stele Ny Carlsberg Glyptothek AEIN 974, where it refers to the aspect of the magician who faces hostile forces. For a translation of that text, see Borghouts, *AEMT,* N° 121 and the translation "grimness." In the present passage, the word is qualified by *=f,* apparently referring to a malevolent being. If so, *dḥr(.t)* refers to an affliction he is attempting to impose upon the Pharaoh. The beings to whom *=sn* refers are attempting to turn back that affliction. Alternatively, it is possible that the word may describe the aspect of the demon here and his adversarial stance.

P. (x + 3: 5) Based on what follows at the beginning of x + 3: 6, the lacuna at the end of the line seems to require a verb.

Q. (x + 3: 6) On the restoration of the suffix pronoun *.sn*, see note R (x + 3: 6), following.

R. (x + 3: 6) The lacuna following the word *wdi* is 4 cm. Given the context of lines 5–8, *wdi=[sn…]* is a possible restoration, but the precise nuance of *wdi* cannot be determined.

S. (x + 3: 6) The reading of the group *rḏw.w stt=f fnd*, "…effluxes, his mucus, nose…" is certain, but the relationship of these three words is unclear. It is possible that *stt=f* and *fnd* go together, giving something like "…his mucus (of) (his) nose…." On *stt*, "mucus," see *WbMT,* pp. 812–14.

T. (x + 3: 7) The beginning of this line presents several difficulties. The initial signs seem to be the final signs of *ḫnm*, "smell" (*Wb.* III 293, 2–6). A verb or noun with such a meaning seems perfectly suited to the present context. The hieratic signs that follow appear to be a writing of or perhaps , neither group yielding much sense. *Wb.* II 384, 8–385, 13 gives the sign (Sign-list G37) as an abbreviated writing of the adjective *nḏs*, "small," but not as an abbreviation of the substantive *nḏs.* For the occurrence of [hieroglyph] with the verb *iri*, see note WW (x + 2: 16) above on the use of [hieroglyph] as a negative determiniative with certain verbs. It is quite possible that the text is corrupt or that a sign or a group of signs has been omitted.

U. (x + 3: 7) The traces of the end of the tail of the sign [hieroglyph] below the word [hieroglyph] *ib*, "heart" point to a restoration of a noun or verb in the lacuna governed by =*f.* The problem with the restoration of a verb is that each verb in this section has =*sn* as its subject. One possible restoration might be *ꜥḥꜥ=f ib=sn*, giving a reading like "he sets their hearts against the enemy...." See Faulkner, *CD*, p. 47, for the phrase *ꜥḥꜥ ib* with such a meaning. Such a restoration, however, would still require establishing to whom the preposition =*f* refers.

V. (x + 3: 7) The signs at the beginning of x + 3: 8 and the space available at the end of this line suggest a restoration of [hieroglyphs] [*mwt.t ḏꜣ ḏꜣ*].*t ḥm.wt rꜣ*, "...dead male, [dead female, male adversary, female adversary], and so on" here. See x + 2: 11 above and x + 3: 12 below for an identical series.

W. (x + 3: 8) The group [hieroglyphs] *r iw n=f* presents several problems. The person to whom =*f* refers remains unclear. In x + 3: 10–12 below, there seem to be references to Seth, Apophis, or a manifestation of the forces of chaos. The prefix pronoun =*f* in the present line could refer to that being. The verb *iw* may be an infinitive—though one would expect the writing *iw.t*—followed by the prepositional phrase *n=f;* its subject would be the beings referred to by the preposition =*sn* of the preceding line, namely the allies of Pharaoh. The pronoun =*f* would then refer to the Pharaoh, the translation being something like "...in order to come for him...." Possibly, [hieroglyphs] is a miswriting of the verb [hieroglyphs], "turn back" (*Wb.* II 406, 2–407, 4). Given the reasonably consistent writing of *rwi* elsewhere in this spell, that seems less likely. But see the variant writings at x + 3: 9 and 13 below.

X. (x + 3: 8) [hieroglyphs] *ꜥḥꜥ* is to be understood as a verb with the meaning "take up a defensive stance" or the like.

Y. (x + 3: 8) [hieroglyphs] *m ḥsi=f* can be read several different ways, as a verb phrase or as a compound preposition. Hannig, *GH* 559 a gives a verb "umkehren" and the phrase *m ḥsi=f*, "um ihn zu treffen." A compound preposition *m-ḥsi* (*Wb.* III 159, 15–17) is known as well with a range of meanings. It can mean "against;" in such a case, the following =*f* here would then refer to Seth, Apophis, or whatever manifestation of chaos is referred to in ll. 10–12. It can also have the localized meaning "in front of." See Gardiner, *EG*[3], p. 582, for such a meaning. The pronoun =*f* would still refer to Seth or the like, with the forces of protection standing in front of the malevolent being to block his path.

Z. (x + 3: 8) The restoration of [hieroglyphs] *i mwt nb*, "O every dead male..." at the end of the line is based on the traces of the sign [hieroglyph] at the beginning of the lacuna and on what follows at the beginning of x + 3: 9.

AA. (x + 3: 9) The restoration of [hieroglyphs] *ḥm.wt r3 nty rwi*, "...and so on who turn back...," fits the lacuna and gives the basic sense required. If the restoration of *nty* is correct, *rwi* would be read as an intransitive participle, "who turn back." An alternative solution would be to restore an imperative here with a meaning like "Turn back!" in place of the pronoun *nty*. A third possibility is that the verbal was preceded by a negative marker; the meaning, then, would be something like "...who do not turn back...."

BB. (x + 3: 9) Restoration at the end of the line is problematic. The relationship of *tm* with the first words of the next line remains uncertain because of the lacuna here.

CC. (x + 3: 10) The first sign of this line, [hieroglyph] =*f*, is likely the subject pronoun of the verb lost at the end of the preceding line.

DD. (x + 3: 10) The scribe has added the supralinear signs [hieroglyphs] to indicate the correct reading of the hieratic writing of the sign [hieroglyph] in the word *s3ḥ*, probably the verb "herankommen" (*Wb.* IV 20, 6–21, 6).

EE. (x + 3: 10) The restoration after *nḥm* is problematic. In lines x + 3: 15–17, the verb appears three times with =*k* as the subject and *Psmṯk* or *pr-ˁ3* as the direct object, followed by a prepositional phrase introduced by *m-ˁ*. It is possible that the subject of *nḥm* is the same person indicated by the suffix pronoun in the phrase *nb=s* that follows.

FF. (x + 3: 10) The writing [hieroglyphs] *nb* with the divine determinative [hieroglyph] (Sign-list G7) establishes its likely meaning as "lord." It is unclear to whom the suffix pronoun =*s* refers.

GG. (x + 3: 10) The group [hieroglyphs] offers two possible readings. The first is *iw sip.n=f*, taking the sign [hieroglyph] as the first sign of the verb [hieroglyphs], the whole group representing an *iw sḏm.n=f.* form. Such a reading offers an apparent parallel to the verb phrase *iw sm3.n=f* in the next line. The second reading is *iw=s ip n=f*, taking the sign [hieroglyph] as the pronoun subject *.s* and the group [hieroglyphs] as the verb *ip*. In this reading, the whole represents an *iw.f sḏm* form + the prepositional phrase *n=f.* Given that the two verbs *sip* and *ip* are closely related in meaning, their nuances being "count," "inspect," and "inventory," either reading would suit the present context. *pEdwin Smith*, 19[5] may offer some insight with the phrase *ḥḏ t3 n ip ir.t ḥr*, "Morning of counting the Eye of Horus...," i.e., "establishing its soundness." The same idea occurs at *CT* 45: *ḥwy-3 ṯw ip=t swḏ3=t m sˁḥ pn nty m-b3ḥ=i*, "Would that you were examined and kept safe in this mummy of yours which is in my presence." *Edfu* VI, 299[13], also a protection text, has the phrase *ḥr sip n=k ꜥ.t=k*, "to assign to you your limbs" in the sense of "to make well." The noun *ẖr.wy*, "testicles," which follows the verb phrase here may contain an allusion to the battle between Horus and Seth, in which Horus was blinded in one eye and Seth was castrated. If such is the case, the pronoun *=f* may refer to Seth; in the preceding lacuna there may have been a parallel clause referring to Horus. Alternatively, the verb *sip* can be used of "assigning" or "consigning" foes to the fire, which may well be what was intended here. On *sip* with such a meaning, see Wilson, *PL*, p. 798.

HH. (x + 3: 10) The writing of *ẖr.wy* is a dual form with the "intrusive" plural strokes found often in such writings, most likely as space fillers.

II. (x + 3: 11) The presence of the sign and the space available in the lacuna after *ꜥ.wy*, "two arms," suit the restoration of the suffix pronoun *=sn*.

JJ. (x + 3: 11) The restoration of the word *smꜣy.wt* is based on the presence of the two signs and the context of the passage; see *Wb.* III 450, 7–9, especially 9, for this word referring to enemies of the king.

KK. (x + 3: 11) *pnꜥ* here is "Feinde niederwerfen" (*Wb.* I 508, 17). There is enough room in the lacuna to restore *pnꜥ.tw=f*, "he is overthrown...," a passive *sḏm.tw=f* form. The presence of the preposition *ḥr* immediately after the verb phrase supports such a reading. The idiom *pnꜥ ḥr*, "turn the face, glance," does not seem relevant here. If the lacuna contained only the determinative (Sign-list A24), the verb may be read as a *sḏm=f* passive form.

LL. (x + 3: 11) The basic discussions of Wennefer are Gardiner, *Miscellanea Academica Berolinensia* II/2, pp. 44–53; Griffiths, *Origins of Osiris*, pp. 57–58; see also Donahue, *JEA* 64 (1978): 146–48. Assmann, *Death and Salvation*, p. 372, says that Osiris is called Wennefer "in his aspect of unchangeable continuation as mummy...." Goyon, *Cérémonial*, p. 115, n. 51, states that the god called *Wnn-nfr mꜣꜥ-ẖrw* is the god of Busiris in his aspect of the revived and divinized king. Perhaps the mention of Wennefer in the present passage is significant. As the god has triumphed over his enemies, so will the king. See the discussion in the Commentary below.

MM. (x + 3: 12) The group may be the particle *ir=k*, assuming the presence of an imperative in the lacuna, or it is the prepositional phrase *r=k*, "against you," with *=k* referring to each of the beings in the list that follows.

NN. (x + 3: 12) The restoration of the group *ḏꜣ.t irr*, "...and female adversary who do(es)...," is based on the traces, the space available, and the sense required.

OO. (x + 3: 12) For the occurrence of the particle *is* in the middle of a sentence, see Gardiner, *EG*³, § 247, esp. the example given at § 247, 5, showing the particle occurring rather late in the sentence, as it does here.

PP. (x + 3: 12) The restoration of *rwi m*, "...turn back from..." at the end of the line is based on the sense required here and on what follows. On the verb *rwi*, see note F (x + 3: 3) above. *pGeneva MAH 15274*, vs. 5^{2-3} provides something of a parallel where a negative protasis is followed by a threat in the apodosis: *ir tm ꜥḥꜥ r sḏm mdw.w=i iw=i ḥꜣꜥ ḫt ḏdw*..., "If (you) don't stop to listen to my words, I shall throw fire (on) Busiris...."

QQ. (x + 3: 13) The group *rwi.kꜣ.tw*[=*k*], "you will be turned back...," is to be understood as a passive *sḏm.kꜣ=f* form. See Gardiner, *EG*³, § 434, for the use of this form to express future consequence in an apodosis; see also Allen, *Middle Egyptian*, 22.10; cf., however, Depuydt, *Conjunction, Contiguity, Contingency*, pp. 201–55, esp. the introductory discussion at pp. 201–7. The signs *.tw* can be read just before the lacuna. Note that the scribe has added the supra linear sign *ꜣ* to correct *rwi* to conform to the writings at x + 3: 3 and x + 3: 4.

RR. (x + 3: 13) The tentative restoration of the word *st*, "place," is based on the traces available and the sense required.

SS. (x + 3: 13) The group *ḫr.wy* occurs before a small break in the papyrus. The lack of any determinative makes the exact reading of this word difficult to ascertain.

TT. (x + 3: 13) The traces after are too faint to allow positive reconstruction, but note that the sign (Sign-list Z6) appears at the end of the break.

UU. (x + 3: 13) *ꜥḥꜥ*, "Menge von Menschen; die grosse Masse" (*Wb.* I 221, 8–9).

VV. (x + 3: 13–14) *ḏd mdw*, "Words to be recited...," fits the available space. It is one of the regularly encountered phrases that begin a coda in this papyrus.

WW. (x + 3: 14) *mḥi*, probably "der Flachs" (*Wb.* II 121, 4–7), although the present writing is not given there. *WbDN*, p. 281, gives *mḥi* used "als Zauberdroge im Zauberspruch/als Droge," citing *pRamesseum 3* B, 3¹; 3³; and *pRamesseum 4* D, 3.

XX. (x + 3: 14) *sfṯ*, "ein Öl" (*WbDN*, pp. 436–37), apparently the same oil that is found in Old Kingdom offering lists where it is written *sfṯ*. Gardiner, *AEO I*, 8*, n. 1, states that it is derived from the cedar-tree. Cf., however, Leitz, *HPBM 7*, p. 74, n. 224, citing *Arzneimittelpflanzen*, pp. 12–20, and the discussion there about *sfṯ* as an oil of unknown origins scented with conifer resin. Concerning its mythological origins, *pSalt 825*, 2³ states that it came from the bloody nose of Geb.

YY. (x + 3: 14) *ibr*, "Laudanum" (*WbDN*, pp. 23–25, where it is said to be used "bei Erkrankungen des Kopfes und des Kopfhaares"). The ingredient *ibr* commonly occurs in medical texts, both in salves and in bandage/application remedies for the head and the eyes. It is even used as a hair-restorer. See also Derchain, *CdE* 30 (1955), pp. 248–49, for its use in certain royal rituals, particularly in sequences that deal with Horus triumphing over his enemies. Based on that use, its appearance here may be significant.

ZZ. (x + 3: 14) The extant hieratic traces show , pointing to *ḥḏr.t. WbDN*, p. 389, citing *pRamesseum 3* A and *pEdwin Smith*, 20^{18}, gives the meaning "ein noch nicht sicher bestimmtes Tier." See Gardiner, *pChester Beatty 3*, p. 16, n.3, and p. 47, n. 3, who proposed the reading "weasel;" Barns, *Ramesseum Papyri*, p. 18, suggested the meaning "a type of fox." See now the comprehensive discussion by Theis, *ZÄS* 138 (2011): 79–86, who proposes the meaning "pig" or "wild boar." An alternative reading would be the word *ḥḏr*, "Art Würmer welche die Leiche fressen" (*Wb.* III 214, 13). This word is not cited by *WbDN*. The loss of the determinative in the lacuna leaves the exact reading open to question.

AB. (x + 3: 14) The traces here show *nḏ šnꜥꜥ*, "ground finely," a commonly encountered term in prescriptions in medical texts, for which see *WbMT*, pp. 493–96 and 756–57, respectively. The phrase is found as well at x + 5: 11 and x + 8: 6 below.

AC. (x + 3: 14) (*Wb.* I 124, 13, as a writing of *wꜥ.t*, "one; together").

AD. (x + 3: 14) is a variant writing of *sḫ3k*, "durchseihen" and "Flüssiges durch (*m*) Tücher seihen" (*Wb.* IV 268, 6–8). See also *WbMT*, pp. 792–93, which discusses the use of this verb with the phrase *m ḥbs*, "…through cloth." The same phrase appears in *pBerlin 3038*, 11^{11} (*Bln* 138); 16^{7} (*Bln* 163h); 20^{4} (*Bln* 185); 20^{5} (*Bln* 186); and 20^{9} (*Bln* 188).

AE. (x + 3: 14) Based on a parallel at x + 8: 6, the restoration at the end of the line would be *di r msḏr*, "place(d) at the ear," bringing this spell to a conclusion. It should be noted that the lacuna at the end of the line leaves just enough room for the writing of *ky*, "Another…," the first word of the new spell.

COMMENTARY

The text of this spell is badly damaged, preventing a substantive reading of the text as a whole, but a number of observations and conclusions may be drawn from its fragmentary remains. As in the preceding spell, the hostile forces include the generic, gendered pairs of enemies. Note also that in an address to various forces at the beginning of the spell there is a clear mention of 𓃀𓂝 *b*, a common designation of Seth.[180] References in a later section of the spell mention Seth again, possibly his injured testicles, and his confederates who are said to present a threat to Pharaoh[181] and his ear. We also encounter several mentions of counter-forces who seem to play an apotropaic function. Unfortunately, most of their names are now lost. There is one reference to *Wnn-nfr*, apparently in a protective role. This juxtaposition of Sethian beings and Wennefer resonates well with a major myth sequence found in the Osirian cycle that centers on Seth's continued attempts to threaten Osiris with annihilation, even after he had killed him.[182] In the present spell, the association of the king with Osiris, particularly in his manifestation as Wennefer, may allude to the impending triumph over the hostile forces by the Pharaoh. In the preceding spell and its parallel text Spell O, the potential threat to the ear of Pharaoh was raised to the level of a possible cosmic conflict; there the conflict was set in the solar myth cycle. Here the cycle may rather be Osirian; just as Osiris experienced victory over Seth and his accomplices, the king will enjoy the same. Note that at the end of the spell at line x + 3: 12–13 we find: "If you do not [turn back from] the ear of the Pharaoh, then [you] shall be turned back…." Just as we see in the preceding spell and its parallel, the conflict is cast in the form of a threat, not a hostile engagement already in play. As noted above in the Introduction, by drawing a parallel between the threat of a physical ailment and a cosmic "drama" whose positive outcome is well-known, a protection text becomes that much more efficacious in its ability to render threatening forces impotent. The spell concludes with a prescription and instructions to place the prescription "at the ear."

180 See n. C (x + 3: 2) above. The badly damaged text here precludes establishing a specific context for the presence of this name.

181 The title *pr-ꜥꜣ* occurs four times; the name Psamtik does not. There are three lacunae where the term *pr-ꜥꜣ* or the name Psamtik can be restored.

182 What has been called "the second death," for which see Zandee, *Death as an Enemy,* pp. 186–88; Grieshammer, *Jenseitsgericht,* pp. 69–70; Hornung, *Höllenvorstellungen,* pp. 33–34; Assmann, *Death and Salvation,* pp. 74ff.

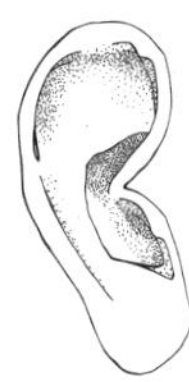

Spell E — Translation with Commentary

COLUMNS X + 3: 14–X + 5: 3) (P. BROOKLYN 47.218.49)

TRANSLITERATION

14. … [*ky*]
15. *rꜣ i rᶜ ḥr.y-tp mꜣᶜ.t wḏᶜ [mꜣᶜ.t] kꜣ m iwnw mi nḥm=k [pr-ᶜꜣ m-ᶜ]*
16. *mwt mwt.t ḥm.wt-rꜣ i wsir ḥḳꜣ [ḏ.t m]i nḥm=k psmṯk m-ᶜ …*
17. … [*i*] … *mi nḥm[=k pr-ᶜꜣ] m-ᶜ ḫft* …
18. ……

COLUMN X + 4

1. … *ir.n …ḫr*
2. … *nn ir=f iwᶜ.w … nn ir=f i… tꜣ ḏr=f ᶜnḫ=f m … …ᶜ.n=f …*
3. *nḥ]m.n=f iꜣw.t n it[=f nḥm].n=f t m-ᶜ ḥkr [mw m-ᶜ]*
4. [*ib*] *ḥbs n ḥꜣw tw … n ꜣḫ i ꜣs.t nṯr.t [wr.t]* …
5. … *sms.t sꜣ.t nw.t mi [nḥm=ṯ] psmṯk m-ᶜ ḫft.w=f mi nḥm.[n=ṯ*
6. *sw m-ᶜ ꜣd sw m smꜣy.wt … sḫm mwt mwt.t ḫft ḫft.t n [pr-ᶜꜣ*
7. [*i*] *nṯr.w rsy.t mḥ.t imn.t.t [iꜣb.t.t irr sḫr].w m-ḫt tꜣ snḏm-ib n* …
8. … *nty irr sḫr.w m-ẖnw kꜣri [irr sḫr.w] m-ḫt tꜣ mi i* …
9. … *irr=tn ᶜ.wt nb n psmṯk … [imi] n=f ib=f ḥr st=f ḥꜣ.ty=f ḥr [st=f]* …
10. *nn thꜣ=f nn wᶜr=f nn gm … [ḫft pf]t mwt mwt.t ḏꜣ ḏꜣ.t ḥm.wt-rꜣ* …
11. … *iw r ᶜḥᶜ.w=f nn rḳi … nn mꜣꜣ s mwt mwt.t nn šni mwt [mwt.t] nn*
12. *iṯi rd.wy=f ḥr šm ḏr.t=f smn … ir s nb s.t nb(.t) rḫy.t nb ḥnmm.t nb(.t) ḥm.wt-rꜣ šm* …
13. … *ir.w ḫpr.w=sn m ẖr.t-nṯr … ᶜ m tꜣ-mri ḫft pr=sn m [ẖr.t-nṯr*
14. [*i*]*rr sḫr.w [m]-ḫt tꜣ is di.t … =tn ḥꜣ psmṯk mki=tn [sw]*
15. [*nḥ*]*m=tn sw m-ᶜ ḥsb sw m-ᶜ i[ꜣd.t] n rnp.t tn m-ᶜ ḏꜣḏꜣ nb m-ᶜ šmm [nb]* …
16. [*m-ᶜ ḥ*]*sb nb pr m rꜣ n nṯr nty ḥwi … tꜣ ḏr=f i psḏ.t ᶜꜣ.t i psḏ.t [nḏs(.t)]*
17. *wḏᶜ mꜣᶜ.t m-bꜣḥ rᶜ mi [wḏᶜ]=tn mꜣᶜ.t n psmṯk nḥm=[tn]*
18. *sw m-ᶜ sbi.w … grg … ḥꜣp.w [n]fr …di.t* …

COLUMN X + 5

1. *ᶜnḫ … nṯr.w … ḳmꜣ*
2. *=sn m … šs nsw wḥm m ᶜnfy (?)*
3. *ṯzw-7 di r tp s ḫft …hrw*

TRANSLATION

14. ....[Another][A]
15. *spell.* O Re, one who has authority[B] over Maat, who administers [justice,][C] Bull in Heliopolis,[D] come, may you save [Pharaoh from][E]
16. a dead male, dead female and so on. O Osiris Heqa[djet, come,][F] may you save Psamtik from [a dead male,][G]
17. [dead female and so on.][H] [O ...6 cm...][I] come, may you save Pharaoh from[J] [the enemy, the fiend,
18. a dead male, dead female, male adversary, female adversary, and so on ...][K]

COLUMN X + 4

1. [...19 cm...][L]
2. [...] he will not produce an heir;[M] he will [not] ...[N] the entire land (?)[O]. He lives on [...][P] he has ...[Q] [...2.5 cm...]
3. he has robbed[R] the office of his father; [robbed] bread from (?)[S] the hungry, [water from][T]
4. the thirsty, the clothing of the naked,[U] [food offerings][V] of the blessed dead.[W] O Isis, [great] goddess [...1 cm...],[X]
5. eldest, daughter[Y] of Nut. Come, [save Psa]mtik[Z] from his enemy like you saved him (?)[AA]
6. from the furious one,[BB] (and) him[CC] from the confederates.[DD] [Overpower][EE] the dead male, dead female, male enemy, female enemy of [Pharaoh].[FF]
7. O[GG] gods of the South, the North, the West, [the East[HH] who govern] throughout the land,[II] who delight the heart of [...2 cm...][JJ]
8. who govern within[KK] the shrine[LL] [who govern][MM] throughout the land. Come then,[NN] ...[OO]
9. may you make [sound][PP] every limb of Psamtik. [Give][QQ] to him his *ib*-heart in its place, his *ḥ3ty*-heart[RR] [in its place so that][SS]
10. he will not go astray;[TT] he will not wander; he will not [... O (?) enemy, fiend][UU] dead male, dead female, male adversary, female adversary and so on. [Do not][VV]
11. come against his multitudes.[WW] He shall not deviate from[XX] [...2.5 cm...].[YY] A dead male, dead female shall not see it.[ZZ] A dead male, [a dead female][AB] shall not pass [...2 cm...] not
12. seize his legs while going forth (?) his hand establishing (?)[AC] [...2.5 cm...]. As for any male, any female,[AD] any commoner, any of the Sun-people and so on[AE] who proceed [...][AF]
13. [...] who make (?)[AG] their forms[AH] in the necro[polis ...] influence[AI] in Egypt as they go forth from [the necropolis][AJ]
14. who govern[AK] throughout the land.[AL] Lo, place [your arms][AM] behind Psamtik. May you protect [him...][AN]
15. [May you save][AO] him from doom (?),[AP] him from [the epidemic] of this year,[AQ] from every fiendish being,[AR] from [every] fever,[AS]

16. [from] every doom (?)[AT] that comes forth from the mouth of the god who floods[AU] … the entire land. O great Ennead, o [small] Ennead[AV]
17. who administer justice[AW] in the presence of Re. Come administer[AX] justice for Psamtik. May you save[AY]
18. him[AZ] from the rebels [...6 cm...] concealed [...][BA] placed [...][BC]

COLUMN X + 5

1. lives[BD] [...12 cm...] gods[BE] [...5 cm...] created (?)
2. they [...11.5 cm...] royal linen,[BF] repeated (?)[BG] [...2.5 cm...]
3. seven knots[BH] which are placed at[BI] the head of a man while[BJ] [...7.5 cm...] day.[BK]

TEXT NOTES

A. (x + 3: 14) Restore [hieroglyphs] *ky*, "Another," written in black to distinguish the beginning of a new spell, as the entire prescription of the preceding spell was written in red. Note that for the writing of [hieroglyphs] *r3*, "spell," the first word of x + 3: 15, the scribe reverts to red ink. See note AE (x + 3: 14) above.

B. (x + 3: 15) *ḥr.y-tp* (*Wb.* III 140, 11) is listed by Leitz et al., *Götterbezeichnungen* 5, p. 394, as an epithet indicating "Bezeichnung von Göttern," specifying Wennefer, Thoth, Khonsu-Thoth, and Khnum-Re. No citations for this phrase qualified by *m3ʿ.t* are offered. Zandee, *pAmunhymnus* 2, p. 228, discusses the phrase in passing but adds little more than the information given in the *Wörterbuch* entry. Kuhlmann, "Gottesepithet," *LÄ* 2 (1977): col. 683, lists *ḥr.y-tp* among the divine epithets used of gods associated with "Regens-Rektum" but only when used with toponyms. See note C (x + 3: 15), following.

C. (x + 3: 15) Based on the phrase *wḏʿ m3ʿ.t m b3ḥ Rʿ* that occurs at x + 4: 17 below, a possible restoration here is [hieroglyphs] *wḏʿ m3ʿ.t*, "judge what is right; administer justice" (*Wb.* I 405, 7–9). Such a restoration also fits the space in the lacuna. It occurs at *Edfu* I, 395[2] in a list of epithets of the god Re. It is also encountered as an epithet of Thoth, for which see *pChester Beatty 8,* rt. 8[5]; *9,* vs. B 4[7]; Goyon, *pConfirmation,* 11[1] and p. 100, n. 170, with references. Borghouts, *pLeiden I 348,* rt. 11[5], cites its use in the Leiden text modifying the phrase *r3 im=f* and gives the translation as "…a mouth is in it which administers justice." The word *wḏʿ* is often translated as "distinguish" or "discern." When employed with the term *m3ʿ.t*, it can mean "separate truth (from falsehood)." On the Egyptian sun-god as judge and savior, see Assmann, *Egyptian Solar Religion,* pp. 190–210.

D. (x + 3: 15) The epithet [hieroglyphs] *k3 m Iwnw*, "Bull in Heliopolis," has several different applications in texts running from the Ramesside Period through the Ptolemaic Period. Originally, it seems to have referred to the so-called "fetish" of Heliopolis, a pillar with the head of a bull, an apparent symbol of the creator god as worshipped in Heliopolis, usually understood to be Atum. It is found as an epithet of Re in the Pyramid Texts. The apparently related epithet *kꜣ wr*, which also has Heliopolitan connections, referred to Re or Atum-Re-Horakhty in his visible manifestation as the Mnevis-bull; see Goyon, *pConfirmation,* p. 92, n. 83, and *Les dieux-gardiens,* p. 430; Zivie, *BdE* 81 (1979): 487 and 489ff; as an epithet of Atum, see Myśliwiec, *Der Gott Atum,* p. 101; also see the discussion by Zandee, *pAmunhymnus* 2, pp. 419–23.

E. (x + 3: 15) The space available at the end of the left fragment suggests the restoration of [hieroglyphs] *pr-ꜥꜣ m-ꜥ*, rather than *psmṯk m-ꜥ*.

F. (x + 3: 16) Restore [hieroglyphs] *Wsir ḥkꜣ ḏ.t mi*, "…Osiris Heqadjet. Come…." In the Theban region, Osiris Heqadjet is perhaps best known from a temple located north of the eastern gate of the Karnak enclosure. This aspect of Osiris had particular importance for the dynasts of the Libyan Period and then for the God's Wives of Amun in the Kushite and Saite Periods who constructed a chapel to him. He was apparently associated with the reaffirmation of kingship and solidarity of the family. See Redford, *JEA* 59 (1973): 16–30.

G. (x + 3: 16) The end of this line and the beginning of x + 3: 17 obviously contained a list of malevolent beings. The traces, however, do not conform to writings of words like [hieroglyphs] *mwt*, "dead male," or the like.

H. (x + 3: 17) The traces at the top of the break at the beginning of the line again do not suggest any confident restorations.

I. (x + 3: 17) A vocative containing the name of a deity and an appropriate epithet most likely occupied this lacuna of 6 cm, paralleling the phrases *Rꜥ ḥr.y-tp mꜣꜥ.t wḏꜥ mꜣꜥ.t* and *Wsir ḥkꜣ ḏ.t* found in the preceding two lines.

J. (x + 3: 17) The traces above the break clearly show [hieroglyphs] *mi nḥm=k*, "Come! May you save…." The traces after that suggest [hieroglyphs] *pr-ꜥꜣ m-ꜥ ḫft*, "…pharaoh from the enemy…."

K. (x + 3: 17) The traces of the first sign of [hieroglyphs], "enemy" justify the restoration of a list of malevolent beings, perhaps the longer list found in x + 3: 7. It continues into what is probably another line of Column x + 3, now lost, since the traces at the beginning of x + 4: 1 do not suit any of the signs of these words. What would follow at the end of the list is uncertain.

L. (x + 4: 1) The blank space above the scant traces at the top of the fragments establishes this as the first line of the column.

M. (x + 4: 2) A possible restoration here is [hieroglyphs] *iwꜥ.w*, "heir," a word which fits the traces and the available space. Although uncertain, these lines may focus on the consequences of not curing or protecting Psamtik. The text here may imply that the triumph of the forces of evil over the Pharaoh would have the same effect as their triumph over the sun-god: order would be destroyed and chaos would reign.

N. (x + 4: 2) The reading of [hieroglyphs] *i3w.t n it.f=f*, "office of his father," is a possibility, but it is a conjecture based only on the first sign and the occurrence of this phrase in the next line.

O. (x + 4: 2) The reading [hieroglyphs] *t3 ḏr=f*, "the entire land," fits the traces.

P. (x + 4: 2) It is possible that *ʿnḫ=f* here is a *sḏm=f* form, corresponding to another earlier form like *mwt=f*, "he will die," or *tm=f ʿnḫ/nn ʿnḫ=f*, "he will not live," the whole expressing the consequences of not curing or protecting the Pharaoh. See note M (x + 4: 2) above.

Q. (x + 4: 2) There are only a few traces in the 2 cm following [hieroglyphs] *ʿnḫ=f*. At the end of that space the signs [hieroglyphs] can be read, but little else.

R. (x + 4: 3) The traces at the beginning of the line suggest the restoration of the group [hieroglyphs] *nḥm n=f*. The numerous lacunae make it very difficult to understand the text and its allusions clearly. The first problem encountered is whether the writing is a *sḏm.n=f* form or an imperative followed by a prepositional phrase. The second problem is establishing the meaning of the verb. *nḥm* can mean "fortnehmen, rauben" (*Wb.* II 295, 12–296, 8). If that is the case, the person to whom =*f* refers would not be Psamtik but one of the malevolent beings; furthermore, the writing would represent a *sḏm.n=f* form and would mean "he has seized…." This part of the spell may refer to the reversal of order that occurs if the threats to Psamtik are not neutralized; the *sḏm.n=f* forms in the passage, moreover, would seem to refer to past events. There may be an allusion to the quarrel of Horus and Seth. The word *nḥm* is used in *pChester Beatty 1*, 1^8 and 4^{10}, to describe wrongful seizures of royal prerogatives and the office of kingship, respectively. Note, however, that texts referring to the threats of cosmic reversal are more commonly couched in future or prospective verb forms, not those that have past reference.

It is also possible that these forms are negative *n sḏm.n=f* forms with the negative word [hieroglyph] *n* occurring in the lacunae before the two writings of *nḥm n=f*. This construction, however, is not attested elsewhere in the papyrus. The pronoun =*f* would then still refer to the malevolent being, and the resulting translation would be: "He cannot rob the office of his father, [he cannot rob] bread from the hand of the hungry, [the water of] the thirsty, the clothing of the naked, the [offerings made] to the blessed dead."

An alternative interpretation is to read the verb *nḥm* as an imperative with a following dative and meaning of "save" here, rather than "seize." In this case, *nḥm n=f* would mean "save… for him …." The pronoun =*f* then would most likely refer to Psamtik. Although such a translation for *nḥm* makes good sense with the first phrase, *nḥm n=f ỉ3t n it=f*, "Save for him the office of his father," it seems a bit strained for what follows. The phrases *nḥm n=f t m-ʿ ḥḳr mw ib ḥbs n ḥ3w* [...] *n 3ḫ* might be translated "Save for him the bread in the hand of the hungry man, the water of the thirsty, the clothing of the naked, [the offerings made] to the blessed dead." Such a reading focuses on the idea that the maintenance of cosmic order and equilibrium is dependent upon the successful protection of the Pharaoh. Each of the phrases above would express the need for the prevalence of Maat. Where the text is better preserved at the end of column x + 3 and from x + 4: 5 onwards to the end of the spell, the format consists of enjoinders to various beings to do something on behalf of the pharaoh.

S. (x + 4: 3) The writing [hieroglyph] occurs here in what appears to be the first element of a series of parallel ideas. It is replaced by the preposition [hieroglyph] in the clauses that follow. The group [hieroglyph] should probably be read *m-ʿ*, "from."

T. (x + 4: 3) The restoration of the noun [hieroglyph] *mw m-ʿ*, "water from...," is based on the context. It seems that some word like "water" or "beer" is required here.

U. (x + 4: 4) For the reading adopted here, see note R (x + 4: 3) above.

V. (x + 4: 4) If the phrase [...] *n 3ḫ*, "...for the blessed dead," continues the preceding string of parallel ideas, it seems that some prerogative of an *akh* is to be restored in the lacuna, most likely a noun denoting a food-offering. See Friedman, "On the Meaning of *Akh* (*3ḫ*) in Egyptian Mortuary Texts," (Brandeis Univ. diss. 1981), pp. 137–38, who discusses the continuing need for food after death. *CT* 39 has the statement *mn n ḥtp-nṯr n nṯr.w pr.t-ḫrw n 3ḫ.w*, "...divine offerings have been established for the gods, invocations offerings for the blessed dead...." *CT* 40 has *m t3 pn ʿnḫ.w m-m im3ḫ.w sbb r ḥtp.w*, "...in this land of the living among the venerated ones who attain to food-offerings..." Bakir, *The Cairo Calendar No. 86637*, rt. 20[2], has *ir.t pr.t-ḫrw n 3ḫ.w*, "Make an invocation-offering to the blessed dead." Statements such as these have been interpreted to mean that the dead not only need food but have a right to it. The large quantities mentioned in the offering lists of stelae and funerary chapels represent the idea of offerings made in perpetuity, or possibly allude to the quantities needed for a communal feast, one that would signify the deceased's ongoing inclusion in the world of social order. Thus, the representation of food offerings in relief and their common mention in funerary texts may emphasize that the deceased has not become socially disenfranchised, but is still a functioning member of family and community.

W. (x + 4: 4) Here the word [hieroglyph] *3ḫ*, "blessed dead," refers not to a malevolent being, but to one threatened by the forces of disorder and chaos, thus paralleling the preceding nouns "hungry man ... thirsty man ... naked man ...."

X. (x + 4: 4) Following the name of Isis are the traces of [hieroglyphs], probably the beginning of the noun [hieroglyphs] *nṯr.t*, "goddess." If so, it may have been followed by the adjective [hieroglyphs] *wr.t*, forming the epithet "great goddess."

Y. (x + 4: 5) I read *smsw.t* as an attributive adjective modifying the last word in the lacuna at the end of x + 4: 4. The phrase *s3.t Nw.t* probably continues the string of epithets of Isis that began in the preceding line.

Z. (x + 4: 5) The proposed restoration of [hieroglyphs] *nḥm=ṯ Psmṯk*, ["…save Psamtik] from his enemy…" is partially based on the context and the appearance of the verb *nḥm* again at the end of the line in what appears to be a parallel clause. The verb *nḥm* here is to be taken in its second sense, "retten, in Schutz nehmen" (*Wb.* II 296, 9–26), commonly constructed with the preposition *m-ʿ*.

AA. (x + 4: 5) Although the restoration of [hieroglyphs] *mi nḥm.n.ṯ=k sw m-ʿ*, "…like you saved him from…," does fit the space available, it is possible that the noun *nṯr* or a divine name like Horus or Osiris should appear here in place of the pronoun [hieroglyphs] *sw*, "him," equating the protection of Psamtik with that of a divinity. For a parallel, see *pChester Beatty 9,* vs. B.17[3–4], which has "…as all the primeval gods were protected, as Isis protected her son Horus against his brother Seth." See also Massart, *pLeiden I 343 +345,* p. 99 n. 6: "I shall repel every evil or bad thing as [so and so (a god)] protected himself against his enemies." A writing of [hieroglyphs] "Horus" or [hieroglyphs] "Osiris" fits the space available at the end of the line following the verb *nḥm*.

BB. (x + 4: 6) [hieroglyphs] *3d*, "der Wütende, der Bedrängte" (*Wb.* I 24, 20–22, but listing its determinatives as [hieroglyph] or [hieroglyph]). The presence of the determinative [hieroglyph] (Sign-list I3), however, is typical of the writing of this word in religious and protection texts. The word *3d* occurs in a number of spells in the Book of the Dead, where it conveys the idea of rage or fury, e.g., *BD* 72, 136 and 151; for the latter spell, see Lüscher, *Untersuchungen zu Tb 151,* pp. 200–201; also Goyon, *pConfirmation,* 8[5], where *ḫsf 3d* is given as an epithet of *ỉn-ḥrt* and is translated as "qui repousse l'agression." For the specific reference of *3d* in the present passage, see note DD (x + 4: 6) below.

The determinative [hieroglyph] (Sign-list I3) may also underscore the notion of crocodile inherent in this word. See *Urkunden VI,* 61[10], for a ritual [hieroglyphs] *nt-ʿ n ḫsf 3d*; the noun *3d* is translated there as "Wütende." See there at 123[3] for the phrase [hieroglyphs] *i nḥm tw m 3d*, and the translation given is "O weiche zurück als Krokodil," with the alternative rendering of the phrase *m 3d* as "in Wut;" see *pBM 10042,* 2[6–7], where it appears twice written [hieroglyphs], and Leitz, *HPBM 7,* p. 33, translates "raging (crocodile)" and "Raging (Crocodile)," respectively; finally, see the discussion by Wilson, in Quirke, ed., *The Temple in Ancient Egypt,* pp. 179–203, esp. 193 on the word *3d*.

CC. (x + 4: 6) The direct object pronoun *sw* probably refers to the deity named in the lacuna at the end of x + 4: 5.

DD. (x + 4: 6) *sm3y.wt*, "Bundesgenossen des Seth, Bundesgenossen der Feinde des König" (*Wb.* III 450, 8–9). A prevalent term in protection texts, it regularly refers to the followers of Seth, to whom the preceding word *3d* may refer.

EE. (x + 4: 6) The traces of the sign (Sign-list S42) before the group point to the writing of the verb *sḫm*; hence, the translation "overpower" is given.

FF. (x + 4: 6) The beginning edge of the cartouche can be seen and the restoration of *pr-ˁ3* best fits the space.

GG. (x + 4: 7) The restoration of *i* "O," fits the space and sense required.

HH. (x + 4: 7) Restore *i3b.t.t*, "East," after *imn.t.t*, "West." This same appeal to the gods of the four cardinal points appears at x + 9: 11–12 below in a lengthy address where it occurs specifically in conjunction with an appeal to the great and small Enneads; note, however, the different order and the somewhat greater elaboration there. *pConfirmation,* 1[10], exhibits the same phrasing and order found in the present passage. See Kessler, *LÄ* 2 (1977): cols. 1213–15 for the orientation and order of the cardinal points in Egyptian texts.

II. (x + 4: 7) The restoration of *irr sḫr.w* is based on the traces and the apparent parallel in the next line and again at x + 4: 14. The phrase *irr sḫr.w m-ḫt t3* is attested from as early as the Old Kingdom. See *Urk.* I, 102[9], where the meaning seems clearly to be "govern throughout the land, i.e., Egypt;" for a later example, see *pLeiden I 343+345,* rt. 5[3], which has *n3 n nṯr.w ḥr ir.t r=k sḫr.t.* The phrase is perhaps best known as an epithet of Khonsu. In Karnak, there was a temple of Khonsu in his aspect of *p3 ir sḫr m w3s.t*, "the one who governs in Thebes," for which see Barguet, *Le Temple d'Amon-Rê,* p. 7; also Meeks, *SO* 8 (1971), pp. 48, 79, and n. 189. Posener, *ACF* 68 (1968): 401–2, suggests that the phrase *irr sḫr.w* designates the divine power to fix and determine the destiny or fate of men. Such a meaning may well be what was intended in the present passage. For a somewhat different interpretation, see Meeks, *RdE* 15 (1963): 44, who in translating a passage in *pBerlin 3048,* a Hymn to Ptah in which this phrase appears, renders *ir=k sḫr.w n 'Imn.tiw*, "Tu (Ptah) t'es préoccupé des Occidentaux…." It is worth noting that the passage there is followed by *dr.n=k ḫft.yw*, "You have driven away the enemy." It seems clear that the endowment this phrase designates gives one power over his enemies and perhaps over the forces of chaos and evil in general.

JJ. (x + 4: 7) The lacuna at the end of the line, following *snḏm ib n*, "who delight the heart of…," likely contained the name of the person(s) to whom *nty* of the next line refers. There seems to be a parallel at x + 4: 14 below, although there is also damage to the papyrus there.

KK. (x + 4: 8) On the writing [hieroglyphs] for the compound preposition *m-ḫnw*, "within," see note R (x + 2: 10) above.

LL. (x + 4: 8) What follows *m-ḫnw* is [hieroglyphs] *k3ri*, "shrine," a term which occurs again at x + 11: 6.

MM. (x + 4: 8) The traces after *k3ri* [hieroglyphs] and at the end of the lacuna suggest [hieroglyphs]. The signs [hieroglyphs] and the fact that the phrase *irr sḫr.w* appears in this spell several times before the prepositional phrase *m-ḫt t3*, "throughout the land," suggest such a restoration.

NN. (x + 4: 8) For the writing of the group [hieroglyphs] with the imperative [hieroglyphs] *mi*, "Come," see *Wb.* II 35, 15–17.

OO. (x + 4: 8) The two signs before the lacuna at the end of the line appear to be [hieroglyphs] perhaps the verb *ni(3)*, abweisen; niederwerfen: Hannig, *GH*, p 391a.

PP. (x + 4: 9) The traces at the beginning of the line are the vestiges of the last sign or two of the partially preserved verb at the end of the preceding line. The suffix pronoun [hieroglyphs] =*tn* would function as its subject, referring back to *nṯr.w* at the beginning of x + 4: 7.

QQ. (x + 4: 9) Possibly restore [hieroglyphs] *imi*, "give," before the prepositional phrase [hieroglyphs] *n=f*.

RR. (x + 4: 9) For a discussion of the terms *ib* and *ḥ3.ty*, see note K (x + 2: 8) above.

SS. (x + 4: 9) A probable restoration here is [hieroglyphs] *ḥr st.f*, "in its place," based on the context, the parallel at the middle of the line, and the space available. For parallels to the idea of locating the heart in its proper place, see *CT* 62 in which Horus comes to his father Osiris to revitalize him; among the statements there is *di n=k ib=k pn n ḫ.t=k sḫ3=k smḫ.t.n=k*, "…who gives to you this heart of yours for your body (so that) you remember what you have forgotten." See also *Djed-Hor,* 83: "He has kept your heart in its place; your heart is under his protection." Ritner, *SAOC* 54 (1992), p. 34, discusses a similar phrase, *ib r st=f*, stating that its basic meaning is "to function correctly;" see also n. 156 there for the citation of several other texts in which the phrase appears. At the end of this line, the preposition *r* should probably be restored to mark the clauses that follow as purpose clauses.

TT. (x + 4: 10) The subject pronoun =*f* in this phrase and the two that follow most likely refer to Psamtik. It is quite possible that these are statements to the effect that Psamtik is intact and healthy; thus, he can and will withstand the assault of the inimical forces.

UU. (x + 4: 10) This lacuna contained both the conclusion of the idea begun at the end of x + 4: 8 and the beginning of a new one. The likely restoration at the beginning of the lacuna is a negated verb of motion, paralleling the verbs in the two preceding negative clauses: "…he will not go astray, he will not wander…." It is possible that a preposition also followed that introduced the relationship between the verb and the string of malevolent beings that follows. Alternatively, the idea may have terminated with the missing verb in the lacuna; a new thought would then follow, an address to a list of malevolent beings introduced by *i*, "O." The traces of the sign (Sign-list Z6) before the word , "dead male," suggest a restoration like *ḫft pft*, "…enemy, fiend…." The inclusion of these words is more typical of the extended vocative phrases found in this papyrus; the shorter lists follow prepositions or serve as direct objects and invariably begin with the term *mwt*, "dead male."

VV. (x + 4: 10) Assuming that this line continues the thought of x + 4: 8–9, then restore , the imperative of the negative verb *imi*, followed by the verb *ii*, "come," or the like, continuing into the beginning of x + 4: 11.

WW. (x + 4: 11) Despite the damage to the papyrus, the hieratic writing is clearly *ʿḥʿ.w*, "Masse" (*Wb.* I 221, 8–9). X + 3: 13 shows a similar writing that lacks the plural strokes.

XX. (x + 4: 11) For *rḳi*, the meaning "jem. befeinden" has been offered (*Wb.* II 456, 9–12); there is a related noun associated with Seth (*Wb.* II 456, 18–20); but see Meeks, *Mythes et légendes*, p. 55, n. 51, who, in a discussion of the apparently reduplicated form *rḳrḳ*, suggests for the simple radical *rḳ* the meanings "(de)part; deviate (from)." Such a meaning accords well the verbs in the preceding line.

YY. (x + 4: 11) The lacuna could continue the idea introduced by *nn rḳi=f*, perhaps a parallel phrase introduced by *nn*.

ZZ. (x + 4: 11) The small lacuna that occurs under the group makes establishing the function of the sign problematic. The pronoun could refer to a feminine noun now lost or be a writing of the masculine pronoun *sw*.

AB. (x + 4: 11) Based on the conjectured width of the gap between column x + 4 and column x + 5, it is possible to fit at least the word *mwt.t*, "dead female," if not one more group of signs.

AC. (x + 4: 12) The traces at the beginning of the line show *iṯi*, "seize." It is possible that this word was preceded by the negative *nn* like the preceding verbs. Immediately following , the group *rd.wy=f*, "his two feet/legs," can be read clearly. One sign can be seen; the other sign is lost in the hole in the papyrus. If *ḏr.t=f* and *smn* are to be taken together, the expected *ḥr* of the First

Present construction has been omitted. Such omissions become more common in writings of this construction from the time of Ramesses III onward; see Černý and Groll, *A Late Egyptian Grammar,* p. 34; see also Winand, *Études de néo-égyptien* 1 *AL* 2 (1992), pp. 413–19, Nos. 635–48, esp. No. 636, for a statistical overview of the presence and absence of *ḥr* in this construction. The traces show the verb *smn*, "establish;" the word that followed *smn* had (Sign-list D26) as its determinative. The long stroke that originates in the lacuna seems to be the remains of the pronoun . Alternatively, if *smn* is a stative form, the translation would then be something like "…his hand is firm…."

AD. (x + 4: 12) Likely restore *s.t nb*(*.t*), "any female," in the lacuna.

AE. (x + 4: 12) For a longer but similar list in a book of protection, see *pChester Beatty 9*, vs. B.12[3–4]. There the invocation begins with *ir rmṯ nb ir.y-pꜥt nb rḫyt nb ḥnmmw.t nb*(*.t*)…, "As for any man, any patrician, any of the common people, any of the sun people…," specifying the group from whom protection is needed.

AF. (x + 4: 12) *šm* seems to be the first verb in a series continuing into the next two lines.

AG. (x + 4: 13) The traces at the beginning of the line show .

AH. (x + 4: 13) For *ḫpr.w*, "form," see the discussion and bibliography in Fischer-Elfert, *ÄA* 60 (1999), p. 177, n. d.

AI. (x + 4: 13) The reading of the word *ḫr.t nṯr*, "god's domain/necropolis," is certain. The writing may be the word "influence," for which see note S (x + 13: 14) below.

AJ. (x + 4: 13) Based on the traces of the sign (Sign-list R8) and the context, the restoration of at least part of the group at the end of the line seems probable. See note AK (x + 4: 14), following.

AK. (x + 4: 14) The beginning of the line reads , with the final signs of *ḫr.t-nṯr* in the lacuna at the beginning.

AL. (x + 4: 14) On the idea of "governing," see note II (x + 4: 7) above.

AM. (x + 4: 14) After the traces that seem to indicate , "arms" is a possible reading, giving the phrase *di ꜥ.wy*, "placing the arms behind (someone)," a standard posture of protection. An alternative would be to read the verb *ꜥḥꜥ*, "stand," or a word with a similar meaning. The preposition *ḥꜣ* (*Wb.* III 8, 14), occurring with verbs meaning "to stand" or "to place," gives the general meaning "schützend hinter jem. stehen, sich hinter jem. stellen."

AN. (x + 4: 14) Restore [hieroglyphs] at the end of the line, reading *mki*[=*tn sw*, "May you protect him…." The whole of this part of the line would read: "Lo, place your arms behind/make yourselves stand behind Psamtik; may you protect him, …."

AO. (x + 4: 15) Restore [hieroglyphs] *nḥm*=*tn sw*, "may you save him…," at the beginning of the line.

AP. (x + 4: 15) For [hieroglyphs] *ḥsb*, a negative meaning seems required here. *Wb.* III 166, 6 gives a verb written [hieroglyphs] with the meaning "zerbrechen" and *Wb.* III 166, 7 a related noun written [hieroglyphs], "Bruch." The entries [hieroglyphs] given at *Wb.* III 166, 11–168, 1, all written with the book-roll determinative, deal with calculation and reckoning. *Wb.* III 168, 4 gives a verb [hieroglyphs], "schlachten;" *Wb.* III 168, 5 has a noun [hieroglyphs], "Messer." Hannig, *GH*, p. 561b gives "Schicksal; Verhängnis," possibly thinking of *Urk.* IV, 5[17]: *ʿḥʿ.n ꜣꜣtꜣ iw n rs.y stk.n šꜣw=f ḥsb=f*, "Then Aata came south; his fate caused his doom (*ḥsb*) to approach." Note, however, that the word written in that text that has been read as *ḥsb* should perhaps be read as *šꜣw* as well; see Quaegebeur, *OLA* 2 (1975): 49–57. In the Brooklyn passage, the unmarked noun *ḥsb* clearly has little or nothing to do with calculation, unless we are to understand this noun as having the idea of "(final) reckoning," similar to ours, for which see Fischer-Elfert, *BSAK* 9 (2003): 110, nn. 1–4; pp. 114–15. Hannig's meanings, "fate; doom," suit the context nicely.

AQ. (x + 4: 15) Based on the initial [hieroglyph] (Sign-list M17) and the group [hieroglyphs] at the right hand edge of the left fragment, the reading [hieroglyphs] *iꜣd.t n rnp.t*, "Not des Jahres = Misswachs, Seuche" (*Wb.* II 431), should be restored. The basic discussions of the "epidemic of the year" are Yoyotte, *Kêmi* 18 (1968): 82–83, who sees the *iꜣd.t* as messengers of Sakhmet; Goyon, *Les dieux-gardiens*, pp. 187–88; Germond, *Sekhmet*, pp. 286–304, particularly on the "epidemic of the year" and its connections with the New Year and the goddess Sakhmet; Leitz, *Tagewählerei*, pp. 213–14 and nn. 32–36; finally Derchain, *CdE* 53 (1978): 51 and n. 4, who sees in this phrase a reference to an annual air- or water-borne disease that came with the rise of the Nile. The phrase also occurs in *pEdwin Smith*, 18^{15-16}; 20^{5-8}; *pCairo 58027*, 4^{7}; *pConfirmation*, passim; and *pLeiden I 346*, 2^{4}; 2^{6}; 2^{7}; and 2^{11}, all of which are texts dealing with protection at the time of the New Year.

AR. (x + 4: 15) [hieroglyphs] is probably to be read *ḏꜣḏꜣ* (*Wb.* V 532–33, 4 gives a word written [hieroglyphs] and [hieroglyphs], meaning "feindlich; Feind").

AS. (x + 4: 15) [hieroglyphs] *šmm*, "fever" (*Wb.* IV 468, 1°17). The adjective *nb*, "every," should be restored at the end of the line.

AT. (x + 4: 16) Restore [hieroglyphs] *ḥsb*, "doom," at the beginning of the line.

AU. (x + 4: 16) For *ḥwi* (*Wb.* III 48, 16–22: "schlagen"), Lopez, *RdE* 24 (1972): 111–15 claims that the meaning "to flood" is a semantic specialization of the verb meaning "to strike" (*Wb.* III 46, 1–47, 24). There may be room for *m* before *tꜣ ḏr=f*, or else the phrase *tꜣ ḏr=f* is an unmarked direct object. On the idea of evil coming forth from the mouth, compare *CT* 165: *wḏꜣ=kwi m-ꜥ sḏb nb pr m rꜣ nṯr nb ꜣḫ nb mwt nb m rnp.t tn*, "I am safe from any evil utterance that comes forth from the mouth of any god, any blessed dead, any dead person in this year." Note the contrast of the latter two terms: *ꜣḫ* refers to the dead who have passed judgment and attained a transcendent state of being, while *mwt* refers to those who did not pass judgment but continue to exist as transient beings. *BD* 78 has the statement *mdw(i) n=i irk wsir di=k wḏb pr m rꜣ=k r=i*, "Speak to me, Osiris. May you grant that what has come forth from your mouth against me be redirected." On the association of evil and the inundation which marks the beginning of the New Year, see the discussion at note AQ (x + 4: 15) above. The god who floods the land with his mouth, if that is what was intended here, is the one who creates the cosmos through the act of spitting, an idea at least as old as the Pyramid Texts. See the remarks of Zibelius, *Studien zu Sprache und Religion Ägyptens* I, pp. 399–407, esp. pp. 406–7.

AV. (x + 4: 16) There is enough room at the end of the line to restore *nḏs.t*, "small." For an invocation to Enneads elsewhere in this text, see, for example, x + 9: 12–13 where they are qualified more specifically and extensively. For the gods who form the great and small Enneads, see Barta, *MÄS* 28 (1973), pp. 53–58.

AW. (x + 4: 17) The sign (Sign-list Z7) or (Sign-list G43) should be restored at the beginning of the line as the initial sign of the verb *wḏꜥ*, "judge, administer."

AX. (x + 4: 17) Restore *wḏꜥ* in the middle of the line, as it suits the sense and the space available.

AY. (x + 4: 17) The sign (Sign-list A24), the determinative of the verb *nḥm*, "save," is partly visible at the end of the line.

AZ. (x + 4: 18) Traces of the dependent pronoun *sw*, "him," can be seen at the beginning of the line.

BA. (x + 4: 18) After the determinative (Sign-list A24) of the word *ḥꜣp.w*, what can be seen is . There is a flake of papyrus obscuring what is written before or possibly , as the two writings are virtually identical in the papyrus.

BC. (x + 4: 18) At the end of the line, the group *di*, "given/placed," is clear, but what follows in the lacuna of 1 cm is lost. The 1.5 cm of blank papyrus seen below the writing of this group indicate that the present line is the final line of column x + 4. The extensive lacunae at the top of the next column, approximately two lines in length, make the restoration at the end of the present line impossible.

BD. (x + 5: 1) The traces at the beginning of this line show [hieroglyphs].

BE. (x + 5: 1) At the middle of the line, the traces suggest the writing of the sign [hieroglyph] (Sign-list F31) or [hieroglyph] (Sign-list R8A).

BF. (x + 5: 2) For [hieroglyphs] *šs nsw.t*, "royal linen," see *Wb.* IV 540, IV B and 542, 2–3. The word occurs in *pLeiden 348 I,* rt. 8[6], where it is similarly written and is the medium upon which a spell is to be written. The same phrase may appear in the demotic magical text *pLouvre E 3229,* rt. 4[5], in a list of ingredients in a prescription; for that text, see Johnson, *Enchoria* 7 (1977), pp. 55–102.

BG (x + 5: 2) The exact meaning of [hieroglyphs] *wḥm m*, "repeated as…" (?) cannot be determined due to the lacunae.

BH. (x + 5: 3) The reading *ṯzw-7* is certain, despite damage to the beginning of the line.

BI. (x + 5: 3) Though somewhat damaged, the signs [hieroglyphs] *di r*, "placed at," are clear.

BJ. (x + 5: 3) The word [hieroglyphs] *ḫft*, "while," after the writing of the word [hieroglyphs] *z*,"man," served to introduce further circumstances for carrying out the instructions of the spell.

BK. (x + 5: 3) The two signs [hieroglyphs] that occur before the rubric which begins the next spell are possibly the vestiges of *hrw*, "day."

COMMENTARY

The text of this spell is also badly riddled with lacunae, but vestiges of the original text offer reasonable evidence for some observations and thoughts about interpretation and meaning. The text as a whole appears to describe, once again, a cosmic conflict, but in this case one in which the positive and negative forces are already drawn up in posture of confrontation. The benevolent forces are named first — Re, Osiris, and possibly Atum.[183] If the restoration of the name of Atum has any validity, these three gods would allude to the ordered cosmos as a whole, as they comprise the god of the cycle of renewal, the god of the cycle of continuation, and the god of the cosmic preexistence and existence.[184] Additionally invoked are Isis, the gods of the cardinal points, and the two Enneads. Among the malevolent forces are the "furious one" and "the companions," references to Seth and his accomplices. There are several other Sethian allusions as well. We also encounter "rebels," "doom," "the epidemic of this year," and "…every doom that comes forth from the mouth of the god who floods…the entire land." The generic hostile forces — dead male, dead female, et al. — are present as well. Thus, the individual gods

183 The restoration is based on context.

184 Assmann, *Death and Salvation,* pp. 371–72.

and groups of gods taken together seem to represent the cosmos at large that is inhabited by both benevolent and malevolent forces.

What seems to be at stake in this spell is not just the well-being of the king, but that of the earthly world as well, normally kept in order by the principle of *maat* as controlled and administered by the king. Here the specific threats to the king that are mentioned do not focus on his ear, but on his whole physical well-being. Note that the divinities are asked to "save" the king[185] from the forces that threaten to assail him.[186] In an unfortunately lacunae-ridden section at the beginning of the text, there may have been a series of descriptions of the earthly world in (potential) disorder and disarray. We can see in these a clear reference to what the outcome will be of a failed effort to preserve the well-being of the king and, thus, the equilibrium of the cosmos. At one point, Isis is asked to save the king from the Sethian beings and the generic hostile forces just as she once saved someone, unfortunately not named, but possibly Horus.[187] If this interpretation is correct, the allusion would be to another mythic "drama," perhaps that in which Horus is bitten by a scorpion and his ensuing illness represents a threat to the balance in the cosmos.[188] The reference may rather have to do with Osiris, given the presence of Seth and his accomplices in the text. The gods of the cardinal points are called upon as well to aid in the protection of the physical well-being of the king, a necessity if he is to function properly: "[Give] to him his *ib*-heart in its place, his *ḥ3.ty*-heart [in its place so that] he will not go astray; he will not wander; he will not [...."[189] The mention of the heart is significant, as the heart is a potent symbol of bodily well-being and also represents the will of the individual. The heart must be in its proper place in order for the body to operate properly as an integrated entity and for the emotional and cognitive life of the individual to continue to function.[190]

A direct appeal to the generic hostile forces follows, with imprecations regarding what they will not be allowed to do, a feature already familiar from the two preceding spells. Individuals identified simply as "any male, any female, any *rḫyt*-person, any of the *ḥnmm.t*-people" are asked to stand in protection behind Psamtik in order to save or protect him from danger. The forces that threaten the king this time are enumerated as "doom...[the epidemic] of this year...every fiendish being...[every] fever every doom that comes forth from the mouth of the god who floods the entire land." Most of these ideas are associated with the coming of the New Year, and a number of them are found or have close parallels in the group of texts found in Crypt B' of the Temple of Nekhbet

185 The name Psamtik occurs five times and *pr-ˁ3* once. There are two lacunae where the name Psamtik or *pr-ˁ3* could be restored.

186 The phrase *mi nḥm=k psmṯk/pr-ˁ3* occurs five times in the first half of the text.

187 For the interpretation that the allusion here is to Horus, see above at note AA (x + 4: 5); the evidence for such an interpretation offered there comes from *pChester Beatty 9*, vs. B.17$^{3-4}$.

188 For examples of texts that preserve this myth, see Klasens, *OMRO* 33 (1952), passim, and Jelínková-Reymond, *BdE* 23 (1956), passim.

189 x + 4: 9–10.

190 Assmann, *Death and Salvation*, pp. 28ff. and p. 421, n. 13, for references.

at Elkab.[191] Finally, there is an appeal to the great and small Enneads who are asked to "administer justice" for the king. The phrase *wḏꜥ mꜣꜥ.t* that occurs here echoes its use as an epithet of Re found at the beginning of the text; thus, we have an example of a *kyklos,* a literary device that frames a text and serves to bring its end back to its beginning.

Overall, then, the spell seems to serve a more general purpose than those encountered earlier, one that is not strictly bound to the protection of the ear. In fact, given its more generalized application, perhaps we should see it as a text from the genre of the protection of the king at the New Year, especially given its close affinities with the texts from the Elkab Crypt.[192] The text lacks a prescription at the end but does give an instruction concerning a thread with seven knots, an apotropaic element found in a number of protection texts.[193]

191 For these texts and a discussion thereof, see the Introduction, pp. 12ff.

192 For a discussion of this genre and examples of texts belonging to it, see the Introduction, pp. 12ff. and pp. 29ff.

193 On the use of knots in protection texts, see p. 31 and n. 159 above.

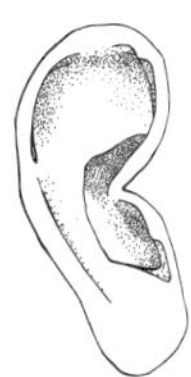

Spell F — Translation with Commentary

COLUMN X + 5: 3–11 (P. BROOKLYN 47.218.49)

TRANSLITERATION

3. *k(y) rꜣ inḏ ḥr=k gi.[w]*
4. *pꜣ gi.w pr … ḥr ibḥ.w ḫn.ty …*
5. *wsir r dr mwt mwt.t … ḏꜣ ḏꜣ.t nty … t …*
6. *nty ḏdf m ꜥ.wt=f … gny.t tp pn … rꜥ s-*
7. *…=f pwy n gi.w … ḫpr.n=i m iwnw … s nwd (?)*
8. *[t]n iw=i m imn.t.t … ḫpr … n ḥꜥ.w=i nty …=k im ḏd-*
9. *-f m-ẖt ꜥw.t …nty … pw]y rmṯ nṯr.w …*
10. *…ꜣ im=f inḏ ḥr=k gi.w … [ḏd mdw] zp-4 pẖr.wt di r=f ꜥfi*
11. *ꜥpnn.t nḏ šnꜥꜥ ḥr ḥsꜣ … [di] r msḏr*

TRANSLATION

3. ....*Another Spell.*[A] Hail to you, *gi.w*-plant,[B]
4. the *gi.w*-plant[C] that comes forth […4 cm…][D] strong (?)[E] upon teeth (?)[F] first (?)[G] […1.5 cm…]
5. Osiris to drive away a dead male, dead female […4 cm…][H] male adversary, female adversary who are [in] […1.5 cm…]
6. who tremble (?)[I] in his limbs[J] […4 cm…] earlobe[K] of this head … Re […1.5 cm…]
7. this his […][L] of a *gi.w*-plant.[M] […3.5 cm…] I came into being in Heliopolis[N] … place […0.5 cm…]
8. this[O] […] I am in the West […] come into being […3.5 cm…] of my body which you […0.5 cm…] therein, trem-
9. -bling[P] throughout the limbs[Q] […] which […3.5 cm…] men, gods, […1.5 cm…][R]
10. … him.[S] Hail to you *gi.w*-plant (?)[T] […3 cm…. *Recite*][U] *four times.*[V] *The remedies*[W] *given to* him[X] (consist of) bee[Y] […1.5 cm…]
11. a worm[Z] ground finely[AA] with a thread[BB] […3.5 cm…] [(and) placed] at the ear.[CC]

TEXT NOTES

A. (x + 5: 3) The rubric *k*(*y*) *r*ꜣ, "Another spell," marks the beginning of a new section. There are no rubrics terminating the preceding section. See x + 2: 6 for a parallel to such a writing.

B. (x + 5: 3) Two small and highly damaged fragments have been placed at the left edge of this column. What can be read shows that they represent what remains of the end of these lines. The initial signs of the word *gi.w*-plant can be read here. For a discussion of that term, see note C (x + 5: 4), following.

C. (x + 5: 4) The first sign of the line may be , although the writing is more typical that of *s*ꜣ, which does not make much sense. , "*gi.w*-plant" (*Wb.* V 157, 11–158, 11) appears again at x + 5: 7 where the text has suffered some damage, but the writing there appears to be similar. *WbDN,* pp. 533–37, discusses two different words, both showing a wide range of writings, one usually transcribed *gi.t,* and the other *gi.w*. They can be virtually indistinguishable, given the variety of spellings they show. *WbDN,* p. 534, states that *gi.t* is a medicinal ingredient applied externally, found only in *pEbers,* citing seven occurrences of the word with five different writings. Further on, at pp. 536–37, it states that *gi.w* represents *Cyperus rotundus* and *Cyperus esculentus,* both technical terms for the sedge plant. Manniche, *Ancient Egyptian Herbal,* pp. 43 and 98, equates *gi.w* with *Cyperus esculentus,* citing Theophrastus, according to whom *gi.w* is only a food; she cites no references for *gi.w* as a medicant. Borghouts, *pLeiden I 348,* rt. 10^8, offers the translation "cypress plants," without commentary. There it is written . Jonckheere, *Le papyrus médical Chester Beatty,* p. 18, n. 5, enumerates several different kinds of "*gi.w*-plants." Germer, *Flora,* p. 248, however, claims that the Egyptians used the term *gi.w* to describe two different plants, one with an edible, oil-bearing tuberous root, the other a weed with an inedible but aromatic root. Cf., however, Germer, *Heilpflanzen,* pp. 146–48, who says that its earlier identification as "Nussgras" is not certain. The problem of determining which term is employed here is compounded by the fact that the word does not occur in a prescription but in the body of a spell for protection. See the discussion in the Commentary.

D. (x + 5: 4) The lacuna that runs vertically through the column here is approximately 3–4 cm, based on a conjectured column width of 19 cm.

E. (x + 5: 4) The sign (Sign-list T12) seems to be what is written here. Its meaning and relationship with the signs that follow are not clear.

F. (x + 5: 4) The word *ibḥ.w*, "Zähne" (*Wb.* I 64, 2–4) appears in conjunction with the *gi.w*-plant at *pEbers,* 83^5 (*Eb* 663), a prescription for treating disorders of the abdomen. Bardinet, *Dents et mâchoires,* pp. 79–80, discusses this passage but notes that the meaning of the phrase *ibḥ n gi.t* remains obscure. Germer,

Arzneimittelpflanzen, p. 340, states that *ibḥ* is part of a plant, namely "Stachel; Dorn." Due to the poorly preserved nature of the papyrus, it is unclear whether a direct connection exists between these two terms here. Also, see note G (x + 5: 4), following, and the Commentary below.

G. (x + 5: 4) It is possible that the word *ḫn.ty* modifies the preceding word *ibḥ*, forming the phrase *ibḥ.w ḫn.tyw*, "first teeth." *pOphiologie,* 2[21], has *ibḥ ḫn.ty Wsir* in a spell recited against the poison of a snake bite. Sauneron, pp. 56–58, gives the translation "dent primitive d'Osiris," seeing a reference in this phrase to one of the "milk teeth" of the god when young. Its role in that spell is directed against the bite and teeth of the malignant force, namely the poison of the snake which has bitten the victim. The phrase *ibḥ n wsir* occurs in *pProphylaxie,* x + 16[18]; see Goyon, *pProphylaxie,* p. 122, n.9. Given the lacunae in the present passage, it is impossible to determine whether the noun *ibḥ.w* refers to part of a plant, for which see note F (x + 5: 4), preceding, or alludes to a role played by the teeth of a divinity. But see the Commentary below.

H. (x + 5: 5) The hieratic traces before the writing of *ḏꜣ*, "male adversary," are too poor to suggest anything. The lacuna may have continued with *ḫft pft*, as in column x + 4: 6 above.

I. (x + 5: 6) *ḏdf*, "Zeichen der Furcht, Schaudern" (*Wb.* V 634, 4–6, giving the writings and). Although the determinatives are not given in the writings cited there, the meanings given for *ḏdf* clearly suit the present context. The word is found in *pLouvre 3233 A–B* 2, a text also connected with protection, for which see Goyon, *BIFAO* 77 (1977): 45–54, pl. 15, and esp. 50, n. 3; see also Koenig, *BIFAO* 79 (1979): 103–19, pls. 38–39, for a copy of the Louvre text just cited, and his comments on the term *ḏdf* at 106–7, n. a. The same verb apparently occurs at x + 5: 10–11, below, as well.

J. (x + 5: 6) Despite damage to the surface of the papyrus, the group *ꜥ.wt=f*, "his limbs…," can be read with certainty.

K. (x + 5: 6) The traces here show , a variant writing of *gry.t* (*Wb.* V 181, 7; *WbMT* 921), meaning "[Teil des Ohres];" the variant writing *gny.t* is given at *Wb.* V 174; Hannig, *GH,* p. 901b gives an entry only for the spelling *gny.t*. Breasted, *pEdwin Smith,* 7[14], translates the phrase *gry.t nt msḏr=f*, "orifice of his ear." Sanchez and Meltzer, *The Edwin Smith Papyrus,* give the translation "auricle of the ear."

L. (x + 5: 7) The traces of *=f* at the beginning of the line governed a noun or verb written at the end of the preceding line.

M. (x + 5: 7) On the *gi.w*-plant, see note C (x + 5: 6) above.

N. (x + 5: 7) The group *ḫpr n=i* can be read either as “I came into being in Heliopolis,” or “…come(s) into being for me in Heliopolis.” The signs that appear at the end of the extant line show something like . Hannig, *GH,* p. 400a gives a verb *nwd*, “abweichen,” with the determinative . I can make little sense of the writing here, however.

O. (x + 5: 8) The traces of what appears to be the demonstrative *tn* can be seen at the beginning of the line.

P. (x + 5: 9) The traces at the end of line 8 and the beginning of line 9 indicate the writing of , the verb at x + 5: 6.

Q. (x + 5: 9) Though damaged, the traces after the preposition *m-ḫt*, “throughout,” clearly show , suggesting the restoration of *ʿ.wt*, “limb; limbs.”

R. (x + 5: 9) There are only a few illegible traces at the end of the line.

S. (x + 5: 10) The reading of the word at the beginning of this line is uncertain, as the sign before is difficult to read. It may be a writing of one of the words spelled , *sw3*, with the meanings “be far from” (Hannig, *GH,* 674b) or “pass by” (ibid., 675a). If that is the case, the sign *s* would have been written at the end of the preceding line. Neither of the entries cited gives that particular spelling, however. Alternatively, it may be the verb , *ḏ3*, “feindlich jemandem entgegenstrecken” (*Wb.* V 514, 4) or “sich feindlich in den Weg stellen” (*Wb.* V 514, 14–16), both of which employ the preposition *m*. If so, the writing of the sign seems somewhat different from its writing elsewhere in the papyrus.

T. (x + 5: 10) The traces following the group *inḏ-ḥr=k*, “Hail to you…,” show , suggesting the reading , *gi.w*, the plant name that appears at x + 5: 4 and x + 5: 7 above.

U. (x + 5: 10) The rubric should be restored as . The statement includes the instruction to recite the text four times, followed by a specification of what *pḫr.wt* should be given to the person whom the text is intended to help.

V. (x + 5: 10) There is damage to the surface of the papyrus, but the reading *zp-4*, “four times,” seems certain. For a parallel in this text, see x + 8: 18 below.

W. (x + 5: 10) For the writing , *pḫr.wt*, “remedies” (*Wb.* I 549, 1–12).

X. (x + 5: 10) Despite the break and damage, the reading at the end of the line is certain.

Y. (x + 5: 10) [hieroglyphs] *ʿfi*, "die Biene" (*Wb.* I 182, 10, written with the determinative [hieroglyph] (Sign-list L2). *WbDN,* pp. 87–88, cites the word as *ʿff* and gives a number of writings, all of which have [hieroglyph] (Sign-list G41) as the determinative. It occurs at *pEbers,* 74[14] (*Eb* 576) in connection with *ʿpnn.t*, the word that follows here as well. On the mythological origins of the bee, see *pSalt 825,* 2[5], where it is stated that it was created from the tears of Re.

Z. (x + 5: 11) [hieroglyphs] *ʿpnn.t*, "Art Wurm oder Schlange" (*Wb.* I 180, 6–7; *WbDN,* pp. 84–86). The word is found in *pEbers,* 74[14] (*Eb* 576) in connection with *ʿff,* "fly," a cognate of *ʿfi*, the preceding word here. According to the *Wörterbuch* entry, *ʿpnn.t* is written in a number of instances with the determinative [hieroglyph] (Sign-list F27) or [hieroglyph] (Sign-list I14). See *WbDN,* pp. 84–86 for the variety of meanings that have been assigned to the word *ʿpnn.t* and the relevant sources cited there. See also Sauneron, *pOphiologie,* p. 114, for his translation "salamandre d'eau," and p. 115, n. 2, where he discusses this choice of translation. Cf., however, Leitz, *HPBM* 7, p. 7, n. 37, who takes issue with such an identification and translation. The word is found in both prescriptions to be ingested and ones that are topical dressings. On its use in medical prescriptions, see Sauneron, *pOphiologie,* p. 191.

AA. (x + 5: 11) On the term [hieroglyphs] *nḏ šnʿʿ*, "ground finely," see note AB (x + 3: 14) above.

BB. (x + 5: 11) [hieroglyphs] *ḥsꜣ*, "Faden; Schnur" (*Wb.* III 166, 4).

CC. (x + 5: 11) Though there is damage to the surface of the papyrus, the traces before [hieroglyphs] *msḏr*, "ear," seem to indicate the writing of [hieroglyphs] *di r*, "…to be placed at…." For a parallel to the phrase *di r msḏr* placed at the end of a remedy and spell, see x + 8: 6 below. The rubrics that follow [hieroglyphs] begin a new spell, though they are faint and somewhat difficult to read.

COMMENTARY

The text of this spell is badly damaged, and what is left is very disconnected, making a coherent reading of the whole very difficult; moreover, a more grounded interpretation of its meaning remains highly problematic. A few observations can be offered. The spell begins with an appeal to the *gi.w*-plant, known chiefly from medical texts, though it does occur in one non-medical text. A passage in the Coffin Texts offers the statement *iw ꜣt=k ḥr pḥwy=k iw ib=i ḥr rdi.t gi.w n itm*, "Your striking power is in your tail (but) my heart gives the *gi.w*-plant to Atum."[194] As the initial clause seems to refer to a scorpion, the context suggests then that the *gi.w*-plant was considered to have not only medical but protective properties as well. If the *gi.w*-plant had thorns, as its connection with the word *ibḥ.w* might suggest, therein may lie its protective powers. A plant with thorns could be seen as a suitable adversary for the sting of a scorpion and the bite of a snake

194 *CT* 112.

in Egyptian thinking. A cursory review of the ingredients found in the prescriptions of medical and protection texts will show that there are some that have real medicinal properties, like those that are analgesics, for example. The powers that some of the others have seem associative at best. Perhaps that is the case with the *gi.w*-plant found in this spell, as the passage in *CT* 112 may suggest. See the Commentary to Spell O below.

Additionally, the statement "I came into being in Heliopolis" of the Brooklyn spell offers a connection to Atum. There may be a further allusion to divine or royal birth as well, one found in the Book of the Dead and in one Late Period papyrus.[195] The mention of Heliopolis certainly has solar associations, and the references to Osiris and one to the West suggest possible connections with the Osirian cycle. It may be significant that neither Psamtik nor *pr-ꜥꜣ* is named, though either word may have occurred in any one of the lacunae. The spell concludes with a prescription that unfortunately offers nothing by way of insight.

195 *BD* 115 makes reference to a number of deities created in Heliopolis, as does *BD* 125. Goyon, *pConfirmation,* p. 95, n. 105, says that Heliopolis is the royal birth place *par excellence*. For a discussion of the presence and role of Heliopolis in protection texts, see the discussion in the Commentary that follows Spell L below.

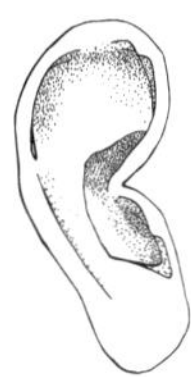

Spell G1 — Translation with Commentary

COLUMN X + 5: 11–X + 6: 12 (P. BROOKLYN 47.218.49)

TRANSLITERATION

11. *… mḏꜣ.t n.t sḥri-*
12. *-.t mwt mwt.t m msḏr nty ẖr… dmḏ.yt n.t ḏḥwty r s-*
13. *ḥtm [sb]i.w m wn=s[n] … ꜥšꜣ ms.w sḫm.ty…sn i ir*
14. *ḏt=f m-ꜥ štꜣ.w=f i ḏsr … gbꜣ.wy=fy i irr mꜣꜥ.t m wiꜣ*
15. *n ḥḥ i wp ir.t=f irr … gm wš tp ꜥꜣ m ꜥ.wy i itm*
16. *irr ẖr.wt=f i ꜥwꜣy … .w i ḥr ꜣwi iw.t.y ꜣẖ.t …*
17. *i ssw ṯtf ḳs(n).w [ḥr] … stẖ ir nšni.w i … tp ꜥšꜣ rn*
18. *.w imn rn=f štꜣ i … n it i wr bꜣ.w m-ꜥ štꜣ …*

COLUMN X + 6

1. *… zp … [p]r m ḏ.t …*
2. *… rn=f i nb n … .w ꜥ n … ir rn=f ḥꜣp.w … [i mnmn]*
3. *[n=f] pt i mnmn n=f tꜣ i … ḥr.t i wdi is.wt irr …*
4. *… sḥtp rḫ.wy m wiꜣ … .f ḏs=f nn rḫ.tw=f i ms.w …*
5. *… =f i ꜥnḫ n ḥnmm.t … =f iṯi sw r ḥr.t i …*
6. *… [rḫ].tw=f i wḏꜣ.wt ꜥšꜣ nbi … dz sḫm-ib i ḳn… [sḫm]*
7. *ib.w i smn tꜣ ir rn … ir=s i smn mꜣꜥ.t m ḥꜣ.t …*
8. *… [i]r mk.t=s ir mwt im i ms.w … ꜥꜣ nrw i sḫm-ib …*
9. *…=f…s wp mw.t=s i ꜥšꜣ ms.w … i zp nšni.ti i sḫm-[ib] …*
10. *… [wḏꜣ].t i ir mꜣꜥ.t ms nw.t … n ḥꜣ.ty n nb=s i šm [ii]*
11. *… i irr grḥ rn wsir … =s pt m sšm=s i s[. …*
12. *… i ir fnd i šm ii … [i]m=s i ir rn=s ḥbs m ꜥ.wy=s*

TRANSLATION

11. ……………………………………….*A book-roll for driving off*[A]
12. *a*[B] *dead male, dead female from the* ear[C] *of one who is suffering* […4 cm…] *compilations of prescriptions*[D] *of*[E] Thoth[F] to[G]
13. *annihilate*[H] *the rebels (when) they are* […4 cm…][I] [O][J] one numerous of forms,[K] overpower[L] … them. (?)[M] O one who made

14. his body from his secrets.[N] O one who separates [...4 cm...] his two arms.[O] O[P] one who does [what is right][Q] in the Barque
15. of Millions.[R] O one who opens his eye,[S] who makes [...4 cm...] — found destroyed[T] — great first born in the arms. (?)[U] O Atum,
16. who provides for his own needs.[V] O robber[W] [...4 cm...]. O long-faced one (?)[X] whose magical power does not exist. (?)[Y]
17. O time[Z] of overflowing/pouring down (?)[AA] harpoons (?)[BB] [...6 cm...] Seth[CC] who made raging. O [...1 cm...] heads (?)[DD] whose names
18. are numerous, who conceals his secret name.[EE] O [...4 cm...] of (his) father. O one whose *Ba*'s are great[FF] together with (his) secrets [...][GG]

COLUMN X + 6

1. [...1.5 cm...] occasion[HH] [...7 cm...] which comes forth from [his] body (?)[II] [...7 cm...]
2. [...1.5 cm...] his name.[JJ] O possessor of [...3 cm...] who has made his name[KK] (?) concealed [O one for whom]
3. the heaven [shakes].[LL] O one for whom the earth shakes.[MM] O ... heaven.[NN] O one who prepares[OO] the crew[PP] who does [...3 cm...]
4. [...1.5 cm... O] one who appeases the Two Companions[QQ] in the Barque[RR] [...3 cm...] himself.[SS] He is not known. O children[TT] [...3 cm...]
5. his [...1.5 cm...][UU] O one who lives on the sun-folk,[VV] he [...3 cm...] removing himself to heaven.[WW] O[XX] [...3 cm...]
6. He [is not known].[YY] O amulets (?)[ZZ] whose flames are numerous(?)[AB] [...3 cm... O] cutter,[AC] violent one.[AD] O strong (?) [...3 cm...]
7. [...1.5 cm...] violent ones.[AE] O one who brings the land into order,[AF] who made [her] name[AG] [...3 cm...] that she does/who does it.[AH] O one who establishes Maat[AI] in the fore [...][AJ]
8. [... made][AK] her protection[AL] (who) made death[AM] therefrom. O children (?)[AN] [...3 cm...] one great of terror.[AO] O violent one[AP] [...1.5 cm...] (?)
9. he [...1.5 cm...] her[AQ] who opened her mother.[AR] O one whose forms are numerous[AS] [...3 cm...] O occasion (when) she was enraged.[AT] O violent [one][AU]
10. [...1.5 cm...Wadjet].[AV] O one who did what is right,[AW] child of Nut[AX] [...3 cm...][AY] for the heart of her lord. O one who goes [and comes] [...2 cm...][AZ]
11. [...1.5 cm...] O one who makes the night (whose) name (?) is Osiris[BA] [...3 cm...] she ... heaven in her following. O [...2 cm...]
12. [...1.5 cm...][BC] O one who made rage.[BD] O one who goes and comes[BE] [...3 cm...] with her. O one who made her name "clothing in her arms."[BF]

TEXT NOTES

A. (x + 5: 11) The beginning of the title of this spell is *mḏꜣ.t n.t sḥri.t mwt mwt.t m msḏr nty ẖr*..., “Book-roll for driving off a dead male, dead female from the ear of one who is suffering...” A short text of *pBerlin 3038,* 6^{11} (*Bln* 71) has a similar heading: *ky sḥri mwt m msdr*, “Another [text] for driving off a dead male from the ear,” followed by a short list of ingredients in a prescription.

B. (x + 5: 12) The traces at the beginning of the line show the signs and (Sign-list A24), the final signs of the verb *sḥri*.

C. (x + 5: 12) The traces after *msḏr*, “ear,” show *nty ẖr*, “...ear of the one who is suffering....”

D. (x + 5: 12) *dmḏ.t*, “Sammelwerk (von Receptsammlungen)” (*Wb.* V 462, 9). See Helck, *MÄS* 31 (1974), p. 132, who supports the general meaning “Summe.” *WbMT,* p. 980, cites five occurrences of this word in the medical texts. Westendorf, *Handbuch* 1, pp. 80–81, discusses the term under his category “Sammelhandschriften.” Sauneron, *pOphiologie,* pp. 53–54, gives further relevant citations and bibliography. See also Schott, *Bücher und Biblioteken,* p. 412, citing Edfu III, 348^{1}: “Bücherkatalog.”

E. (x + 5: 12) Read as the indirect genitive marker *n.t*.

F. (x + 5: 12) The name Thoth in connection with the noun *dmḏ.t* also occurs at *pEbers,* 1^{9} (*Eb* 1): *ir=f dmḏ.t*, “He makes the collection of texts...,” For the writing of the name *ḏḥwty*, “Thoth,” in black ink within a rubric, see Posener, *JEA* 35 (1949): 77–81; see also the references at Goyon, *BdE* 42 (1966): 2 and 28, n. (1).

G. (x + 5: 12) Note that the conjunction is written here in black ink as well.

H. (x + 5: 13) *sḫtm*, “vernichten” (*Wb.* IV 223, 10–224, 7). This word appears quite commonly in protection texts. See *pBerlin 3038,* 8^{8} (*Bln* 99) with the noun *ḫft*, “enemy,” as its direct object; also, *pChester Beatty 8,* vs. 4$^{8-11}$ and vs. 15^{3}; Roccati, *Aeg* 44 (1969): 5–13, a Ramesside text in Turin; *pBM 10209,* 1^{16}; Zandee, *pAmunhymnus,* p. 299, n. 394; finally Goyon, *pConfirmation,* 1^{18}, and especially p. 90, n. 65, for the notion that the writing of the group is a faulty determinative for the root *ḫtm* and a common error in Late Period texts.

I. (x + 5: 13) After *sḫtm*, there is a hole in the papyrus, 1 cm in width, followed by traces showing that should be restored.

J. (x + 5: 13) The restoration of the vocative marker before the adjective *ꜥšꜣ*, "numerous," seems likely.

K. (x + 5: 13) *ms.w*, "Gestalt…eines Gottes" (*Wb.* II 141, 14). For a parallel to the phrase *ꜥšꜣ ms.w*, "one whose manifestations are numerous," see the *Wörterbuch Belegstellen* II 209, 14, which cites *nb ms.w ꜥšꜣ ḫpr.w*, "…lord of forms, one whose manifestations are numerous…," found on an unnumbered stele in Turin and in TT 3. For the term *ms.w* and its range of meanings and their relationship, see Zandee, in Lloyd, ed., *Studies in Pharaonic Religion and Society in Honour of J. Gwyn Griffiths,* pp. 169–85; also Baines, in Porter, *One God or Many?,* pp. 9–78.

L. (x + 5: 13) In the word the reading of only some signs is certain. It appears to be different from *sẖm*, "overpower," as written elsewhere.

M. (x + 5: 13) The pronoun *=sn* is either an object pronoun or a suffix pronoun subject of the verb that precedes it. In the lacuna here, there may have been an infix like *.tw*.

N. (x + 5: 14) For the phrase *i ir ḏ.t=f m-ꜥ štꜣ.w=f*, "…O one who made his body from his secrets…," *pBM 10042,* 4^{2-3} may offer a parallel in the phrase *štꜣ ir.w*, "…one secret of forms…," a divine epithet; see also there at 3^{3}; see, as well, Klasens, *Socle Behague,* p. 108, n. 186. For a relevant discussion of the nature of divine bodies, see Meeks and Favard-Meeks, *Daily Life of the Egyptian Gods,* pp. 53–60, esp. p. 55; for the word *štꜣ* used of the body of a divinity, see Hornung, *Sonnenlitanei,* vol. 1, p. 157, and vol. 2, p. 134, n. 371 for a passage in which the nouns *ẖꜣ.t*, "corpse," and *štꜣ.w*, "secrets," are said to be identical in meaning. See also Darnell, *Enigmatic Netherworld Books,* p. 384, n. 54, for *štꜣ.t*, "secret; mystery" meaning "corpse," but specifically the corpse of Osiris; and ibid. pp. 289–90 with references for *štꜣ.w* meaning the corpse of the sun(-god).

O. (x + 5: 14) *gꜣb.t*, "der Arm" (*Wb.* V 154, 1–5) is a late writing of *gbꜣ* (*Wb.* V 163, 4–12).

P. (x + 5: 14) The single sign (Sign-list A26) is a variant writing of *i*, "O," the vocative marker (*Wb.* I 25). This is the only occurrence of such a writing in this papyrus.

Q. (x + 5: 14) Based on the traces of the sign (Sign-list H6) at the right hand edge of the third fragment of this column, the restoration of the epithet *irr mꜣꜥ.t* seems likely. For *irr mꜣꜥ.t*, "one who does what is right," see *Wb.* II 20, 3–4, and Assmann, *Maât,* p. 124; it is also found as an epithet of Thoth in a demotic magical text in conjunction with the epithet *wḏꜥ mꜣꜥ.t*. See Betz, *Greek Magical Papyri,* p. 288, citing *PDM* lxi, 63–78.

R. (x + 5: 14–15) *wiꜣ n ḥḥ*, “barque of millions” (*Wb.* I 271, 11) is the name of one of the solar barques in which the sun-god makes his nightly journey. The name “barque of millions” is thought to allude to the number of dead who accompany the sun-god on his nightly journey; see Hornung, *ÄA* 7, p. 20. Alternatively, the phrase has been understood to have a temporal sense and is translated “barque of millions of years,” for which see Piankoff, *LJN*, p. 56. Leitz et al., *Götterbezeichnungen* 2, p. 279, see it as the barque associated with the overthrow of Apophis or with the appearance of the god Amun-Re-Harakhty. For its occurrence elsewhere in protection texts, see, for example, Massart, *pLeiden I 343+345*, vs. 9[10–11] and p. 109, n. 16; and Klasens, *Socle Behague*, p. 26 c4.

S. (x + 5: 15) The epithet *wpi ir.t=f*, “One who opens his eye…,” may refer to Horus. Compare *Edfu* IV, 323[8]: “he [Horus] opens his eyes (and) day comes to pass; he closes his eyes (and) night comes to pass.” If the sign (Sign-list G7) is the determinative of the entire phrase *wp ir.t=f*, the epithet may refer to Thoth, who healed the damaged eye of Horus, or to Horus himself, who opened his damaged eye after it was restored.

T. (x + 5: 15) The traces suit *gm wš*, “found destroyed,” indicating the presence of a lacuna in the text from which the scribe was copying.

U. (x + 5: 15) Due to the lacuna in the papyrus and the marker *gm wš*, it is difficult to understand the relationship of to what follows it. A demotic text from the archive of Hor has the phrase *tp ꜥꜣ (n) Wsir*, “Great first-born of Osiris,” as an epithet of Harpocrates, for which see Ray, *The Archive of Hor*, pp. 67 and 71. The translation “great first-born” offered here is, of course, provisional.

V. (x + 5: 16) *irr ẖr.wt=f*, “für jemds. Bedarf an Speisen sorgen” (*Wb.* III 391, 1–3); Leitz et al., *Götterbezeichnungen* 1, pp. 481ff., only give a number of specialized epithets built from *iri ẖr.t*. The phrase is an apt epithet for Atum as the creator god.

W. (x + 5: 16) *ꜥwꜣy*, “robber” (*Wb.* I 171, 3–21); the reference is uncertain, since it cannot be determined if this is a single or compound epithet.

X. (x + 5: 16) The group presents problems. Reading the signs together gives an epithet *ḥr ꜣwi*, “long-faced one,” but this is not attested by the *Wörterbuch* or by any other source to my knowledge. Leitz et al., *Götterbezeichnungen* 5, p. 308, give two epithets that begin with *ḥr.y ꜣw.t*, but neither is qualified by the phrase *iw.t.y ꜣḫ.t*. For *ḥr.y ꜣwi*, they offer the translation “der Gebieter der Opferspeise.” “Long-faced,” though unattested, seems to be a fitting description of Thoth. The epithet *iw.t.yw ꜣḫ.w ḥr=sn*, “…over whom there are no *akh*’s…,” is found in the Book of the Earth, 3[7], there describing malevolent beings called *ꜥḥꜣ.w ḥr*, “the ones with fighter-faces.” Although there may be a connection with this epithet, it is difficult to determine what was intended here, due to the fragmentary nature of the papyrus. Hence, the translation of *ꜣḫ.t* as "power" here.

Y. (x + 5: 16) On [hieroglyphs] *ꜣḫ.t*, see preceding note X (x + 5: 16). In light of the vocative marker at the beginning of the next line, this word would terminate an epithet.

Z. (x + 5: 17) The sense of [hieroglyphs] *i sw ṯtf* is obscure. See the discussion at notes AA (x + 5: 17) and BB (x + 5: 17), immediately following. [hieroglyphs] *sw* is either "Zeit" or "Monatstag;" see Hannig, *GH*, p. 673a–b.

AA. (x + 5: 17) [hieroglyphs] *ṯtf*, "ausgiessen; ausschütten" (*Wb.* V 412,11–413, 2). Of particular interest here is the citation given at *Wb.* V 412, 16 for the verb used in the phrase "das Blut der Feinde vergiessen;" see further at *Wb.* V 412, 23, which calls *ṯtf* "den Fluss mit dem Blut der Feinde." Faulkner, *CD*, p. 308, gives a meaning "flow down," citing *Urk.* IV, 502[5], and a further meaning "overflow," citing *pPrisse* 7[8] and *Peas.* B 1, 294. The verb is constructed with the preposition *ḥr* that occurs here after *ḳs*(*n*).*w*. See also Borghouts, *pLeiden I 348,* rt. 13[4] and n. 310, on the occurrence of the verb *ṯtf* with *ib* as its direct object; he offers the translation "confuses the heart," stating that it literally means "to make the heart brim over," presumably with fear or anxiety. The word appears in *pTurin 54003,* rt. 13, for which see Borghouts, *AEMT,* p. 91 (137), who offers the translation "scatter." See further *pAnastasi 4,* 10[7], where *ṯtf* occurs in a description of the inundation. Commenting on the latter passage, Caminos, *LEM,* p. 175, suggests the translation "pour out; overflow." The term *ṯtf* is found at *pBM 9997,* 6[7], in connection with the word "poison," where the poison is instructed to "flow out." It occurs as well in *pBM 10309,* 2[18], also of the flowing out of poison. For other meanings offered for *ṯtf,* see Roccati, *AnOr* 56, p. 72, 14 for the phrase *ṯtf ḥꜥ.w nb* and p. 167 for the translation "...rinvigorire tutte le membra...;" also Roccati, *pTurin 54003,* p. 26, n. c for the various meanings "spente," "salir," and barbouiller," the latter two offered by Posener in a letter to Roccati. Given the numerous lacunae in the present passage, the sense intended here remains somewhat elusive.

BB. (x + 5: 17) As written, [hieroglyphs] appears to be *ḳs.w* (*Wb.* V 68, 2–69, 4: "Knochen"). The sign [hieroglyph] can also be read *ḳsn.t* or *gn.wt*. None of the words transliterated as *ḳsn.t* or *gn.wt* offer much by way of suggestion. A somewhat similar writing occurs in *pBM 9997,* 2[14] and 4[5], for which see Leitz, *HPBM 7,* pp. 7 and 10, who gives the transliteration *ḳsn.t* and translates it as "evil," presumably based on the presence of the determinative there. The lack of a determinative and the presence of the oblique stroke suggests that the sign [hieroglyph] is an ideogram. If so, *ḳs.w* here may mean "harpoons" (*Wb.* V 68, 1). The verb *ṯtf* can be used metaphorically of weapons "raining down" on one's enemies, for which see *Edfu* III, 255[15]; VI, 83[8–9]; and VI, 64[5]. Thus, a possible reading is "O time of the harpoons raining down on [... and] Seth..." if we are to take the first four words together. Taking *ḳs.w* as "harpoons" and reading *ṯtf* meaning "overflow," the translation "the harpoons brimming over [with blood]" is also possible. The traces of the name of the god Seth just after the lacuna suggest a reading like "O time of the harpoons brimming over [with the blood of] Seth." See *Edfu* II, 75[2]; V, 186[13–14]; VII, 151[15]; and VIII, 11[11] for examples conveying such an idea. Alternatively, reading *ḳs.w* with the meaning "bones," a notion like "bones brimming over [with fear]," akin to our idea of being "terrified to the core," is possible. I have found no examples, however, that would support such a reading. In the Edfu texts, the word *ḳs.w* is usually found with negative associations, largely in the context of apotropaic rituals in which the bones of a hippopotamus, Seth, or the enemies of the king are burnt. For these texts, see Wilson, *PL*, p. 1069.

CC. (x + 5: 17) Traces of the sign [hieroglyph] (Sign-list E21) are evident before the epithet *ir nšni*. The preceding lacuna offers ample room for the phonetic writing of Seth as well as a vocative marker. It is possible that the phrase "…Se]th who made raging…" is to be taken with the three words that occur at the beginning of the line.

DD. (x + 5: 17) There is a small break between [hieroglyph] and [hieroglyph]. It is unclear, then, whether the words [hieroglyph] "heads" and [hieroglyph] "many" go together. If so, they recall an epithet *tp.w ꜥšꜣ.w* that occurs in a Third Intermediate Period religious text, for which see Piankoff, *Mythological Papyri*, No. 20, Scene 3. At the end of the line and at the beginning of the next, the traces seem to indicate [hieroglyph], suggesting rather that *ꜥšꜣ rn.w* should be taken together.

EE. (x + 5: 18) For the phrase [hieroglyph] *imn rn=f*, "whose name is concealed," see the discussion at note D (x + 6: 14) below.

FF. (x + 5: 18) The epithet [hieroglyph] *wr bꜣ.w*, "one whose *ba*'s are great," is found in texts as early as the Old Kingdom, used of gods, kings, and even royal regalia. See Žabkar, *A Study of the Ba Concept in Ancient Egyptian Texts*, pp. 55–67.

GG. (x + 5: 18) At the end of the line, [hieroglyph] *m-ꜥ štꜣ[.w]*, "together with (his) secrets…," can be seen clearly. There is only about 1 cm left at the end of the line, just enough space for the remaining signs of *štꜣ.w*. The beginning of the first line of the next column has only a small lacuna as well. On *štꜣ.w*, see note N (x + 5: 14) above.

HH. (x + 6: 1) The traces show [hieroglyph] *zp*, "occasion." This writing compares favorably with that of the same word found at x + 6: 9 below.

II. (x + 6: 1) The traces at the beginning of the break seem to be vestiges of [hieroglyph] *ḏ.t*, "body."

JJ. (x + 6: 2) The reading of [hieroglyph] *rn.f*, "his name," is beyond question, based on the hieratic traces. It was possibly the object of a participle, now lost from the beginning of the line.

KK. (x + 6: 2) At the end of the lacuna, the group is either *ir.n=f* or *ir rn=f* as taken here. For the epithet *ir rn=f*, see Leitz et al., *Götterbezeichnungen* I, p. 471ff. for derivative epithets. The noun *rn* is found written elsewhere in the papyrus without the determinative (Sign-list A2). See note BA (x + 6: 11) below. For the idea of hidden names, see also note D (x + 6: 14) below.

LL. (x + 6: 2–3) The first word of this line that can be read is *pt*, "heaven." At x + 9: 11 below, the phrase *mnmn=f pt*, "one who shakes heaven," immediately precedes the phrase *mnmn.f tꜣ*, "one who shakes the earth," a variant of which follows here as well. If this epithet began at the end of the preceding line, a probable restoration then is *mnmn n.f pt*, "one for whom heaven shakes." See note MM (x + 6: 3), following.

MM. (x + 6: 3) *mnmn n=f tꜣ* presents several problems. *Wb.* II 80–81, 1–15 cites a verb *mnmn* with the meaning "sich bewegen; etw. fortbewegen;" the determinatives given there are , both of which occur in the writing of this verb at x + 9: 10–11 below; the book-roll determinative is not given. Its presence here may be due to the fact that it is a typical determinative of the non-reduplicated radical *mn*. In an epithet of Min, *mnmn* appears to mean "begatten" (*Wb.* II 81, 16). The phrase occurring below at x + 9: 10–11 is written *mnmn=f tꜣ*. Despite the differences in writing, the two phrases seem to express the same idea, and the meaning of *mnmn* is "schwanken (von der Erde)" (*Wb.* II 81, 5). The epithet "he who shakes the earth" is commonly used of Geb. The theme of shaking the earth is already well-known in the Pyramid Texts and continues into the Ptolemaic Period with more general references to divine or royal epiphany. For a discussion, see Traunecker, *Coptos*, pp. 153–54, n. 1; pp. 341–51, esp. pp. 344–47; Goyon, *pConfirmation*, 3^{19-20} and p. 96, n. 115. See further Parker et al., *Lake Edifice*, p. 58, n. 37, where the phrase *mnmn gb* is explained as an equivalent to *mnmn tꜣ*. *pTurin 1983*, rt. 60 has "We shall save her from the one who shakes the earth and who is called the Mover (*mnmn*);" see Edwards, *HPBM* 4, p. 53, and n. 30 for further texts.

NN. (x + 6: 3) The lacuna ends with what seems to be or possibly *pt*, "heaven," although the former seems more likely, as *pt* is written or elsewhere in this papyrus.

OO. (x + 6: 3) The translation of *wdi* as "prepares" is based on the sense required.

PP. (x + 6: 3) is probably *is.t*, "Gruppe" (*Wb.* I 127, 11–19). It may be a miswriting of *is.wt ḏḥwty*, "crew of Thoth," for which see note ZZ (x + 7: 5) below, where a similar writing appears with one fewer vertical sign. See also Zandee, *pAmunhymnus*, 3^{2}, where this noun is similarly written. The term is also encountered in the Edfu texts as a designation of guardian gods, for which see Goyon, *Les dieux-gardiens*, p. 20, n. 6, and p. 43, n. 8.

QQ. (x + 6: 4) The writing [hieroglyphs] at the beginning of the line seems more certain than [hieroglyphs]. [hieroglyphs] *rḥ.wy* means "die beiden Genossen," referring to Horus and Seth (*Wb.* II 441, 13–15). The phrase *sḥtp rḥ.wy*, "…appeasing the Two Companions," may be an epithet of Thoth, the god who played the role of separating and appeasing the two gods. The more familiar epithet is [hieroglyphs] *wpi rḥ.wy*, "die Beiden trennen," for which see *Wb.* II 441, 14.

RR. (x + 6: 4) The hieratic signs point to a reading and restoration like *m wiꜣ n Rꜥ*, "in the barque of Re."

SS. (x + 6: 4) The phrase *ḏs=f*, "himself," refers to the name of a male deity in the lacuna.

TT. (x + 6: 4) The lack of a determinative for the word [hieroglyphs] *ms.w* makes the translation "children" provisional. It could mean "forms" here, a meaning which is found at x + 5: 13 above.

UU. (x + 6: 5) At the beginning of the line, only [hieroglyphs] can be read for certain; perhaps [hieroglyphs] *mdw.t=f* should be restored, although I am uncertain of its meaning here.

VV. (x + 6: 5) [hieroglyphs] *ḥnmm.t*, "Menschheit" (*Wb.* III 114, 6–13). See Gardiner, *AEO* 1, 111*–12*, as well as Serrano, *SAK* 27 (1999): 353–68.

WW. (x + 6: 5) For the translation of the phrase [hieroglyphs] *iṯi r* as "remove to (a place)," see Caminos, *JEA* 58 (1972): 222 and Column B, l. 15. It is unclear to whom the pronoun *sw* refers.

XX. (x + 6: 5) Restore [hieroglyphs] here.

YY (x + 6: 6) The traces here show [hieroglyphs] *rḫ.tw=f*. Compare the writing of [hieroglyphs] *nn rḫ.tw=f*, "he is not known," at x + 6: 4 above.

ZZ. (x + 6: 6) The translation of [hieroglyphs] *wḏꜣ.w* as "amulets" is provisional. The lack of the determinative [hieroglyph] or [hieroglyph] and the presence of plural strokes make it unlikely that it is the divine name Wadjet. Alternatively, it could be [hieroglyphs] *wḏꜣ.t*, "die Reste" (*Wb.* I 404, 2 gives this as a Late Egyptian writing), but such a reading makes little sense here. See note AB (x + 6: 6), following.

AB. (x + 6: 6) The traces just before the break yield [hieroglyphs] *nbi*, possibly the beginning of any of the words associated with fire (*Wb.* II 244, 3–14). *ꜥšꜣ nbi.wt* is found at *Edfu* III, 34[15] as an epithet of the sun god. If these two words continue an epithet that begins with the word *wḏꜣ.t*, the allusion may be to amulets associated with fire, like *wadjet*-eye amulets or uraei-form amulets. I have yet to find a textual reference to such.

AC. (x + 6: 6) The phrase *ds sẖm-ib* may have been intended as a single epithet here: O cutter, violent one," taking *ds* as a substantive of the verb "schneiden" (*Wb.* V 487, 2–3). The writing , to be read *ds sẖm*, is given as a name of one of the guardian gods in the Edfu texts, for which see Goyon, *Les dieux-gardiens,* p. 88. The particle *i*, "O," after *sẖm-ib* marks the advent of a new idea beginning after the phrase *ds sẖm-ib*. See the discussion at note AD (x + 6: 6), following.

AD. (x + 6: 6) *sẖm-ib*, either "kühn; dreist" (*Wb.* IV 246, 16–17, in particular IV 246, 16 for its use as a divine epithet) or "sich belustigen" (*Wb.* IV 252, 10–253, 7), usually written *sẖmḫ*. The word occurs again at x + 6: 8 below. An epithet meaning "the one whose heart is powerful" is attested as early as the Coffin Texts; see *CT* 473 and *CT* 476; see also Goyon, *Les dieux-gardiens,* pp. 288–90.

AE. (x + 6: 7) Restore [*sẖm*]-*ib*, for which see note AD (x + 6: 6), above.

AF. (x + 6: 7) *smn tꜣ*, "bring the land into order" (*Wb.* IV 134, 1). For this phrase as an epithet of Thoth, see *Edfu* V, 28[6]; VI, 27[7].

AG. (x + 6: 7) The restoration of *rn=s*, "her name," is possible, based on the traces and the occurrence of the suffix pronoun =*s* later in the line.

AH. (x + 6: 7) The group appears directly before a vocative marker, indicating that it ends a vocative phrase. It is possibly a relative form, modifying the preceding word now lost in the lacuna: "…which she did." Alternatively, it may be a participial phrase meaning *ir s*(*w*), "who made herself/him/it," as *s* may be a writing of *sw*.

AI. (x + 6: 7) For the epithet *smn mꜣꜥ.t* (*Wb.* IV 133, 27), "one who establishes Maat," as an epithet of the king , see van Dijk, *GM* 33 (1979): 23, line 2, and 25.

AJ. (x + 6: 7) The traces at the beginning of the lacuna show ; a possible restoration at the end of this line and the beginning of the next is *m ḥꜣ.t wiꜣ n rꜥ*, "in the fore of the barque of Re." For this epithet, encountered most typically of Seth, see, for example, *pLeiden I 346,* 2[12]. See also x + 9: 14 below.

AK. (x + 6: 8) The traces before the word *mk.t*, "protection," suit the writing of *ir*, "made."

AL. (x + 6: 8) The suffix pronoun =*s* refers to the female deity addressed here or is a writing of *sw*.

AM. (x + 6: 8) The epithet *ir mwt*, "one who made death," is used in association with the malign aspect of lion-headed goddesses. See *Edfu* I, 510[18], and VI, 266[3].

See also the discussion by Germond, *Sekhmet,* pp. 52–53 and 93, n. 40; Derchain, *Elkab* 1, pp. 24–25.

AN. (x + 6: 8) On the possible meanings of the word *ms.w*, see note TT (x + 6: 4) above.

AO. (x + 6: 8) *ꜥ3 nrw*, "groß an Schrecken" (*Wb.* II 278, 4, citing it as a divine epithet). It is found as an epithet of Thoth in *pTurin 54053,* for which see Roccati, *AnOr* 56, p. 44, 8. Two similar epithets, used of guardian gods, are found in the Edfu texts: *ꜥ3 snḏ* and *wr nrw*, for which see Goyon, *Les dieux-gardiens,* pp. 82–84 and 99, respectively.

AP. (x + 6: 8) For the epithet *sḫm-ib* used of divinities, see note AD (x + 6: 6) above.

AQ. (x + 6: 9) The suffix pronoun =s ends a vocative phrase that occurred in the lacuna at the beginning of the line.

AR. (x + 6: 9) The hieratic here seems to be (*s*)*wp.t mwt=s*. The initial *s* does not seem to belong with the words that follow. *wp*(*.t*) *mwt.s* could mean "the one who opened her mother," a possible allusion to a first-born child. I can make little sense of the reading as it appears. The reading may be instead, possibly a miswriting of *wps.t* (*Wb.* I 305, 9–10, giving this word as the name of "eine Göttin, welche die Bösen verbrennt"), although none of the lexica attest such a writing for that word. For a discussion of Wepset as a name of the fire-spitting uraeus, see van Dijk, *LÄ* 6 (1986): cols. 1218–20; Junker, *Die Onurislegende,* pp. 82 ff; and Germond, *Sekhmet,* p. 95, n. 56. For Wepset in a protection text, see *pBremner-Rhind,* 24^{11}; 25^{5}; and 25^{9}. The lack of the determinative , usually found with the writing of the names of goddesses in this papyrus, may be due to confusion with the word *wpr.ty*, "die Seitenlocke des Kindes" (*Wb.* I 305, 6).

AS. (x + 6: 9) For the epithet *ꜥš3 ms.w*, "one numerous of forms," see the discussion at note K (x + 5: 13) above.

AT. (x + 6: 9) For the reading *is zp nšni.ti*, compare the identical writing of *nšni* at x + 5: 17 above. The sign that follows *nšni* appears to be , a writing of the 3rd person singular stative ending, giving the translation "…occasion when she was enraged." The allusion may be to the activity of one of the lion-headed goddesses. For *zp*, Bickel, *Cosmogonie,* pp. 58–59 has suggested that the noun has the meaning "activity" or "action" in phrases like this one.

AU. (x + 6: 9) As only can be read, the reading *i sḫm*-[*ib*], "O violent one…," is provisional.

AV. (x + 6: 10) The signs point possibly to the restoration of *wḏ3.t*, "Wadjet."

AW. (x + 6: 10) On the epithet *ir m3ʿ.t*, "one who did what is right," see note Q (x + 5: 14) above.

AX. (x + 6: 10) The epithet *ms Nw.t*, "child of Nut/one whom Nut bore," is a possible reference to either Isis or Nephthys, as the reference here is to a female deity.

AY. (x + 6: 10) It is possible to restore a phrase beginning with the participle *ir* before the group , giving something like "[one who did X] *n ḥ3.ty n nb.s*, for the heart of her lord."

AZ. (x + 6: 10) Following *i šm*, "O one who goes…," a possible restoration is , "…and who comes," based on the parallel *i šm ii*, "O one who goes and comes," that occurs at x + 6: 12 below. In the Edfu texts, it is an epithet of Horus the Behedite; see, for example, *Edfu* IV, 76[11] and 252[5]. The phrase *šm ii* is also used to describe the freedom of movement that the deceased has in the necropolis. See Vernus, *BdE* 74 (1978): 202–3, and idem, *BIFAO* 75 (1975): 54, n. (b), for a more general use of such terms: "…qui visent à exprimer toutes les modalités d'une action en juxtaposant les aspects extremes." The word appears in a number of places in the demotic Book of Thoth but never, it seems, as an epithet. It is used there, for example, to describe the ability of a scribe to start and to stop writing; it is also used to describe the freedom of movement bestowed on the student who wishes to be inducted into the wisdom of Thoth. See Jasnow and Zauzich, *The Book of Thoth,* pp. 215–16, 233–34; 240–41. It is also a fitting description of Thoth in his lunar form, although I have not yet found an example of it used as such.

BA. (x + 6: 11) The group presents several alternatives. appears to be *rn*, "name," without the determinative , a common omission in Late Period hieratic texts. We are left then with a juxtaposition of two nouns giving *i irr grḥ rn(=f) wsir*, "O one who makes night (whose) name is Osiris." It is also possible that the intended reading was *i irr grḥ m rn n Wsir*, "one who makes the night in the name of Osiris," and that the preposition *m* has been inadvertently omitted. Alternatively, but less likely, it is possible that the group is a writing of the verb *grḥ*, "fertig machen" (*Wb.* V 182, 4–183, 3). The phrase would then read *i irr grḥ r3 n Wsir* and be translated as "one who makes complete the mouth of Osiris." One would expect the oblique stroke for the word *r3*, however, to be written next to the signs . The lacunae in the present passage impede certain restoration. One should note the scribal mark above the group , quite possibly an indication that the copyist either had difficulty with the reading here or had made an inadvertent omission. The epithet *irr grḥ* is also found at *Urk.* VI, 119[16].

BC. (x + 6: 12) There are two or three signs, occupying approximately 1 cm, missing at the beginning of the line.

BD. (x + 6: 12) The group [hieroglyphs] may be a writing of [hieroglyphs] *fnḏi* (*Wb.* I 578, 3), an epithet of Thoth; the word written here lacks the expected determinatives [hieroglyphs]. An additional problem is that the word here seems to depend on the preceding word *ir*, given the common occurrence of the construction *ir*(*r*) + noun in this section of the text. *Wb.* I 578, 4 gives a word whose meaning is "das Zürnen," which may be what is intended here. It should be noted, however, that the *Wörterbuch* citations lack the determinative [hieroglyph] (Sign-list F51) found here.

BE. (x + 6: 12) [hieroglyphs]: see note AZ (x + 6: 10) above.

BF. (x + 6: 12) [hieroglyphs] *ḥbs*, "bekleiden; verhüllen" (*Wb.* III 64, 3–65, 17). It is possible that the phrase [hieroglyphs] *ḥbs m ꜥ.wy*, "clothing in her arms," refers to some form of protection. On divinities making or preparing clothing as a means of protection for the deceased, see, for example, *CT* 484–86, where the deceased and Hathor weave clothing for each other. Both are said to wear the clothing, evidently as a means of protection. In those texts, the word play with the verb *ṯz*, meaning both "weave" and "wear," is further developed with another meaning of *ṯz*, "knot; tie;" hence, the word play also makes allusions to magical protection.

COMMENTARY

The section designated here as Spell G1 is not a separate spell, but the introduction to a longer spell. This part of the text is a protracted series of apostrophes and is riddled with lacunae; thus, it seemed best to treat it separately. The spell begins with a reference to Thoth. Next comes a long appeal to what seem to be a number of different deities, none of whom is named directly. Each one, rather, is introduced by an epithet that occasionally allows the identification of the deity. At least thirty-five epithets are used. A number of them consist of the participle *ir* (*r*) followed by a substantive, the whole yielding "O one who made/did X…." The badly damaged state of the papyrus, however, compounds the difficulty of establishing a clear reading and understanding of many of these epithets. That this section of the spell may have come from a prayer to Thoth has been suggested.[196] Some of the epithets encountered are attested for Thoth, some are not. A number of the unattested epithets, however, do seem apt descriptions of Thoth. The apostrophe at the beginning of the next section of the spell, however, reads *ind ḥr=tn m-m rn=tn*, "Hail to you together with your names." The occurrence of the plural pronoun =*tn* twice there suggests that the present section of the text forms an address to a number of different beings. Additionally, the badly damaged state of the papyrus makes the establishment

196 Hans Fischer-Elfert, personal communication, Winter 2010. The present text, however, bears little resemblance to the Turin papyri in which Thoth features prominently; see Roccati, *AnOr* 56, pp. 21–27, 37–64, and 89–123.

of anything far from certain. Note, however, that any epithet encountered having any connection with Thoth has been detailed in the notes above.

Contrast the protracted address that opens this spell and consists almost solely of epithets with the long address to named deities that occurs at the beginng of Spell N below (column x + 9: 8–18). Neither the title *pr-ꜥꜣ* nor the name Psamtik occurs in this section of the spell.

Spell G2 — Translation with Commentary

COLUMN X + 6: 13–X + 8: 1 (P. BROOKLYN 47.218.49)

TRANSLITERATION

13. *ind ḥr=tn m-m rn=tn ḥms=sn m pt wnm=sn m tꜣ iꜥr.wt=sn m pt*
14. *bꜣ(.w)=sn m tꜣ sꜥḥ(.w)=sn m ẖr.t-nṯr rn(.w)=sn imn r ms.w=sn*
15. *ḏ.(w)t=sn pnꜥ r iwn=sn nn rḫ.tw ḥn.tyw=sn ḫtm*
16. *… ꜥšꜣ ḫpr.w smn=tn tp(.w)=tn r nḥb.(w)t=sn irr=sn n ḏ.t zp=sn ꜥnḫ=tn*
17. *[m ib] n ḥnmm.t wnm=tn m ḥꜣ.ty[w] [n] rḫy.t irr šꜥd.w m ḫft*
18. *… wnm=sn m sbi.w m mnw … ꜣd ꜥpp m wḥm iw šfw.t=tn*
19. *… nrw=tn im.y ꜥ.wy=tn is ii=[tn] r dr ḫft pft mwt mwt.t ḏꜣ ḏꜣ-*

COLUMN X + 7

1. *-.t ḥm.wt-rꜣ … w … [r nḥ]ḥ ḏ.t i. … =tn …r … .wt=tn*
2. *mꜣꜣ.n=f imn=tn iw … =tn m-bꜣḥ rꜥ ptḥ m dwꜣ … m ḏḥwty wnn*
3. *ḥr sꜣ wsir sšm rn … tp n b wsir nb-ḥw.t [ꜣs.t] … irr=sn r=f*
4. *imi ir=k nb in.tw … nb n.im=sn ḥr ꜥḥ n … ḥr im.y šn.wt*
5. *ḥr ḫꜣ.wt nt irr mꜣꜥ.t … šb.t im=f im.y-ḫt … [psḏ.t] ꜥꜣ ist ḏḥwty ḏsr.t*
6. *nty m sšm.w=f ḳmꜣ … rḫ.n=f ir.w=f gm … =f štꜣ=f ḥꜣp.w*
7. *m rꜣ-stꜣ.w rḫ.n=f im.y … rḫ=f nty im=s iw di=i … im … didi ḥbs.w n ḥb-*
8. *-s.w didi n=f iꜣw ḫft itn … imi n=k ib=k gm wš… m-bꜣḥ rꜥ ptḥ ḫpri is-*
9. *-ds ḏd tw rꜣ pn r šd … [mḏꜣ.t] tn r ḫft-ḥr n ẖr mḥr ḏd šn.t … rꜣ ḥnꜥ irr*
10. *ir.w n rꜥ itn ḥr tp=f ir.w n ḫpri … [ir.w n] rp.wt sḫm.t ir.w n ḏḥwty [m] wꜣḏ.t r-gs=f ir.w n ir mꜣꜥ.t m*
11. *ḥr n ḫpri ir.w n-9 m ḥr n pꜥ.t rd.wy n nṯr ir.w n-9 m ḥr n rmṯ ḥms m w-r-ꜥ*
12. *ḥms ꜣḫ n-4 ꜥḥꜥ m ir.w m ḥr n rmṯ sš ḥr stp n pꜣḳ(.t) di r ḫḫ n s ḫft*
13. *šni mḏꜣ.t tn ḥnꜥ ini s pn is rdi.t(w) wḏꜣ.t m ḏr.t=f di r ḫḫ=f ir rdi s is*
14. *ḏr.t=f ḥr tp=f ḏs=f ḥnꜥ ḏd=f m ḳꜣ ḫrw=f pr.n=i m ḏdw sḏr.n=i m ꜣbḏw*
15. *ḥr ḫḫ it=i wsir gm=i rwḏ n mḏꜣ.t ḫpr ink ḥr nḏ it=f ḥnꜥ sš*
16. *tp n ꜥꜣ ḳmy gs m ꜥn.tyw di r-ḫft-ḥr n ẖr mḥr šni mḏꜣ.t tb m tb …-*
17. *-mw ḥḏ.t sdm m … sd m pꜣḳ(.t) md n ḥr m ḏr.t wnmi ḥr…n bꜣḳ m*
18. *ḏr.t iꜣbi šni rꜣ pn m ḳꜣ ḫrw ir nn ḫpr rwḏ=k … ḥr ḏd=k sw m ḳꜣ ḫrw mk.t*
19. *pw ꜥꜣ.t m pr mḏꜣ.t ir mtr … mty nty ḥr sš m … [di r msḏr] n s*

COLUMN X + 8

1. *m … m sšrw mꜣꜥ ḥḥ zp*

TRANSLATION

13. Hail to you[A] together with[B] your names. They[C] dwell in heaven, they eat on earth, their uraei in heaven,
14. their *ba*'s on earth, their mummies in the necropolis, their names concealed from their children,[D]
15. their bodies[E] change(d) according to their appearance (?)[F] One does not know the limits of their lifetime,[G] sealed[H]
16. […1 cm…][I] whose forms are numerous.[J] You affix your heads to your necks.[K] They have been made[L] for an eternity and an eternity. You live[M]
17. [on the hearts][N] of the Sun-people;[O] you feed on the hearts of the common people,[P] making a slaughter[Q] against the enemies
18. [of yours].[R] They eat the rebels daily,[S] (when) Apophis [rages][T] again. Your majesty[U]
19. [and] your terror[V] are what is in your arms.[W] Lo, [may you come][X] to drive away the enemy, the fiend, the dead male, the dead female, the male adversary, the female

COLUMN X + 7

1. adversary and so on [from coming against the ear of Pharaoh[Y] forever and][Z] ever. […3 cm…] your […2 cm…] […4 cm…]
2. he has seen that you are hidden[AA] […3.5 cm…] you […][BB] in the presence of Re (and) Ptah[CC] in the morning[DD] […1.5 cm…] by Thoth.[EE]
3. Horus exists,[FF] the son of Osiris, guiding the name (?)[GG] […3.5 cm…] the head of[HH] the Evil One,[II] of Osiris, of Nephthys[JJ] [of Isis…][KK] (so that) they act against him.[LL]
4. Cause indeed[NN] that the lord[OO] be brought[PP] […3.5 cm…][QQ] every […] from them,[RR] with a burnt-offering[SS] to (?) [the followers of (?)][TT] Horus-who-is-in-*šnw.t*[UU]
5. upon an altar of the one who does what is right[VV] […3.5 cm…] mixed[WW] in it, that which is in the following[XX] … of the great Ennead[YY] the sacred crew of Thoth[ZZ]
6. [AB] who are in his[AC] following, [created …][AD] his forms are known to him[AE] found [destroyed] (?) he [… secrets][AF] concealed
7. in Rosetau. He has known what is in […]; he knows what is in it. I gave[AG] […1.5 cm…] therein,[AH] by giving[AI] clothing of the cloth-[AJ]
8. ing given to him.[AK] Praise in front of the sun-disk[AL] […3.5 cm…].[AM] Give your heart to yourself[AN] –found destroyed—[AO] in the presence of Re, Ptah,[AP] Khepri and Is-
9. -des.[AQ] *One should say this spell in order to recite … this [book-roll]*[AR] *in front of one suffering from sickness. Say the recitation* […] *the spell* and make[AS]
10. an image of Re, a sun-disk[AT] upon his head, an image of Khepri,[AU] [an image of a female] statue[AV] of Sakhmet, an image of Thoth, a Wadjet-eye beside him,[AW] an image of the one who has done what is right[AX] with

11. the face[AY] of Khepri, nine[AZ] images with the face of a man[BA] (and) the feet[BC] of a god, nine[BD] images with the face of a man seated[BE] with *w-r-ꜥ*[BF]
12. seated, four[BG] *akh*'s standing with an image [with the face][BH] of a man, drawn on a strip[Bi] of fine linen,[BJ] placed at the neck of a man while
13. reciting the spells of[BK] this book-roll in particular. Bring[BL] this man who is weak,[BM] amulets are placed in his hand (and) placed at his neck. If the man who is weak[BN] places
14. his hand upon his head himself and he says with his voice raised:[BO] "It is from Busiris that I have come forth; it is in Abydos that I have slept,[BP]
15. while searching for[BQ] my father Osiris. I found the strength[BR] of the book-roll come to pass.[BS] I am Horus, avenger of his father" *and draw*[BT]
16. *the head of a dun-colored ass,*[BU] *anointed with myrrh, placed in front of one who is suffering (this) illness.*[BV] *Recite the book-roll* [...3.5 cm...]
17. [...]white ...[BW] *painted*[BX] *with (and) embellished*[BY] *with fine linen, a staff*[BZ] *of* Horus *in the right hand*[CA] *with*[...] *of the moringa-tree*
18. *in the left hand. Recite this spell* [*in*] *a loud* [*voice.*][CB] *If your strength does not come to pass for you,*[CD] *then you shall say it*[CE] *with the voice raised.*[CF] *It is*[CG]
19. *a great protection*[CH] *from the House of Writing.*[CI] *As for (it)* [...2.5 cm...][CJ] *precisely*[CK] *what is in writing in*[CL] [...4.5 cm...] [*placed at the ear*] *of a man*

COLUMN X + 8

1. *with* [...3.5 cm...] *truly effective millions of times.*[CM]

TEXT NOTES

A. (x + 6: 13) In the phrase [hieroglyphs], "Hail to you...," the sign [hieroglyph] (Sign-list G7) is an honorific determinative written with [hieroglyph], used when the address is made to divinities. See for example *pChester Beatty 1,* 2[1], and *pChester Beatty 8,* rt. 9[9–11]. A similar writing can be found in the papyrus at x + 1: 21 above. The beings invoked here are those described in the list of epithets called Spell G1.

B. (x + 6: 13) [hieroglyphs] *m-m* is an apparent reduplication of *m* that has the meaning "together with." See Caminos, *JEA* 58 (1972): 214 and nn. 2 and 3.

C. (x + 6: 13) The suffix pronoun [hieroglyphs] =*sn* probably refers to the deities just invoked and not to the group [hieroglyphs] *rn=tn*, "your names." Such shifts from second person to third person are common in Egyptian texts.

D. (x + 6: 14) *pChester Beatty 9,* vs. B. 17[5–7] provides a parallel here: "O these gods (and) goddesses whose names have been pronounced, who dwell in the sky (but) eat upon the earth, whose uraei are upon their heads, whose *ba*'s are in Busiris, whose mummies are in the necropolis (and) whose names are not known...." For further parallels to the idea that the *ba* and the body inhabit different locales in the afterworld, see, for example, *pCairo 58027,* x + 3[10]: *bꜣ=k m ḥr.t ḫꜥ=k m dwꜣ.t,*

"...your *ba* in heaven, your body in the Netherworld;" and Zandee, *Amunhymnus* 1, pp 188–91. For *imn r*, "sich verbergen (vor jem. *r*)," see *Wb.* I 83, 14.

E. (x + 6: 15) The reading of the word *ḏ.t*, "body," is certain.

F. (x + 6: 15) The phrase *ḏ.(w)t=sn pnꜥ r iwn=sn* is challenging. *pnꜥ* (*Wb.* I 508, 11–509, 9) has a range of meanings, from "turn over" to "overturn; throw down," to "make inverted," among others. It seems to be largely transitive or reflexive. The presence of immediately after *pnꜥ* is, thus, difficult to explain. is given as a writing of *iwn*, "Farbe" (*Wb.* I 52, 10–17), a word that can also mean "Aussehen eines Gottes." That leaves us with several readings, one of which is "...their bodies inverted against their color." The Twenty-fifth Dynasty magical text *pLeiden I 358* has the statement *ntf pꜣ kꜣ pnꜥ iwn*, "he is the bull who reverses his colors," a description of the sacred bull Buchis worshipped at Harmonthis and elsewhere in the Theban region. The Buchis bull was a manifestation of Mut, Re, Atum, and Amun, according to Macrobius, *Saturnalia* 1.21. For this text and these references, see Klasens, *OMRO* 56 (1975): 20–28, esp. 26 and nn. 44–46. The passage there seems to be stating that one power of divinities is to change or reverse their outward appearance. See also Darnell, *Enigmatic Netherworld Books,* pp. 426–48, for an extensive discussion of inversion in the Netherworld, esp. pp. 433–34 and nn. 36–37 for a late text that employs the verb *pnꜥ* to describe an inversion of the normal order of things. For an alternative translation, we take the preposition *r* to mean "according to" and *iwn* to mean "appearance," giving "their bodies changed according to their appearance." Here the idea seems more clearly that the gods have manifest forms and aspects, an idea that seems to make sense in the present passage. Another alternative is to consider that is an error for *inm*, "skin" (*Wb.* I 96, 14–20), as the note "Verwirrung mit *iwn*: 'Farbe'" at the end of the entry explains. *inm* is also found in conjunction with *pnꜥ*. *pEdwinSmith,* 21^{3-4} lists a remedy entitled *pḫr.wt spnꜥ inm* and there translated "Remedies for renewing the skin." Thus, we could understand the phrase *ḏ.(w)t=sn pnꜥ r iwn=sn* meaning something like "their bodies renewed from (?) their skin." *pnꜥ* and *inm* also appear in *CT* 258, also in a description of a god: *ṯwt ḫn ḥr ḥw inmw pnꜥ*, "To you belongs the utterance of Hu (and) whose skin is turned over," with the latter phrase written . As noted above, the problem in the Brooklyn text lies in the presence of the writing . Whatever the case may be here, the spirit of the sentence seems clear, however we translate it. The outward appearance of the gods is complex and unknowable, like their names and their other attributes.

G. (x + 6: 15) *ḥn.ty*, "Bereich; Frist" (*Wb.* III 105, 10–106, 16, especially 106, 15–16, where "jemds. Lebenszeit" is attested).

H. (x + 6: 15) , probably *ḫtm*, "siegeln" (*Wb.* III 350,3–352, 3). The determinative (Sign-list S20) would have been found at the beginning of the next line.

This word may have continued the thought of the preceding idea, namely that knowledge of the life span of the gods is sealed and unknowable.

I. (x + 6: 16) The hieratic traces before the writing of show the vestiges of plural strokes. A possible restoration would be , giving the phrase *ḫtm r3.w*, "whose mouths are sealed."

J. (x + 6: 16) The phrase *ʿš3 ḫpr.w*, "whose forms are numerous," has a parallel in the phrase *ʿš3 ms.w* that occurs at x + 5: 13 and at x + 6: 9 above, for which see note K (x + 5: 13).

K. x + 6: 16 Affixing the head to the neck is a common metaphor in Egyptian texts designating well-being or the triumph over death and disintegration. See, for example, *pLeiden I 348,* rt. 3, 7 where the patient cured of a headache is described as *mn nḥb.t*, "his neck is made firm." See also Manassa, *The Late Egyptian Underworld* 1, pp. 40–41, and Darnell, *Enigmatic Netherworld Books,* pp. 110–15 on headless deities.

L. (x + 6: 16) The phrase *irr=sn* should be read as a *sḏm=f* passive form, with the suffix pronoun *=sn* referring to either "heads" or "necks."

M. (x + 6: 16) The phrase *ʿnḫ=tn*, "you live…," is to be understood as "feed on." See the discussion in the Commentary below on this series of clauses describing the gods feeding on their enemies.

N. (x + 6: 17) The restoration of *ib.w*, "hearts," at the beginning of the line fits the traces and the space available.

O. (x + 6: 17) *ḥnmm.t*, "Menschheit" (*Wb.* III 114, 6–13); see note VV (x + 6: 5) above. The term is often found in lists of the enemies of the sun-god; see, for example, *pChester Beatty 9*, vs. B. 12, 3–4, where the word appears in a list of enemies of the sick.

P. (x + 6: 17) *rḫy.t*, "common people" (*Wb.* II 448, 1–2) is also one of the sub-groups in lists of malign forces. See Koenig, in Kousoulis and Magliveras, *OLA* 159 (2007), pp. 223–38, esp. p. 224, n. 8, and the references there on the original meaning and developed nuances of this word.

Q. (x + 6: 17) *šʿd*, "schneiden" (*Wb.* IV 422, 3–17). The word seems to be a substantive here, hence the translation "slaughter."

R. (x + 6: 18) The restoration of the suffix pronoun *tn*, "yours," at the beginning of the line fits the space and sense required.

S. (x + 6: 18) *wnm*, "essen" (*Wb.* I 320, 15–17) is constructed regularly with the preposition *m* preceding the direct object. On the idea of eating one's enemies, see the discussion in the Commentary.

T. (x + 6: 18) The first sign after the lacuna is . A possible restoration is *ꜣd*, "wütend sein" (*Wb.* I 24, 12–17), although one would expect the writing to be , with the hand-sign over the reptile-sign. The restoration *ꜣd ꜥpp m wḥm* gives "(when) Apophis rages again." See also Hannig, *GH,* p. 18b: "angreifen," as both a transitive and intransitive verb. Based on that meaning, an alternative translation of the phrase is "attacking Apophis again" or even "(when) Apophis attacks again."

U. (x + 6: 18) *šfy.t*, "Majestät; Ansehen eines Gottes" (*Wb.* IV 457, 2–459, 7). For a writing similar to that which occurs here, see the example at 457 marked "*D. 21ff. auch." Here the word stands in parallel construction to the noun *nrw*, "terror."

V. (x + 6: 19) The traces at the beginning of the line suit the restoration of *nrw*, "der Schrecken; der Respekt" (*Wb.* II 277, 11–278, 11). For *nrw*, see Koenig, *RdE* 33 (1981): 33–35.

W. (x + 6: 19) Note that in the writing , the scribe wrote the preposition *m* and then added the sign (Sign-list Z11) above the line, indicating that he had intended to write *im.y*, "what is in…." He also repeated the sign \\ when he added the supralinear sign.

X. (x + 6: 19) The traces just before the lacuna suggest the restoration of , "…(you) come in order to drive away…." An oblique stroke below the line points to the presence of , perhaps the vestiges of the particle *r=f.*

Y. (x + 7: 1) After *ḥm.wt rꜣ*, possibly restore *m ii r msḏr n pr-ꜥꜣ*, "…from coming against the ear of the Pharaoh…."

Z. (x + 7: 1) The traces suit the restoration of *r nḥḥ ḏ.t*, "forever and ever."

AA. (x + 7: 2) The antecedent of the subject of the verb *mꜣꜣ.n=f*, "he has seen," cannot be established with certainty.

BB. (x + 7: 2) The suffix pronoun that occurs at the end of the lacuna may have been the subject of a verb forming a parallel to *imn=tn*, "you are hidden."

CC. (x + 7: 2) At x + 7: 8 below, Re and Ptah appear again in tandem, followed there by Khepri and Isdes.

DD. (x + 7: 2) The traces that follow the sign suggest the restoration *m dw3*, “in the morning.”

EE. (x + 7: 2) Although the papyrus is damaged here at left edge of this column, the signs can be read.

FF. (x + 7: 3) The exact function of , the last word of x + 7: 2, is uncertain.

GG. (x + 7: 3) The exact meaning of the group *sšm rn…* also remains uncertain.

HH. (x + 7: 3) The masculine indirect genitive marker is written here rather than simply , a common writing in Late Period texts.

II. (x + 7: 3) On the word *b* as a designation of Seth or Apophis, see note C (x + 3: 2) above.

JJ. (x + 7: 3) The names *b 3s.t nb.t-ḥw.t* appear to be dependent on the phrase *tp*, “head of.” The reference may be to images that are to be drawn, either the heads of the gods just mentioned here or figures with their heads.

KK. (x + 7: 3) The restoration of Isis in the lacuna seems logical, given the identity of the three gods who precede. The traces at the end of the lacuna seem to show .

LL. (x + 7: 3) The exact syntactical function of the verbal *irr=sn* is unclear.

MM. (x + 7: 4) Here, we encounter a number of problems in the text which itself may be corrupt. The first group of signs appears to be the imperative *imi*, “give; cause.” The relationship of this word to what follows is unclear due to the lacuna.

NN. (x + 7: 4) The group appears to be a writing of the particle (*i*)*r=k*, commonly found with imperatives. See Gardiner, *EG*[3], § 252.2, for such a writing with the initial sign (Sign-list M17).

OO. (x + 7: 4) The hieratic here represents *nb*, “lord.” If this is what the scribe intended, the group *imi ir=k nb in.tw* seems to mean “Cause that a lord be brought…”, a statement whose precise meaning is unclear.

PP. (x + 7: 4) The traces before the break suggest *in.tw*. The lacunae make any determination beyond that impossible.

QQ. (x + 7: 4) I have no suggestions for restoration here.

RR. (x + 7: 4) [hieroglyphs] *nb n.im=sn*, "…every […] from/in them," refers to what precedes it, possibly the drawing of figures. Again, the lacunae preclude an exact understanding. For the writing [hieroglyphs], see F. Junge, *LEG*, p. 89, 2.2.4 (3).

SS. (x + 7: 4) [hieroglyphs] *ꜥḫ*, "Feuerbecken; Opferfeuer" (*Wb.* I 223, 13–16).

TT. (x + 7: 4) Based on the reading of the group at the end of the line, the lacuna may have ended with a term like *šms.w* or *im.y.w-ḫt*, "following/followers." See note XX (x + 7: 4) below.

UU. (x + 7: 4) [hieroglyphs] (*Wb.* IV 498 reading *ḥr im.y šnw.t*); see also Kees, *ZÄS* 64 (1929): 107–12 on the reading of the group [hieroglyphs] as *šnw.t*. Goyon states that the epithet refers to Horus of Sohag, who has close associations with the Pharaoh; see *pConfirmation*, 13[15] and p. 105, n. 209, and relevant bibliography there. Borghouts, *pLeiden I 348*, p. 164, n. 391, suggests that the word play on the town name *šnw.t* and the root [hieroglyphs] *šni*, "conjure; recite spells," may be significant; for this manifestation of Horus appearing on *cippi*, see Sternberg-El Hotabi, *ÄA* 62 (1999), p. 113, No. 9; note that the reading *ḥr im.y-iwf* that is given there seems to be incorrect. For the correct reading, see above.

VV. (x + 7: 5) The group [hieroglyphs] presents several difficulties. Reading *ḥr ḫꜣ.wt* as a prepositional phrase, "upon the altar," connects "altar" somehow with the epithet [hieroglyphs] *irr mꜣꜥ.t*, the likely restoration here. The reading may be *ḥr.y ḫꜣ.wt* (*Wb.* III 226, 18, a priestly title) that occurs at least once as a divine epithet; see Goyon, *pConfirmation*, 16[16] and p. 119, n. 305. Such a reading would require reading *nt* as a writing of the relative *nty*, equating the epithets *ḥry ḫꜣwt* and *irr mꜣꜥt*, and a translation like "…the *ḥr.y-ḫꜣwt*-priest who makes offerings…." For the epithet *irr mꜣꜥ.t*, see note Q (x + 5: 14) above.

WW. (x + 7: 5) [hieroglyphs] *šbi*, "mischen; sich mit jem. gesellen" (*Wb.* IV 436, 4–14).

XX. (x + 7: 5) The phrase [hieroglyphs] *im.y-ḫt*, "who/what is in the following…," can be read just before the break. Its exact meaning here cannot be determined.

YY. (x + 7: 5) The signs [hieroglyphs] at the end of the lacuna suggest the restoration [hieroglyphs] *psḏ.t ꜥꜣ(.t)*, "great Ennead." See note AV (x + 4: 16) above for this phrase.

ZZ. (x + 7: 5) I take this group to be a writing of [hieroglyphs] *is.t ḏḥwty*, "crew of Thoth;" see note PP (x + 6: 3) above.

AB. (x + 7: 6) The book roll determinative [hieroglyph] (Sign-list Y1), visible at the beginning of this line, is the final sign of the word *ḏsr*, "sacred," the last word of the preceding line.

AC. (x + 7: 6) The antecedent of the suffix pronoun =*f* cannot be determined.

AD. (x + 7: 6) Before the lacuna, the group *ḳm3* can be read. Notwithstanding, the loss of the determinative of this word precludes establishing its meaning here.

AE. (x + 7: 6) The reading adopted here of *rḫ n=f irw.w=f* may be a *sḏm=f* passive form and translate "his forms have been known to him." Alternatively, it may be a *sḏm.n=f* form and the translation should be "he has known his forms." A third reading is that *rḫ* is an active participle, with *n=f* serving as a dative, the whole meaning "one who knows his forms (to his advantage)." In any case, the three translations offered are roughly equivalent in meaning.

AF. (x + 7: 6) The hieratic traces just before the lacuna may indicate another writing of *gm wš*, "found destroyed." Note that the traces of *gm* occur roughly in the same place in this line as *gm wš* does two lines below. The length of the lacuna makes any restoration provisional. At the end of the lacuna, the group can be read, the beginning signs of the word *št3.w*, "secrets."

AG. (x + 7: 7) *iw di=i* seems certain.

AH. (x + 7: 7) The signs seem certain despite the fact that a fragment of papyrus has shifted and covers part of the text here.

AI. (x + 7: 7) is a writing of the imperfective active participle *didi*, "giving; placing." *didi ḥbs* is found as an epithet of Osiris in the demotic papyrus *pCG 50058,* line 5.

AJ. (x + 7: 7) The signs at the end of this line and the beginning of the next give *ḥbs.w n. ḥbs.w*, "clothing of the clothing."

AK. (x + 7: 8) *didi n=f* appears to be an imperfective passive participle and a dative phrase; for the form of *didi*, see Gardiner, *EG*^{3}, § 358. In the Coffin Texts, various articles of clothing are referred to as a means of protection. See note BE (x + 6: 12) above.

AL. (x + 7: 8) The traces show .

AM. (x + 7: 8) The signs can be read just before the lacuna.

AN. (x + 7: 8) The traces suit the restoration of the imperative *imi*, "give."

AO. (x + 7: 8) The traces indicate *gm wš*, "found destroyed."

AP. (x + 7: 8) The gods Re and Ptah appear in tandem above at x + 7: 2, for which see note CC (x + 7: 2) above.

AQ. (x + 7: 9) Isdes, "als Götterbezeichnung von Anubis, Thoth und anderen" (*Wb.* I 134, 11–12); see also Grieshammer, *LÄ* 3 (1979): col. 185, who states that the equation of Isdes with Thoth is a late development. Isdes is encountered as a falcon-headed god as early as the Coffin Texts with the epithet "lord of Justice." At *BD* 17 a 13, he is found in conjunction with Seth as one of the Lords of Truth and is also called Lord of the West. In *pJumilhac* 1^{x+17}, Isdes appears as Thoth or Anubis and is responsible for destroying the Companions of Seth; Isdes is found there again at 15^{11} as a form of the *ḳd-i͗(r)-tw*-wolf. See *LJ* 28, where he is found in connection with the sun-god. He is closely associated with the similarly named god Isden, a dog-headed god called the son of Rattaui, also connected with Thoth, for which see Leitz et al., *Götterbezeichnungen* 1, p. 560: "In der Späzeit identisch mit *isdn*." The name Isden clearly seems to be a later development, as the texts cited at Grieshammer, *LÄ* 3 (1979): col. 184 are largely Ptolemaic. Isdes appears again in this papyrus at x + 9: 10 in a long invocation of deities, a list that includes the names of Thoth and Anubis. He probably should be understood here and again at x + 9: 10 in his independent, non-syncretized form.

AR. (x + 7: 9) The restoration of *mḏꜣ.t* before the demonstrative adjective tn is a conjecture based on the context.

AS. (x + 7: 9) At the end of this line, the surface of the papyrus is quite abraded. Before the final words of the line, , the rubrics can be read with reasonable certainty. The faded rubrics, the darkening of and damage to the papyrus, and the small pieces of tape that are holding the fragments in place have made reading this section of the text very difficult. The writing of above the signs indicates that it was a supralinear addition to correct the text. What follows after *ḏd šni͗*[*.t*] cannot be read. at the end of the line is the verb *irr*, as the sign (Sign-list A53) at the beginning of the next line is the noun *ir.w*, "image," consistently written so in this section of the text. A series of images to be inscribed on a strip of linen begins here. Lists of images of gods inscribed on strips of linen to be used as amulets appear frequently in protection texts; see, for example, *pCairo 58027*, 3^{14}, *pKölner 3547*, 3^{7}, and *pChester Beatty* 5, vs. 5^{7-9}.

AT. (x + 7: 10) The word *itn*, "solar disk," is not a separate divine name in this list of images but an element of the image that is to be drawn here. Elsewhere in this passage, the sign , read *ir.w*, "image," immediately precedes the name of each god mentioned.

AU. (x + 7: 10) The traces show , "Khepri."

AV. (x + 7: 10) The traces at the end of the lacuna suggest *rp.wt*, "Frauenstatue," for which see Hannig, *GH*, p. 464b. I thank Dr. Joachim Quack for suggesting this reading.

AW. (x + 7: 10) The writing of the group [hieroglyphs] seems certain, indicating where the image of the *wadjet*-eye is to be drawn.

AX. (x + 7: 10) Only the signs [hieroglyphs] can be made out here: *ir mꜣꜥ.t m*, "…one who has done what is right with…." The noun governed by *m* is written at the beginning of the next line.

AY. (x + 7: 11) I thank Dr. Joachim Quack for checking my readings of the latter part of this column and for suggesting some improved readings of the text here.

AZ. (x + 7: 11) The reading of what looks like [hieroglyphs] is *ir.w n-9*, "nine images." On the construction of cardinals with *n*, seen here beneath the sign *ir.w*, see Graefe, *SAK* 1 (1975): 174–84. Alternatively, it may indicate a writing of the word *mꜣw*, also with the preceding *n*, giving the reading *n mꜣw*, "new." See *Wb.* II 27, 3–4, which cites the abbreviated writing of *mꜣw*, "new," with the single sign [hieroglyph]. Compare the writing of the sign [hieroglyph] in the word *ḳmꜣ* at x + 7: 6 above. New figures, images and media to receive them are common in magical texts. The sudden addition of the adjective "new," however, seems odd here in what is a long list of images; thus, the reading *n-9* is given.

BA. (x + 7: 11) Following [hieroglyphs] *ḥr n*, "face of," the restoration of the traces seems to better suit [hieroglyphs] than [hieroglyphs] *rmṯ*.

BC. (x + 7: 11) The signs [hieroglyphs] have been added as a supralinear group above the signs [hieroglyphs], to indicate the reading *rd.wy*, "legs." The phrase "face of a man (and) legs of a god" here may refer to a human-headed mummiform figure.

BD. (x + 7: 11) On the sign [hieroglyph] (Sign-list U1), see note AZ (x + 7: 11) above.

BE. (x + 7: 11) The sign [hieroglyph] (Sign-list A7) after the writing of *rmṯ*, "man," is curious. It seems to be used as the phoneme *gn* in the writing of [hieroglyphs] *gngn*, the name of the plant given by *WbDN*, pp. 538–39, which occurs in another Brooklyn papyrus, *pBrooklyn 47.218.75+86* (unpublished), a medical text dealing with ailments of the back and the buttocks. None of the words written *gn-* in the *Wörterbuch* shows a writing with this sign as a phonogram, and none give a meaning suitable to the context of the present passage. I take the sign as an abbreviated writing of *ḥms*, "to sit; be seated," as given by Daumas, *Valeurs phonétiques* 1, p. 2, no. 43. Given the presence of the word [hieroglyphs] *is* that soon follows and that may mean "weak," it is also possible that [hieroglyph] is an abbreviated writing of *wrḏ*, "müde sein/werden" (*Wb.* I, 337, 1–338, 7) or *gnn*, "schwach sein, weich sein (Wb. V, 174–75, 17), although neither of these abbreviations is attested. See note BM (x + 7: 13) below.

BF. (x + 7: 11) The writing of [hieroglyphs] *w-r-ꜥ* suggests that it is a loan word, one that is unknown to the lexica.

BG. (x + 7: 12) For the writing of the number "four" with the group [hieroglyphs], see note AZ (x + 7: 11) above. Four *akh*'s are known from a number of texts as guardians of Atum or as the guardians assigned to Osiris by Re; see Goyon, *Les dieux-gardiens,* pp. 412–15, especially p. 414, nn. 3–5.

BH. (x + 7: 12) The restoration of [hieroglyphs] *ḥr n*, "face of," seems probable.

BI. (x + 7: 12) [hieroglyphs] *stp*, "Lappen; Binde" (*Wb.* IV 341, 13–15).

BJ. (x + 7: 12) [hieroglyphs] *p3ḳ*, "Feinster Leinenstoff" (*Wb.* I 499, 11–15, citing the spelling with [hieroglyph] in place of [hieroglyph]). The group *stp p3ḳ*, "strip of fine linen," appears as well at *pEdwin Smith,* 22[13], and *pChester Beatty* 5, rt. 4[7]; see also *pRamesseum* 3, A 23, and *MuK,* 8[3].

BK. (x + 7: 13) [hieroglyphs] *šni*, "beschwören; besprechen" (*Wb.* IV 496, 8–12). The reference here is to the recitation of the texts contained in the papyrus. This verb occurs again at x + 8: 6 and x + 8: 19 below.

BL. (x + 7: 13) A small hole in the papyrus precludes a clear reading of the hieratic group here; the traces show [hieroglyph]. See notes BM–BN (x + 7: 13), following.

BM. (x + 7: 13) Although there is damage to the papyrus here, the group [hieroglyphs] *is* can be read (*Wb.* 1 128, 6–13.) The word has been discussed by Clère, *OLA* 63, pp. 5ff, as a term designating baldness, referring in particular to the bald priests of Hathor. It can also mean "old." See also O'Rourke, *ZÄS* 134 (2007): 166–67, for a discussion of its occurrence in *CT* 1117. Neither the meaning "bald" nor "old," however, seems to have any valence here. The *Wörterbuch* does not give [hieroglyph] as a determinative for other words written *is*; see Clère, *OLA* 63, pp. 22–23, however, who states that by the Late Period the sign [hieroglyph] has become a phonetic determinative for words written both *is* and *3s*. An attractive reading for the word [hieroglyphs] *is* in the Brooklyn text is the adjective given at *Wb.* I 128, 4, "leicht sein," used here possibly in the metaphoric sense of "weak." The end of the spell speaks of "strength" that results from the recitation of this text, lending credibility to the suggested reading.

BN. (x + 7: 13) On the word *is*, see preceding note BM (x + 7: 13).

BO. (x + 7: 14) What follows for roughly one and one-half lines is the recitation of the man described as *is*.

BP. (x + 7: 14) For a parallel to [hieroglyphs] *pr.n=i m ḏd sḏr.n.=i m 3bḏw*, "It is from Busiris that I have come forth; it is in Abydos that I have slept," see *oGlasgow D.1925.79* (= *oColin Campbell 14*), a copy of a portion of a text in *pLeiden I 349,* 3[11]. There we encounter the phrase *ink ḥr pr m ḏdw sḏr m 3bḏw*, "I am Horus who came forth from Busiris, who slept in Abydos." See

McDowell, *Hieratic Ostraca,* pp. 18–19 and pls. xviii–xviiia; and de Buck and Stricker, *OMRO* 21 (1940): 59 for the Leiden text. See also *pBerlin 3038,* 21^{6-7} (*Bln* 190), which has "I am Horus who slept [in…] and passed the day in Abydos."

BQ. (x + 7: 15) *ḥḥi*, "suchen" (*Wb.* III 151, 3–152, 4, especially 151, 3, which gives "eine Person suchen [den Osiris…]").

BR. (x + 7: 15) *rwḏ* here seems to mean "strength" (*Wb.* II 412, 10–12: "Festigkeit).

BS. (x + 7: 15) The translation of the verbal *ḫpr* as "come to pass" is based on passages in other protection texts where the lector claims to have seen the effectiveness or power of a given spell. A slightly different wording is found in *pBrooklyn 47.218.2,* 6^{15} (Guermeur and O'Rourke, forthcoming): "I have seen it happen myself." The same phrase is found in *pHearst,* 2^{10} (*H* 25); also *pBremner-Rhind,* 23^{16} (cf. R.O. Faulkner, *JEA* 23 [1937]: 176); *pEbers,* 69^{17} (*Eb* 509). One other possible reading here is *it=i Wsir gm.n=i rwḏ n mḏꜣ.t ḫpr*, "…my father Osiris (whom) I found strong because (this) book-roll has come into being." The reading as given in the translation above seems preferable, since the point of emphasis in the present passage is the effectiveness of this particular spell.

BT. (x + 7: 15) In the last four and one-half lines of this column and half of the first line of the next column, the rubrics have faded considerably, and the papyrus has darkened somewhat, making the reading of this section of the text very difficult. With the aid of enhanced digital photographs, I have been able to read and restore most sections of the text, except where the surface of the papyrus is damaged. The reading of *hnꜥ sš* at the end of the line seems reasonably certain.

BU. (x + 7: 16) *tp ꜥꜣ*, "head of an ass," is clear. It is followed by *ḳmy*, "falben" (*WbMT,* p. 885). A number of body parts of an ass are known from prescriptions in medical texts, for which see *WbDN,* pp. 76–78. The closest parallel to this phrase is *ḏꜣḏꜣ ꜥꜣ*, "head of an ass," at *pEbers,* 25^{15} (*Eb* 106), suggesting that should be read *ḏꜣḏꜣ* here as well. For the noun *ꜥꜣ*, "ass," qualified by the adjective *ḳmy*, see *WbDN*, pp. 77–78. For the phrase *ꜥꜣ ḳmy,* see also *pBM 10059,* 9^{11-12}; Leitz, *HPBM* 7, p. 69, n. 16; note that Leitz does not translate the word *ḳmy* there.

BV. (x + 7: 16) The correct reading is perhaps *mḥr*, "illness," rather than *mwt*, "death" or "dead male."

BW. (x + 7: 17) The writing of the sign ⊙ in black is perhaps in deference to its use in the name of the god Re.

BX. (x + 7: 17) *sdm*, "schminken" (*Wb.* IV 370, 1–8).

BY. (x + 7: 17) After *sdm* there is the single sign *m*, followed by a small lacuna and then *sd*, “geschmückt sein” (Hannig, *GHB*, 788a).

BZ. (x + 7: 17) The traces support the reading *md n ḥr*, “staff of Horus.” For this object, used by the god to destroy his enemies, see Meeks, *Mythes et légendes*, pp. 92–93, n. 245, and the discussion at pp. 231–33.

CA. (x + 7: 17) The reading of the group *m ḏr.t wnm.t*, “in the right hand,” is fairly certain, despite the faintness of the ink here.

CB. (x + 7: 18) The restoration here is , based on the traces and the occurrence of the same phrase at the end of the line and at x + 7: 14 above.

CD. (x + 7: 18) The hieratic shows *ir nn ḫpr rḏ=k*.... The writing of the sign in black in the verb *ḫpr*, “become,” may be in deference to the use of this sign in the name Khepri. See note BW (x + 7: 17) above.

CE. (x + 7: 18) The traces, though faint in places, show .

CF. (x + 7: 18) Perhaps the idea here is to say the spell “in a louder voice,” reading the word *k3* as a comparative form.

CG. (x + 7: 18) The signs *mk.t*, “protection,” seem clear.

CH. (x + 7: 19) The damaged first signs of the line are .

CI. (x + 7: 19) The institution *pr mḏ3.t*, “House of Writing,” refers to a scriptorium or “reference” library, usually found as part of the larger institution known as the House of Life, for which see Wessetsky, *LÄ* 1 (1975): cols. 783–85; Weber, *LÄ* 3 (1979): cols. 954–57; Gardiner, *JEA* 24 (1938): 157–79; see also Redford, *Pharaonic King-Lists*, pp. 215–29, where he discusses temple libraries and their probable contents; and see Nordh, *Aspects of Ancient Egyptian Curses and Blessings*, pp. 106–26; finally, Jasnow and Zauzich, *The Book of Thoth*, pp. 33–36, and nn. 111–27 for further references. It is possible that the preposition *m* here means “from” and not “in.”

CJ. (x + 7: 19) The traces in the middle of the line show .

CK. (x + 7: 19) The signs *mty* suggest a writing of the adverb *mty*, “precisely; exactly.”

CL. (x + 7: 19) The signs *nty ḥr sš m*..., “...that which is written in...,” are probably the vestiges of something like “...that which is written in this book-roll.”

CM. (x + 8: 1) [hieroglyphs] *m sšrw mꜣꜥ ḥḥ zp*, "truly effective millions of times" (*Wb.* IV 542, 13–16) is quite clear here.

COMMENTARY

This section of text designated as G2 consists of a direct address to the deities invoked in the previous section G1. The beginning of the text describes their particular powers and points out the general state of well-being that these deities enjoy. The initial description "They dwell in heaven, they eat on earth, their uraei in heaven, their *ba*'s on earth, their mummies in the necropolis…"[197] emphasizes the natural state of the divine who were thought to inhabit several spheres of the cosmos simultaneously, just like the blessed dead.[198] The following phrase, "whose names are hidden from their children," lays stress on the mysterious nature of the divine. The idea that the gods possessed names that are hidden and not known is prevalent in Egyptian thought.[199] The Coffin Texts provide early examples: *iw.t.y rḫ nṯr.w rn=f*, "…whose name the gods do not know," found in a list of epithets;[200] *ḫm rn=f ḫmm rn=f*, "whose name is not known and whose name will not be known."[201] On the specific idea of names concealed from one's children, several Late Period texts offer good parallels: *nn rḫ rn=f iwnw=f in ms.w pr(.w) m ꜥ=f*, "His name (and) his aspect are not known by the children who came forth from his body," in a description of the god Amun;[202] see, further, an epithet of Osiris: *i Wsir kꜣ imn.t imn rn=f r ms.w=f*, "O Osiris, Bull of the West, whose name is concealed from his children."[203] What follows is a continuation of the description of the hidden nature of the gods.[204]

The reference to the gods feeding on other beings is well-attested in Egyptian texts. Such an idea appears as early as the Pyramid Texts in the well-known "Cannibal Hymn"[205]

197 x + 6: 13–14.

198 Assmann, *Death and Salvation*, pp. 90ff. As noted at note D (x + 6: 14) above, *pChester Beatty 9*, vs. B. 17^{5-7} offers a very close parallel.

199 The idea was already circulating in the Old Kingdom; see Zandee, *Amunshymnus* 1, pp. 131–33.

200 *CT* 75, a creation text in which the deceased is identified with Shu.

201 *CT* 146, again in a description of the deceased.

202 See Derchain, *pSalt 825*, 9^9; also Klotz, *YES* 6 (2006), p. 165 and pl. 10, l. 30, for a description of the god Amun in a Hymn to Amun in the Hibis Temple: *imn.n=f m rn=f m imn-wr*, "…he hid himself in his name of *imn-wr*…;" for the identity of *imn-wr*, see ibid., p. 117, n. B.

203 *pLeiden I 346*, 2^9, for which see Bommas, *Die Mythisierung der Zeit*, p. 16. For *imn rn=f* as an epithet of the unified Re-Osiris, see Manassa, *The Late Egyptian Underworld* 1, pp. 341–42. For additional examples of the names of gods hidden from their children, see *pBM 10059*, 8^{13-19}; *pIllustré*, 4^3; *pBM 10042*, 7^1; Zandee, *Amunhymnus*, vs. 2^{8-9} and the discussion there at pp. 131–33; and finally, the discussion in Meeks and Favard-Meeks, *Daily Life*, pp. 97–100 and 103–4.

204 See Dunand and Zivie-Coche, *Gods and Men*, pp. 23ff.

205 *PT* 273–74; see the discussion by Eyre, *The Cannibal Hymn*, pp. 153–74.

and is attested in later texts as well.[206] Once the nature and powers of the divinities invoked in the first section of this spell have been outlined, the gods themselves are called upon in the last line of column x + 6 to drive away the malevolent forces, namely the generic ones already familiar from the preceding texts.

Unfortunately, the lacunae in the first twelve lines of the next column are numerous. The restoration of , *m ii r msḏr n pr-ꜥꜣ*, "…from coming against the ear of the Pharaoh…," is conjectural, based solely upon the common occurrence of that phrase in the papyrus as a whole. Little in the way of interpretation can be offered for the next eight lines because of the lacunae, several uncertain readings, and a lack of clarity in the syntax, particularly with reference to the pronouns encountered. What can be said is that a number of divinities are named, among them Re, Ptah, Horus, son of Osiris, Osiris, and Nephthys. In tandem with the latter three is a reference to *tp n b*, "the head of the Evil One," but the context in which all of this occurs is unclear. Horus of Sohag is also mentioned, a manifestation of Horus found on *cippi.*[207] The references to the two manifestations of Horus, to "the Evil One," and to Osiris make possible allusion to the Horus myth in which he avenges his father; the phrase *ink ḥr nḏ it.f* actually ends the text of the spell proper at x + 7: 15, as the list of prescribed ingredients begins there. At line x + 7: 9 there begins a lengthy description of images of individual deities to be drawn on a strip of linen. What follows are detailed instructions about the placement of the linen and the recitation of "the spells of this book roll," apparently by an individual who is designated as *is*. The recitation is a mythological reference to Horus' searching for his father Osiris, with specific mentions of Busiris and Abydos,[208] and the whole is to be read or spoken in a loud voice. In Egyptian thought, the idea of speaking loudly was usually considered an abomination of the gods. The Coffin Texts offer several examples: *im=f nhm sẖꜣ=f bw.t=i bw.t=i pw nhm*, "He should not shout but he should remember what I abominate; shouting is my abomination;"[209] also *im=k nhm bw.t wsir pw nhm*, "You should not shout; shouting is the abomination of Osiris."[210] The idea here may be that the act of speaking loudly is also an abomination of the malign forces who will flee the person who acts in such a manner. The following statement, "I am Horus, avenger of his father," contains the allusion to the Horus myth mentioned above. The *md n ḥr*, "staff of Horus," is mentioned as well, an object used to destroy the enemies of the god.

206 See, for example, *CT* 69, *BD* 79, and *pBM 10042*, 10^{3-4}. For discussions of the annihilation of one's enemies by eating them, see Eyre, *The Cannibal Hymn*, pp. 153–74; Goeb, *BdE* 139 (2004): 143–73, esp. 151–59; Kees, *Tieropfer*, pp. 71–88; Leclant, *MDAIK* 14 (1956): 128–45; and Labrique, *OLA* 51 (1992), pp. 119, 303, and passim for an important discussion of the interconnections of images and texts of food-offering rituals with those of protection rituals in parallel scene sequences in the Edfu temple.

207 For this god, see the citations given at note UU (x + 7: 4) above.

208 For parallels, see the citations given at note BP (x + 7: 14).

209 *CT* 36.

210 *CT* 37. See Koenig, *pBoulaq 6*, pp. 102–3, n.1, for further references; also Assmann, *Death and Salvation*, p. 190; Frandsen, in Clarysse et al., *OLA* 84 (1998), pp. 975–1000.

Despite the fact that the first section of the spell presents obstacles to a coherent reading and the lacunae in the second section create obstacles as well, it seems that, for at least the latter part of the text of the spell, we can connect this text with another myth sequence in which benevolent beings in the ordered cosmos are able to thwart the threats of the malignant forces of chaos.

Several thoughts on the text as a whole and its presence in the papyrus may be offered as well. The mention of the word *msḏr* in the heading of the text *mḏꜣ.t n.t sḥri mwt mwt.t m msḏr nty ẖr…*, "A book-roll for driving off a dead male (and) a dead female from the ear of one who is suffering…," is the only mention of the ear in the text. Given that the title of this spell, however, is found as well in a text in *pBerlin 3038*, whose heading is "Another [text] for driving off a dead male from the ear," it seems highly likely that the present spell was a spell known for the protection of the ear.[211] The instruction at the end of the spell, to place the strip of linen at the neck, not the ear, is, in all likelihood, an instruction to hang the strip of linen from the neck as an amulet.[212] The absence of the name Psamtik or the term Pharaoh anywhere in this lengthy text presents no real problems, as there are other texts of the papyrus in which this is the case as well.[213] As noted above, the title of this spell is found also in *pBerlin 3038,* introduced simply by *ky sḥri*, "Another [text for] driving off…." The presence of the word *mḏꜣ.t* suggests that the exemplar for the present spell may have originally been an independent text; this may explain its length and comprehensive instructions, as the rubric of close to five lines may suggest. What can be said is, given that the text is most likely a spell for protection of the ear and given its length — its forty-seven lines make it the second longest text of the papyrus — the reasons for its inclusion in the papyrus seem obvious.

211 See note A (x + 5: 11) above.

212 See also x + 8: 11 below, where the prescription written on a new strip of papyrus is to be placed at the throat. These amuletic linen strips were first rolled into a small, tight bundle.

213 See Spells J and K below. The presence of numerous lacunae in the present text may also be offered as the reason for their absence.

Spell H — Translation with Commentary

COLUMN X + 8: 1–6 (P. BROOKLYN 47.218.49)

TRANSLITERATION

1. *… ky [rꜣ] … nbỉ.t ꜥẖm=ỉ …*
2. *rdỉ.t(w) n=ỉ… ỉw rdỉ.t(w) {n=ỉ} hh ss[wn].n=ỉ sw rdỉ ḫpr=sn ỉnk ꜣs.t*
3. *ꜥḥꜣ … =s nn dỉ=ỉ sꜣ ḥr n hh [nḥ]m n=ỉ sw nn n pẖr.wt ꜣḫ.y ḥr*
4. *<.t> pr … rꜥ pr m ḥꜥ.w=f ỉnk [dr] st-ꜥ nṯr nṯr.t mwt mwt.t ḥm.wt-rꜣ ỉrr*
5. *hh [m tp m mꜣ]ꜥ m msḏr n psmṯk [ꜥ.]w.s. ḏd mdw ḥr 8 twr.w ṯz.t*
6. *n rw … šnỉ msḏr ỉm ḥnꜥ ḏꜣ[ỉs] nḏ šnꜥꜥ ḥr ỉbr dỉ r msḏr*

TRANSLATION

1. ……………………………………… Another [spell …4 cm…][A] flame[B] [which] (?) I extinguished.[C] […2.5 cm… fire.][D]
2. [Fire] is given to me[E] […] I have […3 cm…][F]. Fire is given {to me}[G] (and) I have [punished (?)][H] him[I] who caused them[J] to come into being. I[K] am Isis[L]
3. who fights […3 cm…] her.[M] I will not give the child Horus[N] to the fire. These effective remedies[O] will [save][P] him for me,[Q] while[R]
4. coming forth […3 cm…][S] of Re, coming forth from his body.[T] I am the one who [drives away][U] the influence[V] of a god, goddess,[W] dead male, dead female and so on who make
5. heat[X] [in the head, in the tem]ple[Y] in the ear of Psamtik, l.p.h. *Recitation over 8 reed plants,*[Z] *a knot*
6. *of* […][AA] […2 cm…] *reciting spells (over)*[BB] *the ear therewith* together with the *ḏꜣ*[*ỉs*-plant],[CC] ground finely[DD] with laudanum (and) placed at the ear.

TEXT NOTES

A. (x + 8: 1) The traces indicate the restoration *ky* [*rꜣ*], "Another Spell." Since the prescription and set of instructions of the preceding spell were written entirely in rubrics, the scribe was required to use black ink to indicate the beginning of a new spell, at least for the word *ky*. This is not the customary practice seen in this papyrus.

B. (x + 8: 1) *nbi.t*, "Flamme; Feuersglut" (*Wb.* II 244, 7–9) can be read clearly.

C. (x + 8: 1) *ʿḫm*, "löschen" (*Wb.* I 224, 15–18). It is possible that the phrase *ʿḫm=i* here is a relative form, modifying the noun *nbi.t* that precedes it, and should be translated "...which I extinguish." One possible restoration is [... *rdi.t*(*w*) *n=i*] *nbi.t ʿḫm=i*, "Fire was given to me which I extinguished ...." *pRamesseum C*, vs. 3^3 has a possible parallel in ...] *n=k ḫt ʿḫm.n=k* ..., "...you...fire (which) you extinguished." See also *BD* 22: *ii.n=i r mrr ib=i m iw nsrsr ʿḫm.n=i sḏt pr*, "I have come according as my heart desires from the Island of Fire. I have extinguished the fire that came forth (there)."

D. (x + 8: 1) The traces at the end of the line show the vestiges of (Sign-list Q7), suggesting the restoration of a word associated with fire.

E. (x + 8: 2) The traces suggest the restoration of *rdi.t*(*w*) *n=i*, "...given to me...."

F. (x + 8: 2) The lacuna ends with (Sign-list N35), a determinative indicating a word like "extinguish." One possibility is the verb , *ʿḫm*, which occurs above at x + 8: 1. Both (Sign-list Q7) and (Sign-list N35) are given as determinatives of this verb (*Wb.* I 224, 15–18).

G. (x + 8: 2) In the writing , the signs have been crossed out with a red stroke. Thus, we are left with *iw rdi.t*(*w*) *hh*.... The context seems to require a passive form here; therefore, I have taken as a passive form introduced by *iw*, reading *iw rdi.t*(*w*) *hh*, "...destructive fire is given ...."

H. (x + 8: 2) and the traces at the beginning of the lacuna suggest the possible restoration of . is *sswn*, "bestrafen" (*Wb.* IV 273, 7–15). Numerous references are given there to its occurrence in connection with Apophis and other enemies of the gods and the king. It occurs in a number of texts in the Edfu temple describing the fiery punishment that Hathor inflicts. See Wilson, *PL*, p. 939, for references; see also *pBM 9997*, 7^{12}, in a text addressed to the poison of a snake-bite.

I. (x + 8: 2) If the restoration of the verb is correct, then the dependent pronoun would refer to one of the evil forces.

J. (x + 8: 2) The antecedent of the suffix pronoun *=sn* remains unclear.

K. (x + 8: 2) The sign *k* at the bottom of the lacuna and the other traces indicate a writing of the independent pronoun *ink*, "I."

L. (x + 8: 2) The writing of the divine name *ꜣs.t*, "Isis," at the end of the line is also found at x + 8: 13.

M. (x + 8: 3) If the sign at the end of the lacuna is the feminine suffix pronoun, its antecedent would be Isis, whose name occurs at the end of the preceding line.

N. (x + 8: 3) The group *s3 ḥr* can be translated either as "son Horus" or as "boy Horus," the rendering adopted here. See Borghouts, *pLeiden I 348,* rt.1[5], 2[9], and p. 55, n. 52, for extensive references.

O. (x + 8: 3) *pḫr.wt*, "remedies;" similarly written at x + 5: 10 above.

P. (x + 8: 3) Despite a small lacuna here, the restoration of *nḥm*, "save," is certain.

Q. (x + 8: 3) The omission of a preposition before , "these…," suggests that *nn n pḫr.wt 3ḫ.(wt)*, "these effective remedies," is to be taken as the subject of the verb *nḥm*, "save," and that the phrase *n=i* is a dative, translated "for me." An alternative translation is "May these effective remedies save him…." Alternatively, the verb may be taken as a *sḏm.n=f* form, with the understanding that the scribe has inadvertently omitted the preposition *m* before the phrase that begins with *nn n*. The translation would then be "I have saved him with these excellent remedies" or the like.

R. (x + 8: 3) The line ends with and the first two signs of the next line are . One explanation is that the group is simply a scribal error. Another is that the scribe originally wrote at the end of x + 8: 3 and the beginning of x + 8: 4, then realized that he had omitted the preposition and chose to add it at the end of x + 8: 3 where there was room, instead of making it a supralinear addition.

S. (x + 8: 4) The lacuna ends with the signs , indicating that a plant name occurred in the last part of the lacuna.

T. (x + 8: 4) The antecedent of the suffix pronoun *=f* is probably the noun *rʿ*, "Re," which occurs in the preceding phrase.

U. (x + 8: 4) The traces suit the restoration of the verb *dr*, "entfernen, vertreiben, beseitigen" (*Wb.* V 473, 1–474, 12), a word encountered frequently in this papyrus.

V. (x + 8: 4) *st-ʿ*, "Bez. für Krankheit" (*Wb.* I 157, 5). *WbMT,* pp. 701–2, gives the additional meanings "Einwirkung; Einwirkungsstelle," citing a number of examples where the word is followed by *nṯr*, *nṯr.t*, *mwt*, or *mwt.t* as direct genitives. The group can also be preceded by the sign (Sign-list R8) in honorific transposition to indicate the "influence of a god." Cf., however, Gardiner, *pChester Beatty 9,* vs. B. 1[1] and p. 106, where he translates as "blows." *pBM 10059,* 13[4] offers a close parallel to the Brooklyn text. The word *st-ʿ* can also have a positive nuance, for which see Vandier, *BdE* 18 (1950): 168–69.

W. (x + 8: 4) The word *nṯr.t*, "goddess," appears only here in the lists of potentially harmful beings encountered in this papyrus.

X. (x + 8: 5) The traces at the beginning of the line point to the word *hh*, "Gluthauch" (*Wb.* II 501, 15–502, 1–8, in particular 502, 6, where it is cited as "Hitze als Krankheit Zustand eines Körperteils"). This word occurs more than thirty times in the Brooklyn papyrus, invariably referring to a destructive power used by the forces of evil against the Pharaoh. For an extensive discussion of this word, see the Introduction, pp. 26ff. above.

Y. (x + 8: 5) The restoration of the phrase *m tp m m3ʿ*, "in the head, in the temple," is based on the space available and the occurrence of this phrase below at x + 9: 3, x + 11: 19–x + 12: 1, x + 12: 4, and x + 13: 1. I cannot explain what appears to be the writing of , unless it is a scribal slip, as many words written *m3ʿ* have that determinative. Compare the similar writing at x + 9: 3.

Z. (x + 8: 5) Although some of the signs are quite smudged here, the reading appears to be *8 n twr.w*. For the construction of a cardinal number and *n* preceding the noun it modifies, see note AZ (x + 7: 11) above. For *twr*, see *Wb.* V 318, 13: "Röhricht;" *WbDN*, pp. 551–52, gives "Rohrpflanze;" Westendorf, *Handbuch* 1, p. 390, translates it as "*twr*-Rohr." Germer, *Heilpflanzen,* pp. 152–53, essentially concurs. Note that it occurs at *pBerlin 3038, 6*[7] (*Bln* 67), a "fumigation" spell for "driving off the influence (*st-ʿ*) of a dead male, dead female," a phrase echoed in the Brooklyn text; it occurs elsewhere in the Berlin papyrus in two spells for "removing the poison of a god, a goddess, a dead male, a dead female…." See *pBerlin 3038, 6*[1–2] (*Bln* 61–62).

AA. (x + 8: 6) There are signs at the beginning of the line which appear to be , of which I can make little sense.

BB. (x + 8: 6) *šni*, "beschwören; besprechen" (*Wb.* IV 496, 2–6) occurs as well at x + 7: 13 above and x + 8: 19 below. See note BJ (x + 7: 13) above for a discussion of its meaning and translation.

CC. (x + 8: 6) The restoration of *ḏ3is* is based on the signs and the traces. It has been given as the name of an unknown plant (*Wb.* V 520, 12–521, 3; *WbDN,* pp. 592–94). Borghouts, *AEMT,* p. 106, n.159 states that it is a poisonous herb but gives no evidence to support this claim. Aufrère, *BIFAO* 86 (1986): pl. IX, 6–9 identifies it as *Lactuca amara,* a type of lettuce that has not only analgesic properties but narcotic ones as well. Miller, *BIFAO* 94 (1994): 349–59, identifies *ḏ3is* as *harmala,* citing its use as an analgesic among its medicinal applications. Germer, *Heilpflanzen,* p. 172, questions its pharmaceutical efficacy.

DD. (x + 8: 6) On the phrase *nḏ šnʿʿ*, "ground finely," see note AB (x + 3: 14) above.

COMMENTARY

The numerous lacunae at the top of this column impede a fully informed reading of the text. The spell is narrated by the goddess Isis and centers on the child Horus, who appears to be threatened by fire. Isis declares that she will play no part in attempting to destroy the child Horus; in fact, she claims responsibility for saving the child and restoring him to health. She then states that she will now save Psamtik by driving away the malevolent forces that are identified as the generic forces of chaos that we have routinely encountered in the papyrus.[214] At the end comes a possible reference to remedies that have emanated from the body of Re, although the lacunae again inhibit a secure reading. The mythological allusions in this spell are similar to those found in the stories about the child Horus who was hidden in the Delta marshes by Isis to protect him from his enemies.[215] The connecting thread between that myth cycle and the present text may lie in the reference to fire, a possible allusion to the heat and pain of the scorpion sting that Horus suffered in an incident central to those myths. Thus, as Isis saved Horus from the fiery bite of scorpion, she will likewise protect Pharaoh by driving away the malignant forces who are attempting to place fire in his ear. It may be significant that the first ingredient in the prescription is a reed-plant commonly found in the marshes of the Delta. The presence of such a plant in the coda of the spell may be an attempt to draw further connections between this text and the Horus myth discussed above.

214 For these beings, see the discussion above, p. 26ff.

215 For texts alluding to that myth cycle, see, for example, Klasens, *OMRO* 33 (1952), passim.

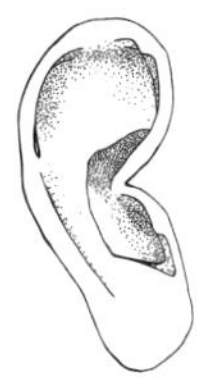

Spell I — Translation with Commentary

COLUMN X + 8: 6–11 (P. BROOKLYN 47.218.49)

TRANSLITERATION

6. … *ky*
7. *rꜣ i͗[w-ms] n [mwt] i͗w-ms n mwt.t i͗w-ms [n] tm sḏm mdw.wt i͗w-ms n*
8. *=sn rm.w tp mw ꜣpd.w m pꜣy=sn n sn-2 nty ẖr mw.t*
9. *wꜥ.t i͗w ḥr sẖti ḏr.t=w wꜣḥ ḥr dmḏ.yt r ḫtm rꜣ.w n mwt mwt.t ḏꜣ ḏꜣ-*
10. *.t nty i͗rr hh m msḏr n psmṯk ꜥ.w.s. ḏd mdw ḥr wiꜣ n rꜥ sš ḥr ḏ-*
11. *-mꜥ n mꜣw.t di͗ r ḫḫ n s hh m msḏr=f*

TRANSLATION

6. ……………………………………………………… *Another*
7. *spell.* A warning for a dead male,[A] a warning for a dead female, a warning for one who does not listen to[B] the words,[C] a warning for them.[D]
8. The fish upon the waters[E] (and) birds in their flight[F] belong to (?)[G] the two brothers who possess one mother,[H]
9. coming[I] upon[J] the net catcher,[K] (their) hands[L] pointing out[M] the appointed time[N] to seal the mouths[O] of the dead male, dead female, male adversary, female
10. adversary who make heat in the ear of Psamtik, l.p.h. *Recitation over* a barque of Re[P] *drawn on a*[Q]
11. *new papyrus roll*[R] *(and) placed at the throat*[S] *of a man (with) heat in his ear.*

TEXT NOTES

A. (x + 8: 7) The particle *i͗w-ms* is one that remains rather poorly understood. The basic discussion of the word still seems to be Gardiner, *Admonitions*, pp. 21–23. There the word occurs as the heading of each new section of the text. Further on in that papyrus, *i͗w-ms* is replaced by *mk=tn*, strongly suggesting that *i͗w-ms* is also a particle and one that stands in initial position. Gardiner offers the neutral translation "forsooth," a rendering that offers little insight into the particle's basic meaning. For *i͗w-ms*, the lexica give "Unwahrheit" (*Wb.* I 52, 7–9) and "aufgestellte Behauptung; als Behauptung erlogen" (Hannig, *GH,* p. 34b). Gunn, *Studies in Egyptian Syntax,* p. 147, n. 5, appears to agree with the meaning given at *Wb.* I 52, 7–9. In his publication of a Middle Kingdom magical text, Roccati, *pTurin 54003,* p. 25, n. g, claims that *iw-ms* is a particle derived from an adverb, basing his interpretation and discussion on a phrase found in *CT* 225: *iw-ms r=f mi ḏd NN,* "*iw-ms*, indeed, like what NN says." Borghouts, *EU* 24.1, p. 133, §33.b.27, identifies only the word *ms* as a particle that "expresses contrariety and surprise."

In the Brooklyn text, *iw-ms* occurs four times in the opening of this spell. It, too, serves as as an introductory word, each time followed by a prepositional phrase introduced by *n*. Three times the preposition is followed by a noun, once by a suffix pronoun. We can rule out the word *n* as the genitive marker, given its occurrence in the phrase [hieroglyphs] *iw-ms n=sn*; suffix pronouns are not so marked. Several different interpretations can be offered. The first is to understand *iw-ms* as the particle discussed above and to take the word [hieroglyph] *n* that follows it as the *nisbe* form of the preposition, *n(y)*, indicating ownership or possession. See Gardiner, *EG*³, §114, 1, where examples are given showing the occurrence of *n(y)* even before suffix pronouns. Following this interpretation, the word *n(y)* would connect the phrases that follow it to *ky r3*, the heading of the spell. Hence, the translation would be "Another spell, indeed, for a dead male, indeed, for a dead female, etc...." The problem with such a reading is that in spells of this sort that have a construction like *ky r3 n*, the person or category of persons that follows is the one whom the spell is intended to benefit. It also relegates *iw-ms* to a position in the sentence that is non-initial, which may or may not be problematic.

Alternatively, we can read *iw-ms* as the noun given at *Wb.* I 52, 7, accepting the basic meaning "lie; untruth." See, for example, Lacau and Chevrier, *Une chapelle d'Hatshepsout* 1, p. 137, l. 25, and p. 140, n. (q) for further references. Again, the sign *n* would be understood as the *nisbe* form *n(y)*, indicating possession. In this case, the translation would be: "Another spell. A lie belonging to a dead male, a lie belonging to a dead female...." This interpretation is greatly weakened by the fact that the referent of the word "lie" seems impossible to establish. It certainly cannot be the body of the text, as that conforms to the content and intent of the other spells in the papyrus, all of which are clearly considered true and effective. It also cannot be the word "spell," and that is the only word that precedes it.

A third interpretation would be to posit a meaning like "woe!" or "a warning!" for *iw-ms*. Such a meaning has already been suggested by Gardiner in his discussion of the word, as he concludes: "Thus, the function of *ms* is here to admonish" (p. 23). The meaning "warning" chosen for the translation of the present passage works both grammatically and contextually. Similarly, such a translation would work well in the passages of the *Admonitions* where it appears. By no means is this to suggest that "warning" is the meaning of the particle *iw-ms*, but rather that such a translation captures its emphatic nuance. Note also, that the translation offered is one that is done so with reservation.

B. (x + 8: 7) *itm*, "Atum," as written seems to make little sense in the context given. It seems better to see a writing of the negative verb *tm* here; the presence of the divine determinative can be explained as a scribal error due to the similarity in writing of the verb and the name of the god Atum in Late Period texts where it is often written without the initial *yod*.

C. (x + 8: 7) The restoration of *mdw.wt*, "words," is based on the traces. The phrase *sḏm mdw.wt*, "hear the words," occurs as well at x + 2: 7 and 10–11 above, and at x + 12: 19 and x + 13: 3 below.

D. (x + 8: 7) It is unclear whether the suffix pronoun =*sn* refers to the individuals just listed or to the group "fish …birds" that follows.

E. (x + 8: 8) *rmw*, "fish," is also written with two signs in *pBrooklyn 47.218.84*, for which see Meeks, *Mythes et légendes*, 7[3], and p. 84, n. 204. The reference to fish and birds is found in several texts in which they refer to manifestations of the enemies of the sun god. See the discussion in the Commentary below.

F. (x + 8: 8) For the occurrence of birds in connection with fish, see *Wb.* I 9, 6 and the references cited in nn. 217–19 below.

G. (x + 8: 8) I have taken the word *n* here, again, as a *nisbe* form.

H. (x + 8: 8–9) *sn-2 nty ḥr(.wy) mw.t wꜤ.t*, "two brothers who possess one mother." I owe the correct reading of the hieratic here to Richard Jasnow. This is likely a reference to Osiris and Seth; see Goyon, *pConfirmation*, 20[9] for a similar epithet: *ms n sn.wy*, "the one who gave birth to two brothers," and ibid., p. 123, n. 341, where he says that it is a probable reference to Nut. The references to these two gods make sense in light of the fact that the spell focuses on strife.

I. (x + 8: 9) *iw* is likely a participle here; an imperative form is ruled out, as the imperative of the root *iy* is *mi*; see Quack, *LingAeg* 12 (2004): 133–36. Despite the simple writing, this form seems to be plural, referring to the "two brothers…" in the preceding phrase. See Gardiner, *EG*[3], § 359.

J. (x + 8: 9) For the various meanings of *iw ḥr*, see Hannig, *GH*, p. 27b.

K. (x + 8: 9) *sḫti*, "Vogelfänger" (Hannig, *GH*, p. 750b). See *Urk.* VI, 69[21] for *mi nḥm.k wi m-Ꜥ sḫti*, "Come, may you rescue me from the bird-catcher…." The occurrence of *sḫti* as an epithet possibly connected with Horus further strengthens the interpretation of the fish and birds above as manifestations of inimical beings.

L. (x + 8: 9) The group following *ḏr.t* is either the *plene* writing of the plural *ḏr.wt* or the Late Egyptian third person plural suffix pronoun =*w*. Such a writing is found at x + 11: 6 below as well.

M. (x + 8: 9) For the meaning of *wꜣḥ* here, see Capart, Gardiner, and van de Walle, *JEA* 22 (1936): 182, where they discuss the idiom *wꜣḥ ḏrt ḥr*, "to point out s.t."

N. (x + 8: 9) *dmḏ.yt*, "die bestimmte Zeit" (*Wb.* V 461, 14–462, 6).

O. (x + 8: 9) On sealing the mouth of the enemy, see Schott, *ZÄS* 65 (1930), pp. 35–42, a publication of selected passages from *pBM 10081* that deal with sealing body parts and places as a means of controlling the forces of chaos. The phrase *ḫtm rꜣ*, "seal the mouth," occurs as well at *pLeiden I 343+345*, vs. 5^{4}. See also *pBM 10042*, rt. 8^{3} and 8^{8}; vs. 1^{3}, 2^{3-4}, and 2^{5-7}. Sealing the mouths of the enemy prevents them from uttering any imprecations or magical spells of their own against Psamtik.

P. (x + 8: 10) The instruction in the prescription to draw a figure of a barque of Re is likely due to the idea that the solar barque was a place of ultimate protection. See the discussion in the Commentary.

Q. (x + 8: 10) The rubric is faded, but the signs *sš ḥr*, "drawn on," can be read.

R. (x + 8: 11) The last two signs of the previous line and the beginning signs of this line give *dmꜥ*, "Papyrus Blatt" (*Wb.* V 574, 4–9).

S. (x + 8: 11) The instruction about the placement of the strip of papyrus on which the spell and prescriptions are to be written indicates that it is an amulet to be worn at the neck. See the discussion on the Commentary below.

COMMENTARY

This spell is one of the more puzzling in the papyrus. Establishing a correct reading of the text has proven as difficult as attempting to determine its meaning. In places the syntax seems uncertain, and there occur a number of enigmatic words that impede a clear understanding of the text where they appear. The beginning of the spell appears to be couched in words of warning to the malevolent forces. Embedded in that warning we once again find the injunction to "hear the words," encountered in Spells C, O, and P.[216] At x + 8: 8, we come upon a reference to fish and birds who seem to be included among the adversarial forces.[217] In a passage in the Book of the Dead, Apophis and his confederates, the traditional enemies of the sun god, are referred to as birds and fish during their

216 x + 2: 7.

217 For a discussion of birds and fish appearing together, see Hornung, *Eranos Jahrbuch* 52 (1983): 455–96; also Klotz, *ZÄS* 136 (2009): 136–40.

attack upon the solar barque: *šʿd.n ḥr tp.w=sn r pt m ꜣpd.w ẖpd.w=sn* [*r*] *š m rm.w ḏꜣ nb ḏꜣ.t nb.t ẖm=sn m Wsir hꜣi=f m pt pr=f m tꜣ iw.t=tn ḥr mw šꜣs=ṯn m-ʿb sbꜣ.w ḥsḳ.n st ḏhwty*, "Horus has cut off their heads in the sky as birds, their buttocks [in] the lake as fish. Every male adversary, every female adversary who lay hold of Osiris N., should he descend from the sky, should he come forth from the earth, should you come by water or should you travel in the company of the stars, Thoth has decapitated them."[218] Note that the heading and coda of this funerary text both mention the barque of Re, a sacred object that appears in the coda of the Brooklyn spell as well. Another New Kingdom religious text recounts a myth in which the sun god regurgitates rebellious gods whom he has swallowed, and they emerge in the form of fish and birds.[219] The enemies of Osiris transformed into birds also appear in the "Ritual of Annihilation of Enemies."[220] See also *pVienna 8426* in a somewhat lacuna-ridden passage: *iꜣd.t=*[*s*] *m ꜣpd.w nšni=s m rm.w m itrw*, "…her pestilence in birds and her rage in the fish in the flood."[221] The same occur again as enemies of Re in the so-called "rite de chasse au filet." Of particular interest is text VIII in Alliot's study of this ritual, in which a hunter (*wḥʿ*) captures fish and birds in his net; these are equated with the Asiatics and bow-people who number among the traditional enemies of the king.[222] Furthermore, birds and fish lie at the core of the technical word *rsf*, found as "a general term for birds and fish caught in the marshes during fishing and fowling expeditions," ostensibly to be used in offering rituals.[223] A possible reference to Osiris and Seth occurs here as well, but not in a context that recalls the Osirian cycle discussed above.[224] Additionally, the mention of *sẖti*, "Vogelfänger," further strengthens the interpretation of the aforementioned birds and fish as members of the group of adversaries in this spell. Note that although there is no prescription given, there are instructions to recite the text over an image of a barque of Re, an image that has clear associations with triumphing over one's enemies and that also plays a role in the Book of the Dead spell discussed above.

As noted above, the papyrus on which the spell is written is an amulet to be worn at the neck. Written prescriptions placed at the throat in cases where the physical affliction occurs in another part of the body are quite common.[225] The genre known as amuletic oracular decrees comprises the best-known texts of this type.[226]

---

218 *BD* 134.

219 *pCairo 86637*, rt. 6^{4-8}.

220 See Burkard, *Osiris-Liturgien*, pp. 66 and 304.

221 Flessa, *pVienna 8426*, p. 54, ll. 11–12.

222 See Alliot, *RdE* 5 (1946): 57–118, esp. 83–89; also, Posener, *ACF* 75 (1975): 405–12; Koenig, in Kousoulis and Magliveras, eds., *OLA* 159 (2007), pp. 223–38; for a discussion of birds as the enemies of Re or Osiris, see Meeks, *Mythes et légendes*, pp. 230ff.

223 Wilson, *PL*, p. 592. For an example of such a use, see *pBerlin 3053*, 15^{3}.

224 See the Commentary to Spell D.

225 For examples of spells having such an amuletic function, see *pLeiden I 348*, vs. 2: a spell for chasing away nightmares; ibid., rt. 4^{5-9}, a spell against headaches; and *pLeiden I 346*, 1^{1-2} and 1^{5}, a spell against the demons of the last day of the year and against the *iꜣd.t*-plague of the year.

226 See Edwards, *HPBM* 4, passim.

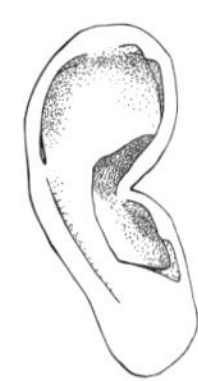

Spell J — Translation with Commentary

COLUMN X + 8: 11–15 (P. BROOKLYN 47.218.49)

TRANSLITERATION

11. *…ky rꜣ tp-ꜥ.wy ỉr.t ḥr ỉꜣd.t-*
12. *=s ỉw ꜣd=k r=s ỉw ꜣd=s r=k nsb ḫr ssd m pt nꜣ.w [w]ḥꜣ.w*
13. *ḫnsw.w m tꜣ pr ḫt ḥr ỉꜣb[.t.t] n ꜣs.t r wḥm n nb-ḥw.t dr nbd m*
14. *nhs ṯz-pẖr ỉw ỉr.n nṯr.w ỉwy=sn ꜥnw ii m wp.t ḏd mdw ḥr*
15. *ỉr.w n ḥr ỉr.w n b sš ḥr msḏr n s*

TRANSLATION

11. ……………………………….Another *spell* before[A] the Eye of Horus (and) its torment(er).[B]
12. You rage[C] against it (and) it rages against you. May the enemy[D] be devour(ed)[E] (so that) the *ssd*-binding[F] (is) in heaven, eye-disease[G]
13. (and) swelling[H] (are) on earth. Fire comes forth upon the left (side)[I] of Isis and again upon that of Nephthys.[J] Drive away the fiend[K] as
14. the Seth-animal[L] and vice-versa. The gods have made their malice[M] turn back[N] the one who comes with a message.[O] *To be recited over*
15. an image of Horus (and) an image of the Evil One drawn upon the ear of a man.[P]

TEXT NOTES

A. (x + 8: 11) Reading *tp ꜥ.wy* as the preposition "vor" (Hannig, *GH*, p. 926a).

B. (x + 8: 11) The group written *ỉꜣd.t* presents difficulties. It may be the noun "Not; Mangel" (*Wb.* I 35, 16–18), a word that fits the context. Thus, the translation would be "…the Eye of Horus (and) its torment/damage." None of the lexica, however, shows a writing with the determinative (Sign-list F51). It may be the verb *ỉꜣd*, "elend sein; Mangel leiden" (*Wb.* I 35, 9–12). In this case, the sign is to be understood as the suffix pronoun referring to the Eye and serving as the subject, hence the translation: "…the Eye of Horus. It is in torment." Either reading makes sense describing the damaged eye of Horus and may account for the presence of the determinative [hieroglyph] that suggests a connection with the body. Alternatively, it may be the noun "Frevler; Feind" (*Wb.* I 35, 13–14); Meeks, *AL* 1 (1977), p. 14 gives a meaning "l'ennemi," suggesting a comparison with Coptic **ОТ**. Following that interpretation, the translation would then be "…the Eye of Horus (and) its tormenter/enemy," and the noun *ἰ3d.t* would clearly refer to Seth. Several statements in this spell describe reciprocal activity, and the prescription at the end of the spell involves recitation over images of both Horus and Seth. The only problem with such an interpretation is again the presence of the determinative [hieroglyph] and the lack of a "negative" determinative that one would expect if the word [hieroglyphs] *ἰ3d.t* referred to Seth.

C. (x + 8: 12) [hieroglyphs], "wütend sein" (*Wb.* I 24, 12–17, especially 15, where this verb is cited with the preposition *r* and the meaning "lostoben gegen"). The paronomasia with the preceding word *ἰ3d.t* should be noted.

D. (x + 8: 12) Beginning here and continuing into the next line, the text is difficult. [hieroglyphs] *ẖr* presents the first problem. It may be the noun used "als verächtliche Bez. für Feind" (*Wb.* III 321, 7–322), although neither of the determinatives [hieroglyphs] is given in the *Wörterbuch* entry. Alternatively, it could be the noun "Blutbad" (*Wb.* III 322, 6–323, 7, citing the determinative [hieroglyph] (Sign-list T30). That word occurs in *BD* and in Ptolemaic Period texts "als Beiwort von Dämonen," referring specifically to the sacrificial victims in apotropaic rituals. See also Wilson, *PL*, p. 746, who gives it as a generic term for sacrificial animals, attested from the Old Kingdom through the Roman Period. If *ẖr* is a verb, it would mean "fällen" (*Wb.* III 319–321, 5, where the determinatives [hieroglyphs] are given and both transitive and intransitive meanings). The context, however, seems to call for a noun, not a verb, as the first word of the clause is *nsb*, which is unquestionably a verb. Comparing the writing found here with that of the word *ἰ3d.t* above, which also lacked the determinatives that one might expect, a case for reading *ẖr* as "enemy" here can be made.

E. (x + 8: 12) [hieroglyphs], "etw. verschlingen; etwas ablecken" (*Wb.* II 334, 11–14). For a somewhat extended meaning of this verb, see Goyon, *Cérémonial*, p. 145, 2, for the phrase *nsb=f r ḫft.yw=k* and the translation "elle est dardée contre tes ennemis," the suffix pronoun *=f* there referring to the tongue of Osiris-Khentiamentiu. The present context seems to require the meaning "devour" or "swallow." See note D (x + 8: 12) above.

F. (x + 8: 12) The word [hieroglyphs] *sšd* could be either the noun "Binde" (*Wb.* IV 301, 3–10) or the verb "mit einer Binde schmücken" (*Wb.* IV 301, 12–13). It can have positive associations, as in the description of the wrapping of a mummy or binding of a wound. Hannig, *GH*, p. 769a gives the meanings "Binde (*a. mit Zauberspruch*);" *sšd n s3*, "Binde des Schutzes." Wilson, *PL*, p. 935 gives it as "head band," one that has royal associations and one that can be used as a physical symbol of unification. It is also used as a bandage for the finger of Osiris in *PT* 519; see Manassa, *The Late Egyptian Underworld* 1, pp. 25–26. As will be seen from the discussion in the Commentary, the noun *sšd* can be used metaphorically, having close associations with the Eye of Horus. See notes G (x + 8: 12) and H (x + 8: 13), following.

G. (x + 8: 12) A small hole in the papyrus prevents an exact reading of the sign that immediately follows, quite likely the first sign of the word whose remaining signs [...]*ḥ3* can be seen here. Possible restorations would be *mḥ3*, "an unknown disease" (*WbMT,* p. 386), found in *pChester Beatty 6,* vs. 1^{5}; the traces less likely suit *nḥ3*, "uneben; rührig" (*WbMT,* p. 471, citing *pEbers,* 108^{17}–109^{2} [*Eb* 874a], where it qualifies the noun *ʿ3.t*, "Geschwulst"). *Wb.* II 290, 5–14 cites a similarly written adjective: "wild; schrecklich; gefährlich." The traces of something before seem to rule out *ḥ3*, "Krankheit" (*WbMT,* p. 583). The most attractive reading may be *wḥ3.w*, "etwas Krankhaftes das unter Umständen zum Tode führen kann" (*Wb.* I 347, 8–10). That word is written mostly as a plural, which would explain the preceding group *n3* as the plural definite article. The traces don't rule against such a reading. Furthermore, Hannig, *GH,* p. 209a gives it as "Augenkrankheit," which seems relevant here as well. It appears in a text on the sarcophagus of Ankhnesneferibre: *šp ḥr=tn mi ḥr n wḥ3*, "May your faces be blinded like the face of the *wḥ3*-fiend," the *wḥ3*-fiend standing parallel to the enemies of Re; see Sander-Hansen, *Die religiösen Texte auf dem Sarg des Anchnesneferibre,* pp. 121–22. Again, note the association of the term *wḥ3* with eye-disease and blindness. On the broader meaning of blindness in Egyptian thought, see Darnell, *Enigmatic Netherworld Books,* pp. 171–73, esp. n. 36.

H. (x + 8: 13) *ḫns.w*, "Geschwülste" (*Wb.* III 300, 12–14 gives *ḫns.yt*, written with plural strokes, as a derivative of Khonsu). The meaning "swelling" is evidently based on Khonsu's lunar associations. *WbMT,* p. 661 follows in giving that meaning and an additional meaning "Krankheit des Kopfhaares." Hannig, *GH,* p. 606b, under *ḫns.yt* gives "Krankheit (nässender Auschlag [m] am Kopf)." Additionally, the article *n3* may also qualify *ḫns.w*, which may be plural here. The word *ḫns.w* ends a string of three nouns whose relationship to what precedes remains unclear. The group can at least be divided into parallel pairs. The phrase "*sšd*-binding in heaven" seems to resonate with the phrase "eye disease (and) swelling on earth." As noted above, the word *sšd* seems positive in its meaning and application, while both of the nouns [*w*]*ḥ3.w* and *ḫns.w* appear to have negative overtones. The apparent absence of a verb here impedes further observation and interpretation. One suggestion for rendering its meaning is to posit the accidental omission of the word *iw* before this string of nouns. Restoring *iw* gives *iw sšd m pt n3 wḥ3.w ḫns.w m t3*, "The *sšd*-binding (i.e., the restored Eye of Horus) is in heaven, the *wḥ3.w* disease and swelling on earth." The meaning of this section of the text would be that if the enemy of the Eye of Horus is subdued, here "swallowed," then harmony is restored. The Eye is in its proper and secure place in heaven and the threats to it, here in the form of eye disease and swelling, are left behind on earth. I really have little else by way of suggestion. See the Commentary below.

I. (x + 8: 13) *i3b.t.t*, "left side" (*Wb.* I 30, 14). The left side appears again at Spell K, x + 8: 18, below. On the significance of the right and left sides, see Spell B, note A (x + 1: 21) above.

J. (x + 8: 13) The preposition *n* after *r wḥm*, "again," suggests that the phrase *n nb-ḥw.t*, "…of Nephthys," stands parallel to the phrase *n 3s.t*, "…of Isis."

K. (x + 8: 13) *nbd*, "der Böse, als Bez. des Apophis und des Seth" (*Wb.* II 247, 6–7). The word has been discussed by Kees, *ZÄS* 59 (1924): 69–70, who associates this demon or aspect of Seth with the darkness of night, an idea that seems relevant here. See Klasens, *SocBehague,* p. 32 c.1 and p. 37 c.3, where he offers the translation "demon of the dark;" see also Wilson, *PL,* pp. 508–9 for further references to its connections with Seth. The darkness alluded to here may be linked to or be a metaphor for blindness, also mentioned in this spell.

L. (x + 8: 14) *nhs*, "Bez. des Seth als Tier" (*Wb.* II 287, 14–16). See Goyon, *Kêmi* 19 (1969): 41, who believes the term is a surname of Seth; also Wilson, *PL,* pp. 530–31 for further references to its connections with Seth.

M. (x + 8: 14) The group *iwy* presents difficulties. What is left of the determinative is a vertical stroke that is damaged at the top. The verb governing this noun means to "avert" or "turn away," suggesting a negative idea like "evil" or "malice." A word *iw.yt*, "Böses; Sünde," is given at *Wb.* I 48, 11–13. See Borghouts, *AEMT,* p. 71 (95), where such a word appears in the phrase *iw n nṯr*, which is translated "divine plague." If the damaged vertical sign written that can be seen after *iwy* here is (Sign-list R8), we may be dealing with a similar idea. Another possible reading is , "klagen" (Hannig, *GH,* p. 32a). The translation "The gods have made their weeping turn back…" seems somewhat odd, despite the references to eyes and eye disease in the text.

N. (x + 8: 14) *ꜥn*: either "umwenden" (*Wb.* I 188, 13–189, 7) or "wiederum" (*Wb.* I 189, 8–16). The former meaning is adopted here.

O. (x + 8: 14) After *ii m*, "…come with…," the traces seem to show , a writing that is well-attested for the word *wp.t*, "message; mission" (*Wb.* I 303, 8–304, 5) in the Late Period, for which see M. Vallogia, *Recherches sur les "messagers,"* p. 19. The phrase *ii m wp.t* means "kommen mit einem Auftrag (mit einer Botschaft)" (*Wb.* I 304, 4). For parallels, see *pLeiden I 348,* rt. 3[3]: *ii.n=f m wp.t Rꜥ n Ptḥ*, "He has come with a message of Re for Ptah;" and rt. 10[1]: *ii.n=f m wp.t n.t ḏḥwty r ḏsr-tp*, "He has come with a message of Thoth for Djeser-tep." See also

Goyon, *pProphylaxie,* p. 18, for a discussion of a phrase known from a number of texts: *ii.n=i m iwnw m ipw.ty n spꜣ*, "I have come from Heliopolis as a messenger of Sepa…." In funerary texts, the deceased is at times described as bearing a message from his father or from Re that contains the commands and will of the god and that serves as a diplomatic document to ensure safe passage. See, for example, *PT* 214, 262, 578; see also Assmann, *Death and Salvation,* pp. 144ff. Note that all of the examples cited have a positive context, whereas the present passage appears to require a word whose valence is negative. The related word *wpw.tyw*, "messengers" (*Wb.* I 304, 6–11) is frequently found in lists of dangerous beings, for which see Vallogia, op. cit., pp. 48–63; also Germond, *BSEG* 2 (1979): 23–29. The word *wpw. tyw*, "messengers," however, seems not to be written with the determinative 𓀗. The lacuna precludes an exact reading of the text here, but the text seems to imply that the gods in their role of protection have turned back the one described as *ii m wp.t*, seemingly a being with hostile intent. Note that an alternative translation can be offered, one that does not substantially change the meaning of the text as read: "The gods have made their malice. The one who comes with a message has been turned back."

P. (x + 8: 15) See the discussion in the Commentary, following.

COMMENTARY

Spell J is another text that presents challenges to the establishment of its meaning. The problems stem from its somewhat loose and seemingly convoluted syntax. The spell begins with the description of an apparent confrontation between an unnamed being, simply described as "you," and the Eye of Horus. The conflict here alludes to the mythological struggle between Horus and Seth in which the Eye of Horus was damaged, as the presence of the words *iꜣd.t*, "tormenter," *ẖr*, "enemy," *nbd*, "fiend," and *nhs*, "Seth-animal," strongly suggest. A parallel to the idea of the "raging of a divine Eye" can be found in a Late Period text where the Eye of Re is said to rage (*ẖꜥr*) against the god because he has allowed three other divinities to come into being in her absence. To appease the wrathful Eye, Re places it on his brow, where it becomes the uraeus that exercises power over the entire land.[227] Now, the raging Eye of Re has been shown to be strongly interconnected with the raging Eye of Horus,[228] but in this text the allusion is clearly and only to the Eye of Horus.

The text next mentions the *sšd* diadem, known from early dynastic times as a head-band that seems to have had Libyan origins.[229] More importantly, the noun "*sšd*-fillet"

227 *pBremnerRhind,* 27[3], and Faulkner, *JEA* 23 (1937): 172 and 182, n. 27, 3; see also Junker, *Onurislegende,* p. 158.

228 For a comprehensive discussion of the the two and their interconnections, see Darnell, *SAK* 24 (1997): 35–48.

229 See Bruyère, *FIFAO* 16 (Cairo 1939), p. 176 on its origins and pp. 180–81 for its function as part of a composite crown like the *atef*-crown. See also Goyon, *pConfirmation,* 1[16] and esp. pp. 87–88, n. 34 for an illustration of this object, seemingly used to bind the crowns of

has associations with the Eye of Horus that are found already in the Pyramid Texts.[230] Given that the present spell focuses, at least partially, on the Eye of Horus, a passage in the Edfu temple may have particular relevance. In an address to Horus, the king states *šsp.n=k ir.t=k m sšd*, "You have received your eye, namely the *sšd*-cloth," the latter representing the white crown.[231] The significance here is the connection between the *sšd*-fillet (i.e., white crown) and the word "eye," a focal point of the present text. A link between the *sšd*-fillet and the Eye of Horus occurs in a number of the Underworld Books, where the *sšd*-fillet has associations with regeneration and transfiguration.[232] If the text is restored as suggested above, then the nouns *sšd* and *ḫns.w* would stand in contrasting clauses. If we understand the noun *sšd* here as a metaphor for the Eye of Horus, as the Edfu text indicates, then it is the eye that has lunar associations and that waxes and wanes according to a set pattern. The noun *ḫns.w* and its possible lunar associations could be seen in a negative light. The basic meaning of *ḫns.w*, "swelling," could be used to indicate the waxing phase of the moon, but there is nothing inherent in the word that necessarily implies its corresponding waning cycle. Perhaps the contrast between the two lies in the fact that *sšd*, as the Eye of Horus, is part of the ordered and normally functioning cosmos, whereas *ḫns.w* is part of the disordered, non-functioning realm, as it cannot swell and abate according to a fixed pattern or principle. Thus, it belongs with its proper fellow "eye disease."

Next, Isis and Nephthys are named in a context that remains unclear but has to do with fire. No prescription is given, but the rubric concluding the spell states that it should be "recited over an image of Horus and an image of Seth drawn upon the ear of a man."[233] This instruction offers further evidence that the present text is connected to the myth of the struggle between Horus and Seth, offering another example of allusion to a cosmic conflict, a *topos* that we have seen in a number of the preceding spells. Furthermore, in the present text, the drawing of images on the ear may further equate the ear with the locus of an original cosmic conflict, the outcome of which has already been determined.[234] Although the name of Psamtik and the term Pharaoh are both absent from the text, the focus of the spell on Horus and his protection from Seth likely contains direct allusions to the protection of the king as Horus from his assailants. Moreover, the single reference to the ear at the end of the text offers a logical reason for its inclusion in the present compilation.

Upper and Lower Egypt together. In his discussion of binding, Ritner, *Mechanics*, does not mention the word *sšd*.

230 *PT* 519, for which see Manassa, *The Late Egyptian Underworld* 1, pp. 25–26.

231 *Edfu* I 393^{4}.

232 See Manassa, *The Late Egyptian Underworld* 1, pp. 25–26, 142, 415–16, esp. 142.

233 For parallels to drawing images on the body, see *pLeiden I 348*, rt. 12^{6-7}, where a recipe concludes with: "This spell should be recited over two images of Thoth drawn on the hand of a man." See also ibid., rt. 12^{10}, where a prescription concludes with nineteen images to be drawn on the belly of a man, *ḥr mny im.f*, "on the sore spot on him."

234 For a discussion of such magical images, see Eschweiler, *OBO* 137 (1994), pp. 254–56.

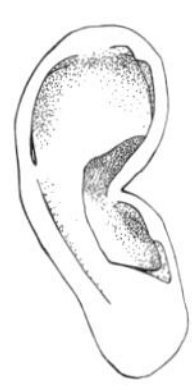

Spell K — Translation with Commentary

COLUMN X + 8: 15–18 (P. BROOKLYN 47.218.49)

TRANSLITERATION

15. *…ky rꜣ ḥr ḥr=k mwt nb mꜥbꜣ.yt rhn iḳr*
16. *m ḏbꜣ.w nbi.t ẖnd rwd n kꜣ ṯꜣ nb mꜥbꜣ.yt nn wṯs=k*
17. *n=i m ḥr nn sbi=k r=i m b wꜥr rhn iḳr ẖdb m mꜥbꜣ.yt ẖr*
18. *=tw ḥr sꜣ.t wbd.ti ḥr iꜣb.t.t ḥr ḥr=k mwt wšr ḏd mdw zp-4*

TRANSLATION

15. …………………………………*Another spell.* Upon your face,[A] dead male. The Lord[B] of the Tribunal,[C] the excellent ram[D]
16. with a harpoon[E] of fire,[F] the binder[G] with the sinew (?)[H] of the bull[I] of the Lord of the Tribunal.[J] You shall not inform against[K]
17. me as Horus. You shall not rebel against me as the Evil One. Flee the excellent ram[L] (or) be killed[M] by a spear.[N]
18. You are fallen[O] upon the ground,[P] branded[Q] upon the left side.[R] Upon your face, dead male. Dry up.[S] *To be recited four times.*[T]

TEXT NOTES

A. (x + 8: 15) The phrase *ḥr ḥr=k*, "Upon your face…," occurs routinely in protection texts as a command to the forces of evil to place themselves in posture of submission. See, for example, Klasens, *SocBehague*, p. 81, n. 4.

B. (x + 8: 15) The writing for the masculine form *nb* is commonly encountered in Late Period texts. The writing may have been influenced by the fact that it stands in apposition to the following noun *rhn* that looks feminine but is not.

C. (x + 8: 15) Establishing a correct understanding of the group presents something of a challenge. The noun *mꜥbꜣ.yt*, "der Gerichtshof der Dreissig" (*Wb.* II 46, 16–17) is used to indicate any board of high authority, in particular a tribunal of the gods. Grieshammer, *ÄA* 20 (1970), pp. 97ff., says that it was originally the name of an Old Kingdom court but used later of tribunals encountered in mythological texts and those dealing with the Netherworld; Gardiner, *pChester Beatty 1,* p. 14, n. 3, claims that it was the traditional grand jury of Egypt; so Caminos, *CLEM,* p. 234, based on *pAnastasi* V, 9[5–6] and 21[5–6]. Sauneron, *Esna* V, pp. 257ff., states that the word refers to the first thirty gods or divine manifestations created by Neith; Parker et al., *The Edifice of Taharqa,* p. 85, supports Sauneron's interpretation and sees the number thirty as referring to the sum of the ten *ba*'s, the ten names, and the ten *ka*'s of Amun, called "the *mꜥbꜣ.yt* of the beginning."

There is another word *mꜥbꜣ.yt* (*Wb.* II 47, 1–3, "Art Speer"), written with the determinatives [hieroglyph], [hieroglyph], or [hieroglyph]. The presence of the determinative [hieroglyph] and the lack of determinatives like [hieroglyph], [hieroglyph], or [hieroglyph], however, speak against a reading of [hieroglyphs] as "Art Speer." Both of the words read *mꜥbꜣ.yt* are found in epithets with the word *nb*, "lord." The first, *nb mꜥbꜣ.yt*, "Lord of the Tribunal of Thirty," is used as an epithet of the god Khnum; see, for example, *pChester Beatty 9,* vs. B. 16[8]; *pLeiden I 346,* 1[3]; *Edfu* I, 52[4] and VI, 56[4]. Given the presence of the word *rhn*, "ram," immediately following, one may be tempted to see in *nb mꜥbꜣ.yt* an epithet of the god Khnum. Cf., however, Behrens, *LÄ* 6 (1986): cols. 1243–45, who states that only the terms *bꜣ* and *šf* are used generally of Khnum and that *rhn* is used solely as a designation of the god Amun. See also note D (x + 8: 15) that follows. The second epithet, *nb mꜥbꜣ.yt*, "Lord of the Harpoon," is found in a number of texts referring to gods in roles of protection. It is a common epithet of Horus of Edfu and of one of the Guardian-gods of Edfu when they are combatants of the enemy of the sun god, for which see Goyon, *Les dieux-gardiens,* pp. 50–52. It is also found on two "healing statues" that date to the 4th century BC: *Turin Suppl. 9 + Florence 8708,* where it occurs as an epithet of Shu, son of Re; and *Turin 3031,* where it is used as an epithet of Onuris; see Kákosy, *Egyptian Healing Statues,* pp. 54 and 64, and 104, respectively. The epithet is also found in Text VII from the Elkab Crypt, for which see Capart, *CdE* 15 (1940), p. 25, and the discussion in the Introduction at pp. 12ff. above. In one of the Edfu texts mentioned above (*Edfu* VI, 56[4]), the god Khnum assists the king in the enforcement of Maat by netting his foes, a passage that may be of relevance, given the apparent reference to a net or trap in this text. As noted above, accepting this writing as "lord of the harpoon" is certainly weakened by the presence of the determinative [hieroglyph] and the lack of the determinative [hieroglyph]. Towards the end of the present text, we encounter a word written [hieroglyphs] that seems to read *mꜥbꜣ.yt* as well. The context there indicates that it is a weapon, in all likelihood; thus, we do seem to have the presence of the word *mꜥbꜣ.yt*, "spear," in this spell. Though the determinatives in the word [hieroglyphs] do seem to indicate the word "Tribunal (of Thirty)," there is a most probably a connection between the two words found in the text. See further at note N (x + 8: 17) below.

D. (x + 8: 15) [hieroglyphs] is a writing of [hieroglyphs] *rhn*, "der heilige Widder des Amun; Widdersphinx" (*Wb.* II 441, 1–3), although the determinative [hieroglyph] (Sign-list F27) is not given there. The writing of *rhn* as it appears here is also found in *pBologna 1094,* 10[11], for which see Gardiner, *LEM,* p. 10., l. 6. *WbMT* does not cite this word, although it is found in both *pHearst* and *pEbers*. The essential discussion of this word is Cabrol, *OLA* 97 (2001), pp. 74–76, 93, 268, 351–52, and 377–417, who offers the meanings "ram" and "ram-sphinx" and demonstrates the close connections that this word has with Amun and his cult in Thebes. Behrens, *LÄ* 6 (1986): cols. 1243–45, also connects *rhn* solely with Amun.

E. (x + 8: 16) *m ḏbꜣ.w* could be the prepositional phrase "als Belohnung für; als Ersatz für" (*Wb.* V 559, 11–14). Note, however, that only the writing with plural strokes is given there. An alternative explanation is to take the group as the verb "verstopfen" (*Wb.* V 558, 9–15) and to understand the preceding sign *m* as the negative imperative marker. The translation would then be "Do not stop fire," a reading not without its own problems. The word *ḏbꜣ.w* seems to have the more abstract derivative meaning "punishment" (*Wb.* V 556, 5–10) here, as fire seems to be used as a means of punishment at the end of the spell. An interesting solution is to see a writing of the word *ḏbꜣ*, meaning "Die Harpune des Horus in Edfu" (*Wb.* V 560, 6). Wilson, *PL*, pp. 1229–30 sees in that word a possible derivative of the word *ḏbꜣ* meaning "punish." The occurrence of words written *mbꜥ.yt* in the present text may be seen to support such a reading.

F. (x + 8: 16) The fire mentioned here is possibly the agent intended to dry up the inimical force, as can be seen in x + 8: 18 below.

G. (x + 8: 16) For *ẖnd*, *Wb.* III 312, 15–314, 18 offers "treten; gehen," but without the determinatives ; Hannig, *GH*, p. 609b, gives the exact writing of the word in the Brooklyn text and the meaning "Flechter;" see also Westendorf, *KoptHWb*, p 559. In *pAnastasi* 2, 2[7], the word *ẖnd* is written . In his translation of that text, Caminos, *CLEM*, p. 42, suggests the meaning "tie up," giving support to the reading adopted here.

H. (x + 8: 16) *rwḏ*, "Bogensehne; Sehne" (*Wb.* II 410, 2–6). On its meaning in the passage, see note I (x + 8: 16), following.

I. (x + 8: 16) *ẖnd m rwḏ n kꜣ ṯꜣi*, possibly "…bind with the sinew of a <male> bull." The closest parallel that I have found is in Schott, *Urk.* VI, 5, an execration ritual performed on an image of Seth. There we encounter *snḥ m rwḏ n iḥ dšr*, "Bind (the image of Seth) with the tendon of a red ox."

J. (x + 8: 16) For the group , see note C (x + 8: 16) above.

K. (x + 8: 16) *wṯs*, "aussprechen; verherrlichen; anzeigen; verraten" (*Wb.* I 384, 1–2; the entry there does not give the signs as possible determinatives.) The determinative (Sign-list D54) is found with a number of words spelled *ṯs* (*Wb.* V 405,1–407, 15). See Wilson, *PL*, p. 272, who also sees the difficulty in trying to make distinctions between the writings *ṯs* and *wṯs*. See, for example, *CT* 349 (B1Bo text): *ntf ṯs ṯw…swt wṯs=f ṯw*, where the two spellings clearly stand for a single verb. Here *wṯs* seems to require a negative meaning as suggested by the parallel phrase *nn sbi=k r=i m b*, "You shall not rebel against me as the Evil One." Thus, a translation like "You shall not denounce/proclaim against me as Horus" seems warranted. The preposition *n* here may be an error for *r*. It is also possible that the determinatives indicate a meaning like "rise up," to be taken in a negative sense like "revolt."

L. (x + 8: 17) For *rhn*, see note D (x + 8: 15) above.

M. (x + 8: 17) *ẖdb*, "töten" (*Wb.* III 403, 3–13). The problem here is whether the verb is a passive participle or an active imperative. Whatever the case may be, it parallels the verb *ḫr* that follows. For the occurrence of these two verbs together, see Wilson, *PL*, pp. 778–79.

N. (x + 8: 17) The writing after the preposition *m* seems to be . *Wb.* II 47, 1–3 gives a writing for the word *mꜥbꜣ.yt*, "Art Speer." Based on that, I am taking as a writing of *mꜥbꜣ.yt*, "spear," as well. This word echoes the phrase *nb mꜥbꜣ.yt* above with obvious and appropriate word play, and there may be connections with the phrase *m ḏbꜣ.w* above as well.

O. (x + 8: 18) *ḫr*, "fallen" (*Wb.* III 319–321, 5). The pronoun =*tw* may indicate a writing of the stative here.

P. (x + 8: 18) The traces suggest *sꜣ.t*, "Erde" (*Wb.* III 423, 7–424, 12).

Q. (x + 8: 18) *wdb*, "brennen" (*Wb.* I 297, 1–6). It is also used of burning food offerings, especially animals, in apotropaic rituals. Thus, it may be the noun "das Brennen; der Brand; die Brandwunde" (*Wb.* I 297, 3; *Wb.* I 297, 7–9). It is unclear which word is intended here; the general sense, nonetheless, seems clear. The noun occurs twice in *pLeiden I 348*, at vs. 3[1–2], as a term for a burn that the child Horus has suffered. In its first occurrence in that text, the burn was caused by the flame of Sakhmet. See also Wilson, *PL*, pp. 220–21, for this word used in Ptolemaic texts to describe the destruction of enemies.

R. (x + 8: 18) *iꜣb.t.t*, "linke Seite" (*Wb.* I 30, 14). It also occurs at x + 8: 13 above.

S. (x + 8: 18) *wšr*, "trocknen, verdorren" (*Wb.* I 374, 10–19). It should be noted that the spell here speaks of fire and branding, perhaps an allusion to the phrase *m ḏbꜣ.w nbi.t* above.

T. (x + 8: 18) For a parallel to *ḏd mdw zp-4*, "to be recited four times," in this papyrus, see x + 5: 12 above.

COMMENTARY

The spell begins and ends with the exhortation "Upon your face, dead male," offering an example of a *kyklos,* a literary device that frames a text and serves to bring its end back to its beginning. At the outset, we encounter two epithets: *nb mꜥbꜣ.yt* and *rhn iḳr*. As discussed above, the epithet *nb mꜥbꜣ.yt* may mean "Lord of the Tribunal" or "Lord of the harpoon," describing any number of divinities who play apotropaic roles. The epithet *rhn iḳr*, "excellent ram," despite its obscurity has clear associations with the god Amun. The noun *rhn*, "ram," appears twice in a Turin magical text, there written with the divine determinative.[235] Its first occurrence may be relevant for our text: *hꜣi iꜥr.t tꜣ ḫft.t rhn sꜣ siw*, "Come down, (oh) cobra, you enemy of the ram, (he) the son of the sheep."[236] In his discussion of this passage in the Turin text,[237] Borghouts notes that the use of the term *rhn* is usually restricted to the god Amun but then argues for a more generalized interpretation of the word in the Turin text, given that the "ram" there is called "the son of the sheep, with the looks of Seth, a master of mysteries, the offspring of Min, the offspring of Geb." He suggests a meaning "recliner," citing its connection with the verb *rhn*, "lean."[238] It is worth noting that in *oNash* 14, a parallel to the Turin text, the word *nḫn*, "child," appears in place of the term *rhn* found in the Turin text; perhaps this substitution is an indication of the difficulty that even an ancient scribe had with the word *rhn*. The word is found again at *pChester Beatty 7,* vs. 1[6], in a simile describing Seth's attack on the goddess Anat: *iw=f ḥr pꜣy mi pꜣy rhn*, "he leaps like a ram leaps." Cf., however, Jonckheere's remark: "En j2 c'est *rhnw*...mais pour lesquels il nous est impossible de suggérer une traduction."[239] Whatever the word's intended meaning, we see that, at least in the Turin text, the *rhn*-ram appears as an enemy of one of the traditional nemeses of the sun god; Borghouts has clearly established in his study that the term *rhn* can refer to a divine protector. The epithet *rhn iḳr*, "the excellent ram," seems unattested. Cabrol, however, does document an epithet *rhn nfr* used of Amun, Amun-Re, and even Ptah.[240] Thus we have further support for understanding *rhn* as a divine force or manifestation, notably associated with Amun, whose task it is to subdue a malevolent being.

Of even greater importance for our purposes is the fact that the noun *rhn* has apparent connections with the ear. On a New Kingdom stela,[241] an image of a ram is accompanied by the inscription *rhn imn-rꜥ sḏm ḥtp* (or *msḏr ḥtp*), "The ram of Amun-Re, the one who listens benevolently" (or "the benevolent ear").[242] The epithet *sḏm/msḏr ḥtp* occurs

---

235 *pTurin 54051, f*or which see Roccati, *AnOr* 56, p. 77, ll. 9 and 11.

236 For the text and translation, see Borghouts, *RdE* 32 (1980): 33–46, esp. 33–34.

237 See n. 236, preceding.

238 *Wb.* II 440, 4–8.

239 *Jonckheere, Le papyrus médical Chester Beatty,* p. 47.

240 Cabrol, *OLA* 97 (2001), pp. 386ff.

241 *Copenhagen AEIN.I.N.1676,* for which see Guglielmi, *HÄB* 37 (2001), pp. 54–68.

242 Guglielmi, *HÄB* 37 (2001), p. 68.

on another stela dedicated to Amun as well, *Avignon A60;* there Amun is shown in the form of a goose.[243]

Thus, the two epithets of our text appear to refer to divinities who are asked to play an apotropaic role. If *nb mꜥbꜣ.yt* refers to the "lord of the Tribunal of Thirty," there may be a possible allusion to the tribunal held after the struggle between Horus and Seth to resolve the inheritance of kingship. If that interpretation is correct, this section of the spell then resonates with sections of the preceding spell, in which allusions to the damage done to the Eye of Horus were encountered. In the present text, Horus is mentioned, as is Seth in his manifestation as *b*, the Evil One. On the other hand, if *nb mꜥbꜣ.yt* means "lord of the harpoon," the reference may be to Onuris, well-known as an apotropaic deity. The occurrence of the writing at the beginning of the text and the writing at the end, both of which can be read *mꜥbꜣ.yt*, suggests a strong connection between the two. The appearance of the latter in the phrase *ẖdb m mꜥbꜣ.yt*, "killed by a spear," seems to indicate an apotropaic function and perhaps indicates a judicial one as well. If the writing indicates the presence of a tribunal with judicial powers, then the phrase *nn wṯs=k n=i*, "You shall not inform against me…," has a more meaningful context. Establishing a clear, overall interpretation and understanding of the text continues to be somewhat elusive because of the number of epithets whose specific references still remain uncertain. What can be said, even in the face of these difficulties, is that the text has all of the marks of a protection text, with its appeal to beings who play an apotropaic role and with its insistent declarations to the malevolent force, here simply named "dead male," that his threats have been reversed. Neither Psamtik nor *pr-ꜥꜣ* is mentioned in the spell, a circumstance that obtained in the preceding spell as well. No prescription is given; the text concludes with a short rubric consisting of the simple instruction to recite the spell four times.

243 Guglielmi, *HÄB* 37 (2001), pp. 54–68.

Spell L — Translation with Commentary

COLUMN X + 8: 18–X + 9: 5 (P. BROOKLYN 47.218.49)

TRANSLITERATION

18. *… ky rꜣ*
19. *n šnỉ hh n … ꜣ.t ỉnḏ ḥr=k rꜥ nb … ḥr smsw*

COLUMN X + 9

1. *m ỉwnw ꜥḫm n s… ẖr=k ḫft nb [ḫft.t] nb.t mwt nb mwt.t nb(.t) ḏꜣy [nb]*
2. *ḏꜣy.t nb(.t) kꜣp nb ỉmn nb sn ỉr.w=f nb nty ỉrr hh m msḏr n pr-ꜥꜣ ꜥ.(w.s.)*
3. *m ỉwf=f m mꜣꜥ=f m ḥꜥ.w=f nb m ꜥ.wt=f nb ỉ.ptn rdỉ sw m ḳd m rs.y*
4. *sḫꜣ sw r bỉn=f m ẖr.t-nṯr ỉn ỉt<=f> psmṯk kꜣ m ỉwnw*
5. *sḫr=f mwt nb mwt.t nb.t ḏꜣy nb ḏꜣy.t nb.t hh nb tꜣwḥ ỉm*

TRANSLATION

18. ……………………………………………………………Another
19. spell *for reciting spells (against)*[A] *the heat of* [*the ear* …2 cm…][B] *time.*[C] Hail to you, Re, Lord of[D] […3 cm…] child,[E] Horus the Elder[F] who is

COLUMN X + 9

1. in Heliopolis, divine manifestation[G] of […2 cm…] you make fall every male enemy, every [female enemy], every dead male, every dead female, [every male adversary]
2. every female adversary, every *kꜣp*-demon,[H] every *imn*-demon[I] who makes every form[J] of his unrecognizable,[K] who makes heat in the ear of Pharaoh, l.p.h.,[L]
3. in his flesh, in his temple, in all his body, in all these limbs of his, who gives it in sleep,[M] in wakefulness.[N]
4. Remind[O] him[P] (?) of[Q] his evil in the necropolis. It is[R] the father of Psamtik,[S] the Bull in Heliopolis,[T]
5. who will cause to fall[U] every dead male, every dead female, every male adversary, every female adversary, (and) every heat that makes a disturbance[V] therein.

TEXT NOTES

A. (x + 8: 19) For [hieroglyphs] *šni*, see note BK (x + 7: 13) above. *Wb.* IV 496, 8 cites its use with the name of a disease following as a direct genitive, as is the case here.

B. (x + 8: 19) Restore, probably, [hieroglyphs] *msḏr*, "ear," at the beginning of the lacuna.

C. (x + 8: 19) Note the use of black ink for the writing of the sign [hieroglyph] (Sign-list N5) and the presence of the divine determinative in the word [hieroglyphs] *ꜣ.t*, "time." The presence of these signs may be due to their use in the writing of the name of the god Re.

D. (x + 8: 19) On the writing of [hieroglyphs] for [hieroglyph], see note B (x + 8: 15) above.

E. (x + 8: 19) [hieroglyph] (Sign-list A17) is the determinative of [hieroglyphs] *ḫrd* or [hieroglyphs] *šri*, both of which mean "child." Alternatively, it could be an ideogram for either of those words.

F. (x + 8: 19) The traces show a writing of [hieroglyph] *smsw*, "elder." The phrase *ḥr smsw* appears as an epithet of the god Haroeris, for which see Kurth, *LÄ* 2 (1977): cols. 999–1003, especially col. 999.

G. (x + 9: 1) [hieroglyphs] *ꜥḫm*, "Götterbild" (*Wb.* I 225, 4, citing it as a variant writing of [hieroglyphs]); also Hannig, *GH*, p. 158b, under *ꜥḫm*; alternatively, Zandee, *Death as an Enemy*, p. 194, sees it as a demoniacal animal.

H. (x + 9: 2) [hieroglyphs] *kꜣp*, "als Bez. eines Krankheitsdämons (neben *imn*)" (*Wb.* V 105, 1, citing *pHearst*, 7^{4-6} [*H* 85]). *BD* 151 refers to a demon whose name is *kꜣp-ḥr*, "Hidden of Face," who also appears in the so-called standard texts of "magical bricks," which are essentially drawn from the text of *BD* 151. See Heerma van Voss, *LÄ* 6 (1986): col. 1402. For Ptolemaic texts in which the term is used of Seth in both crocodile and hippopotamus form, see Wilson, *PL*, p. 1082.

I. (x + 9: 2) For [hieroglyphs] *imn*, "Name des Krankheit bringenden, spukenden Toten" (*Wb.* I 84, 14, again citing *pHearst*, 7^{4-6} [*H* 85]). For a discussion of these demons, see Borghouts, *pLeiden I 348*, p. 68, n. 98; Sauneron, *pOphiologie*, p. 114 who discusses the similarly written word [hieroglyphs] *imn.w* as it occurs in that text and assigns the meaning "dard," claiming to see a parallel in the present passage. Note that he makes the assertion "Le mot *imnw* n'est pas jusqu'ici connu…."

J. (x + 9: 2) [hieroglyphs] *ir.w*, "form," has the additional determinative [hieroglyph] (Sign-list Z6) to emphasize that the manifestations of this malign force are inherently dangerous.

K. (x + 9: 2) *sn*, "seine Gestalt unkenntlich machen" (*Wb.* III 457, 12–13, esp. 457, 13 for the use of this verb in connection with the noun *ir.w*, "form").

L. (x + 9: 2) The two hieratic strokes that follow the writing of *pr-ꜣʿ*, "pharaoh," are a common abbreviation for *ʿ.w.s*, "life, prosperity and health," in Late Period texts. See Möller, *HP* 3, p. 67, n. 2.

M. (x + 9: 3) *ḳdd*, "der Schlaf" (*Wb.* V 79, 7–8).

N. (x + 9: 3) seems to be a writing of the word *rs* found at *Wb.* II 451, 2–12, which essentially means "wakefulness; vigilance;" both meanings fit the present context. It may be a writing of "der Traum" (*Wb.* II 452, 1–4), the presence of *tp* a scribal error originating from the writing of the words *rs* that have that sign. For the dangers associated with dreams, see Szpakowska, in Kousoulis, *OLA* 175, pp. 63–76. Here it seems that what is needed is not a link between the two ideas of sleep and dream, but rather an emphasis on the antithesis between sleep and wakefulness. Such a contrast would emphasize that the threats of the malevolent beings were constant, not just nocturnal occurrences. See, for example, Koenig, *pDeM*, 40, 1, where inimical forces are described as "those who come at night, in the day, at any time;" a further parallel can be found at x + 12: 8 below.

O. (x + 9: 4) *sḫꜣ*, "sich erinnern; gedenken" (*Wb.* IV 232, 12–233, 26). The context suggests that it is to be taken as an imperative.

P. (x + 9: 4) The dependent pronoun *sw*, "him," seems to refer to one of the malevolent beings.

Q. (x + 9: 4) The hieratic sign appears to be although the damage to the papyrus makes certainty difficult. Elsewhere in this text, the sign is simply written as a straight horizontal line with no flourishes.

R. (x + 9: 4) The particle *in* introduces the noun *it=f*, an emphatic subject of the verb *sḫrw=f* which follows at the beginning of x + 9: 5. See Vernus, *YES* 3 (1989), pp. 55–60.

S. (x + 9: 4) The writing *in it=f psmṯk kꜣ m iwnw* presents problems. As written, the relationship between the word *it=f* and the name Psamtik appears to be one of apposition. Such a reading would make Psamtik both the one threatened and his own savior, a puzzling but possible interpretation. It may be that is an error for . The name Psamtik would then be a direct genitive: "It is the father of Psamtik, the Bull in Heliopolis…." See note T (x + 9: 4), immediately following.

T. (x + 9: 4) The epithet *kꜣ ỉwnw*, “Bull in Heliopolis,” has several different functions in texts from the Old Kingdom to the Ptolemaic Period. Originally, it seems to have referred to the so-called “fetish” of Heliopolis, a pillar with the head of a bull, seemingly a symbol of the creator god as worshipped there, usually understood to be Atum. It is found as an epithet of Re in the Pyramid Texts. All of this simply reinforces the idea that Re is the father of Horus, i.e., the king. The apparently related epithet *kꜣ wr*, also having Heliopolitan connections, referred to Re, and Atum-Re-Horakhty as well, in his visible manifestation as the Mnevis-bull; see Goyon, *pConfirmation,* p. 92, n. 83, and *Les dieux-gardiens,* p. 430; Zivie, *BdE* 81 (1979): 487 and 489ff.; see further the discussion by Zandee, *pAmunhymnus* 2, pp. 419–23. Note that the god Re is invoked at the beginning of the spell as well. Such an interpretation may further argue for the emendation suggested at note S (x + 9: 4) above.

U. (x + 9: 5) See Vernus, *YES* 3 (1989), pp. 55–60.

V. (x + 9: 5) *tꜣwḥ* (*Wb.* V 233, 8, meaning undetermined). Hannig, *GH,* p. 916a, gives “stören.” Faulkner, *CD,* p. 294, citing Merikare 2, 8 offers the meaning “make mischief;” Quack, *Studien Merikare,* p. 21, gives the translation “Aufrührer,” but see his qualifying note at p. 21, n. b.

COMMENTARY

This spell begins with an appeal to divinities associated with Heliopolis to throw down[244] the numerous malevolent forces that “make heat in the ear of the Pharaoh.” Heliopolis played a major role in certain Egyptian creation myths as the place of the primeval hill of sand on which the creator god took his first stand; it was also the location of the *benben,* the pillar on which the *benu*-bird, symbol of the reborn sun, perched.[245] After an initial address to Re, Haroeris is invoked to cause the undoing of the inimical forces. Haroeris is a figure routinely encountered in protection texts.[246] Here his name occurs with the epithet *ỉm.y ỉwnw*, “the one who is in Heliopolis,” for which see a New Kingdom group statue in Berlin: *ḥtp di nsw ḥr wr nṯr ꜥꜣ ỉm.y ỉwnw*…, “An offering which the King gives (and) Haroeris, great god who is in Heliopolis….”[247] In Heliopolitan myths, Haroeris appears both as a brother of Osiris and as Osiris himself in his form of murdered victim of Seth.[248] Following the invocation of Haroeris comes a listing of the hostile forces from

244 *sḫr=k*, “You will make fall…”: x + 9: 1 and 5.

245 Zivie, *BdE* 81 (1979): 477–98.

246 See, for example, Borghouts, *pLeiden I 348,* rt. 11^{6}; Jelinkova-Reymond, *Djed-Hor,* p. 33; *Edfu* VI, 148^{9}, the text known as “Schutz des Hauses.” For a discussion of this god and his confusion with the younger Horus, son of Isis, see Anthes, *StudAeg* 9 (1983): 120–21.

247 Berlin 4422, for which see *ÄIB* 2, p. 50.

248 Meltzer, *Oxford Encyclopedia of Ancient Egypt* 2, p. 120.

whom Psamtik needs protection. The list given here, however, has been expanded from those previously encountered to include two new nemeses: the *kꜣp*-demon and the *imn*-demon. Both are known from a single passage in the medical text *pHearst.*[249] Note that the phrase *hh n msḏr*, "the heat in (or of) the ear," is also named as one of the adversarial forces.[250] The spell concludes with a reference to the Bull of Heliopolis. In certain texts, he is found as the manifestation of a solar god in his aspect of creator.[251]

The Heliopolitan references that frame this text thus associate it with an important solar myth focused on the act of creation. A passage in another Brooklyn papyrus, although damaged, may be significant here.

> *ii.n=pr-ꜥꜣ ꜥ.w.s. min m iwnw snty.n=f tꜣ pr.n=f im=f ḫpr.n=f m pꜣt=f ḫpr=f*
> *rḫ.n=ʾItm nty pr-ꜥꜣ ꜥ.w.s. mꜣꜣ st=f irr mḫr.w=f*
> *rdi mꜣꜥ.t m st=s … ḥr hnꜥ stḫ rdi sn.wy…sn im.y iwnw nst=sn…*

> "Pharaoh, l.p.h., has come today from Heliopolis. He has established [the ground plan of] the land from which he has emerged. He has come into being in his primeval time of his coming into being. Atum has understood that Pharaoh, l.p.h., sees his place and makes his rule [in it], establishing Maat in [her] place…Horus together with Seth, the Two Brothers place their […] which is in Heliopolis…their seats…."[252]

This association of Pharaoh with Heliopolis occurs in a rite dealing with the (re)confirmation of royal power at the time of the New Year. Thus, there appears to be a possible point of connection between the Bull of Heliopolis, a manifestation of Atum-Re-Harakhty as demiurge, and Pharaoh as creator, at least as outlined in *pConfirmation.* The mention of Horus and Seth in connection with Heliopolis resonates with the mythic allusions to Haroeris that occur at the beginning of the spell, but also alludes to the myth cycle of the contention between Horus and Seth as well.[253] Therefore, the text brings into play two fundamental Egyptian myths, one focusing on creation and the solar cycle, the other on the myth of the contending of Horus and Seth.

In addition, the name of Heliopolis is often written as [hieroglyphs] in Late Period hieratic texts.[254] The presence of the sign [hieroglyph] in this writing certainly suggests, at least on the visual

249 See notes H and I (x + 9: 2).

250 See x + 9: 5.

251 Zivie, *BdE* 81 (1979): 491. In the texts cited in this reference, the bull referred to is called *kꜣ sty*, "the bull that spills [his seed]," interpreted as a reference to the demiurge Atum-Re-Horakhty.

252 *pBrooklyn 47.218.50* (*pConfirmation*), 2^{19-20}; see also Goyon, *Confirmation,* p. 59 and pp. 91–92, nn. 77–80.

253 It is worth noting that the restorations that Goyon has suggested for the lacuna show that he interprets the Heliopolitan allusions in the text as connected with cosmic conflict and disorder. See *Confirmation,* p. 92, n. (80) esp.

254 Note, however, that it is consistently written [hieroglyphs] in both *pBrooklyn 47.218.49* and *pBrooklyn 47.218.84* (*Mythes et légendes*)

level, a connection between Heliopolis and the ear.[255] Meeks has discussed the important connections between hearing and Heliopolis in the Late Period, particularly as the place *par excellence* where one "understands or hears something," "hearing" understood in the legal sense of the word. Already in the Old Kingdom, Heliopolis was understood to be the meeting place of the tribunal that adjudicated the suits between Horus and Seth and between Osiris and his adversaries.[256] Heliopolis was, thus, the place where cases were "heard," again in the legal sense.[257] In *Mythes et légendes,* we encounter a goddess associated with Heliopolis whose name was *sḏm.t-nb.t*, "she who hears everything."[258] In that text, Heliopolis was also stated to be the location of the resting place of four relics: the eyes of Horus, the thumb of Atum, the hand of Haroeris, and the ear of Horakhty,[259] the latter god seen as the incarnation of the sun in its course of eternal renewal.[260] The relic of the ear of Horakhty is not known from elsewhere,[261] but its connection with Heliopolis offers an important key for the interpretation of our spell. The efficacious power of the present spell to protect the ear seems to stem from its references to deities and locations that have implied associations with the ear. Thus, its power is not stated explicitly but implicitly and suggestively, and subtly so. We have already seen that the same situation obtained in the preceding text.

255 See Sauneron, *RdE* 8 (1962): 191–94 for a discussion of the hieratic writing of the name of the city of Heliopolis and its correct reading, delineating the difference between the hieratic writings of the signs [illegible] and [illegible].

256 Note that the *mꜥbꜣ.yt*-tribunal played such a role in the preceding spell.

257 Meeks, *Mythes et légendes,* pp. 185ff.

258 ibid., esp. pp. 186–87.

259 *pBrooklyn 47.218.84,* x + 3^4.

260 Meeks, *Mythes et légendes,* p. 188. Meeks notes that the writing of *msḏr* when referring to the relic employs the hieratic sign for the human ear, not the bovine sign used in the writing of Heliopolis.

261 ibid., p. 188: "L'oreille de Horakhty n'est pas autrement connue également."

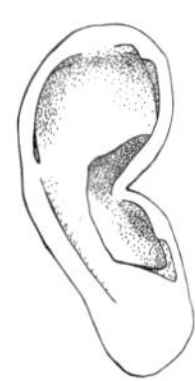

Spell M — Translation with Commentary

COLUMN X + 9: 5–7 (P. BROOKLYN 47.218.49)

TRANSLITERATION

5. *...ky*
6. *r3 šp=k mwt mwt.t d3y d3y.t ii m kkw r ir.t hh m msdr n*
7. *pr-ʿ3 hr wbn rʿ m pt hr ḥtp wsir [m] hr.t-ntr*

TRANSLATION

5. .... *Another*
6. *spell.* Flow out,[A] dead male, dead female, male adversary, female adversary, you who come in the darkness[B] to make heat in the ear of
7. Pharaoh. Then Re will rise in heaven (and) then Osiris will set[C] in the necropolis.

TEXT NOTES

A. (x + 9: 6) *šp*, "ausfließen" (*Wb.* IV 443, 14–444, 7). The word occurs commonly in spells dealing with scorpion bites where either the poison, the scorpion itself, or both are ordered to leave the body of the one bitten and to fall upon the ground. See *MuK* 1^{9}; *pChester Beatty 7*, rt. 1^{4} and p. 56, n. 2; and *pLeiden I 348*, rt. 3^{2}, where it occurs in an address to a *mw.t št3.w*, "a hidden vessel," in the head which is causing a headache. It also appears in *pChester Beatty 9*, vs. B. I^{2} in an address to *hft*, "enemy," a usage that conforms closely to that in the present text.

B. (x +9: 7) For the epithet *ii m kkw*, "who comes in the darkness," referring to a malign being, see *MuK* 1^{9}, where a malevolent demon is so described. It should be noted that the address to the evil being there also begins with the phrase *šp=k*, "Flow out...." The intent of the demon described in that text is to harm or take away the child whom the magical spells are to protect.

C. (x + 9: 7) The non-enclitic particle *hr* introduces two verbal clauses indicating result here; see Vernus, *YES* 3 (1989), pp. 61–84, esp. pp. 71–77.

COMMENTARY

This short spell is reminiscent of apotropaic texts normally addressed to scorpions and their poison. What is emphasized here is that the harmony of the body of the one threatened corresponds to cosmic order. The normal cycle of Re rising and Osiris setting will take place only after the disease demon has "flowed out." The idea that Re and Osiris are complementary manifestations of the rising and setting sun seems to have been fully developed by Dynasty 21; see Niwinski, *JEOL* 30 (1987–88), pp. 89–106, who traces the development of the unification of these two eschatological concepts; see also Darnell, *Enigmatic Netherworld Books*, passim, who discusses their development during the New Kingdom. The term *pr-ʿꜣ* occurs once. As in the preceding two spells, no prescription or instructions are given.

Spell N — Translation with Commentary

COLUMNS X + 9: 7–X + 12: 16 (P. BROOKLYN 47.218.49)

TRANSLITERATION

7. … *ky.t-ẖt rꜣ.w nw kꜣp*
8. *msḏr dr hh rwi mwt mwt.t m msḏr i rꜥ i itm i ḫpri i šw*
9. *i tfnw.t i gb i nw.t i wsir i ḥr i stẖ i ꜣs.t i nb.t-ḥw.t i ḥw*
10. *i siꜣ i wp-wꜣ.wt i inpw i isds i mnmn=f pt i mnmn*
11. *=f tꜣ i iri i sḏm i ḏḥwty i nṯr.w rsy.t i nṯr.w mḥ.t i nṯr.w*
12. *imn.t.t i nṯr.w iꜣb.t.t i psḏ.t ꜥꜣ.t im.y pt i psḏ.t ꜥꜣ.t im.y tꜣ i*
13. *psḏ.t ꜥꜣ.t im.y.w ẖr.t-nṯr i pꜣ-4 bik.w ꜥꜣ.w nty ḥms*
14. *m ḥꜣ.t wiꜣ n rꜥ ḫft wbn=f m ꜣḫ.t iꜣb.t.t n.t pt ḫft ḥtp=f m ꜣḫ.t imn.t.t n.t pt*
15. *i tꜣ-4.t iꜥr.wt ꜥꜣ.w(t) nty m ꜥḥꜥ n wiꜣ n rꜥ i pꜣ miw ꜥꜣ*
16. *nty rs r mskt.t n rꜥ ḫft wbn=f m ꜣḫ.t iꜣb.t.t n.t pt i nṯr.w i.pw nb.w*
17. *ḥr ꜥšꜣ iꜥr.wt i tꜣ-4.t wḏꜣ(w.t) ꜥꜣ.w(t) nty hms ḫft ḥr n nb=sn*
18. *i… w nb ḥḥ nꜣ ir … ḏt i …i ḏsr.w štꜣ.w ḥr*

COLUMN X + 10

1. *i ḥḥ n nṯr.w nn rḫ [rn=s]n m pt tꜣ dwꜣ.t i nn n nṯr.w nṯr.wt nb.w i d-*
2. *-m.tw rn=sn mi dr=tn mwt mwt.t hh m msḏr n psmṯk ꜥ.(w.s.) nn irr=f*
3. *šꜥd=f im=f nn ḫꜣꜥ=f ꜣtp=f r=f nn mhi=f ib=f nn ir=f dḥr.t*
4. *ḥꜣ.ty=f nn ir=f wšꜥ m ḥꜥ.w=f nn irr ḥnḥn m šm=f nn ir=f ftft m ḥꜥ.w=*
5. *=f nn wnm=f m iwf=f nn nḥm=f rꜣ=f nn iṯi=f mdw.wt=f nn šp=f ir.ty=fy nn idn=f ꜥnḫ.wy=*
6. *=fy ḥꜣ=k ḫft pft mwt mwt.t ḥm.wt-rꜣ irr hh m msḏr n psmṯk iw=k pr.tw iw s-*
7. *-šm=k n=i sšm.yw n nṯr.w ꜥꜣ.w di=k rḫ=sn ḥr nb.w m-ꜥ nb šfꜥꜣ*
8. *pḥ.ty ꜥšꜣ rn.w wsr.w ꜥḥꜥ.w nb ḫpr.w štꜣ.w m st imn*
9. *iw wṯs.n=k mꜣꜣ=k nb nn ḥꜣp.w im=f ḫft mꜣꜣ=k is r=k šp ir.ty=k ḥr nn mꜣꜣ=k iw w-*
10. *-ṯs=k r tꜣ im mꜣꜣ=k nṯr.w sšm=k pt hꜣ=k {tꜣ} r dwꜣ.t rḫ=k im.y=s ḏd=k*
11. *sšm n wsir wnn-nfr m ẖr.t-nṯr nn rḫ.tw sḥwr tw nṯr.w im.y wr.t ḫpr*
12. *m sp tpy i ḫft pft mwt mwt.t ḏꜣy ḏꜣy.t ḥm.wt-rꜣ pꜣ hh tꜣ hh.t*
13. *nty m msḏr n psmṯk ꜥ.(w.s.) in iw bn sḫꜣ.n=k pꜣ ḏd i.ir=k mꜣꜣ mn m st š-*
14. *-tꜣ mi pt rsy.t iw ḥr=f m bꜣ ir.ty=fy m nsr.t iw ꜥ.wy=fy m miw rꜣ=f m*
15. *tꜣw i ḫft pft mwt mwt.t ḏꜣ ḏꜣ.t ḥm.wt-rꜣ nty m msḏr n pr-ꜥꜣ iw ḏd=k mꜣꜣ=i sšm m*

16. *ꜣḫ.t iꜣb.t.t n.t ḥr.t iw ḏd=k kfꜣ=i ꜥfn.yt špss mꜣꜣ=i tp n ḥw.t-ḥr.t*
17. *m sšm štꜣ imn i ḫft pft mwt mwt.t ḏꜣ ḏꜣ.t ḥm.wt-rꜣ nty irr hh m msḏr*
18. *[n] pr-ꜥꜣ ꜥ.w.s. iw ḏd=k ii.n=i m rꜣ-stꜣ.w pw ḥr sšm wꜣ.wt … ii m grḥ*
19. *… ii inpw m ḏdw sdwḫ.n=[f] wsir m wꜥb[.t] twy … .f is*

COLUMN X + 11

1. *wsir ꜣs.t sḏr ḥr ḫ.t=sn ḥr swḏꜣ n wnn-nfr ḫr ir=k m-ḏr ḏd=k sw i ḫft [p]ft*
2. *mwt mwt.t nty irr mḥr tn m msḏr n psmṯk iw ḏd=k mꜣꜣ=i ir.wt r wsir in …*
3. *is ir.t nb.t gmḥ sn šp ḥr-ꜥ mi ḏd=k štꜣ.w m iṯi šw m-ꜥ=k [ḥꜥp]i*
4. *ꜥḳ m ḫr.t-nṯr nḏri.n=f ḫt im.y=s i ḫft pft mwt mwt.t nty m tp ꜥnḫ.wy n pr-ꜥꜣ*
5. *iw ꜥḥꜣ=k r rḫ.wy sn.wy in gb ir.y-pꜥ.t nṯr.w r rꜣ mꜣꜥ.t iw ḏd=k nm-*
6. *–ꜥ ḫft n rꜥ m sḫm nṯr.w nb.w im.y.w kꜣri=sn is psḏ.t šn*
7. *ḥr ḥr=sn mi ḏd=k r pꜣ-4 nṯr.w hꜣi m pt iw ḥr=sn m bik ꜥ.wy*
8. *=sn m mꜣi mdw.w=sn šm=sn ḫnm.w sꜥḳ=sn r imi m sḫm*
9. *dr mwt mwt.t hh m mꜣꜥ n psmṯk i ḫft pft mwt mwt.t ḥm.wt-rꜣ [nty] m msḏr*
10. *n pr-ꜥꜣ iw ḏd=k sšm m ḫr-ꜥḥꜣ nṯr.w m-ḫt=sn wṯs=k sšm r rw.ty*
11. *im.y.w-ḫt nṯr ꜥꜣ ꜥnḫ=st sḏr iw nṯr.w šm=sn ḥr tp=sn*
12. *m ḫr ꜣḫ=sn nn wnm=sn nn siw=sn ḥr ꜥnḫ=sn m mꜣꜥ.t iw nṯr.w nty im=*
13. *=s sḏr=sn m šnw sḏ.t inḥ m išrw nn mꜣꜣ sn ir.t nb.t ir nty ḥr*
14. *mꜣꜣ=w šp=f ḥr-ꜥ wn im miw mḥ-7 ꜥnḫ=f m tp=f hw nn tkn=f in ir.t nb.t wp-*
15. *-ḥr=f ḏs=f mk psḏ.t ḫr-ꜥḥꜣ dr=sn mwt mwt.t ḏꜣy ḏꜣy.t ḥm.wt-rꜣ nty*
16. *irr hh m msḏr n psmṯk i ḫft pft mwt mwt.t ḏꜣ ḏꜣ.t nty irr hh m tp*
17. *m mꜣꜥ m msḏr n pr-ꜥꜣ m-ḏr ḏd=k ii.n=i m sḫm mꜣꜣ.n=i ḏꜣḏꜣ nṯr.w ḥms ḥr*
18. *bḥd n b[iꜣ] … ꜥ.wy=sn ḥr sꜣṯ.w iw … .w m rn=sn r dd rn=f m ḥm=f*
19. *pḫ=f … ꜣt i ḫft pfy mwt [mwt.t ḏ]ꜣ ḏꜣ.t irr hh [m tp m mꜣꜥ] m ꜥnḫ.-*

COLUMN X + 12

1. *–.wy n psmṯk ꜥ.w.s. rḫ=k ḏd=k pr iwnw nfr nb rnp nfr rꜥ nb*
2. *ir rmṯ nṯr.w m ḥꜥ.w=fy rwi kkw m-ḫt ḫpr=f nty nb r-ḏr nsw nṯr.w ḥḳ-*
3. *–ꜣ ꜥꜣ rn=f i ḫpri rꜥ dr=k mwt mwt.t ḏꜣ ḏꜣ.ṯ pꜣ hh tꜣ hh.t nty m tp n*
4. *pr-ꜥꜣ i ḫft pft mwt mwt.t dꜣ dꜣ.t nty m tp m mꜣꜥ m msdr n pr-ꜥꜣ m-ḏr ḏd=k mꜣꜣ=i sšm*
5. *n kꜣri štꜣ m pt wꜣ r ḫ-n-r-m ḥr tꜣ iw=f ꜣmm dwꜣ.t štꜣ.w*
6. *ḏw ir=k mwt mwt.t ḥm.wt-rꜣ irr hh m msḏr n pr-ꜥꜣ nn ḏw is r psmṯk i ḫft pft*
7. *mwt mwt.t ḏꜣ ḏꜣ.t ḥm.wt-rꜣ pꜣ hh tꜣ hh.t pꜣ nk sn m rꜥ pꜣ sd ks-*
8. *–ks r ꜥnḫ.wy n psmṯk nty ii r hꜣi r-r=f m grḥ m rꜥ m nw nb dr.tw*
9. *rwi.tw ḫr.tw sḫri.tw nn wꜣḥ=k m tp m mꜣꜥ m ꜥnḫ.wy n pr-ꜥꜣ iw nꜣ nṯr.w nb.w*
10. *r di.t wꜣ=k r pr-ꜥꜣ mi wꜣ ns n msḥ r=f m ꜣw ḏ.t sp-sn ḏd mdw ḫft rꜥ*
11. *wbn=f m ꜣḫ.t=f ḥnꜥ sš nn n nṯr.w nb.w ḥr mḥ.t n mꜣw.t iw tit ḥr in gs m bit iꜥ*
12. *… m ḥnḳ.t nḏm.t swri in s nty ḫr mḥr m tp nty ḫr hh m ꜥnḫ.wy ḥnꜥ sš=f ḥr stp p-*
13. *–ꜣḳ iw nṯr m sšm=f gs m tp.t ꜥn.tyw rdi wḏꜣ.t r ḫḫ n s ir*
14. *snb=f gs=f m bit ḫꜣꜥ r mw ir tm=f snb gs wḏꜣ.wt mrḥ.t gs msḏr is*
15. *tm m ꜥf.wt ṯḫb m ibr rꜥ nb ḥnꜥ sḏm=fy m ṯꜣw.t n ꜥf.wt ṯḫb*
16. *bit mi.t.t*

TRANSLATION

7. ....*Other spells for fumigating*[A]
8. *the ear,*[B] *driving away heat, turning back a dead male, a dead female from the ear.* O Re![C] O Atum! O Khepri![D] O Shu!
9. O Tefnut! O Geb ! O Nut ! O Osiris! O Horus![E] O Seth! O Isis! O Nephthys![F] O Hu!
10. O Sia![G] O Wepwawet! O Anubis! O Isdes![H] O he who shakes the heaven![I] O he who shakes
11. the earth![J] O god who sees! O god who hears![K] O Thoth![L] O Gods of the South! O Gods of the North! O Gods
12. of the West! O Gods of the East![M] O Great Ennead which is in heaven! O Great Ennead which is on earth! O
13. Great Ennead which is in the necropolis![N] O Four Great Falcons[O] who sit
14. in the prow of the barque of Re[P] when he rises in the eastern horizon of heaven, when he sets in the western horizon of heaven!
15. O Four Great Uraei[Q] who are in the entourage[R] of the barque of Re! O Great Cat[S]
16. who guards over the *mskt.t*-barque of Re when he rises in the eastern horizon of heaven![T] O all these gods
17. (of) numerous faces (and) uraei![U] O Four Great protectors who sit in the presence of their Lord![V]
18. O [...3 cm...] all ... eternity, those who do[W] [...1.5 cm...] eternity.[X] O [...3 cm...] O sacred ones whose faces are secret.[Y]

COLUMN X + 10

1. O millions of gods [whose names][Z] are not known in heaven, (on) earth, (or in) the Duat![AA] O all these gods (and) goddesses! O
2. (you) whose names are pronounced![BB] Come! May you drive away a dead male, dead female, heat from the ear of Psamtik l.(p.h.). He[CC] shall not make
3. his slaughter in him.[DD] He shall not hurl his load[EE] against him. He shall not make his heart forgetful.[FF] He shall not make
4. his heart bitter.[GG] He shall not make a gnawing[HH] in his body, not make a holding back when he goes forth.[II] He shall not make a trembling[JJ] in his body.
5. He shall not eat from his flesh.[KK] He shall not take away his mouth.[LL] He shall not seize his words.[MM] He shall not blind his eyes.[NN] He shall not make deaf his ears.[OO]
6. Get back you, enemy, fiend, dead male, dead female and so on who make heat in the ear of Psamtik. You are come forth.[PP]
7. You lead the manifestations[QQ] of the great gods to me, so that you may let everyone[RR] and everything[SS] know them, (their) great majesty,[TT] whose
8. numerous powers,[UU] powerful names (in)[VV] all periods of time, whose forms are secret in the hidden place.[WW]

9. You have arisen.[XX] You see everything (and) there is nothing concealed in it. When you look,[YY] indeed, your eyes are blinded because of[ZZ] these things (that) you see.[AB]
10. You rise (up) to the land therein.[AC] You see the gods. You guide heaven.[AD] You descend {earth[AE]} to the Duat (so that) you may know what is in it, (so that) you may speak of an image[AF] of
11. Osiris Wennefer in the necropolis which is not known.[AG] The gods who are in the West[AH] who came into being
12. on the First Occasion[AI] curse you.[AJ] O enemy, fiend, dead male, dead female, male adversary, female adversary and so on, male heat, female heat
13. who are in the ear of Psamtik, l.(p.h.). Do you not remember[AK] the statement that you made:[AL] "See[AM] (god) so and so[AN] in the secret place[AO]
14. like the southern heaven,[AP] his face that of a *ba,* his eyes of fire,[AQ] his arms those of a cat,[AR] his mouth of
15. fire."[AS] O enemy, fiend, dead male, dead female, male adversary, female adversary and so on who are in the ear of Pharaoh. You say:[AT] "I see the image[AU] in
16. the eastern horizon of heaven." You say: "I uncover its noble *ʿfn.t*-cloth.[AV] I see the head of Hathor,[AW]
17. namely[AX] a secret (and) concealed image." O enemy, fiend, dead male, dead female, male adversary, female adversary and so on, who make heat in the ear
18. of Pharaoh, l.p.h. You say: "It means I have come from Rosetau while following the paths[AY] [...3 cm... coming on the] night[AZ] (when)[BA]
19. Anubis [came][BC] from Busiris. He embalmed[BD] Osiris[BE] in this Place of Purification[BF] [...1 cm...] He [...3 cm...]. Indeed,

COLUMN X + 11

1. Osiris (and) Isis[BG] sleeping upon their bellies,[BH] while protecting Wennefer." Fall, indeed,[BI] afterthe moment[BJ] you say it.[BK] O enemy, fiend
2. dead male, dead female who make this illness[BL] in the ear of Psamtik. You say:[BM] "I see what has been done[BN] to Osiris[BO] by [...]"[BP]
3. Indeed, every eye which sees them[BQ] is blind immediately. Likewise,[BR] you tell[BS] the secrets (?)[BT] when the sunlight[BU] is taken from you[BV] and [Hapi][BW]
4. enters from the necropolis.[BX] He has plundered[BY] the things that are in it.[BZ] O enemy, fiend, dead male, dead female who are in the head, (in) the ears of [Pharaoh],[CA]
5. you are fighting against the Two Companions, the Two Brothers. Is[CB] Geb, the prince of the gods,[CD] against the utterance[CE] of Maat? You say[CF] (that)
6. the enemy of Re is sleeping[CG] in Letopolis.[CH] All the gods are in their shrines. Lo, the Ennead is in fear (?),[CI]
7. upon their faces. Likewise,[CJ] you speak about[CK] the four gods who descend from heaven,[CL] their faces (those) of a falcon, their arms
8. (those) of a lion.[CM] They speak (and) they go forth united.[CN] They enter into the tent[CO] in Letopolis
9. driving away the dead male, dead female, heat from the temple of Psamtik. O enemy, fiend, dead male, dead female and so on who are in the ear

10. of Pharaoh. You speak of the image(s) in Kheraha [CP] (and) (?) the gods [CQ] who are in their following. You carry [CR] the images to the outside [CS]
11. who are in the following of the Great God. They are alive,[CT] (but) sleeping,[CU] while the gods proceed,[CV] their chiefs [CW]
12. in possession of their powers.[CX] They do not eat, they do not drink because they live on Maat.[CY] The gods who are in
13. it,[CZ] they sleep in the ring of fire,[DA] surrounded [DB] by a Sacred Lake.[DC] No eye shall see them.[DE] If (there is) one whom [DF]
14. they see,[DG] he is blinded immediately. There exists there a cat [DH] of seven cubits;[DI] he lives with [...] its head.[DJ] (As for) the *hiw*-serpent,[DK] it shall not [DL] be approached by anyone except [DM]
15. him himself.[DN] Behold the Ennead of Kheraha.[DO] They drive away the dead male, dead female, male adversary, female adversary and so on who
16. make heat in the ear of Psamtik. O enemy, fiend, dead male, dead female who make heat in the head,
17. in the temple, in the ear of Pharaoh since you say: "I have come from Letopolis. I have seen the Divine Tribunal [DP] sitting upon
18. the thrones of metal [DQ] [...2 cm...] their arms upon the ground."[DR] [...1.5 cm...] in their names to say his name [...] when he does not know (it)[DS]
19. cut through [DT] [...2.5 cm...] moment. O enemy, fiend, dead male, [dead female, male][DU] adversary, female adversary who make heat [in the head, in the temple] in the ears [DV]

COLUMN X + 12

1. of Psamtik, l.p.h. You know and you say that beautiful Iunu [DW] comes forth, lord of renewing beauty every day,
2. who made men (and) the gods from his body, who turns away the darkness after he comes into being, who is lord of all, king of the gods,
3. great ruler is his name.[DX] O Khepri, Re, may you drive away the dead male, dead female, male adversary, female adversary, the male heat, the female heat who are in the head of
4. Pharaoh. O enemy, fiend, dead male, dead female, male adversary, female adversary who are in the head, in the temple, in the ear of Pharaoh after the moment you say, "I see the image
5. of the secret shrine [DY] in heaven it being far from [DZ] *ḫ-n-r-m* (?)[EA] upon earth. He grabs hold of[EB] the secret Duat."[EC]
6. Evil against you,[ED] dead male, dead female, and so on who make heat in the ear of Pharaoh – indeed, there is no evil against Psamtik. O enemy, fiend,
7. dead male, dead female, male adversary, female adversary and so on, male heat, female heat, the rapist who transgresses by day [EF], the "tail" [EG] that dances [EH]
8. against the ears of Psamtik, who comes to descend against him [EI] by night, by day (and) at any time. You are turned away,
9. you are repelled, you are fallen, you are driven off. You will not endure in the head, in the temple, in the ears of Pharaoh. All of the gods

10. [will cause][EJ] you to be far from Pharaoh like the tongue of the crocodile is far from him,[EK] for the length of eternity and of eternity. *To be recited* when Re
11. rises in his horizon and draw all of these gods upon a new *mḥt*-bowl,[EL] an image in color[EM] smeared with honey. Wash[EN]
12. [...][EO] with sweet beer (to be) drunk by a man who is suffering illness in his head, who is suffering heat in his ears, and he draws upon a strip[EP] of
13. fine linen[EQ] a god in his image.(?) Smear with fine oil,[ER] myrrh,[ES] place amulets at the throat of a man. If
14. he is healthy, he is smeared with honey added to water.[ET] If he is not healthy, smear the amulets with oil (and) smear the ear. Lo
15. not [...] with the *ʿft*-plant,[EU] immersed[EV] in laudanum every day and paint his eyes[EW] with a part[EX] of the *ʿft*-plant immersed
16. (in) honey likewise.

TEXT NOTES

A. (x + 9: 7–8) [hieroglyphs] *ky.t ẖt n k3p*, "Other spells for fumigating...;" For *ky.t ẖt* as the plural of *ky*, "other," see Gardiner *EG*[3], §98; also Allen, *Middle Egyptian*, 6.7; Borghouts, *EU* 24.1, p. 102, § 24.b.1.

B. (x + 9: 8) The full phonetic writing of [hieroglyphs] *msḏr*, "ear," occurs only here in the papyrus.

C. (x + 9: 8) The invocation beginning with [hieroglyphs] *i rʿ*, "O Re!" is a long petition to certain deities to come as agents of protection for the king. Such lists are common in protection texts. *pChester Beatty 5*, 4[1], for example, has a shorter list in which many of the names of the gods invoked here are found, although in a different order. *pChester Beatty 8*, r. 10, has several lists of invoked deities which are similar to the present one. See Borghouts, *pLeiden I 348*, pp. 168–69, n. 405, for references to further examples of such appeals to the pantheon.

D. (x + 9: 8) The three deities invoked at the beginning of this long apostrophe, Re, Atum, and Khepri, are manifestations of the sun god.

E. (x + 9: 9) Beginning with Shu and ending with Nephthys are the names of the gods who form the Heliopolitan Ennead, excluding Atum. The occurrence of the name Horus is perhaps unusual, unless we see in this name a reference to *ḥr wr*, the "Elder Horus," a god encountered in Spell L above. The presence of the name of the latter among the members of the Heliopolitan Ennead should come as little surprise, given the close associations that *ḥr wr* had with Heliopolis; see the discussion in the Commentary to Spell L; see also note O (x + 2: 9) above for a reference to a text naming Horus as one of the children of Nut. See also note F (x + 9: 9), following. On the confusion of Horus and Haroeris, see Anthes, *StudAeg* 9 (1983): 120–21.

F. (x + 9: 9) The close proximity of the name of Atum in the preceding triad may imply its assumed presence here, thus forging a close bond between the first two groups of deities named in the invocation. See the discussion in the Commentary. On the inclusion of Horus in this grouping, see note E (x + 9: 9) above.

G. (x + 9: 10) The pair Hu and Sia are personifications of "utterance" and "perception."

H. (x + 9: 10) On the god Isdes, see the discussion at note AQ (x + 7: 9) above.

I. (x + 9: 10–11) [hieroglyphs] *mnmn*, "schwanken (von der Erde)" (*Wb.* II 80–81, 1–15). See note J (x + 9: 9), following.

J. (x + 9: 11) The epithet "he who shakes the earth" usually refers to Geb. The theme of shaking the earth is already well-known in the Pyramid Texts and continues into the Ptolemaic Period with more general references to divine or royal epiphanies. For a similar pairing, see notes LL and MM (x + 6: 3) above. See also the discussion in the Commentary below.

K. (x + 9: 11) The names of the two gods [hieroglyphs] and [hieroglyphs] are to be read *iri*, "the god who sees," and *sḏm*, "the god who hears." Known from texts and representations that date as early as Dynasty 18, they often appear in conjunction with Thoth, as they do here, and Seshat. See Meeks, *Génies*, p. 59 and pp. 82–83, nn. 238–40; Brunner-Traut, *Fragen an die altägyptische Literatur*, pp. 125–45, for a discussion of their history.

L. (x + 9: 11) [hieroglyphs] is a writing of *ḏḥwty*,"Thoth" (*Wb.* V 606), found as early as the Middle Kingdom.

M. (x + 9: 11) An address to the gods of the four cardinal points occurs in the same order in *pChester Beatty 8*, rt. 10[5], and *pConfirmation*, 1[9]. On the orientation and order in which the four cardinal points appear, see Kessler, *LÄ* 2 (1977): cols. 1213–15.

N. (x + 9: 13) The grouping of heaven, earth, and the necropolis parallels a similar sequence of heaven, earth, and the Duat found in x + 10: 1 below.

O. (x + 9: 13) The first of three groups of four deities. See note Q (x + 9: 15), note V (x + 9: 17), and the Commentary, all below.

P. (x + 9: 14) On the iconography of solar boats, see Assmann, *Solar Religion*, pp. 49–51; Thomas, *JEA* 42 (1956): 79, n. 3, suggests that the Egyptians used the term [hieroglyphs] *wỉꜣ n rꜥ*, "barque of Re," generically to describe the solar barque; additionally, the terms *mꜥnd.t* and *mskt.t* were not the names of two separate barques, but different terms to designate the solar barque in its daily and nightly appearances. See also *pConfirmation,* 10[14] and 11[5], where the names Isis and Nephthys are used of the night barque and the day barque, respectively.

Q. (x + 9: 15) See note O (x + 9: 14) above, note V (x + 9: 17), and the Commentary below.

R. (x + 9: 15) [hieroglyphs] *ꜥḥꜥ*, “Menge von Menschen” (*Wb.* I 221, 8–9).

S. (x + 9: 15) [hieroglyphs] *pꜣ miw ꜥꜣ*, “the Great Cat” (*Wb.* II 42, 1–3) is a manifestation of the sun god. Note that it is the only single deity named in this section where all of the other divinities are found in groups of four.

T. (x + 9: 16) Since the term *mskt.t* is usually used of the solar barque crossing the night sky, the connection between this barque and the eastern horizon seems somewhat peculiar, unless the texts refers to its presence in the eastern horizon before dawn. See *pBremner-Rhind,* 28[14] as well. Derchain, *Hathor Quadrifons,* p. 28, n. 20, discusses the general confusion in the employment of solar barque terminology in Late Period texts. See also note P (x + 9: 14).

U. (x + 9: 17) This epithet seems to refer to all of the gods invoked thus far. In all likelihood, the uraei refer to the symbols of protection that appear on the headgear of divinities.

V. (x + 9: 17) It is unclear whether the word *wḏꜣ.t* here has the generic meaning “protector” or whether it is to be understood literally as “*wḏꜣ.t*-eye.” On groups of four deities, see notes O (x + 9: 14) and Q (x + 9: 15) above, and the Commentary below.

W. (x + 9: 18) The phrase [hieroglyphs] *nꜣ ir*[.*w*], “those who do/make…,” continues the epithet in the lacuna that ended with *nb.w nḥḥ*.

X. (x + 9: 18) The traces at the end of the lacuna suggest a writing of [hieroglyphs] *ḏ.t*, “forever; eternity.”

Y. (x + 9: 18) The word *ḏsr.w*, followed by *štꜣ.w ḥr.w*, forms a single vocative: “O sacred ones whose faces are secret/mysterious,” as the following line, column x + 10: 1 begins with a vocative marker.

Z. (x + 10: 1) The restoration of the phrase [hieroglyphs] *rn=sn*, “their names,” seems certain. The reference to “millions” is routinely encountered in religious texts and is one way the Egyptians expressed the idea of “infinite.” See, for example, *BD* 65: *ḥms rꜥ m-ḫnt ḥḥ=f*, “Re sits before his millions.” For a discussion, see Meeks and Favard-Meeks, *Daily Life,* pp. 33–34.

AA. (x + 10: 1) On the association of heaven, earth, and the Duat, see note N (x + 9: 13) above.

BB. (x + 10: 1–2) [hieroglyphs] *dm*, "aussprechen" (*Wb.* V 449, 8–450, 6). See *pChester Beatty 8*, rt. 10[9–10], where it occurs in a somewhat similar phrase: "Hail to you, gods and goddesses. I pronounce (*dm*) [your] names." The idea expressed here is that all of the gods whose names have just been pronounced are called upon to come to the aid of Psamtik. Pronouncement of their names indicates that the speaker has a knowledge of their essence and, thus, has power over them.

CC. (x + 10: 2) *nn irr=f* refers to the agent of the disease. Note that in this series of parallel sentences that begin with *nn* + prospective, the verb *iri* shows three writings: [hieroglyphs], [hieroglyphs], and [hieroglyphs]. See the discussion above at pp. 21ff.

DD. (x + 10: 3) The pronoun in *im=f* refers to Psamtik, not to the ear.

EE. (x + 10: 3) [hieroglyphs] *nn ḫꜣꜥ=f ꜣtp=f r=f*, "He shall not hurl his load against him." See *pLeiden I 348*, vs. 11[10] and p. 31 for the phrase *ꜥḳ r ẖ.t=f ḫꜣꜥ=f ꜥꜣ sšm=f*, which Borghouts translates "…who has entered his belly so that he could leave behind the influence (?) of his manifestation." The sense of the verb *ḫꜣꜥ*, at least in these contexts, seems to be that of abandoning something undesirable or of leaving something where it does not belong.

FF. (x + 10: 3) For [hieroglyphs] *mhi ib*, "make the heart forgetful," see *pEbers*, 101[8] (*Eb* 855) where it occurs in conjunction with *ꜣḳ ib*, another disease affecting the heart. A gloss there explains the two: "It is the (harmful) activity of the lector-priest which does it. It enters into the lungs as disease and (it) turns out that the heart goes astray under its influence." In that passage, the term *ẖr.y-ḥb*, "lector-priest," is the equivalent of "magician," i.e., one capable of reading or reciting a text correctly. In the present passage, the construction *nn mhi=f ib=f* suggests that *mhi* is a verb, not the noun as in *pEbers*. The sense here also seems to require a verb that is transitive and has a causal meaning. See also Piankoff, *Coeur*, pp. 46–47, where he discusses a number of passages in which this phrase appears, most of them literary texts. A similar idea occurs in *CT* 62: *di=(i) n=k ib=k m-ḫn.w ẖ.t=k sḫꜣ=k sḫm.t.n=k*, "I place your heart within your body for you (so that) you may remember what you have forgotten."

GG. (x + 10: 3–4) For [hieroglyphs] *dḥr ḥꜣ.ty*, "bitterness of heart; make the heart bitter," see the discussion at note O (x + 3: 5) above.

HH. (x + 10: 4) [hieroglyphs] *wšꜥ*, "das Beissen" (*Wb.* I 370, 14). A close parallel occurs at *pEbers*, 72[19] (*Eb* 556) and 73[19] (*Eb* 563) in the phrase "driving away…gnawing (*wšꜥ.w*) in the body of a man." The word occurs above as well, for which see note LL (x + 2: 13).

II. (x + 10: 4) *ḥnḥn*, "Negiert: (nicht) zurückgehalten werden [beim Gehen]" (*Wb.* III 115, 8). Either the scribe has omitted the subject of *ir*, probably the suffix pronoun =*f* found in all of the parallel phrases, or the text was intended to be read as is. See *pBM 10059,* 5[1], and Leitz, *HPBM 7,* p. 60, for the translation "tremble," a meaning that suits the present context as well.

JJ. (x + 10: 4) *ftft*, "springen; hüpfen" (*Wb.* I 581, 3–6). *Wb.* I 581, 7 offers "Verbum" citing *pSallier 2,* 14[5], a hymn to the Nile. For that text, see Helck, *Der Text des 'Nilhymnus,'* p. 75, who, in the phrase *pꜣ tꜣ r ꜣw ftft*, translates the verb as "hüpft." See also van der Plas, *EU* 4 (1986), pp. 145–46, who offers the translation "gambade." *WbMT,* p. 308 gives the meaning "springen." The word appears in *pEbers,* 108[14] (*Eb* 873) in a similar phrase referring to the activity of *št.w*-vessels: "*št.w*-vessels that hop (*ftft*) between these limbs." In that text and the Brooklyn text, the word seems to refer to a pulsation, throbbing, or spasm of some sort.

KK. (x + 10: 5) For a parallel to the phrase *nn wnm=f m iwf=f*, "he shall not feed on his flesh," see, for example, *BD* 163 which focuses on the protection of the corpse and *ba* against beings who would consume them. Note that the scribe of the papyrus consistently writes both *im.y* and *wnm* with the sign \\.

LL. (x + 10: 5) Beginning with *nn nḥm=f rꜣ=f*, "he shall not take away his mouth," there occur several statements that refer to threats of having one's physical or natural powers taken away. See the discussion in the Commentary below.

MM. (x + 10: 5) On the loss of the power of speech, see the Commentary below.

NN. (x + 10: 5) On the threat of blindness, see, for example, *pBremner-Rhind,* 10[27]; *pBM 10042,* vs. 1[4-5] and 1[11]; Leitz, *HPBM 7,* p. 47, nn. 132–33. See also Brunner, *LÄ* 1 (1975): cols. 828–34; Darnell, *Enigmatic Netherworld Books,* pp. 171–73, esp. n. 36; and the discussion in the Commentary below.

OO. (x + 10: 5) On deafness as a threat, see, for example, *pBM 10042,* vs. 1[4] and 1[11]; see also Grieshammer, *LÄ* 6 (1986): cols. 241–42 and the discussion in the Commentary below.

PP. (x + 10: 6) The suffix pronoun =*k* in the verb phrase *iw=k pr=tw* apparently refers to each of the individual malignant forces just addressed. Here, the one reciting the text claims to have power over the agent of disease at this point and gives him a series of explicit instructions.

QQ. (x + 10: 6–7) *iw sšm=k n=i sšm.w n nṯr.w ꜥꜣ.w* offers several possible translations. *Wb.* IV 285 gives as a "spät" writing of *sšm* (*Wb.* IV 285, 7–287, 10), a verb whose basic meanings are "lead; guide." Elsewhere in the papyrus, the scribe has written *sšm* simply without an initial *s*. The writing that follows here points to one of two similarly written nouns, both again read *sšm* (*Wb.* IV 290, 14–291, 16), that essentially mean "manifestation of a god." Hence, the translation offered is "you lead to me the manifestations of the great gods." Faulkner, *CD*, p. 247, gives a meaning "business; conduct" for the noun *sšm*; Borghouts, *EU* 24.1, p. 474b, offers a similar idea with his "state of affairs." Thus, the sentence could then be translated "You guide the (state of) affairs of the great gods for me." Another possibility is to take the noun as a writing of "leader" (Hannig, *GH*, p. 764a) and read as *sšm.w* or *sšm.yw*, yielding the translation "You guide the leaders of the great gods to/for me." Such a reading seems much less likely. On *sšm* meaning "manifestations," see also Manassa, *The Late Egyptian Underworld* 1, p. 270, n. a, where she notes that *sšm*-images were typically hidden from view, even during divine processions. See n. WW. that follows.

RR. (x + 10: 7) The pronoun =*sn* seems best understood as the object of the verb *rḫ*; the phrase *ḥr nb m-ʿ nb*, "everyone and everything," functions as the subject. The idea here is that the force(s) of chaos intend to commit a sacrilegious act by making images visible to all when they should be kept hidden.

SS. (x + 10: 7) The word *nb*, "everything," is complementary to *ḥr nb.w*, "everyone."

TT. (x + 10: 7–8) The point of reference of the string of epithets *šf.yt ʿ3 pḥ.ty ʿš3 rn.w wsr ʿḥʿ.w nb* is unclear. They refer either to "the great gods" mentioned earlier in the line or to the immediately preceding phrase "everyone." A similar string of epithets can be found at *pLeiden I 346*, 2^{10-11}.

UU. (x + 10: 8) For *pḥ.ty*, te Velde, *Seth*, p. 38, argues for the more abstract meaning "potency," as does Westendorf, *ZÄS* 92 (1966): 142 ff; see also Hollis, *Two Brothers*, pp. 89–90 and nn. 2–9.

VV. (x + 10: 8) The scribe may not have omitted the preposition *m*, as temporal adverbials are commonly used without prepositions in Middle Egyptian.

WW. (x + 10: 8) For parallels to *ḫpr.w št3.w m st imn*, "whose forms are secret in the hidden place," see *pBM 10042*, 4^{2-3}, where *št3.w ir.w* is used as an epithet of Amun. See also *pLeiden I 348*, vs. 11^{2} for *št3.w ḫpr.w* as an apparent epithet of the gods. The idea of a "hidden place" or "places" is encountered frequently in funerary texts. See, for example, *CT* 2; *CT* 33–35; *CT* 115; *CT* 118; *CT* 143; *CT* 728; and *BD* 15. For a discussion of the nature of the manifestations of the gods, see Meeks and Favard-Meeks, *Daily Life*, pp. 53–60; Assmann, *Solar Religion*, pp. 136–42; and see n. QQ above and the source cited there.

XX. (x + 10: 9) *iw wṯs.n=k*, "You have arisen," appears to be an *iw sḏm.n=f* form. Its grammatical relationship with the surrounding text is unclear. The group may stand for the writing of . The phrase would then be translated "...in order to rise up for you." See note YY (x + 10: 9), following.

YY. (x + 10: 9) *iw wts.n=k m33=k nb.t nn ḥ3p im=f ḫft m33=k is rk šp ir.ty=k ḥr nn m33=k* appears to be a single idea whose meaning is "You have arisen, you see everything, nothing hidden in it. When you look, indeed, your eyes are blinded because of the things which you see." The sentence begins with what appears to be an *iw sḏm.n=f* clause, a common narrative verbal construction in Middle Egyptian. In the phrase *nn ḥ3p im=f* that follows, the verbal *ḥ3p* could be either a participle or a *sḏm=f* form whose pronominal subject has been inadvertently omitted. If it is a participle, it could modify the preceding word *nb*, thus indicating that it is "everything which is not hidden." If *ḥ3p* refers to the suffix pronoun =*k*, used as the subject of the three verbs in this part of the passage, then the being addressed is marked as "without being hidden from it." If it is a *sḏm=f* form, its omitted subject could be either =*k* or =*f*. For parallels to the idea of seeing what is hidden in the Underworld or in the "secret place," see, for example, *CT* 61: *wn=k wsi.w ḥr psḏ.t m3=k sšt3.w ntt im=s*, "You open the windows over the Ennead (so that) you may see the secrets which are in it."

ZZ. (x + 10: 9) *ḥr* here is a conjunction meaning "because of" (*Wb.* IV 443, 10–11).

AB. (x + 10: 9) *is rk šp ir.ty=k ḥr nn m33=k*, "...indeed, your eyes are blinded because of the things which you see" suggests that the agent of the disease has been struck blind after being lured into looking at what is forbidden. For a parallel, see *pGeneva MAH 15274*, rt. 7^2 for *šp=tw nn m33=tw*, "you are blind, you do not see," an address by a magician to poison informing it of its complete defeat; also *pVatican 19a*, 2^4 for a similar address to poison, for which see Suys, *Or* 3 (1934): 63–87; Massart, *pLeiden I 343+345*, rt. 2^7, has *mi r-bn=s k3 mn ir.ty*, "Come outside so that your eyes will be blinded."

AC. (x + 10: 10) The hieroglyph at the end of line 9 indicates a writing of *wṯs* rather than *ṯs*. For *wṯs*, see *Wb.* I 382, 16–383, 17, but note that it does give the determinative . The same word is written somewhat similarly at x + 8: 16, there with the determinative . The apparent lack of an object suggests that the verb is intransitive as the translation indicates. Following the verb phrase, we have what appears to be *r t3 i*[*m*], "towards the land therein."

AD. (x + 10: 10) *sšm*, "guide; govern," seems certain. See *BD* 127; 148; and 182 for examples of beings who serve as guides in heaven or in the Underworld. See note QQ (x +10: 6-7) above.

AE. (x + 10: 10) [hieroglyphs] *h3i*, "angreifen; annehmen; werfen" (*Wb.* II 475, 1–4). The word [hieroglyphs] following *h3i* has been crossed out with a red stroke, the text now reading *h3i=k r dw3.t*, "You descend to the Duat." Given the use of supralinear signs in the papyrus, it seems that the scribe was not copying from a text that read "You descend (from) earth to the Duat," as the word *m* would have been added instead.

AF. (x + 10: 11) The writing [hieroglyphs] with the determinative [hieroglyph] (Sign-list G7) points to the noun *sšm*, "image; manifestation," for which see note QQ (x + 10: 7) above.

AG. (x + 10: 11) The phrase [hieroglyphs] can be translated several ways, but the only sensible reading based on the context is *is rḫ.tw*, "which, indeed, is not known" or "which, indeed, one does not know." For a discussion of the problems encountered here, see also notes AH (x + 10: 11), AI, and AJ (x + 10: 12), following.

AH. (x + 10: 11) The writing [hieroglyphs] is difficult. The initial sign seems more likely to be [hieroglyph] than [hieroglyph], as the presence of the tick over the sign makes clear, and comparison of the writing here and the last sign of line x + 10: 9 corroborates such a reading. Gauthier, *DG* III, p. 131, gives a place written [hieroglyphs], identified as a "région de la Syrie septentrionale, non identifiée, très probablement voisine de l'Euphrate." That reading seems unlikely here, since a location with mythological associations seems to be what is needed. I know of no other word spelled *rw* or *rr* written with the sign [hieroglyph] and the determinative [hieroglyph]. Daumas, *VP* 1, 234, cites a reading *mr* for the sign [hieroglyph], opening the possibility that [hieroglyphs] is a writing of the noun *mrw*, given at *Wb.* II 109, 5–8: "Wüste;" note, however, that a writing with the sign [hieroglyph] is not attested there or in any of the lexica. Furthermore, the reading *mrw* and the generalized meaning "desert" in the present passage seems odd, and I have found no attestation of the epithet *im.y mrw* used of the gods or any noun for that matter. An alternative is to understand the hieratic as [hieroglyphs] *pri*, "battlefield," although the present writing is also not attested for that word by the *Wörterbuch* or found in any Egyptological lexical tools. A "battlefield" connected with "the First Occasion" could refer to the place where the creator god subdued the malevolent forces for the first time. Again, there is no attestation of the epithet *im.y.w pri*. Additionally, the hieratic favors [hieroglyph] more strongly than [hieroglyph]. A third but least likely reading is [hieroglyphs] *šnʿ.t*, a writing of the word "underworld; tomb." See Lesko, *DLE* 3, p. 158; Ruffle, *JEA* 50 (1964), pp. 177–78. The problem with such a reading is the clear presence of the letter *r* here. Perhaps the best solution is to read the sign [hieroglyph] as *w*, as attested by Daumas, *VP* 1, p. 231, No. 355, or, even better, as *wr*, following Wilson, *PL*, p. 243. Such a reading would give the epithet *nṯr.w im.y.w wr.t*, "…the gods who are in the West/necropolis…," attested by *Wb.* I 73, 9–13, a reading that makes good sense here; note, however, that the writing with the sign [hieroglyph] is not cited there or given by Wilson under the entry for *im.y.w wr.t* on p. 70. I thank Joachim Quack for the idea that the group [hieroglyphs] might somehow be a writing of *wr.t*.

AI. (x + 10: 11–12) The group [hieroglyphs] *ḫpr m sp tp.y*, "…came into being on the First Occasion," could modify either the place name [hieroglyphs] *wr.t* or the noun [hieroglyphs] *nṯr.w* occurring in the preceding line.

AJ. (x + 10: 12) [hieroglyphs] *sḫwr*, "verfluchen" (*Wb.* IV 213, 4–6). For a parallel to this idea of the gods cursing the malignant forces, see *pLeiden I 343 +345*, vs. 1[1-6], which lists gods and other beings who curse the force of evil.

AK. (x + 10: 13) If the reading [hieroglyphs] is correct, *in iw* introduces an interrogative sentence, for which see *EG*[3], § 491–92. Such questions are frequently rhetorical, for which see Sweeny, *LingAeg* 1 (1991): 315–31. The negative marker *bn* usually indicates that the verb it precedes is a prospective form, for which see Junge, *LEG*, 22.1–22.5. The traces after *sḫꜣ*, however, seem to indicate the writing of the signs [hieroglyphs]. One does not expect a *sḏm.n=f* form preceded by the Late Egyptian particle *bn*. Either *n* is an error, or the phrase [hieroglyphs] may simply serve as a dative providing a reference point for the being(s) addressed. The translation in such a case would be "Does (one) not remember for you?", i.e., "Does (one) not remind you?" There appear to be other Late Egyptian forms in this section of the text, for which see note AL (x + 10: 13), following.

AL. (x + 10: 13) In the group [hieroglyphs] *pꜣ ḏd i.ir=k*, the verbal *ḏd*, marked by the definite article *pꜣ*, is a substantive. If it is inanimate, a translation like "statement" seems warranted; if animate, the translation would be "…the one who says/will say what you are doing…." The group [hieroglyphs] seems to be a writing of the Egyptian relative form *i.ir=k*; one would expect the writing of *ir* to be [hieroglyph] or [hieroglyph]. In every other instance in the Brooklyn text where *irr* is preceded by a vocative marker, the verbal in question has been an unmodified participle. An alternative translation to the one given is "the one who says what you should do/have done."

AM. (x + 10: 13) I take the verbal form [hieroglyphs] *mꜣꜣ* to be an imperative.

AN. (x + 10: 13) The group written [hieroglyphs] or possibly [hieroglyphs] *mn* is puzzling at first. The same writing appears in *pBrooklyn 47.218.2*, x + 8[20] (Guermeur and O'Rourke, forthcoming) in a context that offers little insight as well. One problem of interpretation lies in writing of the determinative here. If the determinative is the sign [hieroglyph] (Sign-list G7), it indicates the writing of a divine name or epithet, possibly that of the god Min, although his name is typically written [hieroglyphs]. Phonetic writings of his name with [hieroglyph], however, are known from the Pyramid texts. For [hieroglyph], *Wb.* II 64, 13–65, 2 gives the meaning "der und der;" the addition of the divine determinative would give the equivalent "god so and so." Alternatively, we can understand the final sign as [hieroglyph], whose writing is identical to that of [hieroglyph] in this papyrus. The meaning of this word then would simply be "so and so." A third, but less plausible solution is to see a writing of the name of the god Amun here and conclude that the scribe has inadvertently omitted the initial sign [hieroglyph]. A possible solution is that indicates that the name of the god inhabiting this secret place is also secret and unknowable. See note BB (x + 10: 2) above.

AO. (x + 10: 13) *st št3*, "secret place," seems certain.

AP. (x + 10: 14) On *pt rsi.t*, " the southern heaven," see Kessler, *LÄ* 2 (1977): cols. 1213–15. For a parallel to the connection of *pt rs.t* with the word *št3.w*, see *oLeipzig 42*, rt. 4, in Gardiner and Černý, *HO* 1 (1957), pls. III and IIIA, rt. 1^4; see also *LJ*, 5; *pCairo 86637*, rt. 5^3 and rt. 5, n. 4; finally, see *pBremner-Rhind*, 27^{22}, where the "southern heaven" is said to be where Orion binds his foe.

AQ. (x + 10: 14) Here begins the description of a composite being. These are well-known in Egyptian thought, with the god Bes being the best-known. *pIllustré*, 2^{1-2} and 4^9–5^2 offer textual descriptions of two such deities, one with nine faces and one with seven faces; there are also several vignettes in that papyrus illustrating these gods as well; see figs. 1–3 there. Such beings are actually manifestations of the creator god who, by thus presenting himself, is able to terrorize whatever malevolent forces are plaguing an individual. See also the remarks of Sauneron, ibid., pp. 11–16. For parallels to a being with eyes of fire, see *PT* 255: *...iw.k3 wnis ḥr=f m wr pw nb 3t... rdi.k3=f nsr n ir.t=f pḫr=s ḥ3=ṯn di=s nšn m ir.w ir.wt...*, "...then Unas will come, his face will be (that) of the great one, the lord of assault...then he will put (forth) the flame of his eye; it will encircle you (and) it will put raging on those who do deeds [of evil]...." See also *pCairo 58027*, 2^{3-4}, which refers to an image of Pharaoh "with eyes of fire." In *BD* 125, Horus appears with "his Two Eyes of Flame coming forth from Letopolis." For the reading of as *b3.(w)*, see Drioton, *JEA* 35 (1949): 120.

AR. (x + 10: 14) The epithet "arms of a cat" may refer to the manifestation of the sun god as the "Great Cat," for which see note S (x + 9: 15) and note Z (x + 13: 15) below.

AS. (x + 10: 14) For parallels to a being with a "mouth of fire," see *Wb.* II 335, 14, citing *Urk.* V, 62 and *Amduat* 2, p. 16; see also *pConfirmation*, 16^{9-10}.

AT. (x + 10: 15) Borghouts, *pLeiden I 348*, rt. 6^5 and n. 170, discusses at length the use of the phrase *iw ḏd.k in* apostrophes such as this. He states that this phrase is used to introduce the intentions of the inimical forces, an interpretation which makes sense here. It may be that knowledge of the intentions of malignant forces effectively neutralizes them.

AU. (x + 10: 15) On the word *sšm*, "image," see note QQ (x + 10: 7) above.

AV. (x + 10: 16) The term *ʿfn(.t) špss*, "noble *ʿfn.t*-cloth" is associated with a number of deities, both male and female. See Eaton-Krausss, *SAK* 5 (1977): 23–25, especially 24, n. 25, regarding its connections with the goddess Hathor; also Egberts, *EU* 8 (Leiden 1995), pp. 136–37, n.7, for a discussion of its royal associations;

also Smith, in Bareš et al., *Egypt in Transition,* pp. 403ff., on Nephthys wearing the *ˁfn.t*-veil as a sign of mourning at the death of Seth. The reference to unwrapping here seems to focus on the unveiling of an image that has been wrapped to ensure its secrecy and to prevent it from being known. See, for example, *CT* 271: *ink mꜣ kfꜣ sꜣ ḥw.t-ḥr*, "It is I who saw the unclothed one, the son of Hathor." See also *BD* 63: "I am the heir who unwrapped the Elder, the weary one." The term *ˁfn.t* is also used of the mummy bandages of the dead which are unwrapped during the night journey of the sun god in order to allow the deceased to see the god as he travels through the Underworld. In such a context, the act of unwrapping is associated with rebirth and resurrection.

AW. (x + 10: 16) On the presence of the goddess Hathor in this context, see note AV (x + 10: 16) above.

AX. (x + 10: 17) The word *m* appears to be the direct object marker here.

AY. (x + 10: 18) [hieroglyphs] *sšm wꜣ.t*, "einen Weg weisen" (*Wb.* IV 286, 11–13). The writing of *pw* here may indicate the presence of a gloss.

AZ. (x + 10: 18) The traces of what must be [hieroglyphs] can be seen above the lacuna, suggesting the restoration *ii m grḥ*, "…come in the night." Due to the lacuna, however, the exact reading remains uncertain.

BA. (x + 10: 18) The introduction of the subordinate conjunction "when" is based on the assumption that this part of the text is connected with what follows.

BC. (x + 10: 19) There is a loss of approximately 2 cm at the beginning of this line. The first sign that can be read is [hieroglyph], suggesting the presence of a verb of motion like *ii* or *šm*.

BD. (x + 10: 19) For [hieroglyphs] *sdwḫ*, restore [hieroglyphs], "balsamieren" (*Wb.* IV 368, 6–7), a word that accords well with the presence of Anubis in the preceding phrase.

BE. (x + 10: 19) [hieroglyphs] is a writing of the name of *wsir*, Osiris (*Wb.* I 359), a writing found as well at x + 11: 2 below. The writing with the egg-sign (Sign-list H8) is known as early as the Coffin Texts; see Altenmüller, *Synkritismus,* pp. 42–52.

BF. (x + 10: 19) The signs [hieroglyphs] *wˁb.t*, "Balsamierungsstätte" (*Wb.* I 284, 4–5) seem clear. The writing of [hieroglyphs] that follows is the demonstrative *tw.y*, "this." For a parallel, see, for example, *CT* 55: …*m-ẖn.w ˁ.wy inpw m wˁb.t*, "one who is within the arms of Anubis in the place of embalming."

BG. (x + 11: 1) Based on the traces, restore [hieroglyphs] *wsir ꜣs.t*, "Osiris (and) Isis."

BH. (x + 11: 1) For this posture as a gesture of deference, see, for example, *CT* 39: …*m3ʿ.t r is.t ʿ3.t r nḏ r3 n p3.wt ḥr.y p3.w.w ḥr ḳ3b=sn ir.w nḏ r3*…, "…Maat at the great chamber to greet the primeval god who is above the primeval gods who are on their bellies (and) making greetings…."

BI. (x + 11: 1) The particle [hieroglyphs] indicates that [hieroglyphs] *ḫr*, "fall," is an imperative.

BJ. (x + 11: 1) [hieroglyphs] *m-ḏr*, "als; seit" (*Wb.* V 593, 15–594, 5) in the sense of "at the moment when."

BK. (x + 11: 2) =*k* seems to refer to one of the malignant forces, and the object pronoun *sw* probably refers to the speech of that being.

BL. (x + 11: 2) For an exact parallel to [hieroglyphs] *nty irr mḥr tn*, "who makes this illness," see *pLeiden I 348*, rt. 6^{4-5}.

BM. (x + 11: 2) On the meaning and use of the phrase *iw ḏd.k*, see note AT (x + 10: 15) above.

BN. (x + 11: 2) The group [hieroglyphs] is most likely the passive participle *ir.wt*; hence, the translation "what has been done" is given here.

BO. (x + 11: 2) For [hieroglyphs] *wsir*, see note BC (x + 10: 19) above.

BP. (x + 11: 2) The final sign of the line is [hieroglyph] (Sign-list Z6), indicating that a name or a term designating one of the forces of evil occupied the lacuna.

BQ. (x + 11: 3) For the syntax of [hieroglyphs] *is ir.t nb.t gmḥ sn šp ḥr-ʿ*, it seems better to read [hieroglyphs] *gmḥ* as an imperfective participle with [hieroglyphs] *sn* as its direct object rather than as a *sḏm=f* form. The antecedent of the pronoun *sn* is, in all likelihood, the secret things which are not to be seen. For [hieroglyphs] *gmḥ*, "sehen" (*Wb.* V 170, 8–171, 11), see also *pBM 10059*, 16^5. For a similar idea, see *pIllustré*, 2^2 and especially 5^2, where Sauneron translates "Si quiconque vivant le voyait, ils mourraient…." At p. 27, n. (ii), Sauneron explains his translation "quiconque" for *ir.t nb* as "…un terme évoquant pluralité." An alternative translation would be "Everyone whom they see is blinded immediately," reading *gmh=sn* as a *sḏm=f* form. This translation echoes the statement in column x + 11: 13–14 below: "If (there is) one whom they see, they see, he is blinded immediately." The problem we then face is determining to whom =*sn* refers.

BR. (x + 11: 3) The translation of the phrase [hieroglyphs] *mi ḏd=k* given at Gardiner, *EG*³, § 170 is "according as you say." It seems that here this phrase introduces a new series of statements; hence, the translation "Likewise, you say…" is given. The phrase occurs again at x + 11: 7 below.

BS. (x + 11: 3) On the phrase *ḏd.k*, see note AS (x + 10: 15) above.

BT. (x + 11: 3) In [hieroglyphs] *št3.w m iṯi šw*, the word written [hieroglyphs] *št3.w* appears to be a writing of one of the words meaning "secret" or "hidden." I cannot explain its relationship to the words that follow.

BU. (x + 11: 3) The text is challenging here. The sign [hieroglyph] *m* seems best taken as a temporal conjunction with a meaning like "when." [hieroglyphs] *šw* is apparently "das Licht; die Sonne" (*Wb.* IV 430, 6–431, 12), but the presence of the determinative [hieroglyph] (Sign-list G7) means that it could be the name Shu. The group *m iṯi šw* could mean "... when Shu seized...," but that translation presents problems since there seems to be no direct object, unless the signs [hieroglyphs] represent the beginning of the writing of a noun like *mk.t*, "protection." A rendering "...when Shu seized protection..." seems odd. By reading the verb *iṯi* as a passive form and understanding the writing [hieroglyphs] to refer to light, a translation that better suits the context can be offered. See note BV (x + 11: 3), following.

BV. (x + 11: 3) [hieroglyphs] could be the particle *mk*, a writing of the noun *mk.t*, "protection," the verb *mki*, "protect," or the preposition *m-ꜥ* with a suffix pronoun *k*. The best reading seems to be the latter, given the context. With a passive form of the verb *iṯi*, the group [hieroglyphs] is *m-ꜥ=k*, "from you;" the whole phrase *m iṯi šw m-ꜥ=k* means "...when the (sun)light is taken from you." The idea of light having been taken away accords well with the reference to blindness that immediately precedes. A major problem in this passage is the relationship of the phrases and clauses. See notes BT and BU (x + 11: 3) above.

BW. (x + 11: 3–4) The traces at the end of this line and the sign [hieroglyph] at the beginning of the next indicate a restoration of [hieroglyphs] *ḥꜥpi*, "Hapi."

BX. (x + 11: 4) For Hapi's connections with the necropolis, *pSallier 2*, 4[7] (a hymn to the Nile) states that Hapi dwells in the Underworld; see van der Plas, *Hymne du Nil*, p. 95.

BY. (x + 11: 4) [hieroglyphs] *nḏri*, "fassen; packen" (*Wb.* II 382, 18–383, 25). See van der Plas, *Hymne du Nil*, pp. 174–75, where Hapi is described as one who seizes and plunders. See also *pBM 10309*, 1[18], where *nḏri* describes the seizing power of the heat of poison.

BZ. (x + 11: 4) The pronoun =*s* refers to the preceding *ẖr.t-nṯr*.

CA. (x + 11: 4) The traces at the end of the line seem to be [hieroglyphs] *pr-ꜥ3*, "Pharaoh," a writing especially common in the New Kingdom.

CB. (x + 11: 5) The particle [hieroglyph] *in* appears to be the interrogative marker here. Gardiner, *EG*[3], § 493, states that the interrogative word *in* is used to introduce questions that show surprise on the part of the questioner. See also Sweeny, *LingAeg* 1 (1991): 315–31, on this particle as a marker of rhetorical questions. Since there is no verb in this sentence, one would expect *in iw* instead. See Černý and Groll, *LEG,* 61.2.10, citing Ex. 1484 given at 57.6, which gives an example of *in* introducing a noun qualified by a long adjectival relative clause. Note, however, that the sentence in the Brooklyn text has an adverbial predicate.

CD. (x + 11: 5) *ir.y-pʿ.t nṯr.w* is an epithet of Geb known as early as the Pyramid Texts and Coffin Texts; see, for example, *PT* 480; *PT* 570; *CT* 131.

CE. (x + 11: 5) The group appears to be a writing of the preposition *r* followed by the word *rꜣ*, "utterance." Alternatively, it may be *r-gs* and the reading would be "at the side of Maat."

CF. (x + 11: 5) On the use and meaning of the phrase *iw ḏd=k*, see note AT (x + 10: 15) above.

CG. (x + 11: 6) The writing at the end of x + 11: 5 and the beginning of x + 11: 6 is *nmʿ*. It could be the verb "schlafen" (*Wb.* II 266, 7–10), although the determinative is not given for that verb. Hannig, *GH,* p. 413a, gives the meanings "verkleiden; verblenden," apparently citing *Wb.* II 266, 11–13. I can find no parallel for the idea of the enemy "sleeping" or "disguised" in Letopolis.

CH. (x + 11: 6) Numerous spells in the Pyramid Texts, Coffin Texts, and Book of the Dead enumerate Letopolis among the places where the original cosmic conflict was said to have taken place. See Wainwright, *JEA* 18 (1931): 159–72, for convenient access to the citations of many of these texts. Much of his discussion, however, is dated and should be used with caution. Letopolis is found in *pBrooklyn 47.218.84,* 7^{10}–9^{2}; see Meeks, *Mythes et légendes,* pp. 17–19 and his commentary there, pp. 226–39.

CI. (x + 11: 6) The traces suggest the restoration of the verb *šnʿ*, "abweisen; nicht zurückgehalten werden" (*Wb.* IV 504, 5–505, 12). A more attractive alternative, however, is the intransitive "scheu sein; sich scheuen" (*Wb.* IV 505, 13). *CT* 150 provides a parallel: *snḏ nṯr.w nrw rf im.y.w kꜣr.w=sn*, "The gods are afraid; indeed those who are in their shrines are frightened."

CJ. (x + 11: 7) On the phrase *mi ḏd=k*, see note BR (x + 11: 3) above.

CK. (x + 11: 7) The addition of the preposition *r* seems to indicate that the address here is directed to the four deities just mentioned. Alternatively, it is possible that *r* means "against."

CL. (x + 11: 7) See note V (x + 9: 17) above.

CM. (x + 11: 7–8) I have yet to find a parallel for such a composite being. See, however, at x + 10: 14–15 above for the description of another composite deity.

CN. (x + 11: 8) In this passage, could be a nominal or verbal form, although the writing certainly does look like the noun *mdw.wt*, "words," as it is written in this papyrus. I take the writing as the verb phrase *mdw(i)=sn* that stands parallel to the following verb phrases *šm=sn* and *sꜥḳ=sn*; hence, the reading *mdw(i)=sn*, "they speak." The following signs suit the reading of *ẖnm.w*, possibly a participial form of "vereinigen mit…; sich vereinigen mit…" (*Wb.* III 377, 4–381, 4). I take it as a verbal adjective modifying the pronominal subject of the preceding verb. An alternative but less likely explanation is that we have the noun *mdw.wt*, and the phrase means "their words go forth in unison," i.e., the four gods all speak at once or speak in agreement.

CO. (x + 11: 8) is *imꜣw*, "das Zelt" (*Wb.* I 81, 1–7), or possibly a writing of *imḥ.t*, one of two words used to designate the necropolis in Letopolis where the relic of Osiris was preserved (the other word is *imḥḏ.t*). The writing of the second does seem a bit peculiar and may be a corrected writing of . See Meeks, *Mythes et légendes*, 5[7] and p. 59, n. 72 and pp. 74–75, and n. 157 especially for a discussion of these words and the sources cited there.

CP. (x + 11: 10) Kheraha is also one of the locations connected with the primal cosmic conflict. It is found in *pBrooklyn 47.218.84*, 7[3-10]; see Meeks, *Mythes et légendes*, pp. 16–17 and the commentary at pp. 221–26. It is worth noting that in that Brooklyn papyrus, the descriptions of Keraha and Letopolis are contiguous; see also Gardiner, *AEO* II, 135*–136*.

CQ. (x + 11: 10) *nṯr.w* may be an appositive to *sšm.w*, and the translation should read "You speak of the images in Kheraha, (namely) the gods who are in their following." Such an interpretation, however, raises the question of the antecedent of the suffix pronoun =*sn* in the prepositional phrase *m-ḫt=sn*.

CR. (x + 11: 10) *wṯs* can have the meaning "hochheben" or "verkünden" (*Wb.* I 382, 16–383, 17, but without the determinative). If it is the latter, the translation would be "You proclaim the images to the outside." Wilson, *PL*, p. 272, offers a verb written with the determinative meaning "carry," certainly a variant of the former. That is the reading adopted here.

CS. (x + 11: 10) Written at the end of x + 11: 10 and at the beginning of x + 11: 11 is *r rw.ty*, "to the outside" (*Wb.* II 405, 6–12, citing the two determinatives).

CT. (x + 11: 11) In *ꜥnḫ=st sḏr iw nṯr.w šm=sn*, the dependent pronoun *st* is the subject of the verb *ꜥnḫ*, see Borghouts, *EU* 24.1, p. 86, § 19.b.2, citing the dependent pronoun as the subject in an ascriptive clause where the predicate is an adjective. The translation is then "they are alive…", a phrase that seems to refer to the images mentioned in the preceding sentence. See note CU (x + 11: 11), following.

CU. (x + 11: 11) The bare verbal *sḏr*, "sleeping," is apparently a participle modifying the pronominal subject of the preceding verbal phrase *ʿnḫ=st*. Bringing the *sšm*-images outside of the shrines where they reside, if that is the idea here, would constitute a sacrilege. See note QQ (x + 10: 6–7) above.

CV. (x + 11: 11) *iw nṯr.w šm=sn*, "while the gods proceed," should be construed as an *iw sḏm=f* form with the subject *nṯr.w* standing in anticipatory emphasis.

CW. (x + 11: 11) is somewhat puzzling. *ḥr-tp=sn* may be prepositional phrase describing how the gods go forth; see *EG*³, § 178. Alternatively, *ḥr.y-tp* may be the substantive meaning "chief; superior;" in that case, the phrase would mean "their superior(s)," again referring to the gods. Note, however, that *hry-tp* is written as if it were singular. That is the reading adopted here, although it is provisional.

CX. (x + 11: 12) is puzzling. The reading seems to be *m ẖr ꜣḫ=sn*, "in possession of their *akh*'s" or "in possession of their power." The antecedent of the pronoun =*sn* would be the noun *hry-tp* as I am reading the text.

CY. (x + 11: 12) On the eating habits of the gods, see Meeks and Favard-Meeks, *Daily Life*, pp. 63–66.

CZ. (x + 11: 13) The antecedent of =*s* is unclear.

DA. (x + 11: 13) *šnʿ sḏt* or *šnʿ (nt) ḫt*, "ring of fire;" both readings are cited by Leitz et al., *Götterbezeichnungen* 7, p. 102. This *topos* is known from *BD* 136B as one of the places of danger that the sun barque has to pass by.

DB. (x + 11: 13) *inḥ*, "umgeben" (*Wb.* I 99, 3–130).

DC. (x + 11: 13) *išrw*, "der heilige See" (*Wb.* I 135, 6). The determinative (Sign-list Q7) is not given there but probably derives from its writing with the verb *ꜣšr*, given at *Wb.* I 21, 4–9; "grillen; das Gegrillte," an interpretation suggested by Jequier, *BIFAO* 19 (1922), p. 226. The writing of the determinative in the word *išrw* is encountered in Ptolemaic texts. See, for example, Sauneron, *MIFAO* 107 (Cairo 1983), pl. 6, no. 7, 1 and pl. 11, no. 11, 35 and 41. The *Wörterbuch* entry incorrectly identifies the term *išrw* as limited to the Mut precinct at Karnak; see now Gessler-Löhr, *HÄB* 21, passim, but esp. pp. 401–24 on *išrw* at Egyptian temples associated with lion-headed goddesses; see, additionally, Sauneron, *BdE* 90 (1983), pp. 77–84; also Yoyotte, *RdE* 14 (1962): 101–10.

DE. (x + 11: 13) On the hidden nature of the gods, see the discussion and references given at note WW (x + 10: 8) above.

DF. (x + 11: 13) The reading [hieroglyphs] *ir nty ḥr*, "As for one who...," seems certain, beginning a new sentence.

DG. (x + 11: 14) The text has the writing [hieroglyphs]. As [hieroglyphs] *w* can only be the Late Egyptian suffix pronoun, the reading is either *m33=w*, as taken above, or understood as (*ḥr*) *m33 w* with the pronoun taken as the direct object of an infinitive, thereby giving "As for anyone who sees them...." This text has a number of Late Egyptian forms and syntactical patterns that make the reading difficult.

DH. (x + 11: 14) [hieroglyphs] *miw*, "cat," is certain. Given the context and the presence in this passage of the *hiw*-serpent, a manifestation of Apophis, we should see the cat, in turn, as a manifestation of the sun god. See, for example, *CT* 759; Sauneron, *pOphiologie*, p. 121 and p. 190, n.2. See *pBM 10042*, rt. 9^{2-3} for the phrase (twice) *ntk nḫt mḥ-7*, "you are a giant of seven cubits;" and Leitz, *HPBM* 7, p. 45, n. 116 for the suggestion that seven cubits is an allusion to the full moon; see there for other texts relevant to the discussion.

DI. (x + 11: 14) If *wn im miw mḥ 7* is to be taken together, note that the adverb *im* seems to have been inadvertently written before the noun *miw*. Otherwise, the writing of *im* directly after *wn* is difficult to explain.

DJ. (x + 11: 14) There is a blank space of approximately 1 cm between the writing of the preposition [hieroglyph] and the group [hieroglyphs]. It may simply reflect a scribal error and the compound prepositional phrase *m-tp=f* was intended, for which see Hannig, *GH*, p. 924a: "oben auf; an der Spitze von; von." I can make little sense of the statement "He lives on top of him/it," as there does not seem to be a clear antecedent for the pronoun *=f*. Possibly, the scribe has inadvertently omitted a word or faithfully copied an exemplar that had a gap here as well. Alternatively, the translation may be "he lives on (i.e., 'eats') his head" or something equivalent. Additionally, the syntactical function of the word "*hiw*-serpent" is unclear. If it has been added to clarify the noun phrase *tp=f*, I am at a loss for a parallel for a cat with the head of a *hiw*-serpent. Because of the uncertainty of what was intended here, I have indicated a lacuna in the translation, and the referent of the pronoun *=f* remains unfortunately unclear.

DK. (x + 11: 14) [hieroglyphs] *hiw*, "Bez. für die im Schlangenzauber zu vernichtende Schlange" (*Wb.* II 483, 20–22 and *Wb.* II 483, 15–17, as a term used of Seth). See Ward, *JNES* 37 (1978): 23–34, especially 26–29; also Brunner-Traut, *LÄ* 2 (1977): cols. 27–30.

DL. (x + 11: 14) Despite a small break in the papyrus and the fact that one fragment has been placed upside down here, the negative marker [hieroglyph] *nn* can be read with certainty. [hieroglyphs] is *tkn*, "nahe sein; nahe kommen" (*Wb.* V 333, 10–335, 12), a verb whose nuance has to do with cautiously approaching anything sacred.

DM. (x + 11: 14) [hieroglyphs] *wp* can be read with certainty. For the translation of *ir.t nb* as "anyone," see note BO (x + 11: 3) above.

DN. (x + 11: 15) The identity of the being to whom these pronouns refer remains unclear.

DO. (x + 11: 15) On Kheraha in this context, see note CP (x + 11: 10) above.

DP. (x + 11: 17) [hieroglyphs] *ḏ3ḏ3*, "tribunal" (*Wb.* V 528, 1–529, 20). On the Tribunal of Letopolis, see, for example, *CT* 337 and 338. A gloss at *BD* 18 states that the Great Council of Letopolis consists of Horus Khenty-irty and Thoth.

DQ. (x + 11: 18) [hieroglyphs] *bḥd.w*, "Thron" (*Wb.* I 470, 3–5). The traces preceding the lacuna show [hieroglyphs], suggesting the restoration of *bi3*, "Metall; Kupfer" (*Wb.* I 436, 1–438, 5). In the word *bi3*, it is possible to see specific connections with Letopolis, for which see Wainwright, *JEA* 18 (1931): 165–66.

DR. (x + 11: 18) The traces seem to indicate a writing of [hieroglyphs] *s3ṯ.w*, "Erde" (*Wb.* III 423, 7–424, 12).

DS. (x + 11: 18) The traces at the end of the line seem to be [hieroglyphs] *m ḫm=f*, "…when he forgets/does not know…"

DT. (x + 11: 19) [hieroglyphs] *pḫ3*, "durchschlagen" (*Wb.* I 542, 12–543, 7). The determinative [hieroglyph] (Sign-list T30) is not given there but is suitable, given its basic meaning. See Koenig, *pBoulaq 6,* rt. 11[2], for this word with the meaning "open." I cannot make sense of its exact meaning here because of the lacunae.

DU. (x + 11: 19) Despite the lacuna of 1.5 cm, the restoration is certain.

DV. (x + 11: 19) The traces, the available space at the end of this line, and the writing of the group [hieroglyphs] at the beginning of the first line of the next column suggest the restoration of [hieroglyphs] [*m tp m m3ʿ*] *m ʿnḫ.wy*, "in the head, in the temple, in the ears…"

DW. (x + 12: 1) [hieroglyphs] *iwnw*, "Iunu" (*Wb.* I 53, 21–22, as a designation of the creator god worshipped at Heliopolis). This is also an epithet of the god Atum, for which see, Myśliwiec, *HÄB* 8, pp. 101–2. Additionally, it was used as a designation of Osiris as a mummy, for which see Goyon, *pLouvre I 3079,* 141, 11 and p. 110, n. 2. Considering the epithets that follow, a connection with the creator god seems the more likely one.

DX. (x + 12: 3) On these epithets of the creator god, see Myśliwiec, *HÄB* 8, passim.

DY. (x + 12: 5) For secret shrines and secret places, see note WW (x + 10: 8) above.

DZ. (x + 12: 5) Beginning here and for the remainder of this line, numerous problems occur, and it is quite possible that the text is corrupt. [hieroglyphs] *wꜣ r* is "fern sein" (*Wb.* I 245, 5–11; Quack, *LingAeg* 3 [1993]: 59–79). It seems to be used as an imperative here.

EA. (x + 12: 5) The writing of [hieroglyphs] suggests that it is a loan word, one unattested in the lexica. It may be a magical name; see, for example, *pBremner-Rhind*, 32[34], which gives [hieroglyphs] as one of the names of Apophis. But as written here, the word has none of the determinatives that one would expect in such a writing. Understanding the writing *ẖ-n-r-m* to be a scribal error for *ẖ-n-r* offers little help, as none of the meanings given in the entries at *Wb.* III, 298, 5–299, 2, where the words showing *ẖnr* written as a loan word are found, suggests anything leading to a satisfactory reading of the text. Note that the phrase *ẖnr r-gs ḥr.t* occurs in *pProphylaxie* at x + VIII[8], with *ẖnr* written there as [hieroglyphs]; see Goyon, *pProphylaxie*, pp. 47–48.

EB. (x + 12: 5) [hieroglyphs] *ꜣmm*, "mit der Faust ergreifen" (*Wb.* I 10, 17–21).

EC. (x + 12: 5) The phrase [hieroglyphs] *dwꜣ.t štꜣ.w*, "secret Duat," occurs in a phrase found in vignettes representing the setting sun in Books of the Dead of Dynasty 21. See, for example, Niwinski, *OBO* 86 (1989), p. 39, fig. 2. It also recalls the name of the burial mound of the deceased gods at Esna, described in *Esna* III, No. 196, 2 as "it is the mysterious Duat which no man sees." See Sauneron, *Esna* V, p. 319 and p. 320, n. (c).

ED. (x + 12: 6) A parallel to the phrase [hieroglyphs] *ḏw r=k*, "Evil against you," followed by the name of one of the malevolent forces is found at *pBremner-Rhind*, 29[22]: *ḏw=k r=k sbi*, "Your (own) evil against you, rebel."

EF. (x + 12: 7) I have no exact parallel for the epithet [hieroglyphs] *pꜣ nk sn m rꜥ*, "the rapist who transgresses by day." [hieroglyphs], *nk*, is used of sexual assault, rape, as well as copulation. For examples, see *pBM 10042*, vs. 7[10], where it has that valence.

EG. (x + 12: 7) [hieroglyphs], read *sd*, "der Schwanz" (*Wb.* IV 363, 3–364, 2). In all likelihood, a derogatory meaning seems wanted here, paralleling *pꜣ nk*. See note EH (x + 12: 7), following.

EH. (x + 12: 7) [hieroglyphs] *ksks*, "tanzen" (*Wb.* V 141–142, 3); Brunner-Traut, *ÄF* 6, pp. 33 and 79. The proximity of *sd* and *ksks* calls to mind *pBoulaq 6*, rt. 8[2]: *iw=k ksks m rd=k iw=k snb sd.t=k*, "You dance with your feet (and) you are healthy right up to your tail." Koenig, *pBoulaq 6*, pp. 82–83, n. f, notes that the phrase *snb n sd.t=k* appears to be a replacement for the more usual *snb n mwt=f*, "healthy up to his death." If *sd.t*, "tail," can also mean the more figurative "end," i.e., "death," then the meaning here may be "…the death that dances against the ears…," with *sd* being a virtual synonym for *mwt*, "dead male."

EI. (x + 12: 8) is presumably to be read *h3i r-r=f*, "descend against him." The verb *h3i* is commonly used of those who advance with hostile intent against others.

EJ. (x + 12: 10) There is approximately 1 cm of text missing at the beginning of this line. What can be read is . This coupled with the group *iw nṯr.w nb.w* at the end of the preceding line gives *iw nṯr.w nb.w r di.t,* a future expressed as subject + *r* + infinitive. This verbal governs the following clause *w3.w=k*, the whole giving "all of the gods will cause you to be far from…."

EK. (x + 12: 10) *ns*, "tongue," can be read with certainty despite a tear in the papyrus. The idea expressed here is a peculiar one for which I have yet to find an exact parallel. The crocodile is a well-known symbol of the forces of chaos.

EL. (x + 12: 10) On the use of the *mḥ.t*-bowl in magical prescriptions, see note M (x + 2: 4) above.

EM. (x + 12: 11) What is written here is clearly . It is probable that the scribe intended the word *iwn*, "Farbe" (*Wb.* I 52, 9–18). The sign (Sign-list N25) may be an error due to the similarity of *iwn* to *in.t*, "das Tal" (*Wb.* I 93, 2–14).

EN. (x + 12: 11) *iʿ*, "waschen; reinigen" (*Wb.* I 39, 2–17). It occurs in conjunction with beer, an ingredient that does occur at the beginning of the following line.

EO. (x + 12: 12) At the beginning of the line is what appears to be vaguely like , a writing that makes little sense. The writing looks nothing like , a determinative commonly found with the word *iʿ*. What these traces represent is likely the object of the verb *iʿ*, suggesting an original writing like "Wash [x] with sweet beer…." See *pLeiden I 348*, rt. 12[11]–13[3], where the same combination of *mḥt*-dish, beer, and the term *iʿ* is found.

EP. (x + 12: 12) *stp*, "strip of linen," can be restored here based on the traces.

EQ. (x + 12: 12–13) The phrase *stp p3ḳ.t*, "strip of fine linen," occurs at x + 7: 12 above.

ER. (x + 12: 13) *tp.t*, "fine oil" (*WbDN*, pp. 554–55).

ES. (x + 12: 13) *ʿn.tyw*, "myrrh" (*WbDN*, pp. 250–79).

ET. (x + 12: 14) *ẖ3ʿ r mw* is unknown to the *Wörterbuch.* It appears in a gloss in the Kadesh Inscription of Ramesses II, describing the king's treatment of the Prince of Aleppo with *ḫ3ʿ sw ḥm=f r mw*, "His Majesty throws him in the water;" see Kitchen, *RI* 2, p. 138. Note, however, that this verb occurs with the generalized meaning of separation in *pBM 9997*, 2[11]; see Leitz, *HPBM* 7, p. 7, n. 31. It does not appear there with the preposition *r* as it does in the Brooklyn text. A parallel is possibly provided by the phrase *ḫ3ʿ r ḫt*, "Feuer legen," given by Hannig, *GH*, p. 581a.

EU. (x + 12: 15) The *ʿf.t*-plant is known from prescriptions in a number of texts, in various spellings. *pBerlin 3038*, vs. 2[10] (*Bln* 201) gives a writing similar to that here. *WbDN*, p. 87, equates it with *Melilotus officinalis*, "honey clover," citing a study by Dawson, for which see *JEA* 20 (1934), p. 41. Cf., however, Germer, *Heilpflanzen*, p. 40, who states that Dawson's identification is unsupportable, as honey clover is not native to Egypt; see further the discussion by Germer, *Untersuchungen*, pp. 218–19; Manniche, *Egyptian Herbal*, p. 120, claims that *ʿf.t* is better identified as a lettuce. Whatever it may be, it is also a plant to be avoided at certain times, as *pCairo 86637*, 1[3] proscribes eating the *ʿf.t*-plant on the third day of Akhet.

EV. (x + 12: 15) [hieroglyphs] *tḫb*, "eintauchen in" (*Wb.* V 326, 1–11).

EW. (x + 12: 15) [hieroglyphs] appears to be a writing of *ir.ty=fy*, "his eyes," here referring to his eyelids.

EX. (x + 12: 15) [hieroglyphs] *t3* (*WbDN*, pp. 561–62, meaning "Teil" when affixed to the names of plants). Here, the phrase "painted with a part of the *ʿf.t*-plant…" must refer either to an external application of the plant steeped in honey or to the use of the *ʿf.t*-plant as the device by which the patient will be painted with honey.

COMMENTARY

This spell of sixty-six lines is the longest single text preserved in the papyrus.[262] Briefly stated, the structure of the text comprises lengthy invocations to protective deities and direct addresses to the forces of hostility and chaos, including protracted statements about what they individually have said. The spell repeatedly affirms what the hostile forces cannot and will not accomplish in their attempts to assail Pharaoh.[263] The spell concludes with a lengthy prescription and instructions for its application.

The text begins with a long invocation of thirteen and one-half lines to numerous gods or groups of deities, more than thirty of whom are mentioned by name. The invocation begins with an address to Re, Atum, and Khepri, manifestations of the solar deity: Re denoting the sun god proper or in his appearance at the summit of the sky; Atum referring to his manifestation as the setting or dying sun; Khepri used of the rising or reborn sun.[264] The deities mentioned next are members of the Heliopolitan Ennead or have close

262 It represents more than 26% of the overall text of the papyrus.

263 The name Psamtik occurs ten times and the title *pr-ʿ3* nine times.

264 See Assmann, *LÄ* 1 (1975): col. 936, and *LÄ* 2 (1977): cols. 764–65; Allen, *YES* 2 (1988), pp. 10–11; Assman, *Solar Religion*, passim., but especially p. 39, n.10.

connections with Heliopolis and the Heliopolitan creation myth. The next pair mentioned, Hu and Sia, have connections with the solar god through their roles in the daily progression of the solar barque.[265] Thus far, we have three groups of deities, presented as a tightly interlocked triplet. The first group is linked to the second through Atum and his membership in the Heliopolitan Ennead. The third group, Hu and Sia, are tied to the first group, the manifestations of the solar deity, through the role they play in the successful daily journey of the solar barque. Thus, what may appear to be an invocation of individual, randomly named gods at the beginning of this text is actually a tightly bound unit.

Anubis, Wepwawet, and Isdes,[266] the next three gods mentioned, all have connections with Osiris and the mummification of Osiris in particular.[267] Their presence appears to introduce a shift to a different cosmic cycle, that of the Osirian myth. The next two deities are addressed only indirectly through epithets: "he who makes the heaven shake" and "he who makes the earth shake." Known from as early as the Pyramid Texts, the shaking of the sky and the earth is thought to occur at significant moments, like divine or royal epiphanies or at some change in the cosmic cycle, such as the ascent of the dead, transfigured king to the sky or his rebirth.[268] Many of these texts have clear associations with Geb when he is assisting the king;[269] others show Thoth in connection with Osiris, recently raised from the dead.[270] All have clear ties to the resurrection of Osiris or the king. Thus, by extension, the gods who shake the sky and the earth have Osirian connections as well. The next two gods, invoked simply as *iri*, "the god who sees," and *sḏm*, "the god who hears," have well-established connections with Thoth, the god invoked next in the text,[271] who also appears in certain myths from the Osirian cycle.[272] In the Pyramid Texts, Thoth plays a role in refashioning Osiris, thereby linking him to the god Anubis and the mummification of Osiris.[273] The eight gods invoked here, beginning with Wepwawet and ending with Thoth, are all somehow connected with the myth of the embalmed and divinized Osiris. Additionally, several of the epithets encountered have associations with Geb, and

265 See Meeks, *Génies,* p. 5 and p. 82, nn. 232–37; Goyon, *pConfirmation,* p. 91, n. 72, with references; Allen, *YES* 2 (1988), p. 38; Altenmüller, *LÄ* 3 (1980): cols. 65–68 and esp. col. 66 for the association of these gods with Heka and other aspects of magic.

266 On Isdes, see note AQ (x + 7: 9) above.

267 The process through which Osiris became the first *akh,* or "transfigured other."

268 For a discussion, see Traunecker, *OLA* 43 (1992), pp. 153–54, n. 1, pp. 341–51, and pp. 344–47 especially; Goyon, *pConfirmation,* 3^{19-20} and p. 96, n. 115. See further Parker et al., *Lake Edifice,* p. 58, n. 37, where the phrase *mnmn Gb* is explained as an equivalent to *mnmn tꜣ*. Additionally, *pTurin 1983,* rt. 60, an oracular amuletic decree, has the phrase "We shall save her from the one who shakes the earth and who is called the Mover (*mnmn*);" see Edwards, *HPBM* 4, p. 53 and n. 30 there.

269 See, for example, *PT* 690 (in a description of the king who is likened to Osiris); *PT* 508–509 (the king ascends to the sky); *PT* 553 (the king raises himself and ascends to the sky); *PT* 685 (the rebirth of the king).

270 See *PT* 477.

271 See the citations above at note K (x + 9: 11).

272 Boylan, *Thoth,* pp. 136ff.

273 See, for example, *PT* 368 and 448.

may offer further allusions to the earthly realm. The gods invoked thus far collectively represent the cosmos in their associations with the sky, the earth, and the underworld.

The gods of the cardinal points and the gods of the great Enneads of heaven, earth, and the necropolis are also found in an Osirian context.[274] The unity of the four cardinal points taken together with the Enneads of heaven, earth, and the necropolis is possibly an attempt to stress the universal nature of this group of gods invoked, who, like the gods invoked before them, embrace the entire cosmos.

What follows is an invocation of four more divine agents, three of which are given as tetrads: four falcons, four uraei, and four protectors.[275] Groups of four gods or goddesses, functioning as tutelary deities, are often encountered in Egyptian religious texts. The number four is likely derived from the cardinal points or from the four regions that form the cosmos.[276] Among such groups are the Four Sons of Horus, well-known from funerary texts and vignettes. A quite common group encountered in protection texts is "the four *šps.wt*-goddesses," four hippo-headed goddesses who guard the newborn and are often associated with the House of Ptah.[277] In a text on the Metternich stele, they guard over the child Horus.[278] They are also found in *pCairo 58027*, a royal protection text, as "watchers" of Osiris. In that text, the four comprise Sakhmet, Bastet, Wadjet, and Smithis, who are invoked to keep certain demonic forces "far from his [the king's] sleeping-place (*ḥnk.t*)."[279] Again, in their role as protectors of the bedroom, they are found in *pBrooklyn 47.218.2*, x + 5^{9} [280]. They are also connected with the protection of the four corners of rooms in houses.[281] Texts also mention four spirits who guard over Osiris.[282] Four falcons are often shown as part of the retinue of state ships, apparently aspects of the god Monthu and not Horus.[283]

Falcons and *wadjet*-eyes are also a dominant motif in the decoration of the sterns and rudders of ships, where their function is apotropaic, as it clearly is here.[284] *pChester Beatty 8* has a passage in which four falcons (there called *si3.w*, not *bik.w* as here) sit in the prow

274 See, for example, their occurrence in a book of protection for Osiris, *pMMA* 35.9.21, col. 27/9, for which see Goyon, *Le papyrus d'Imouthès*, p. 67; pls. XXVI and XXVIA, l. 9.

275 The individual gods mentioned who precede the tetrads are all discussed in the Text Notes above.

276 Note that the tetrads almost directly follow the invocation of the gods of the four cardinal points.

277 See, for example, *pChester Beatty 9*, vs. B, 14^{9-10}; simply designated as *t3-4 šps.wt*, see *pChester Beatty 4*, rt. 6^{11}; *pChester Beatty 8*, vs. 1^{8} and 2^{1}.

278 See Sander-Hansen, *AA* 8 (1956), p. 44, l. 83, and p. 46, n. 83.

279 See Pries, *SAGA* 27 (2009), pp. 20–21, n. 121.

280 Guermeur and O'Rourke, forthcoming.

281 See Ritner, *JARCE* 27 (1990): 36 ff; see also, Koenig, *pBoulaq 6*, pp. 106–7, n. e for further texts in which the four *šps.wt* are found; Goyon, *Les dieux-gardiens*, pp. 115–17, 413–15, and 471; Assmann, *Solar Religion*, pp. 16–37 and 189.

282 *pChester Beatty 6*, vs. 2^{5-6}.

283 See Borghouts, *LÄ* 4 (1982): cols. 200–204.

284 See Altenmüller, *LÄ* 2 (1977): cols. 93–98.

of the solar barque, their role being to overthrow Apophis.[285] In the Book of the Dead vignette called *BD* 126, four baboons sit one each at a corner of the Pool of Fire. In exemplars of *BD* 126 that include text, the four baboons are said to be in the prow of the sun barque.

In the Books of Day and Night, we encounter uraei in the following of the serpent *mḥn.t*, forming part of the entourage of the sun barque,[286] and four uraei who "sting the enemy of fire quickly, rowing before the flame."[287] In the vignettes of the latter text, these uraei form a barrier or margin between the scene in which they occur and the next that shows the destruction of Apophis.[288]

In the company of the three groups of foursomes encountered in this section, we also meet *pꜣ miw ꜥꜣ*, "the Great Cat," an epithet of the sun god whose earliest attestation seems to be in the Coffin Texts.[289] Its association with Re is found as well in the Book of the Dead.[290] In the New Kingdom religious text known as *The Litany of Re*, a cat labeled *miw ꜥꜣ* appears in a row of figures, all identified as manifestations of the sun god. All of the figures are mummiform except the one named *miw ꜥꜣ*, who is shown as a large crouching cat.[291] This same figure appears with Osirian connections in the Karnak Taharqa chapel in a list of the Osirian forms of Re drawn from the aforementioned *Litany of Re*.[292] At Edfu, Re-Harakhty appears both as a cat and as a lion.[293] Additionally, in New Kingdom Books of the Dead, in a passage found at the end of *BD* 151, the deceased says: *ink miw ꜥꜣ im.y st mꜣꜥ.t nt wbn šw.t im=f*, "I am the great cat that is in the place of truth from which sunlight rises."[294] What seems a bit peculiar in the Brooklyn text is that the being designated as *miw ꜥꜣ* is said to be guarding the barque of Re when he rises in the morning.

The gods invoked thus far are now described as having numerous faces and uraei. References to gods who possess these features are common in protection texts, their main role being that of apotropaic or tutelary beings.[295] This description refers, undoubtedly,

285 *pChester Beatty 8*, vs. 7[3]. They also appear in *pTurin 54051*, 77, 3 in the prow of the solar barque. Borghouts, *pLeiden I 348*, p. 184, nn. 449 and 424, discusses gods who precede the solar barque or are found in its prow, like the four baboons mentioned in the text of *BD* 126.

286 *LJN* 5.

287 *LJN* 10.

288 On uraei and other snakes playing an apotropaic role in texts of the solar cult, see Assman, *Solar Religion*, pp. 16–37.

289 *CT* 335.

290 *BD* 15, the New Kingdom version of *CT* 335.

291 See Piankoff, *The Litany of Re*, 13, § 67; and Hornung, *AH* 2 (1975) 1, 64 and 2, 115, n. 152; See also *Urk* VI, 69[4] and 129[9–10], where the cat appears as a manifestation of the sun god.

292 See Parker et al., *Lake Edifice*, p. 33, n. 47, for this later version of the so-called *Litany of Re*.

293 *Edfu* V, 218[18] and 269[19].

294 See, for example, von Dassow, ed., *The Book of Going Forth by Day* (Book of the Dead of Ani), pl. 33.

295 See, for example, *pIllustré*, 2[1–2], where a deity having nine faces is encountered. An accompanying vignette (fig. 2) illustrates that being as well, showing not only his multiple faces, but uraei on the tops of his feet and cobras at his knees as well. The epithet is found at *pConfirmation*, 11[10], referring to Bastet, a goddess with benign and malign aspects.

to the multiple powers of manifestation and modes of protection that the gods have and to their unknowable nature.

This section closes with an address to *t3-4.t wḏ3.(w)t ʿ3.w(t)*, possibly referring to the apotropaic motif found in the barque of Re that was discussed above,[296] but actually concludes with a final address to a group of beings who are identified simply as *ḏsr.w št3.w ḥr.w*, "sacred ones whose faces are secret…." The epithet *št3.w ḥr* is known from the Book of the Dead[297] and the genre of "mythological" papyri,[298] where beings so described play a protective role.

Extended addresses like that found here are a common feature of protection texts.[299] Here, the deities invoked are called upon to protect Psamtik by driving away the malevolent forces. What follows are twelve statements that announce what the hostile force will not be permitted to accomplish. The first group of these (x + 10: 2–5) focuses on threats designed to interfere with the normal functioning of physical powers. The second group (x + 10: 5) centers on the deprivation of the abilities to speak, see, and hear. Numerous parallels for these ideas are found in descriptions of what the righteous have done to their enemies.[300] References to gods who threaten to take away physical powers are known as well and are especially prevalent in the oracular amuletic decrees.[301] The singular suffix pronoun *=f* is used in these statements, perhaps to show that the one who recites the text has power over each individual member of the agents of chaos.[302] The hostile forces are then addressed directly, and a detailed description is given of a number of actions that they either have taken or intend to take. Most of the exploits described here are the typical attempts to violate the normal cosmic order by the forces of chaos. By drawing attention to these violations, the speaker acknowledges that he knows what the hostile forces have attempted in the past, and such knowledge gives him an awareness of what

296 See n. 284 above.

297 E.g., *BD* 65.

298 See, for example, Piankoff, *Mythological Papyri*, Nr. 24, sc. 3. (*pMMA* 25.3.1).

299 See note C (x + 9: 8) above.

300 *pLeiden I 348*, rt. 13^{8-9}, states that the actions of "cutting off a hand," "closing the mouth," and "blinding an eye" will happen to the "dead ones" who might assail the god Horus-Seth as he sallies forth at night; *pBremner-Rhind*, 27^{10-11} says of the evil foe: "I have cut away his flesh from his bones, I have broken his legs, I have cut off his arms, I have closed his mouth and his lips, I have drawn his teeth, cut away his tongue from his gullet, taken away his speech, blinded his eyes, taken away his hearing…."

301 See Edwards, *HPBM* 4, passim. For a somewhat similar idea, see *CT* 23, which states that nothing evil can or will befall the deceased: *n ip.t(w)=k n ḏdḥ.t=k n ẖnnr.t=k n inṯ=k n s3t=k n rdi.t=k m ẖb.t dd.t sbi.w im=s…*, "You are not to be examined; you are not to be taken into custody; you are not to be imprisoned; you are not to be fettered; you are not to be guarded; you are not to be put in the execution place where the rebels are put…." See also Nordh, *Curses and Blessings*, passim, for a comprehensive discussion.

302 In the direct address to the hostile forces that follows soon after, the singular suffix pronoun *=k* is employed as well.

their present and future intentions are. He claims, further, that as a result of their transgressions. they are to be blinded[303] and cursed.[304]

Next follows a section of approximately thirty lines in which the hostile forces are addressed. The structure of this section consists primarily of statements about the intentions of the hostile forces; the verbs employed in each of these clauses are second person singular forms addressed to the hostile forces. Stating their intentions aloud may be seen as an attempt by the one reciting the text to bring their activities into closer focus in order to neutralize or invalidate them.[305] Equally important and noteworthy is that these statements touch on certain mysteries and secrets of the otherworldly realms. They reveal knowledge that is supposed to remain hidden and to which only a few should have access. It is perhaps significant that the forces of chaos named in the apostrophes throughout the spell are the generic beings: "enemy, fiend, dead male, dead female, etc." Such beings fall clearly into the category of the "uninitiated," those to whom virtually all such knowledge has been denied. The dead males and dead females can be thought of as "non-*akh*'s," beings that cannot properly function in any realm of the divine, as they have been denied the wherewithal to do so. Note that through their actions they are trying to make known what should not be done or said. Thus, they routinely attempt to reverse the principle that what is not to be known must remain securely hidden and that the secret places of the otherworldly realms are not to be transgressed.[306] As their intentions are to disrupt the order and proper functioning of the cosmos, the disclosure of what should not be revealed offers a quintessential example of what may be called "cosmic reversal." Their words and actions prove futile, however, because they lack true knowledge of the essence of the secrets of the otherworld; thus, they are bound to fail. The speaker who addresses them speaks from a vantage point of knowledge and simply points to the futility of their attempts to disrupt what is the normally prescribed cosmic order. The result of all of this is that at the end of the text, beginning at x + 12: 6, the malign forces are simply described as "driven away, repelled, fallen, driven off" and thereby incapable of "enduring in the head, the temple, and the ears" of the Pharaoh. Nonetheless, they continue to remain a negative force that must be routinely and repeatedly dealt with. It is a point of interest that the hostile forces are "driven away, repelled, fallen, driven off," only to return to attempt to disrupt things at a later time. That is because they do not threaten the cosmos from without but from within; they are, ironically, part of the structure of the ordered realm. Thus, personifications of chaos like Seth and Apophis, dead males and females, male and female adversaries, et al. cannot be eliminated without bringing the cosmos to a standstill. But they can and must be neutralized, even if only momentarily.[307]

303 x + 10: 9.

304 x + 10: 11–12.

305 See Borghouts, *pLeiden I 348*, rt. 6^5 and n. 170.

306 DuQuesne, *DIE* 36 (1996): 25–38; also Assmann, *Death and Salvation,* pp. 186ff.

307 Instructive here is Assmann's discussion of the nature of "death as enemy," for which see Assmann, *Death and Salvation,* pp. 64–86.

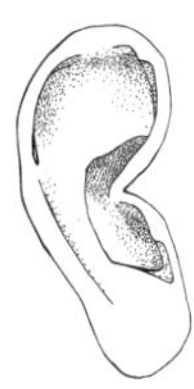

Spell O — Translation with Commentary

COLUMNS X + 12: 16–X + 13: 10 (P. BROOKLYN 47.218.49)

TRANSLITERATION

16. *ky rꜣ n dr hh m msḏr hh dy.t ꞽmꞽ ꞽꞽ r=ꞽ ꞽs ꞽ-*
17. *–r=f tn r sꜣ.wy bꜣ.wy pr [m] šrꞽ n rꜥ dr=tn ẖr nꞽꜣ dꞽdꞽ sḫm rꜥ sḫm pn*
18. *[bꞽk] nsb rꜣ … sd ẖt=k ḥsḳ=k ḏꜥm=k m ꞽrr hh m msḏr n pr-ꜥꜣ ꞽ-*
19. *… ꞽr=k m ꞽꞽ r msḏr=f [sḏm] mdw.wt nw rꜥ rꜥ nb nn … sw ntf ptḥ n rꜥ pn nn sḫm[=k] m*

COLUMN X + 13

1. *msḏr n psmṯk ꜥ.w.s. m ꞽb=f m mꜣꜥ=f m ḥꜣ.ty=f m ḥꜥ.w=f nb i.ptn ḥr ntt ntf ꞽnm*
2. *pr m wsꞽr ꜥb.wy ꞽm=f n ḫn.ty-ḫm šn.w ḥr tp=f m ḥr sꜣ ꜣs.t ꞽw*
3. *ꜥnḫ.wy=fy m-ẖnw wḏꜣ.t sḏm mdw.wt nw rꜥ m ꜣḫ.t ꞽꜣb.t.t n.t pt ꞽ ḫft pft mwt [mwt].t*
4. *ḥm.wt-rꜣ ꞽrr mḥr tn r psmṯk ꜥ.(w.s.) m snf bꜥbꜥ m dšr.t=f gs m ṯr*
5. *n ꜥmꜥ.t ꞽr.n=f m ꜥb.w nṯr.w ḏd=f sḫd=f m ḳs.w=f wnm=f m tbn=f wšꜥ=f m ḥꜥ.w=f nb*
6. *ꞽr.n=f bw.t rꜥ rdi.n=f ꜣtf r tp=f nrꞽ=f ꞽm.y.w ꞽꜣt=sn dgꜣ nṯr.w tp-ꜥ-*
7. *–.wy=sn mꜣꜣ=sn sw <m> ḫt ḥm sn ꞽr.w=f m hꜣ ḥr pr-ꜥꜣ m ꞽꞽ r=f ntf ḥr sꜣ*
8. *ꜣs.t sꜣ ḥꜣ sꜣ ꞽꞽ sꜣ ḏd mdw ḥr snf ꜥꜣ ḳmy snf n msḏr n dꜣg.yt šw.t bnw*
9. *snwḫ ḥr mrḥ.t ꜥd ꜥnḫ gs s ꞽm nty ẖr hh sꜥḳ m mwt mwt.t m msḏr*
10. *ḥnꜥ ꞽr n=f wḫꜣḫ ẖ.wt ḥnꜥ dl.t(w) pẖr.wt nb msḏr*

TRANSLATION

16. *Another spell for driving away heat from the ear.* Heat! Roar![A] Do not come against me. Go,[B] you,
17. indeed, against the Twins,[C] the Two *Ba*'s[D] who came forth [from] the nostril[E] of Re. May you drive away[F] the one possessing evil (?)[G] by placing[H] an image[I] of Re, this image
18. [of a falcon,] (?)[J] licking[K] the mouth,[L] … your weapon[M] has been broken,[N] you behead[O] your *ḏꜥm*-scepter.[P] Do not make heat[Q] in the ear of Pharaoh,
19. …indeed[R] Do not come against his ear. [Listen to] the words[S] of Re every day. You will not […1 cm…][T] him. He is Ptah on this day.[U] You will not gain power[V] in

COLUMN X + 13

1. the ear of Psamtik, l.p.h., in his *ib*-heart, in his temple, in his *ḥ3ty*-heart,[W] in all this body of his because to him belongs the skin[X]
2. that comes forth from Osiris, the horns on him belong to *ḫnty-ḫm*,[Y] the hair on his head[Z] (is) from Horus, the son of Isis.
3. His ears are within the Sound Eye.[AA] Hear the words of Re in the eastern horizon of heaven.[BB] O enemy, fiend, dead male, dead female
4. and so on, he who makes this sickness against Psamtik, l.(p.h.)[CC] in blood,[DD] immersed in his red-blood, smeared with the blood[EE]
5. of an *ʿmʿ.t*-woman,[FF] he has acted with the enmity of the gods.[GG] He who says that he will go down[HH] into his bones, he will feed upon his head, he will chew on all his body,[II]
6. he has done the abomination of Re. He has placed the *atef*-crown upon his head.[JJ] He terrorizes those who are in their primeval mounds.[KK] The gods (who were) their predecessors hide[LL] when
7. they see him. Fall back![MM] Retreat! Pass by! (O) one whose nature is evil![NN] Do not assail[OO] Pharaoh![PP] Do not come against him! He is Horus the son of
8. Isis. A protection behind a protection, there comes a protection.[QQ] *Words to be recited over the blood of a dun-colored ass,*[RR] blood of the ear of a bat,[SS] the feather of a phoenix[TT]
9. brought to a boil with *mrḥ.t*-oil,[UU] (and) goat fat.[VV] Smear a man therewith who is suffering from heat that is caused to enter by a dead male, a dead female into the ear
10. (and) make for him an examination within[WW] and the remedies are placed at his ear.

TEXT NOTES

A. (x + 12: 16) The sign (Sign-list V11) in the word is to be read *dy*; thus, the word here is *dy.t*, "Geschrei; Gebrüll" (*Wb.* V 466, 10–467, which gives the incorrect transcription *dni*). See *pBM 9997,* 7[2], Leitz, *HPBM* 7, p. 19, for an identical writing and the translation "a cry." It appears as well at *pBM 10059,* 3[3] and 16[3]. *hh dy.t* are the first words of the spell proper, possibly forming a vocative phrase; if so, it is odd that the vocative marker is not employed, as it is routinely elsewhere in the papyrus. The two words *hh dy.t* may be appositives or refer to two distinct entities. The appearance of the pronoun =*tn* at the beginning of the next line suggests the latter, or perhaps *dy.t* is a true plural here. In either case, may have Sethian connotations. The god Seth is commonly described as the god who "roars;" see te Velde, *Seth,* p. 20. Note, however, that *dy.t* does not appear in te Velde's discussion, as he focuses on verbs, listed at pp. 22–23, all of which mean "roar" and are written with the Seth-animal determinative. Borghouts, *pLeiden I 348,* pp. 25–26, states that the "loudly roaring one" is an epithet of the demon Akephalos, "the headless one." This epithet is found largely in later texts as an anagram of the name Seth, according to te Velde, *Seth,* pl. XII, 2. The translation "roar" is given for *dy. t* at the above cited *pBM 10059*, 16[3], for which see Leitz, *HPBM* 7, p. 82: "Youthful bull, fearsome of roar...." *pBrooklyn 47.218.2* (Guermeur and O'Rourke, forthcoming), in a section of spells that address crying children, provides a parallel at x + 8[1]: [hieroglyphs] *im=k wdi dy.t m ḫrw=k*, "You shall not emit a cry with your voice." It is also possible that [hieroglyphs] *dy.t* is a personification here and means "Roarers!"

B. (x + 12: 16) The reading of the four signs at the end of the line appears to be [hieroglyphs]. The first three signs suggest the imperative *is*, "gehe!" (*Wb.* I 126, 8–16). The final sign would be the first sign of the particle *(i)r=f* that continues into the next line; the whole group yields the translation "Go indeed!" See *pLeiden I 346*, 1[6], for a parallel.

C. (x + 12: 17) [hieroglyphs] is probably best understood as *s3.wy*, "das Kinderpaar" (*Wb.* III 412, 8–12, referring to Shu and Tefnut). *CT* 783 has a noun written *s3.wy=ky* followed by the names Shu and Tefnut. Given that the phrase *b3.wy*, "the two *Ba*'s," that follows here is a common designation of Shu and Tefnut as well, the translation "the Twins" seems likely. For a discussion of twins, both human and divine, see Baines, *Or* 54 (1985): 461–82. See also note D (x + 12: 17), following.

D. (x + 12: 17) [hieroglyphs] is certain. The first hieratic sign is that given at Möller, *HP* 3, 602, there transliterated as *k3t*; see, however, Gardiner, *Sign-list* Aa4 (=W10*), where the transliteration *b3* is given. The reading *b3.wy*, "Two *Ba*'s," is adopted here (*Wb.* I 412, 12; Hannig, *GH*, p. 238a–b; neither give this writing). Parker et al., *Lake Edifice*, p. 45, nn. 57 and 59, identify the Two *Ba*'s as they appear there as Shu and Tefnut. Zabkhar, *Ba Concept*, p. 37, states that the being named "the-one-who-has-two *ba*'s" embodies the *ba* of Re and the *ba* of Osiris. Numerous passages in the Coffin Texts state that the deceased is the possessor of two *ba*'s; see, for example, *CT* 69 and 696. Several passages make reference to the "House of the Two *Ba*'s," for which see *CT* 50 and 630. The Two *Ba*'s appear in *CT* 945, another spell in which various parts of the body are associated with specific deities. There it is the spine that is said to be the Two *Ba*'s. A passage in *BD* 17 states that "It means Osiris when he entered Busiris. He found the *ba* of Re (and) one embraced the other. Then (they) became the two *Ba*'s." The identification with Shu and Tefnut is further confirmed by what follows; see note E (x + 12: 17).

E. (x + 12: 17) On the act of sneezing and its connection with the origin of divine *Ba*'s, see Žabkar, *Ba Concept*, p. 96, who cites *CT* 75: *nf.n=f wi m šr.t=f*, "He [Re] sneezed me [Shu] out from his nostril...," and also *CT* 191: *nf.[n=f] wi m šr.t=f*, "he has sneezed me out from his nostril...." For a somewhat different act of creation emanating from the nose, see *pSalt 825*, 2[3], where there is a reference to blood from the nose of Geb falling to earth and forming pine trees.

F. (x + 12: 17) The subject of [hieroglyphs] *dr*, "drive away," is [hieroglyphs] *=tn*, the antecedent of which remains unclear.

G. (x + 12: 17) The group presents difficulties. The presence of indicates that is a substantive. The only substantive listed in the lexica written *ni* or *niꜣ* is the word *ni.wt*, "Böses" (*Wb.* II 201, 7). It is found in *CT* 335 in the phrase *dr=(i) iw=i ḫsr=(i) ni.wt=i*, "…I have dispelled my wrongdoing (and) I have driven out my evil." The meaning "evil" attributed to the word *ni.wt* in the Coffin Text passage seems based on the occurrence of the word *ḏw.wt* in the parallel passage in *BD* 17: *dr.i iw=i ḫsr.i ḏw.wt=i*. None of the *CT* exemplars show the determinative in the writing of *ni.wt*, but all show the determinative where preserved. Note that several of the words spelled *ni/niꜣ* do show the determinative. For lack of a better suggestion, I have translated the word written as "evil." Note that there are several other oddly written words in this spell.

H. (x + 12: 17) The group *didi* is the imperfective active participle.

I. (x + 12: 17) *sḫm*, "Göttliche Wesen; Göttliche Macht" (*Wb.* IV 243, 5–245, 2). Goyon, *pLouvre I 3079*, 149, 2, translates *sḫm* as "effigy," an extension of the meanings of the *Wörterbuch.*

J. (x + 12: 18) After a lacuna of approximately 2 cm, the sign (Sign-list G5) can be read. As it is not followed by the determinative (Sign-list G7), it is probably the determinative of *bik*, "falcon," and not the name "Horus."

K. (x + 12: 18) *nsb*, "etw. verschlingen; etwas ablecken" (*Wb.* II 334, 11–14). Vandier, *pJumilhac,* 16[3–4], 16[12], where it is translated "lêcher." Goyon, *pLouvre I 3079,* 145, 2, p. 116, n. 62, gives the translation "est dardée." See the discussion at note D (x + 8: 12) above.

L. (x + 12: 18) What follows is either or a vertical sign damaged in the middle.

M. (x + 12: 18) The group *ḫt=k*, "your staff/weapon," is certain.

N. (x + 12: 18) The traces suggest *sḏ*, "zerbrechen" (*Wb.* IV 373, 8–375, 7). The phrase *ḫt=k* seems to be its subject. *Urk.* VI, 19[14] provides a parallel in *ḥsḳ. n=f ḫt*, "er hat Holz gefällt…." See also notes O–P (x + 12: 18), following.

O. (x + 12: 18) *ḥsḳ*, "abhauen; enthaupten" (*Wb.* III 168, 14–169, 2), used in connection with "der Feind." It occurs in *pJumilhac* 1[x + 7], 2[18], 18[9] and 18[12], 20[6], and 22[10], all passages in which the intended meaning is clearly "decapitate." At 3[19] of the same text, the verb is used of "cutting off" the phallus and testicles. In *pLeiden I 343+345*, vs. 24[3–4], it denotes the "cutting off" of hands and feet.

P. (x + 12: 18) Based on the traces that follow, I am reading the sign (Sign-list S40) as the beginning of the noun *ḏꜥm*, "Art Szepter der Himmel" (*Wb.* V 537, 4–11).

Wilson, *PL*, p. 1225, states that the *ḏꜥm*-sceptre had the head of Seth or that of a snake. Such a detail makes it an interesting figurative object of the verb *ḥsḳ*, "behead." The image in *ḥsḳ=k ḏꜥm*, "you behead your *ḏꜥm*-sceptre," is clearly one of depriving the enemy of any form of power. The two verb phrases here seem to imply that the actions of the malevolent forces are essentially counterproductive and will backfire on them, another example of the reversals or inversions that we see in these texts.

Q. (x + 12: 18) The sign *m* is the negative imperative, beginning a new vetitive clause: "Do not make…."

R. (x + 12: 19) Following the lacuna of 2 cm at the beginning of the line, can be read. I think that the reading of the prepositional phrase *ir=k* seems preferable to that of the particle *(i)r=k*, as there does not seem to be enough space for the writing of another imperative.

S. (x + 12: 19) *sḏm mdw.wt*, "Hear the words…," is common in protection texts, addressed to the agents of disease and disorder and is often followed by an enumeration of the dire consequences that will befall them if they do not listen. For parallels, see Massart, *MDAIK* 15 (1957), vs. 5^{2}: *ꜥḥꜥ sḏm mdw*, "Stop! Hear the word," addressed to a scorpion; *pLeiden I 346*, 3^{5}: *ḥꜣ=i r sḏm mdw.t nṯr.w*, "Get behind me to hear the word of the gods!," addressed apparently to the speaker's *ka*; *pBoulaq 6*, rt. $8^{5–6}$: *im sḏm=ti mdw.t ḏd=ti imn*, "Hear the word which Amun is saying," addressed to Horus; *pBoulaq 6*, rt. 10^{4} and rt. 11^{1}: *ꜥḥꜥ im sḏm mdw.t pꜣ nṯr*, "Stop! Hear the word of the god!," addressed to beings acting irreverently; *pTurin 54051*, 79, 5: *sḏm mdw.t*, "Hear the word;" *pLeiden I 343 + I 345*, rt. 7^{1}: *sḏm ḫrw štḫ*, "Hear the voice of Seth!;" ibid., vs. 17^{2}: *kꜣ sḏm=k nꜣ n mdw.w i…*, "You will hear the words, O […]," likely addressed to a group of malevolent forces. The same phrase is found in Spell C (x + 2: 7 and 10–11) and Spell I (x + 8: 7) above.

T. (x + 12: 19) A single word appears to be lost in the lacuna of 1 cm here. A verb with a meaning like "come against," "gain power over," or "prevail against" is required. See note J (x + 2: 8) above, where the text has the verb *ḫsf*; the traces here show a partial horizontal line that does not suit such a reading.

U. (x + 12: 19) The construction of *ntf* + noun is commonly encountered in magical texts, particularly when introducing a series of statements addressed to the inimical forces explaining why they will fail (or have already failed). *BD* 42 provides a parallel with *ink Rꜥ n hrw nb*, "I am Re every day." Interestingly enough, what follows there is a statement also about hostile forces not gaining power. See also the discussion at note YY (x + 2: 16) above.

V. (x + 12: 19) The parallel at x + 2: 8 has *nn ḫsf=tw*, "One shall not make war…." See note T (x + 12: 19) above.

W. (x + 13) On the terms *ib* and *ḥ3.ty*, see note K (x + 2: 8) above.

X. (x + 13: 1) The parallel at x + 2: 9 above is again slightly different. There the statement is *ntf inm pr m ḥꜥ.wt* [*n Wsir*], "to him belongs the skin that comes forth from the body of Osiris." The skin of Osiris is likely a symbol of cyclical rejuvenation and permanence. See Barbash, *YES* 8, p. 76 and n. 80 there for references. *CT* 106, a text in which the deceased lays claim to empowerment, has a reference to the skin of Osiris: *dr.n=i nkn m ẖnw Wsir*, "I have driven away the injury from the skin of Osiris." On the skin of Horus, see *pBM 10059*, 2^{2-3}, and Leitz, *HPBM* 7, pp. 55–56. The association of a specific body part with a specific deity found in *pBrooklyn 47.218.49* is completely unlike those that occur in any other sources, to my knowledge. Several different prepositions are used here before the name of each deity, thus creating some questions about the relationship of the anatomical parts and the names that follow. A comparable passage in *pBudapest 51.1961*, 3^{5}, gives a list of body parts, each associated with a specific deity, for which see Kákosy, *Acta Antiqua Academiae Scientiarum Hungaricae* 19: 3–4 (1979), pp. 159–77. *In pLeiden I 348*, rt. 5^{4}–6^{2}, a list of parts of the body and their connections with specific deities, the body part is always introduced by *iw* and the name or epithet of the god by the preposition *m*. The same construction is found in *BD* 42.

It is possible, however, that the idea here reflects, in an abbreviated form, another type of statement found commonly in protection texts. Such statements claim that a part of the body is said to be under the protection of a specific deity. In the Leiden text cited above, a string of such statements immediately precedes the section that has *iw* + body part + *m* + name of deity. The different prepositions used in the Brooklyn text, however, seem to imply that the anatomical parts of the Pharaoh come from or belong to an individual deity, not that each part is simply associated with a god. The initial clause of these parallel statements, *ntf inm pr m wsir*, "To him belongs the skin that comes forth from Osiris," seems to support such an interpretation. It is worth noting that in this passage, and in its parallel above in Spell C, all of the body parts are associated with a manifestation of Horus, the divine embodiment of kingship, except one that is associated instead with Osiris.

Y. (x + 13: 2) The epithet *ḫn.ty-ḫm*, "Foremost One of Letopolis," refers to a manifestation of Horus known as *ḥr ḫn.ty ir.ty* or *ḥr mḫn.ty ir.ty*, the chief god of Letopolis. Originally a falcon-headed god, he became associated with Horus in the Old Kingdom. On the connections between Horus and Letopolis, see Junker, *Der sehende und blinde Gott,* passim, but especially pp. 45–58. See Darnell, *Enigmatic Netherworld Books,* pp. 171–73, esp. n. 36 on the broader notions of blindness in Egyptian thought. This manifestation of Horus is attested early in religious literature; see, for example *CT* 50, *CT* 322, and *CT* 335. He appears as well in *BD* 17 and *BD* 78, where he plays an apotropaic role. For his association with healing, see Spiegelberg, *ZÄS* 57 (1922), pp. 70-71. The manifestation of Horus associated with Letopolis appears often in later religious texts as well. *pLeiden I 346,* 2^{9-10}, states that *ḫn.ty-ḫm* is Horus the Elder; see Bommas, *pLeiden I 346,* pp. 86–88. The names *ḥr mḫn.ty ir.ty* and *ḥr ḫn.ty-ẖm* are found in *pChester Beatty 9,* vs. B., 7^{2-3}, in an address to Horus in his manifest forms. The epithet *ḫn.ty-ẖm*, also referring to the god *ẖnty-ir.ty*, occurs in *pLeiden I 343+345,* vs. 23. For further references to the name *ḥr ẖnty-ir.ty*, see Goyon, *BIFAO* 65 (1965): 8; Jelínková-Reymond, *BdE* 23 (1956), § 6, pp. 29 and 34, n. 1; *pLeiden 348 I,* rt. 8^{8}, where *ẖnty-ẖm* appears as the deity who has cut off the heads of the speckled snakes and has, in turn, restored them. He then revives the gods and puts their heads back on as well.

Z. (x + 13: 2) In the parallel at x + 2: 9–10 above, the scribe has added plural strokes to the word *ḥr* and has written the preposition *n* before the word *tp* as well.

AA. (x + 13: 3) On the *Wadjet*-Eye as a place of protection, see the discussion at note R (x + 2: 10) above.

BB. (x + 13: 3) The parallel at x + 2: 10–11 above has the additional phrase *hrw nb*, “every day.” On the instruction to listen to the words of Re, see note S (x + 12: 19) above.

CC. (x + 13: 4) The parallel at x + 2: 12 has the term *pr-ꜥꜣ* in place of the name *Psmṯk.*

DD. (x + 13: 4) The parallel at x + 2: 12 has *mḥ m*, “filled with,” before *snf*, “blood.” The more complete writing seems to make better sense. *bꜥbꜥ*, “trinken” (*Wb.* I 447, 1–4) appears in a number of texts, where it has been variably translated as “se plonger,” “wade,” “bathe.” These translations are discussed by Ward, *SAK* 5 (1977): 274–78, who traces the etymology of both *bꜥbꜥ* and *bꜣbꜣ* and argues for the basic meaning “bathe” for the former. Given the occurrence of *bꜥbꜥ* in the present passage followed by the preposition *m*, Ward’s conclusions about its meaning make sense here: “bathed in blood” = “immersed in blood;” the phrase would parallel the following *gs m ṯr*, “smeared with red-(blood).” It is worth noting that Budge, *The Book of the Dead* (London 1909), p. 509, had already anticipated Ward in translating the same phrase “…shall wash himself clean in your blood, and he shall bathe in your gore….” Cf., however, Goyon, *Les dieux-gardiens,* p. 275, n. 4, and p. 364, n. 5, who, for the verb *bꜥbꜥ*, persists in following the meaning “trinken” as given by the *Wörterbuch.*

EE. (x + 13: 4) *ṯr*, “blood,” is certain. See note BB (x + 2: 12) above.

FF. (x + 13: 5) The term *ꜥmꜥ.t* likely refers to a menstruating woman, for which see O’Rourke, *ZÄS* 134 (2007): 165–71. Note that the sign (Sign-list D52) was added as a supralinear sign. See note GG (x + 2: 13) above.

GG. (x + 13: 5) The parallel at x + 2: 13 has *[ir.n=]f ꜥb.w=f r pr-ꜥꜣ*, “[He has done] his enmity against Pharaoh.” The sense here parallels that thought, though the wording is different.

HH. (x + 13: 5) [hieroglyphs] *sḫd* may be "mit dem Kopf nach unten sein" (*Wb.* IV 265, 8–266, 10). The entry does not give [hieroglyph] (Sign-list A24) as a determinative. The parallel at x + 2: 13 seems to have the verb [hieroglyphs] *sb*, "climb over," occurring there at the end of a lacuna. A parallel to this curious phrase may be found in Jelínková-Reymond, *Djed-Hor*, § 6, 29, l. 1: *sḫd ḳs.wt n Wsir n=f*, with the translation "Renverse les os d'Osiris pour lui!" given at p. 33 and the cautionary remark at p. 33, n.7, "…la signification n'est pas claire". Wilson, *PL*, pp. 917–18, cites this verb as used to describe the action of the flood and gives translations such as "go down to/into; fall headlong into," citing Gardiner, *JEA* 30 (1943): 53; such a meaning makes better sense here. It is also possible that the verb [hieroglyphs] *sb* of the parallel is actually a writing of [hieroglyphs] *sb*, "go; travel."

II. (x + 13: 5) *wšꜥ* is "etw. kauen; etw. zerbeissen" (*Wb.* I 370, 6–13). For parallels to the inimical forces feeding on the unsuspecting or the sick, see *pBM 10042*, 10[3–4]: *nty wnm.w m iwf swri.w m snf*, "those who feed on flesh and drink blood;" see also *pLeiden I 343+345*, vs. 4[9], for the phrase *wšꜥ ḳs.w*,"chewer of bones," as an epithet of the disease or disease-demon *ꜥḫw*. On gods feeding on their enemies, see the Commentary to Spell G2 above. See also note HH (x + 10: 4) above.

JJ. (x + 13: 6) The text follows the parallel at x + 2: 14, with a few minor differences. x + 2: 14 has *ꜣtf m tp-ꜥ*, "*atef*-crown from before," in place of *ꜣtf r tp=f*, "*atef*-crown upon his head" or "*atef*-crown towards his head." See the discussion at notes OO–RR (x + 2: 14) above.

KK. (x + 13: 6) For a similar writing of [hieroglyphs] *iꜣt*, see *pEdwin Smith*, 20[10]; Breasted translates *iꜣt* as "snare," taking it to be the word given at *Wb.* I 36, 8–11. A somewhat similar writing occurs in *pBM 10309*, 2[13], for which see Leitz, *HPBM 7*, p. 29 and pl. 10, where he translates it as "mounds." A singular form of the phrase also occurs in *pBM 9997*, 3[15], for which see Leitz, *HPBM 7*, p. 9, n. 54 and pl. 3, who notes that *im.y-iꜣt=f* is a word for a snake and gives references. Here, we likely have the phrase found in *pBM 10309*, "those who are in their mounds," mentioned above. Note the absence of a determinative such as the mound determinative [hieroglyph] (Sign-list N30) or the town sign ⊗ (Sign-list O49) given at *Wb.* I 35, 8. A reference to a god who is *nb iꜣt*, "Lord of his Mound," occurs in *pLeiden I 348*, rt. 3[6], with the writing of the word *iꜣt* there as [hieroglyphs]. However, that same text has the identical writing at vs. 11[5] for the word *ꜣt*, "time;" such a spelling for *ꜣt* is apparently common in the New Kingdom, for which see Borghouts, *pLeiden I 348*, n. 410. Given the occurrence of the temporal phrases *m tp-ꜥ*, "from before," and *nṯr.w tp ꜥ.wy=sn*, "the gods who were their predecessors," in the present passage, the *iꜣt*-mound may refer to the burial places of the primeval deities mentioned. The *Djeme*-mound in Thebes, located on the west bank at Medinet Habu, was such a place, serving as the focal point in the *Djeme*-festival celebrated at Thebes. During this festival, the god Amun left the Karnak temple to visit the deceased primeval gods at their burial site. On the *i3t*-mound as a term suggesting a burial site, see Darnell, *Enigmatic Netherworld Books,* p. 291. See also note RR (x + 2: 14) above.

LL. (x + 13: 6) *dgi*, "verborgen sein" (*Wb.* V 496, 8–14). Here it is written with the determinative (Sign-list A5); at x + 2: 15 above it is written with the determinative (Sign-list A30).

MM. (x + 13: 7) The sign *m* that is written before the imperative *ḫt* seems to be an error by assimilation, stemming from the writing of the common preposition group *m-ḫt*.

NN. (x + 13: 7) The writing seems certain; it may be a writing of *ir.w* given at *Wb.* I 114, 14, "Bez. für böses Wesen," as that seems to be the only writing of an *iri*-derived word that has both the initial *yod* and the determinative. See the discussion at note WW (x + 2: 16) above.

OO. (x + 13: 7) On *h3i* and its negative connotations, see note XX (x + 2: 16) above.

PP. (x + 13: 7) In place of the phrase *ḥr pr-ʿ3* here, the parallel at x + 2: 16 has simply *ḥr.f.*

QQ. (x + 13: 8) On the commonly encountered phrase *s3 ḥ3 s3 ii s3*, "a protection behind a protection, there comes a protection," see note ZZ (x + 2: 16) above.

RR. (x + 13: 8) The rubric is very faded here, and only the group *snf ʿ3 ḳmy*, "blood of a dun-colored ass," can be read with certainty. On the use of this animal in prescriptions, see note BU (x + 7: 16) above. See also the Commentary below.

SS. (x + 13: 8) On this ingredient, see note AC (x + 2: 17) above.

TT. (x + 13: 8) On this ingredient, see note AD (x + 2: 17) above.

UU. (x + 13: 9) On *mrḥ.t*-oil, see *WbDN*, pp. 250–79.

VV. (x + 13: 9) The ingredient *ʿd ʿnḫ*, "goat fat," is not given in *WbDN*. See the Commentary below.

WW. (x + 13: 10) In the phrase, the first word is *wḫ3ḫ*, "suchen" (*Wb.* I 353, 14–354, 7). See Jelínková-Reymond, *Djed-Hor,* § 2, 28–29 and p. 17, n. 9, where *wḫ3ḫ* is so written for *ḫ3* with the meaning "to examine a patient;" so Hannig, *GH,* p. 213a for *wḫ3*, "suchen (Person, Sache, Verlorenes)." Such a reading seems possible here. The word written is given by *Wb.* III, 356 as a plural writing of *ẖ.t*, "belly," and thus, by extension, as the idea of "within."

COMMENTARY

Spell O is largely a parallel to Spell C (x + 2: 6–18) found earlier in the papyrus, but the text here is better preserved. The two texts differ at the very beginning, but then largely conform to each other. They are simply two versions of the same spell, as the notion of a specific and fixed archetype seems unknown to the Egyptians.[308] The beginning of Spell C is badly damaged and thus offers little to the present discussion. The present spell begins with an address to forces that pose a threat to an individual referred to in the first person. The assailants are told to direct their threats instead against the Twins and the Two *Ba*'s who have come forth from the nostril of Re. The text is unfortunately damaged here; a number of words are missing and the meanings of several words and allusions remain unclear. The parallels to the text of Spell C begin in the last line of Column x + 12 and continue to the end of the spell at Column x + 13: 10. Although the texts differ in wording in places, they essentially speak to the same idea. They focus on threats to the ear and, subsequently, the temple, heart, and body of Psamtik, all of which are said to be unassailable because a number of his individual body parts have close associations with specific deities; among those mentioned are Osiris, Horus Khenty-Khem, Horus son of Isis, and Wadjet. The source of the threat is again the generic forces that have been encountered almost routinely in this papyrus.[309] What is interesting here is that the hostile forces are said to be "bathed in blood," a possible allusion to their involvement in some cosmic conflict.

References to beings immersed in blood, from gods to demons, are numerous. Early religious texts offer a number of examples: an epithet of Re, *bꜣ ỉm.y dšr=f*, "the *ba* who is in his red-blood;"[310] a being described as *rdi.n n=k bꜣ pf ỉm.y dšr.w=f ỉm.y-dšr.w=f*, "that ram who is in his blood has given to you what is in his blood;"[311] there is also a demon called *dšr.ty ḫn.ty ḥw.t ỉns*, "Bloody one who is foremost in the House of Red Linen."[312] New Kingdom texts give further evidence: *wꜥb=f m snf=tn bꜥbꜥ=f m dšr.w=tn*, "He becomes pure (*wꜥb*) in your blood, he bathes (*bꜥbꜥ*) in your red-blood;[313] there are also beings described as "the blood-covered ones."[314] In a passage in the West Semitic Balu-myth, the goddess Anat is so described: "…as to her knees she wades in the blood of the soldiers, to her neck in the gore of fighters."[315] A Late Period text describes beings "in their blood."[316] Note that many of these texts have clear references to conflict.

Throughout the text, the statements addressed to the inimical forces take the form of both negative and positive injunctions that are reinforced through references to count-

308 See Quack, *Die Lehren des Ani*, p. 17.

309 See the discussion in the Introduction above at pp. 26ff.

310 *PT* 854.

311 *CT* 226.

312 *CT* 335; the same deity is found in *pLeiden I 347*, 4^7 as well.

313 *BD* 134. Note the alliterative wordplay between *wꜥb* and *bꜥbꜥ*.

314 *The Book of Caverns*, 6, 39; Pl. 135 (7) P.

315 See Pardee, *The Context of Scriptures* 1, pp. 250–51.

316 See Koenig, *pBoulaq 6*, p. 120, n.d, with references.

er forces that play an apotropaic role. The first of these mentioned is "the words of Re in the eastern horizon of heaven," an expression also found at x + 2: 7 and x + 2: 10–11 above.[317] This phrase may allude to the successful rise of the sun in the eastern sky after the defeat of Apophis in the conflict that played a part in the daily solar cycle. The second element of protection comes in the enumeration of deities, each of whom is connected with a particular anatomical part of the king. Such lists of body parts and their associations with various deities are common in the genre of protection texts.[318] In the present text, it seems that the anatomical parts mentioned come from or belong to the deities named and, thereby, offer powers of protection, in this case, the divine protection of the Pharaoh. The third source of safeguard mentioned is the *Wadjet*-Eye or "Sound Eye." The idea of shelter provided within the *Wadjet*-Eye is quite familiar. For example, in two Coffin Texts that focus on the mobility of the deceased after he is reborn, we find the statement *ink rꜥ n hrw pn (ṯz-pẖr) ink ḥr m-ẖn.w ir.t=f*, "I am the sun of this day (and vice-versa); I am Horus within his Eye."[319] In the Book of the Dead, we encounter the phrase *ink im.y wḏꜣ.t*, "I am one who is within the Sound Eye,"[320] and again, "The Eye of Horus has encompassed you; you are hidden deep within it; it casts its magical protection about your flesh."[321] In a New Kingdom protection text, we find *ink šw twt n rꜥ ḥms=i m-ẖn.w wḏꜣ.t it=f*, "I am Shu, image of Re. I sit within the Sound Eye of his [*sic*] father."[322] In all of these texts, the emphasis is placed on *wḏꜣ.t* as a site of protection. Note that in the present text, it is the ears, the anatomical focal point of the majority of the texts of the papyrus, that are said to be "within the Sound Eye."[323] Further on, we find the *atef*-crown, a well-known symbol of protection.[324] Worn by Re, Osiris, Horus, or the King, the *atef*-crown was considered to be the visible manifestation of Re's power on earth, especially the power to strike fear in the hearts of others. The act of putting on the *atef*-crown and its resultant effect is described in a number of texts. In a Coffin Text, we find *mꜣ.n=kwi m ꜣtf=i ꜥꜣ rdi.n n=i rꜥ smn n.i tm psḏ.t ḥtp.ti ḥr.s*, "I am seen with my great *atef*-crown that Re gave to me (and) that Atum (and) the Ennead made fast for me,

---

317 The apotropaic function of the imperative *sḏm mdw* is discussed at note S (x + 12: 19) above.

318 See, for example, in *pLeiden I 343+345*; *pChester Beatty 7*, vs. 2^{5}–5^{11}; *pVatican* 2^{7}–4^{11}; the basic study of such lists is Massart, *Analectica Biblica. Studia Biblica et Orientalia* III. *Oriens Antiquus* (1959), pp. 227–46; see Ritner, *Mechanics*, p. 40, n. 181, for additional relevant bibliography; important also is Walker, *BACE* 4 (1993), pp. 82–101, esp. pp. 83–84, where he remarks on the lack of conformity among such lists and the absence of anything approaching a rigid canon.

319 *CT* 107 and *CT* 110; the word *ir.t*, "eye," there refers to *wḏꜣ.t*, the restored Eye of Horus.

320 *BD* 42.

321 *BD* 15.

322 *pBM 10042*, 7^{2-3}; in this text *wḏꜣ.t* refers to the Eye of Re. For a discussion of the relationship and interchangeability of the Eye of Horus and the Eye of Re, see. n. 323, following.

323 See Darnell, *SÄK* 24 (1997): 35–48, for a discussion and further texts.

324 For a discussion of the *atef*-crown and its meaning, see Zandee, *pAmunhymnus* 2, pp. 535–38 and 630–37; and Derchain, *CdE* 30 (1955): 225–87.

(they) being pleased by it." The text later continues: *wd=i sḏb.w nw ḫft.yw=i iw=f ḫsf im=i...iw ḫft.yw=i ḫr ḫr snḏ.t m33=sn w(i)*, "I put up obstacles for my enemies when he [*sic*] comes contending with me...my enemies fall through fear of me when they see me."[325] Another text in that corpus has *3tf=i m wp.t=i nrw.t=i m ḥ3.t=i di=s nrw=i n nṯr.w*, "...my *atef*-crown on my brow, my terror on my forehead (so that) it would give my terror to the gods."[326] The Book of the Dead has references to Osiris putting on the *atef*-crown during his reign in Heracleopolis Magna in order to strike terror in the hearts of the other gods, further attesting to general connections between the *atef*-crown and the intent to instill fear in others.[327] *pLouvre E 3661* provides a passage in which the act of donning the *atef*-crown makes one the "lord of terror."[328] *pBM 10288* outlines in great detail the story of Horus putting on the *atef*-crown, an action which causes his face to swell, an obvious etiological or eponymous myth whose purpose is to explain a later derived etymology of the name Harshef as "swollen of face."[329] Finally, the hostile forces are ordered to withdraw, and the Pharaoh is now said to be Horus, the son of Isis, both of whom feature largely in stories of protection in Egyptian myth.[330]

The prescription of Spell C, most of which has been lost, can for the most part be restored from that of Spell O, as the two seem to follow each other fairly closely. Several thoughts on the nature of Egyptian "medical prescriptions" should be offered. In studies of ingredients found in medical and protection texts, the focus has been generally on attempting to identify what these ingredients actually are. Over the course of time, a number of plants and animals have been identified and, in quite a number of those cases, the actual "medicinal" value of some of them has been established and subsequently challenged. There are still, however, many words that represent a variety of animals, vegetables, and minerals whose identities remain absolutely unknown. Additionally, we encounter a number of ingredients whose presence in such lists seems to border on the bizarre. In the prescription of the present text, for example, we meet the ingredients *snf ꜥ3 ḳmy*, "blood of a dun-colored ass," *snf n msḏr n d3g.yt*, "blood of the ear of a bat," and *ꜥd ꜥnḫ*, "goat fat." Further study may reveal that these three ingredients actually do have valid medicinal properties, but a few thoughts can be offered about their presence in this prescription. The ass and the goat are animals that have Sethian associations and thus were thought to have certain powers, albeit negative ones. The blood from the ass and bat has connections as well with certain ideas presented in the body of the text. At x + 13: 4–5, the enemies who are attempting to assail the king are described as "...in blood, immersed in his red-blood, smeared with the blood of an *ꜥmꜥ.t*-woman...." Reversal and inversion are central ideas in Egyptian thought. The power of Sethian elements and that of blood as a well-recognized life force make these very elements powerful weapons to

325 *CT* 313.

326 *CT* 334; it is possible that the second phrase, *nrw.t=i m ḥ3.t=i*, refers specifically to the uraeus on the front of the crown.

327 *BD* 175 and *BD* 183.

328 See Ledrain, *RT* 1 (1870): 92.

329 See Caminos, *JEA* 58 (1972): 205–24.

330 See, for example, the collection of texts found in Klasens, *OMRO* 53 (1952) = (*SocBehague*).

be used against the forces of chaos. Using the very powers associated with the malevolent forces against them is a most effective way to neutralize them. The Egyptians well understood the potency and value of fighting fire with fire.[331]

We can see that the texts of both Spell C and Spell O as a whole show many of the features of a traditional protection text. The menacing forces are identified by name. The text addresses them directly and forcefully, stating unequivocally what they will and will not be allowed to do. It is worth noting that the spell focuses not on the defeat of hostile forces already engaged in conflict; rather, their activity is construed as a potential threat, one that must be warded off apotropaically through the intervention of forces that are specifically enumerated and that routinely play roles in the maintenance of cosmic order. As a group, the protective constituents largely have solar connections through Re and Horus, although there is one clear reference to Osiris. Although neither Seth nor Apophis are directly named, the allusions to the former are present in the references to the ass and the goat encountered in the coda of the spell, an echo of the probable Sethian associations of the word *dy.t* found at the beginning of the text. Once again, the mythological allusions are to threats to the cosmos and the (re)establishment of cosmic equilibrium. By associating the attempt to assail the ear of Pharaoh with the idea of cosmic conflict, the successful outcome of the protection of Pharaoh's ear becomes (hopefully) guaranteed.

---

331 On the nature of such inversions, see Lucarelli, *SAT* 11 (2006): 210ff. On the mythological and religious associations of certain ingredients found in medical prescriptions, see Győry, in P. Kousoulis, ed., *OLA* 175 (2011), pp. 154–55.

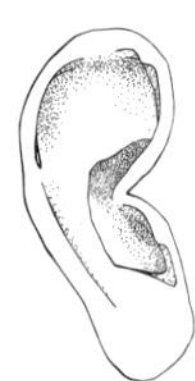

Spell P — Translation with Commentary

COLUMN X + 13: 10–19 (P. BROOKLYN 47.218.49)

TRANSLITERATION

10. … *ky rꜣ hꜣ mwt ir.y msḏr n psmṯk*
11. *bḥn.tw smꜣ.n=i tw m.t is ii.tw m.t wr.t ii.tw hꜣ.tw=tn sḫn.t.t=tn*
12. *ʿb.t=s r imn.t.t iꜣb.t.t r rsy.t mḥ.t ʿb.t=s r imn.t.t im.y.w-ḫt ḥr ʿb.t=*
13. *s r iꜣb.t.t im.y.w-ḫt b ʿb.t=s r rsy.t im.y.w-ḫt ḥr ʿb.t=s r mḥ.t.t*
14. *im.y.w-ḫt b ḥꜣ=k wd ʿ=f m msḏr n psmṯk ḥwi.tw ib snk … ḫr*
15. *ḏd=s rn=k pwy wnm=s smꜣ tw bik ḥsḳ tw miw ḥm sbi*
16. *imi=k wd ʿb=k m msḏr n psmṯk [ʿ.w.]s. šm=k sḫtḫt inn=i wr.t …*
17. *di=s ḫt ḥr=k nb ḏd=k r pr-ʿꜣ pꜣ hh tꜣ hh.t ḏd šn=k r=k bw.t=k … s …*
18. *nn iw=k [r] msḏr n [pr-ʿꜣ] … ḏ[d] mdw ḥr bit ḥs [m]iw ḥs msḥ.t hs … wm …*
19. *p[ꜣ]ḳ …*

TRANSLATION

10. …………………*Another spell.* O[A] dead man, belonging to[B] the ear of Psamtik.
11. You are cut up.[C] I have slain you.[D] Behold, indeed,[E] she is come.[F] Behold[G] the Great One,[H] she is come near you.[I] You shall let[J]
12. her[K] horn[L] pass first to[M] the West, the East, to the South, the North,[N] her horn to the West (and) those who are in the following of Horus,[O] her horn
13. to the East (and) those who are in the following of the Evil One,[P] her horn to the South (and) those who are in the following of Horus,[Q] her horn to the North
14. (and) those who are in the following of the Evil One.[R] Back you, who would place his influence[S] in the ear of Psamtik. The greedy fiendish one[T] is struck,[U] …
15. […] she shall say[W] this name of yours (you) whom she will devour.[X] The falcon has slain you.[Y] The cat has decapitated you.[Z] Retreat, rebel.[AA]
16. Do not place your horn[BB] in the ear of Psamtik, [l.p.]h.[CC] (If) you are proceeding,[DD] turn back. I will bring the Great One[EE] […1.5 cm…]

17. (so that) she puts fire[FF] upon each of you (when) you speak[GG] against Pharaoh. O[HH] male heat! O[II] female heat! Your (own) spell is said against you and against your abomination [...2 cm...]
18. You shall not come [against][JJ] the ear of [Pharaoh].[KK] *Recitation over honey,*[LL] feces of [a cat], feces of a crocodile,[MM] feces[...][NN] [...2 cm...]
19. fine linen[OO] [...16 cm...]

TEXT NOTES

A. (x + 13: 10) *h3*, the vocative marker, is the only occurrence of this word in the papyrus. Gardiner, *EG*[3], § 87, states that this word is employed more rarely than *i* or *i*; see also Allen, *Middle Egyptian,* 16.8.4; Borghouts, *EU* 24.1, p. 134, § 34.1, says that it is "like [*i*] but with the sense of an appeal." He also states that it is common.

B. (x + 13: 10) The group appears to be a writing of the *nisbe*-adjective *ir.y*, "belonging to."

C. (x + 13: 11) *bḥn*, "zerschneiden" (*Wb.* I 468, 10–17). The word occurs with this meaning at *pBremner-Rhind,* 22[4]. It seems to make better grammatical sense to understand as the second person singular of the stative. For the writing of *.tw* as a stative form, see Allen, *Middle Egyptian,* 17.2, who states that this writing is found often in New Kingdom texts; see also Černý and Groll, *LEG*, 12.3.2.c. *pBM 9997,* 7[11], provides an excellent parallel employing the stative, *iw=ṯ ḫr.ti bḥn*[*.ti*]; see Leitz, *HPBM* 7, p. 20, for the translation "You are felled and dissected...." An alternative reading is to understand that the supralinear signs *n=i* that are written over the next verb phrase are to be taken with both verbs here. If so, then the text would read "I have cut you up."

D. (x + 13: 11) . The group was a supralinear addition, giving the reading *sm3.n=i tw*, a *sḏm.n=f* form with dependent pronoun direct object *tw* and translated "I have slain you." Since the scribe wrote the dependent pronoun *tw* directly after the verb, perhaps an error by assimilation stemming from his writing of the stative in the preceding clause, he had to write the group *n=i* above the line.

E. (x + 13: 11) *m.t* (*Wb.* II 36, 6–7) is discussed at Gardiner, *EG*[3], § 23, here followed by the non-enclitic particle *is*. The feminine form *m.t* is used in place of the masculine form *m.k*, given that the subject of the ensuing verbal forms is feminine. For the writing, see, for example, Schott, *Urk.* VI, 9[21] and 11[4]. A similar combination, *mi.tn is*, occurs at Gardiner, *Admonitions,* rt. 7[1] et al., who notes that there it marks the beginning of each new section of the complaints.

F. (x + 13: 11) I take the verbal form as the 3rd pers. sing. fem. stative *ii.ti*.

G. (x + 13: 11) On *m.t*, see note E (x + 13: 11) above.

H. (x + 13: 11) *wr(.t)*, "The Great One," is an epithet used to designate a number of goddesses, most of whom are found among the lion-headed goddesses who function as the royal uraeus, like Sakhmet, Isis, Hathor, and Bastet. See the discussion in the Commentary below.

I. (x + 13: 11) *h3.wt*, probably "Nachbarschaft, Nähe" (*Wb.* II 477, 1–478, 18), commonly used with the preposition *m* or *r* to express a locative idea; it also has a temporal meaning, so "in your time" is also possible; note, too, that the preposition is commonly omitted. Borghouts, *EU* 24.1, p. 456b, offers "interests; affairs" The verb phrase should again be understood as a 3rd pers. sing. fem. stative.

J. (x + 13: 11) A tear in the papyrus here presents problems. What can be read with certainty is . The object is *ʿb=s*, the whole reading "…you shall let her enmity/horn pass first to the West…." A different reading takes *sẖn.t* as an imperative and *=tn* as a dependent pronoun used to give the imperative emphasis. See Borghouts, *EU* 24.2, p. 88, § 19.d, for this construction with 2nd person pronouns. The translation then would be "You, let her enmity/horn pass first to the West…."

K. (x + 13: 12) The pronoun that qualifies *ʿb* throughout this passage is written both as and as *s*, the latter a Late Egyptian writing of the suffix pronoun, for which see Junge, *LEG*, p. 52, 2.1.2 (1). The pronoun apparently refers to the noun "Great One." The context suggests that it should be translated as "her" throughout the passage.

L. (x + 13: 12) On *ʿb.t*, "horn," as a metaphor for force or power used against one's enemies, see the discussion at note HH (x + 2: 13) above and in the Commentary below.

M. (x + 13: 12) It is possible that the preposition *r* here means "against" and not "to."

N. (x + 13: 12) The goddess places her horn in the direction of the four cardinal points as a gesture of protection. See the discussion in the Commentary below.

O. (x + 13: 12) On the connections between Horus and the West, see Kessler, *LÄ* 2 (1977): col. 1214 and col. 1215, n. 22.

P. (x + 13: 12) The epithet *im.y-ḫt stẖ* is found at *SocBehague*, 89. In the Coffin Texts, two disparate groups of beings in the followings of Horus and Seth also occur, for which see *CT* 775. On Seth's connections with the East, see Kessler, *LÄ* 2 (1977): col. 1214 and col. 1215, n. 21.

Q. (x + 13: 13) On Horus' connections with the South, see Kessler, *LÄ* 2 (1977): col. 1214.

R. (x + 13: 13) On Seth's connections with the North see Kessler, *LÄ* 2 (1977): col. 1214.

S. (x + 13: 14) The word written is commonly used in protection texts as a synonym for *st-ꜥ*, "influence," invariably that of a malevolent being. Sauneron, *pIllustré*, 4[2] and p. 25, n. i, explains the word as having the literal meaning of hostility from the hand (of a god). For the idea of establishing an evil influence somewhere, see *pLeiden I 348,* rt. 1[3], which has the phrase *nn wḥm=s wdi nbḏ im=s*, "(she) will not put the Evil One in it again." The verb *wdi* can also have the meaning "extend," as it is commonly found in the phrase *wdi ꜥ.wy*, "extend the arms (in a gesture of adoration)."

T. (x + 13: 14) *ib*, perhaps "Bez. des Apophis" (*Wb.* I 60, 16, where the writing given is and is attested as "spät"). No such writing is attested by Leitz et al., *Götterbezeichnungen* I, 204ff., under the entries spelled *ib*. It may be a "vocalized" writing of , "Evil One" (*Wb.* I 410, 9), for which see note C (x + 3: 2) above.

U. (x + 13: 14) *ḥwi*, "schlagen" (*Wb.* III 46, 1–48, 15).

V. (x + 13: 14) Damage to the surface of the papyrus at the end of the line presents problems. What can be read appears to be . For *snk*, see Hannig, *GH*, p. 724a: "Gier; gierig sein." It is also possible that *snk.t*, "Sehnsucht" (Hannig, *GH*, p. 724a) was written here.

W. (x + 13: 15) The sign at the beginning of the line is the determinative of [.]*ẖr*, the last word of the preceding line. The writing of *rn*, "name," with the determinative (Sign-list Z6) underscores the nature of the being who is addressed here. For a similar writing of the word *rn* with determinative (Sign-list Z6), see *Urk.* VI, 29[6]. The suffix pronoun subject =*s* presumably refers to the "Great One" mentioned in line x + 13: 11 above.

X. (x + 13: 15) *wnm=s*, "she devours," is clear, but there is difficulty in trying to determine how this verb phrase fits with what precedes and follows. The translation offered above is, of course, provisional.

Y. (x + 13: 15) On the falcon and its role in apotropaic texts, see the Commentary below.

Z. (x + 13: 15) On the cat and its role in apotropaic texts, see the Commentary below.

AA. (x + 13: 15) The traces at the end of the line show the writing of the noun *sbi*, "rebel," a designation of Apophis or any of the enemies of the sun god or of Osiris.

BB. (x + 13: 16) *ꜥb* seems best translated here as "horn," as in the parallel occurrences above. The image comes from a personification of the agent of illness who causes pain by inserting a sharp horn in the ear of the patient. See the references at note L (x + 13: 12) above.

CC. (x + 13: 16) The traces in the small lacuna following the name of Psamtik point to a restoration of *ꜥ.w.s*, "life, prosperity, and health."

DD. (x + 13: 16) The context seems to require taking *šm=k*, "You proceed," as the protasis of a conditional sentence or as a concessive clause.

EE. (x + 13: 16) In the lacuna of 1.5 cm that follows *inn=i wr.t*, "I will bring the Great One…," the determinative (Sign-list G7) of the word *wr.t*, "Great One," was likely written, but what follows is uncertain. A new syntactical unit seems to begin the next line. On *wr.t*, see note H (x + 13: 11) above.

FF. (x + 13: 17) On the use of fire against enemies in Egypt, see the discussion in the Commentary below.

GG. (x + 13: 17) The traces suggest that should be restored here.

HH. (x + 13: 17) The article *pꜣ* seems to be the vocative marker.

II. (x + 13: 17) Read the article *tꜣ* as the vocative marker here as well.

JJ. (x + 13: 18) There is enough room for the restoration of the preposition *r*, "against."

KK. (x + 13: 18) There is enough room for the restoration of *pr-ꜥꜣ*, "pharaoh."

LL. (x + 13: 18) Despite the faded and damaged state of the papyrus here, the rubricized word that immediately follows the instruction *ḏd mdw ḥr* is clearly *bit*, "honey."

MM. (x + 13: 18) The reading of *ḥs [m]iw ḥs msḥ*, "…feces of a cat, feces of a crocodile…," is based on a parallel found in *pBerlin* 6[10] (*Bln* 70), a spell that shares some similarities with the present text. Its heading is *kꜣp nt dr hh.yt n.t ꜥḳ m rw.t*, "Fumigation-text for dispelling heat that enters from the outside." That said, the writing of what I am reading as *msḥ* does seem a bit odd; the initial sign looks more like and there are apparently one or two signs before that I can make little sense of.

NN. (x + 13: 18) The reading is also uncertain and at present offers little for restoration.

OO. (x + 13: 19) The traces indicate [hieroglyphs] *p3ḳ*, "fine linen," which occurs at x + 7: 12 and again at x + 12: 12–13, for which see notes EK and EL (x + 12: 12–13). The traces in the preceding line indicate a prescription, of which *p3ḳ* or *stp p3ḳ* would form a likely part.

COMMENTARY

The spell begins with an address to a "dead male who belongs to the ear of Psamtik." Unlike the texts that precede this one, the enemy described here seems to have already been rendered impotent.[331] What follows is an invocation to a goddess, simply called *wr.t*, "the Great One."[332] More an epithet than an actual name of a divinity, the goddess so described is often found exercising the power of destructive fire, as she does in x + 13: 16–17 below. Found as early as the Pyramid Texts, she appears as late as Roman Period temple texts. Here, *wr.t* should be understood as a term designating a manifestation of any one of the goddesses connected with and called the Eye of Re. They function as the royal uraeus and play apotropaic roles. It is possible that the epithet was used intentionally to avoid specifying which of these goddesses is meant.[333] Here, she uses her horn[334] as a means of protection by pointing it to the four cardinal points, a gesture often found in protection texts.[335] The malignant force is then addressed and told to "get back." Again, we find several statements that describe the assailant as already defeated, here killed by agents described as the falcon and the cat. The cat and the falcon are encountered in apotropaic rituals, often in tandem.[336] The hostile agent is then told not to place his horn in the ear

331 "You are cut up. I have slain you."

332 See note E (x + 13: 11) on the identification of the being addressed as feminine.

333 See Borghouts, *pLeiden I 348*, pp. 186–88, n. 461, who lists some of the texts in which *wr.t* appears. See also Germond, *Sekhmet*, pp. 119–28, for a discussion of this role played by Sakhmet as "Eye of Re," "Uraeus," and "Flame." See also, Darnell, *SAK* 22 (1995): 47–95, and idem, *SAK* 24 (1997): 35–48. She is also connected with the "epidemic of the year," for which see the discussion at note AQ (x + 4: 15) above. Johnson, *The Cobra Goddess*, confines her discussion largely to the Old Kingdom.

334 On the word *ʿb* as a metaphor for force or power used against one's enemies, see the discussion at Note HH (x + 2: 13).

335 On the role of the cardinal points in gestures of protection, see *pBM 10042*, vs. 1^{2-3} and Leitz, *HPBM 7*, p. 47: "Let protection fall for me to my south and my north and my west and my east." See also Goyon, *Le Papyrus d'Imouthès*, pp. 66ff., a section of a book of protection in which four balls of clay used to protect Osiris are thrown to the cardinal points. For parallels to the use of horns as a means of protection, see two passages in the Dendera temple where Isis says to the king: *di=i n=k iʿr.t.ṯ* [*sic*] *m ḥ3.t=k ḥr wḏ ʿb=s r ḫft.iw=k*, "I give to you your uraeus on your forehead while ordering its horn/enmity against your enemies" (*Dendara* I, 151^{9}), and *di.i ʿb.t bin r ḫftiw nbw…*, "I give your evil horn/enmity against all the enemies of…" (*Dendara* VIII, 56^{2-3}).

336 See, for example, *pChester Beatty 8*, vs. 1^{1-2} and 1^{4}, where the possessor of a prophylactic text is said to be both a cat and a falcon. *pBrooklyn 47.218.2*, x + 4: 5 (Guermeur and O'Rourke, forthcoming) has the statement [hieroglyphs] *dr.n tw miw.t*

of Psamtik but rather to turn back, for the recitation of the text brings the Great One to the king's aid. Fire is identified as the instrument of destruction that she will use against him. The use of fire against one's enemies is well-known in Egypt. Execration rituals often include the burning of figurines; the most extensive example of this practice can be found in the rituals published in *Urk.* VI.[337] A passage in the *Osorkon Chronicle* may refer to an actual burning of individuals who were responsible for rebellion in Thebes.[338] In the final few legible lines of the spell, an address to male and female heat[339] states that they shall not come against Pharaoh. Here the papyrus shows considerable damage, and we can read only a few words of the prescription and its instructions.

The central figure in the spell, described *wr.t*, "the Great One," is one of the lion-headed goddesses associated with the divine uraeus who were considered dangerous beings, particularly during the liminal periods of the year, like the New Year.[340] They have a long history as apotropaic figures who confront the forces of disorder in a violent and bloody manner. As such, the role that the Great One plays in the present text is much the same. The forces of chaos meet their like and their match in her. Any success on their part is essentially nullified by her presence. Note that in a number of places in the text, the malevolent forces are not threatened, but are said to have been already neutralized.[341] It is worth noting that in this spell, the Great One seems to function as a singular agent of protection. She is not one of a number of beings who have been gathered to protect Pharaoh. Her strong sense of protection may be connected to the fact that she is cast as the mother of the king in late temple texts in Egypt.[342] The fierce protectiveness of the lioness was well-known to the Egyptians, for whom she offered a potent symbol of divine maternal protection that came with a powerful arsenal, including horns and fire.[343]

ḥm.t ḥm.n tw bik, "The female cat has driven you away; the falcon has turned you away." It occurs there in an amuletic spell for the protection of a pregnant woman against still birth. See also Sauneron, Ophiologie, p. 121 and p. 190, n. 2, for a formula pronounced against the "venom of the abominable one" or the "venom of the red one (i.e., Seth)," in which is found the threat *miw sd* that Sauneron translates "que le chat [le] coupe!"

337 See Schott, *Bücher und Sprüche gegen den Gott Seth,* passim.

338 See Caminos, *AnOr* 37 (1958), pp. 48–51, and the discussion in Ritner, *Mechanics,* pp. 157–59; see also Zandee, *Death,* pp. 133–42.

339 For the nature of this malevolent agent, see the Introduction, pp. 26ff.

340 For this goddess and her activities during these times, see the Introduction, pp. 12ff.; see also the texts collected and discussed in Goyon, *BdE* 141. See also Germond, *AH* 9, passim, for the presence of Sakhmet in such texts.

341 See, for example, x + 13: 13, 15, and 17.

342 See, for example, *Dendara* I, 23^{9}; *Kom Ombo* 133^{3}; *Deir Chelouit* II, 89^{6}.

343 See above on the metaphorical meanings of these two.

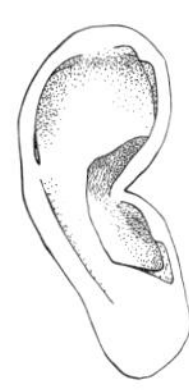

Spell Q — Translation with Commentary

COLUMN X + 13: 19–X + 14: 7 (P. BROOKLYN 47.218.49)

TRANSLITERATION

19. … *[ky] rꜣ* …

COLUMN X + 14

1.	*…mn.t … tm …*	*… tm=k ṯz … wỉꜣ …*
2.	*… ḏd.tw rꜣ pn ḥr …*	*… ỉꜣ n t …*
3.	*… r msḏr m mnw …*	*… dr tm.yt m msḏr n s … [ky] rꜣ s*
4.	*… ỉꜣw …*	*… nb nṯr.w mn ỉb … mrḥ …*
5.	*… psḏ.t mi …*	*… šd=k pr-ꜥꜣ m-ꜥ … msḏr … šn*
6.	*… mw.t wr.t …*	*… ḏs.s m-ḫt=s mi wnm=s […] mwt mwt.t*
7.	*… hh m msḏr [pr-ꜥꜣ] …*	*… ḏd mdw zp … ky rꜣ mi*
8.	*… pḏ*	

TRANSLATION

19. … *Another spell*[A]…

COLUMN X + 14

1. […][B] not[C] […] You shall not […][D] [.] barque[E] […]
2. […] One shall recite this spell over[F] […] […][G] of bread […]
3. […] against the ear daily […] dispelling *tm.yt*[H] from the ear of a man…[…][I] *[Another] spell*
4. […] praises[J] […] the lord of the gods[K] god so-and-so heart (?)[L] [.] *mrḥt*-oil […]
5. […] Ennead. Come[M] […] may you rescue Pharaoh[N] from […] ear […] Recite
6. […] great mother in […] herself in her following, like(wise)[O] she eats […] dead male, dead female
7. […] heat in the ear [of Pharaoh.][P] *Recite*[Q] … *times* … *Another spell.* Come[R] […]
8. … cense (?)[S]

TEXT NOTES

A. (x + 13: 19) The rubricized sign in the middle of x + 13: 19 is possibly what is left of the introductory phrase *ky rꜣ*, "Another spell," indicating the beginning of a new section. The fragmentary text at the end of the preceding spell at x + 13: 18–19 clearly has words typically found in prescriptions. From what is extant at the bottom of the sheet of papyrus on which Column x + 13 is written, line 19 is the last line of the column.

B. (x + 14: 1) The initial signs of the column do not offer any suggestions for reading the text here.

C. (x + 14: 1) The reading of the signs is all that is really clear at the beginning of this line.

D. (x + 14: 1) The sign (Sign-list S24) appears to be written here. The sign below seems to be the sign .

E. (x + 14: 1) Only the three signs can be read, possibly *wiꜣ*, "barque."

F. (x + 14: 2) The rubric *ḏd.tw rꜣ pn ḥr* with the sign *ḥr* written in black ink, can be read clearly.

G. (x + 14: 2) A word ending in *-iꜣ*, with a bird determinative, can be read.

H. (x + 14: 3) The reading of the words *dr tm.yt*, "drive away *tm.yt*…," seems certain. *tm.yt* is a sickness caused by demons, according to *WbMT*, pp. 952–53. It occurs in *pBM 10059*, 3^{1-3}, for which see Leitz, *HPBM* 7, p. 55, n. 32, who states that it is "clearly a skin disease."

I. (x + 14: 3) After the group *msḏr n z*, "…ear of a man…," the word is written in red, likely indicating the beginning of a new spell.

J. (x + 14: 4) The group *iꜣw*, "praise," can be read.

K. (x + 14: 4) The reading of the phrase *nb nṯr.w*, "lord of the gods," seems certain.

L. (x + 14: 4) The signs can be read. For *mn* as "god so-and-so," see note AN (x + 10: 13) above.

M. (x + 14: 5) The traces show , the imperative *mi*.

N. (x + 14: 5) The reading *šd=k pr-ꜥꜣ m-ꜥ* seems sure.

O. (x + 14: 6) *ḏs.s m-ḫt=s mi*.... It is unclear whether to read *mi* as the beginning of *mi.tt*, thus ending a clause, or as the conjunction *mi*, continuing the thought here.

P. (x + 14: 7) *hh m msḏr pr-ꜥꜣ*, "...heat in/from the ear [of Pharaoh...]," is likely.

Q. (x + 14: 7) The rubric is very faded, but *ḏd mdw zp*, "Recite (x) times...," can be read for certain.

R. (x + 14: 7) After the group *ky rꜣ*, "Another spell," the imperative *mi* can be read clearly.

S. (x + 14: 8) The final text of the papyrus ends here. The word *pḏ*, "(den Weihrauch) räuchern; jem. beräuchern" (*Wb.* I 568, 17–18) may be a final instruction here: "Incense!" An alternative reading is *pḏ nmt*, "wide of stride," a common epithet of divinities. *CT* 837 has this as an epithet of Osiris in his manifestation as Orion. Goyon, *pConfirmation,* 10[10] and pp. 99–100, n. 162, gives it as an epithet of the god Ophois in his battle with the god Seth. He cites several references there to it as an epithet of Horus. See also Wilson, *PL,* pp. 383–84, for its use in "martial" contexts. The proper reading here is unfortunately impeded by the lacuna.

COMMENTARY

The end of the papyrus is badly fragmented, but four small text groups can be established. The first has signs from the beginning of Column x + 14, though the initial signs of the column are unreadable, as the papyrus is frayed and the surface is damaged. The second has signs from the middle of the column. The third and fourth offer only a few signs each that don't allow for much restoration. The way in which the fragments are currently placed gives a column width of ca. 19 cm, thus conforming very closely to the width of the other columns of the papyrus. Essentially, only a few words or phrases of the text can be read here. The column finishes at the beginning of line 8, with the single word *pḏ. pr-ꜥꜣ* occurs once and there is one lacuna where either the name Psamtik or *pr-ꜥꜣ* could be restored.

Bibliography

Allen, J.P. *Genesis in Egypt: The Philosophy of Ancient Egyptian Creation Accounts,* YES 2 (New Haven: Yale Egyptological Seminar, 1988).

———. *Middle Egyptian. An Introduction to the Language and Culture of Hieroglyphs* (Cambridge: Cambridge University, 2000).

Allen, T.G. *The Book of the Dead or Going Forth by Day,* SAOC 37 (Chicago: University of Chicago, 1974).

Altenmüller, B. *Synkretismus in den Sargtexten,* GO (IV Reihe: Ägypten) 7 (Wiesbaden: Harrassowitz, 1975).

Altenmüller, H. "Die Altägyptischen Apotropaia" I–II (Ludwig-Maximilians-Universität, Munich, PhD diss., 1965).

———. "Apotropaikon," in *LÄ* 1 (1975): cols. 355–58.

———. "Falke," in LÄ 2 (1977): cols. 93–98.

———. "Hu," in *LÄ* 3 (1979): cols. 65–68.

———. "Magische Literatur," in *LÄ* 3 (1979): cols. 1151–62.

———. "Totenglaube und Magie," in A. Roccati and A. Siliotti (eds.), *La Magia in Egitto ai tempi dei faraoni: Atti, convegno internazionale di studi, Milano, 29–31 ottobre 1985* (Verona: Rassegna internazionale di cinematografia archeologica: Arte e natura libri, 1987), pp. 131–46.

———. "Ein Zaubermesser des Mittleren Reiches," *SAK* 13 (1986): 1–27.

———. "Ein Zauberspruch zum 'Schutz des Leibes,'" *GM* 33 (1979): 7–12.

Anthes, R. "Egyptian Mythology in the Third Millenium BC," *Ägyptische Theologie im dritten Jahrtausend v. Chr.,* StudAeg 9 (1983): 89–132.

———. "Die Vorführung der gefangenen Feinde vor den König," *ZÄS* 65 (1930): 26–35.

Assmann, J. "Chepre," in *LÄ* 1 (1975): cols. 934–40.

———. *Death and Salvation in Ancient Egypt* (Ithaca: Cornell University, 2005).

———. *Egyptian Solar Religion in the New Kingdom* (London: Kegan Paul International, 1995).

———. "Gott," in *LÄ* 2 (1977): cols. 756–86.

———. *Maât. Gerechtigkeit und Unsterblichkeit im alten Ägypten* (Munich: Beck, 1990).

———. "Magic and Theology in Ancient Egypt," in P. Schäfer and H.G. Kippenberg (eds.), *Envisioning Magic. A Princeton Seminar and Symposium* (Leiden: Brill, 1997), pp. 1–18.

Aufrère, S. "Études de lexicologie et d'histoire naturelle, VIII–XVII," *BIFAO* 86 (1986): 1–32.

Baines, J. "Egyptian Deities in Context: Multiplicity, Unity, and the Problem of Change," in B.N. Porter (ed.), *One God or Many? Concepts of Divinity in the Ancient World* (Chebeauge: Casco Bay Assyriological Institute, 2000), pp. 9–78.

———. "Egyptian Twins," *Or* 54 (1985): 461–82.

Bakir, A. *The Cairo Calendar No. 86637* (Cairo: General Organisation for Govt. Print. Offices, 1937).

Barbash, Y. *The Mortuary Papyrus of Padikakem. Walters Art Museum 551,* YES 8 (New Haven: Yale Egyptological Seminar, 2011).

Bardinet, T. *Dents et mâchoires dans les représentations religieuses et la pratique médicale de l'Égypte ancienne,* Studia Pohl: Series Maior 15 (Rome: Editrice Pontificio Istituto Biblico, 1990).

———. *Les papyrus médicaux de l'Égypte ancienne* (Paris: Fayard, 1995).

Barguet, P. *Le livre des morts des anciens Égyptiens* (Paris: Editions du Cerf, 1967).

———. *Le Temple d'Amon-Rê à Karnak. Essai d'exégèse* (Cairo: IFAO, 1962).

———. *Le Papyrus N. 3176(S) du Musée du Louvre,* BdE 37 (Cairo: IFAO, 1962).

Barns, J. *Five Ramesseum Papyri* (Oxford: Griffith Institute, 1956).

Barta, W. *Untersuchungen zum Götterkreis der Neunheit,* MÄS 28 (Munich: Deutscher Kunstverlag, 1973).

von Beckerath, J. *Handbuch der ägyptischen Königsnamen,* MÄS 20 (Munich: Deutscher Kunstverlag, 1984).

Behrens, P. "Widder," in *LÄ* 6 (1986): cols. 1243–45.

von Bergmann, E. *Das Buch vom Durchwandeln der Ewigkeit* (Wien: K. Gerold's Sohn, 1877)

Betz, H.D. (ed.) *The Greek Magical Papyri in Translation, Including the Demotic Spells* (Chicago: University of Chicago, 1992).

Bickel, S. *La cosmogonie Égyptienne,* OBO 134 (Fribourg: Universitätsverlag, 1994).

Bidoli, D. *Die Sprüche der Fangnetze in den altägyptischen Sargtexten,* ADAIK 9 (Glückstadt: Augustin, 1976).

Bierbrier, M., rev. [G. Vittmann, *Priester und Beamte im Theben der Spätzeit: Genealogische und prosopographische Untersuchungen zum Thebanischen Priester- u. Beamtentum d. 25. und 26. Dynastie* (Wien 1978)], *BiOr* 36 (1979): 306–9.

von Bissing, F. "Über die Kapelle im Hof Ramesses II im Tempel von Luxor," *Ex Actorum Orientalium Volumine VIII Excerptum* (1929): 129–62.

———. "Über die Kapelle im Hof Ramesses II im Tempel von Luxor," Ex *Actorum Orientalium Volumine XVI Excerptum* (1937): 190–202.

Black, J.R. "The Instruction of Amenemope: A Critical Edition and Commentary—Prolegomenon and Prologue" (Ph.D. dissertation, University of Wisconsin-Madison, 2002).

Bommas, M *Die Mythisierung der Zeit. Die beiden Bücher über die altägyptischen Schalttage des magischen pLeiden I 346*, GO (IV Reihe: Ägypten) 37 (Wiesbaden: Harrassowitz, 1999).

Borghouts, J.F. "*3ḫ.w* (akhu) and *ḥk3.w* (hekau). Two Basic Notions of Ancient Egyptian Magic, and the Concept of the Divine Created Word," in A. Roccati and A. Siliotti (eds.), *La Magia in Egitto ai tempi dei faraoni: Atti, convegno internazionale di studi, Milano, 29–31 ottobre 1985* (Verona: Rassegna internazionale di cinematografia archeologica: Arte e natura libri, 1987), pp. 29–46.

———. "The Edition of Magical Papyri in Turin: A Progress Report," in A. Roccati and A. Siliotti (eds.), *La Magia in Egitto ai tempi dei faraoni: Atti, convegno internazionale di studi, Milano, 29–31 ottobre 1985* (Verona: Rassegna internazionale di cinematografia archeologica: Arte e natura libri, 1987), pp. 257–69.

———. *Ancient Egyptian Magical Texts*, Nisbada 9 (Leiden: Brill, 1978).

———. *Egyptian. An Introduction to the Writing and Language of the Middle Kingdom*, 2 vols. EU 24 (Leiden: Peeters, 2010).

———. *The Magical Texts of Papyrus Leiden I 348*, OMRO 51 (Leiden: Brill, 1971).

———. "Magical Texts," in S. Sauneron (ed.), *Textes et langages de l'Égypte pharaonique. Cent cinquante années de recherches, 1822–1975: Hommage à Jean-François Champollion*, BdE 64/3 (Cairo: IFAO, 1974), pp. 7–19.

———. "Magie," in *LÄ* 3 (1979): cols. 1137–51.

———. "Month," in *LÄ* 4 (1982): cols. 200–204.

———. "The Ram as Protector and Prophesier," *RdE* 32 (1980): 33–46.

Breasted, J.H. *The Edwin Smith Surgical Papyrus*, OIP 3–4 (Chicago: University of Chicago, 1930).

Brunner, H. "Blindheit," in *LÄ* 1 (1975): cols. 828–34.

Brunner-Traut, E. "Esel," in *LÄ* 2 (1977): cols. 27–30.

———. *Frühformen des Erkennens: Am Beispiel Altägyptens* (Darmstadt: Wissenschaftliche Buchgesellschaft, 1990).

———. "Der Sehgott und der Hörgott in Literatur und Theologie," in J. Assmann, E. Feucht, and R. Grieshammer (eds.), *Fragen an die altägyptische Literatur. Studien zum Gedenken an Eberhard Otto* (Wiesbaden: Reichert, 1977), pp. 125–45.

———. *Der Tanz im alten Ägypten nach bildlichen und inschriftlichen Zeugnissen*, ÄF 6 (Glückstadt: Augustin, 1992).

Bruyère, B. Rapport sur les fouilles de Deir el Médinah (1934–1935). Troisième partie: Le village, les décharges publiques, la station de repos du col de la Vallée des Rois, FIFAO 16 (Cairo: IFAO, 1939).

Buchheim, L. "Die altägyptische Ohrenheilkunde und ihre Bedeutung für unsere Kenntnis der altägyptischen Medizin," *Medizingeschichte im Spektrum* (Wiesbaden: Franz Steiner, 1966), pp. 30–39.

———. "Die Seuchenbeschwörungen im Chirurgischen Papyrus Edwin Smith (verso)," *Sudhoffs Archiv* 47 (1963): 199–208.

———. "Das Verdikt der 'nicht behandelbaren Krankheit' in der altägyptischen Medizin," *Sudhoffs Archiv* 49 (1965): 170–84.

Buck, A. de *The Egyptian Coffin Texts*, 7 vols. (Chicago: University of Chicago, 1935–1961).

Buck, A. de and B.H. Stricker "Teksten tegen Schorpioenen naar Pap. I 349," *OMRO* 21 (1940): 53–62.

Budge, E.A.W. *The Book of the Dead. An English Translation of the Chapters, Hymns, etc. of the Theban Recension, with Introduction, Notes, etc.* (London: Kegan Paul, Trench, Trübner, 1909).

Burkard, G. *Spätzeitliche Osiris-Liturgien im Corpus der Asasif-Papyri*, ÄAT 31 (Wiesbaden: Harrassowitz, 1995)

Cabrol, A. *Les Voies Processionelles de Thèbes*, OLA 97 (Leuven: Peeters, 2001).

Caminos, R. "Another Hieratic Manuscript from the Library of Pwerem Son of Kiki (Pap. B.M. 10288)," *JEA* 58 (1972): 205–24.

———. *The Chronicle of Prince Osorkon*, AnOr 37 (Rome: Pontificium Institutum Biblicum, 1958).

———. *Late Egyptian Miscellanies*, Brown Egyptological Studies 1 (Oxford: Oxford University, 1954).

———. *Literary Fragments in the Hieratic Script* (Oxford: Griffith Institute, 1956).

———. "Magic for the Dead," in A. Roccati and A. Siliotti (eds.), *La Magia in Egitto ai tempi dei faraoni: Atti, convegno internazionale di studi, Milano, 29–31 ottobre 1985* (Verona: Rassegna internazionale di cinematografia archeologica: Arte e natura libri, 1987), pp. 147–59.

———. "Papyrus Berlin 10463," *JEA* 49 (1963): 29–37.

———. "A Prayer to Osiris," *MDAIK* 16 (1958): 20–24.

———. *A Tale of Woe from a Hieratic Papyrus in the A.S. Pushkin Museum of Fine Arts in Moscow* (Oxford: Griffith Institute, 1977).

Capart, J. "Les sept paroles de Nekhabit," *CdE* 15 (1940): 21–29.

Capart, J., A.H. Gardiner, and B. van de Walle "New Light on the Ramesside Tomb-Robberies," *JEA* 22 (1936): 169–93.

Castelli, C. "Credenze magiche dell'antico Egitto: Modalità mentale primitiva o categoria persistente del pensiero?" in A. Roccati and A. Siliotti (eds.), *La Magia in Egitto ai tempi dei faraoni: Atti, convegno internazionale di studi, Milano, 29–31 ottobre 1985* (Verona: Rassegna internazionale di cinematografia archeologica: Arte e natura libri, 1987), pp. 121–27.

Cauville, S. "L'hymne à Mehyt d'Edfou," *BIFAO* 82 (1982): 105–25.

Černý, J. *Paper and Books in Ancient Egypt, An Inaugural Lecture Delivered at University College, London, 29 May, 1947* (London: H.K. Lewis & Co., 1952).

———. "Questions adressées aux oracles," *BIFAO* 35 (1935): 41–58.

Černý, J. and S.I. Groll *A Late Egyptian Grammar*, 3rd updated edition (Rome: Biblical Institute, 1984).

Chassinat, E. *Le manuscrit magique copte no. 42573 du Musée du Caire*, BdEC 4 (Cairo: IFAO, 1955).

———. "Les papyrus magiques 3237 et 3239 du Louvre," *RT* 14 (1893): 10–17.

———. *Un papyrus médical copte*, MIFAO 31 (Cairo: IFAO, 1921).

Chassinat, E. and F. Daumas *Le Temple de Dendara,* 9 vols. (Cairo : IFAO, 1934–1987).

Chassinat, E. and Le Marquis de Rochemonteix *Le temple d'Edfou,* 14 vols. MAFC 10–11; 20–31 (Cairo: IFAO, 1897–1934).

Crum, W.E. "An Egyptian Text in Greek Characters," *JEA* 28 (1942): 20–31.

Daressy, G. "Quelques inscriptions provenant de Bubastis," *ASAE* 11 (1911): 187–91.

Darnell, J.C. "The Apotropaic Goddess in the Eye," *SAK* 24 (1997): 35–48.

———. *The Enigmatic Netherworld Books of the Solar-Osirian Unity: Cryptographic Compositions in the Tombs of Tutankhamun, Ramesses VI and Ramesses IX,* OBO 198 (Fribourg: Universitätsverlag, 2004).

———. "Hathor Returns to Medamûd," *SAK* 22 (1995): 47–95.

Daumas, F., et al. *Valeurs phonétiques des signes hiéroglyphiques d'époque gréco-romaine,* 4 vols. (Montpellier: Université de Montpellier, 1988–1995).

Dawson, W.R. "Studies in the Egyptian Medical Texts," *JEA* 18 (1932): 150–54.

———. "Studies in the Egyptian Medical Texts-II," *JEA* 19 (1933): 133–37.

———. "Studies in the Egyptian Medical Texts-III," *JEA* 20 (1934): 41–46.

———. "Studies in the Egyptian Medical Texts-IV," *JEA* 20 (1934): 185–88.

———. "Studies in the Egyptian Medical Texts-V," *JEA* 21 (1935): 37–40.

De Meulenaere, H. "Sebek à Elkab," *CdE* 44 (1969): 13–21.

Deines, H. von and H. Grapow *Grundriss der Medizin der alten Ägypter* (Berlin: Akademie-Verlag, 1954–73).

———. *Wörterbuch der ägyptischen Drogennamen,* Grundriss der Medizin der alten Ägypter 6 (Berlin: Akademie-Verlag, 1959).

———. *Wörterbuch der medizinischen Texte,* Grundriss der Medizin der alten Ägypter 7/1–2 (Berlin: Akademie-Verlag, 1961).

Depauw, M. *A Companion to Demotic Studies,* Papyrologica Bruxellensia 28 (Brussels: Fondation Égyptologique Reine Élisabeth, 1997).

Depuydt, L. *Conjunction, Contiguity, Contingency. On Relationships Between Events in the Egyptian and Coptic Verbal Systems* (New York: Oxford University, 1993).

Derchain, P. "Bebon, le dieu et les mythes," *RdE* 9 (1952): 23–47.

———. "La couronne de la justification. Essai d'analyse d'un rite ptolemaique," *CdE* 30 (1955): 225–87.

———. *Elkab I: Les monuments religieux à l'entrée de l'Ouady Hellel* (Brussels: Fondation Égyptologique Reine Élisabeth, 1971).

———. "En l'an 363 de sa majesté le roi de haute et basse Égypte Re-Harakhty vivant par delà le temps et l'espace," *CdE* 53 (1978): 48–56.

———. *Hathor Quadrifons. Recherches sur la syntaxe d'un mythe égyptien* (Istanbul: Nederlands Historisch-Archaeologisch Instituut in het Nabije Oosten, 1972).

———. "De la magie à la méditation," in A. Roccati and A. Siliotti (eds.), *La Magia in Egitto ai tempi dei faraoni: Atti, convegno internazionale di studi, Milano, 29–31 ottobre 1985* (Verona: Rassegna internazionale di cinematografia archeologica: Arte e natura libri, 1987), pp. 47–55.

———. *Le papyrus Salt 825 (B.M. 10051), rituel pour la conservation de la vie en Égypte* (Brussels: Palais des académies, 1965).

van Dijk, J. "The Birth of Horus According to the Ebers Papyrus," *JEOL* 262 (1979–1980): 10–25.

———. "The Luxor Building Inscription of Ramesses III," *GM* 33 (1979): 19–27.

———. "Wepset," in *LÄ* 6 (1986): cols. 1218–20.

Donahue, V.A. *"pr-nfr," JEA* 64 (1978): 143–48.

Drioton, E. "Sarcasmes contre les adorateurs d'Horus," *Mélanges Syriens offerts à M. Réne Dussaud* (Paris: P. Geuthner, 1939), pp. 495–506.

Dunand, F. and C. Zivie-Coche *Gods and Men in Egypt. 3000 BCE to 395 CE* (Ithaca: Cornell University, 2004).

DuQuesne, T. "Anubis Master of Secrets (*ḥry-sštꜣ*) and the Egyptian Conception of Mysteries," *DIE* 36 (1996): 25–38.

Eaton-Krauss, M. "The *khat*-headdress to the End of the Amarna Period," *SAK* 5 (1977): 21–39.

Ebbell, B. *Altägyptische Bezeichnungen für Krankheiten und Symptome* (Oslo: Dybwad, 1938).

Edel, E. "Beiträge zum ägyptischen Lexikon II," *ZÄS* 81 (1956): 6–18.

———. "Beiträge zum ägyptischen Lexikon III," *ZÄS* 81 (1956): 68–76.

———. "Beiträge zur ägyptischen Grammatik," *ZÄS* 84 (1959): 105–13.

Edwards, I.E.S. *Oracular Amuletic Decrees of the Late New Kingdom,* HPBM, 4th ser., 2 vols. (London: Trustees of the British Museum, 1960).

———. "Kenhikhopshef's Prophylactic Charm," *JEA* 54 (1968): 155–60.

———. "Some Magical Aspects of the Pyramids," in A. Roccati and A. Siliotti (eds.), *La Magia in Egitto ai tempi dei faraoni: Atti, convegno internazionale di studi, Milano, 29–31 ottobre 1985* (Verona: Rassegna internazionale di cinematografia archeologica: Arte e natura libri, 1987), pp. 161–69.

Egberts, A. *In Quest of Meaning. A Study of the Ancient Egyptian Rites of Consecrating the Merit-Chests and Driving the Calves,* 2 vols. EU 8 (Leiden: Nederlands Instituut voor het Nabije Oosten, 1995).

Erichsen, W. *Demotisches Glossar* (Copenhagen: E. Munksgaard, 1954).

Erman, A. *Neuägyptische Grammatik.* Zweite, völlig umgestaltete Auflage (Leipzig: W. Engelmann, 1933).

———. *Zaubersprüche für Mutter und Kind aus dem Papyrus 3027 des Berliner Museums* (Berlin: Verlag der Königlichen Akademie der Wissenschaften, 1901).

Erman, A. and H. Grapow *Wörterbuch der Ägyptischen Sprache,* 6 vols. (Leipzig: J.C. Hinrichs, Berlin: Akademie-Verlag, 1926–1963).

Erman, A., H. Grapow, H. and W. Erichsen *Wörterbuch der Ägyptischen Sprache. Die Belegstellen,* 7 vols. (Leipzig: J.C. Hinrichs, Berlin: Akademie-Verlag, 1940–58).

Eschweiler, P. *Bildzauber im alten Ägypten,* OBO 137 (Fribourg: Universitätsverlag, 1994).

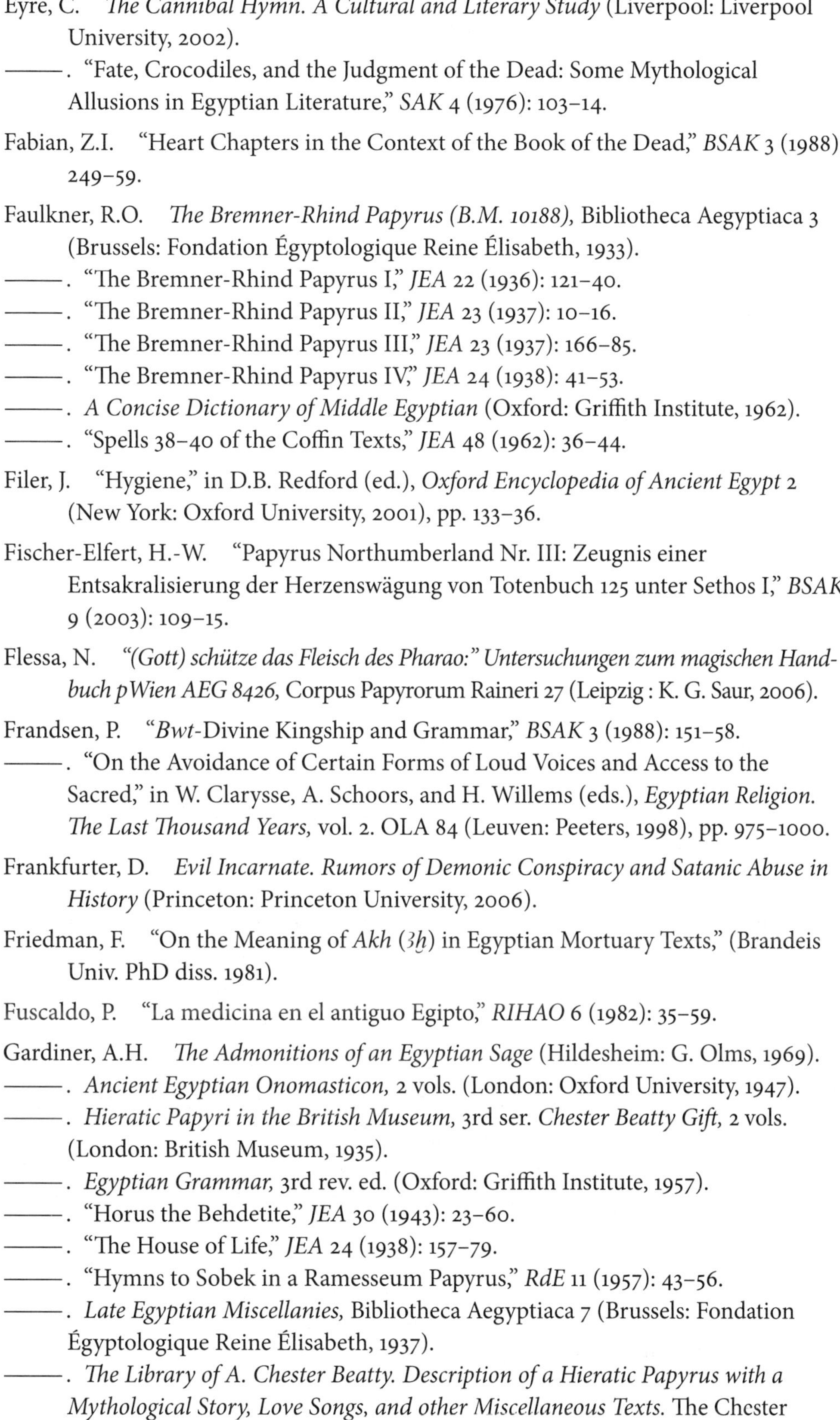

Eyre, C. *The Cannibal Hymn. A Cultural and Literary Study* (Liverpool: Liverpool University, 2002).

———. "Fate, Crocodiles, and the Judgment of the Dead: Some Mythological Allusions in Egyptian Literature," *SAK* 4 (1976): 103–14.

Fabian, Z.I. "Heart Chapters in the Context of the Book of the Dead," *BSAK* 3 (1988): 249–59.

Faulkner, R.O. *The Bremner-Rhind Papyrus (B.M. 10188),* Bibliotheca Aegyptiaca 3 (Brussels: Fondation Égyptologique Reine Élisabeth, 1933).

———. "The Bremner-Rhind Papyrus I," *JEA* 22 (1936): 121–40.

———. "The Bremner-Rhind Papyrus II," *JEA* 23 (1937): 10–16.

———. "The Bremner-Rhind Papyrus III," *JEA* 23 (1937): 166–85.

———. "The Bremner-Rhind Papyrus IV," *JEA* 24 (1938): 41–53.

———. *A Concise Dictionary of Middle Egyptian* (Oxford: Griffith Institute, 1962).

———. "Spells 38–40 of the Coffin Texts," *JEA* 48 (1962): 36–44.

Filer, J. "Hygiene," in D.B. Redford (ed.), *Oxford Encyclopedia of Ancient Egypt* 2 (New York: Oxford University, 2001), pp. 133–36.

Fischer-Elfert, H.-W. "Papyrus Northumberland Nr. III: Zeugnis einer Entsakralisierung der Herzenswägung von Totenbuch 125 unter Sethos I," *BSAK* 9 (2003): 109–15.

Flessa, N. *"(Gott) schütze das Fleisch des Pharao:" Untersuchungen zum magischen Handbuch pWien AEG 8426,* Corpus Papyrorum Raineri 27 (Leipzig : K. G. Saur, 2006).

Frandsen, P. "*Bwt*-Divine Kingship and Grammar," *BSAK* 3 (1988): 151–58.

———. "On the Avoidance of Certain Forms of Loud Voices and Access to the Sacred," in W. Clarysse, A. Schoors, and H. Willems (eds.), *Egyptian Religion. The Last Thousand Years,* vol. 2. OLA 84 (Leuven: Peeters, 1998), pp. 975–1000.

Frankfurter, D. *Evil Incarnate. Rumors of Demonic Conspiracy and Satanic Abuse in History* (Princeton: Princeton University, 2006).

Friedman, F. "On the Meaning of *Akh* (*ꜣḫ*) in Egyptian Mortuary Texts," (Brandeis Univ. PhD diss. 1981).

Fuscaldo, P. "La medicina en el antiguo Egipto," *RIHAO* 6 (1982): 35–59.

Gardiner, A.H. *The Admonitions of an Egyptian Sage* (Hildesheim: G. Olms, 1969).

———. *Ancient Egyptian Onomasticon,* 2 vols. (London: Oxford University, 1947).

———. *Hieratic Papyri in the British Museum,* 3rd ser. *Chester Beatty Gift,* 2 vols. (London: British Museum, 1935).

———. *Egyptian Grammar,* 3rd rev. ed. (Oxford: Griffith Institute, 1957).

———. "Horus the Behdetite," *JEA* 30 (1943): 23–60.

———. "The House of Life," *JEA* 24 (1938): 157–79.

———. "Hymns to Sobek in a Ramesseum Papyrus," *RdE* 11 (1957): 43–56.

———. *Late Egyptian Miscellanies,* Bibliotheca Aegyptiaca 7 (Brussels: Fondation Égyptologique Reine Élisabeth, 1937).

———. *The Library of A. Chester Beatty. Description of a Hieratic Papyrus with a Mythological Story, Love Songs, and other Miscellaneous Texts.* The Chester

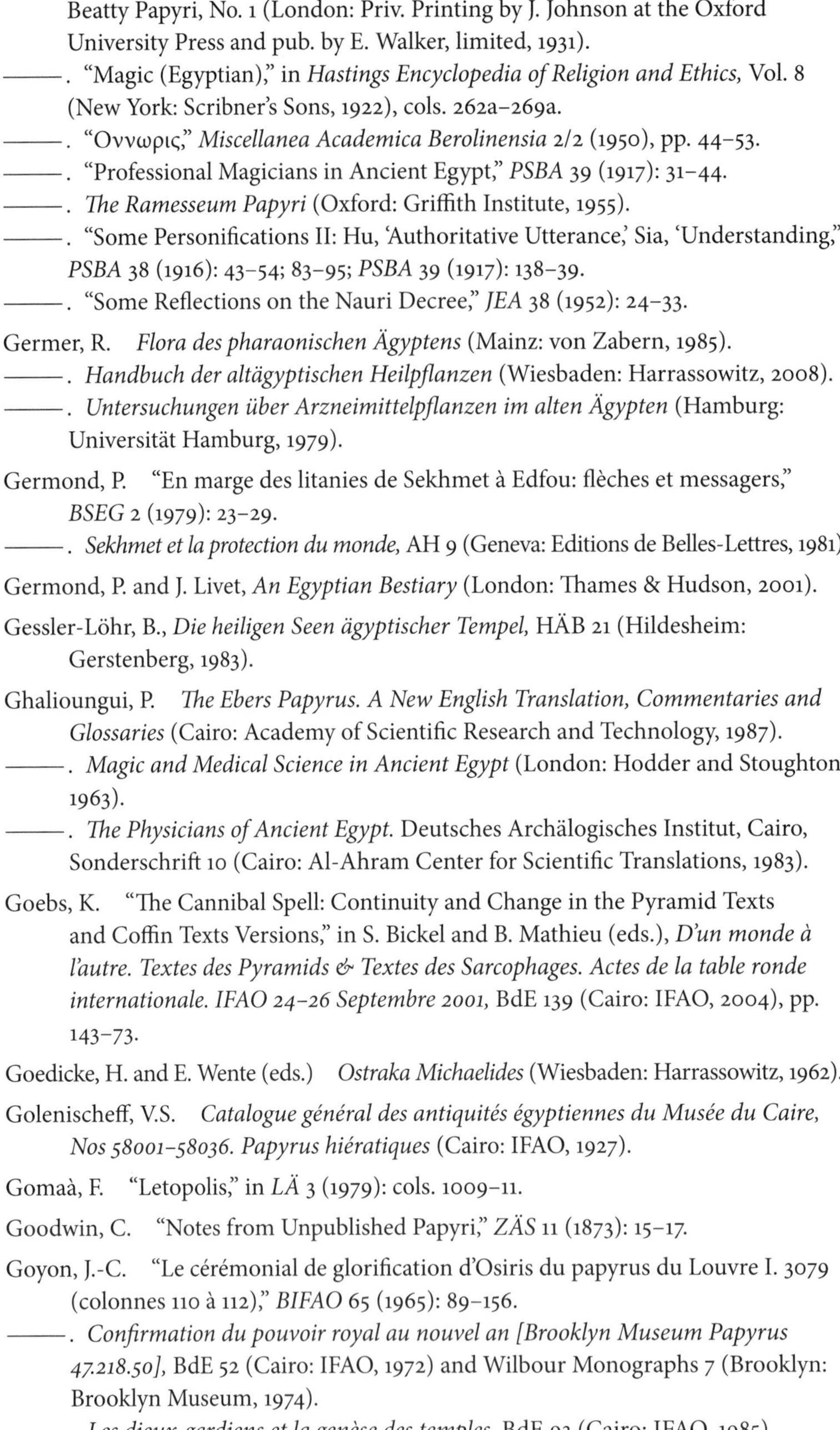

Beatty Papyri, No. 1 (London: Priv. Printing by J. Johnson at the Oxford University Press and pub. by E. Walker, limited, 1931).

———. "Magic (Egyptian)," in *Hastings Encyclopedia of Religion and Ethics,* Vol. 8 (New York: Scribner's Sons, 1922), cols. 262a–269a.

———. "Ονvωρις," *Miscellanea Academica Berolinensia* 2/2 (1950), pp. 44–53.

———. "Professional Magicians in Ancient Egypt," *PSBA* 39 (1917): 31–44.

———. *The Ramesseum Papyri* (Oxford: Griffith Institute, 1955).

———. "Some Personifications II: Hu, 'Authoritative Utterance,' Sia, 'Understanding,'" *PSBA* 38 (1916): 43–54; 83–95; *PSBA* 39 (1917): 138–39.

———. "Some Reflections on the Nauri Decree," *JEA* 38 (1952): 24–33.

Germer, R. *Flora des pharaonischen Ägyptens* (Mainz: von Zabern, 1985).

———. *Handbuch der altägyptischen Heilpflanzen* (Wiesbaden: Harrassowitz, 2008).

———. *Untersuchungen über Arzneimittelpflanzen im alten Ägypten* (Hamburg: Universität Hamburg, 1979).

Germond, P. "En marge des litanies de Sekhmet à Edfou: flèches et messagers," *BSEG* 2 (1979): 23–29.

———. *Sekhmet et la protection du monde,* AH 9 (Geneva: Editions de Belles-Lettres, 1981).

Germond, P. and J. Livet, *An Egyptian Bestiary* (London: Thames & Hudson, 2001).

Gessler-Löhr, B., *Die heiligen Seen ägyptischer Tempel,* HÄB 21 (Hildesheim: Gerstenberg, 1983).

Ghalioungui, P. *The Ebers Papyrus. A New English Translation, Commentaries and Glossaries* (Cairo: Academy of Scientific Research and Technology, 1987).

———. *Magic and Medical Science in Ancient Egypt* (London: Hodder and Stoughton, 1963).

———. *The Physicians of Ancient Egypt.* Deutsches Archälogisches Institut, Cairo, Sonderschrift 10 (Cairo: Al-Ahram Center for Scientific Translations, 1983).

Goebs, K. "The Cannibal Spell: Continuity and Change in the Pyramid Texts and Coffin Texts Versions," in S. Bickel and B. Mathieu (eds.), *D'un monde à l'autre. Textes des Pyramids & Textes des Sarcophages. Actes de la table ronde internationale. IFAO 24–26 Septembre 2001,* BdE 139 (Cairo: IFAO, 2004), pp. 143–73.

Goedicke, H. and E. Wente (eds.) *Ostraka Michaelides* (Wiesbaden: Harrassowitz, 1962).

Golenischeff, V.S. *Catalogue général des antiquités égyptiennes du Musée du Caire, Nos 58001–58036. Papyrus hiératiques* (Cairo: IFAO, 1927).

Gomaà, F. "Letopolis," in *LÄ* 3 (1979): cols. 1009–11.

Goodwin, C. "Notes from Unpublished Papyri," *ZÄS* 11 (1873): 15–17.

Goyon, J.-C. "Le cérémonial de glorification d'Osiris du papyrus du Louvre I. 3079 (colonnes 110 à 112)," *BIFAO* 65 (1965): 89–156.

———. *Confirmation du pouvoir royal au nouvel an [Brooklyn Museum Papyrus 47.218.50],* BdE 52 (Cairo: IFAO, 1972) and Wilbour Monographs 7 (Brooklyn: Brooklyn Museum, 1974).

———. *Les dieux-gardiens et la genèse des temples,* BdE 93 (Cairo: IFAO, 1985).

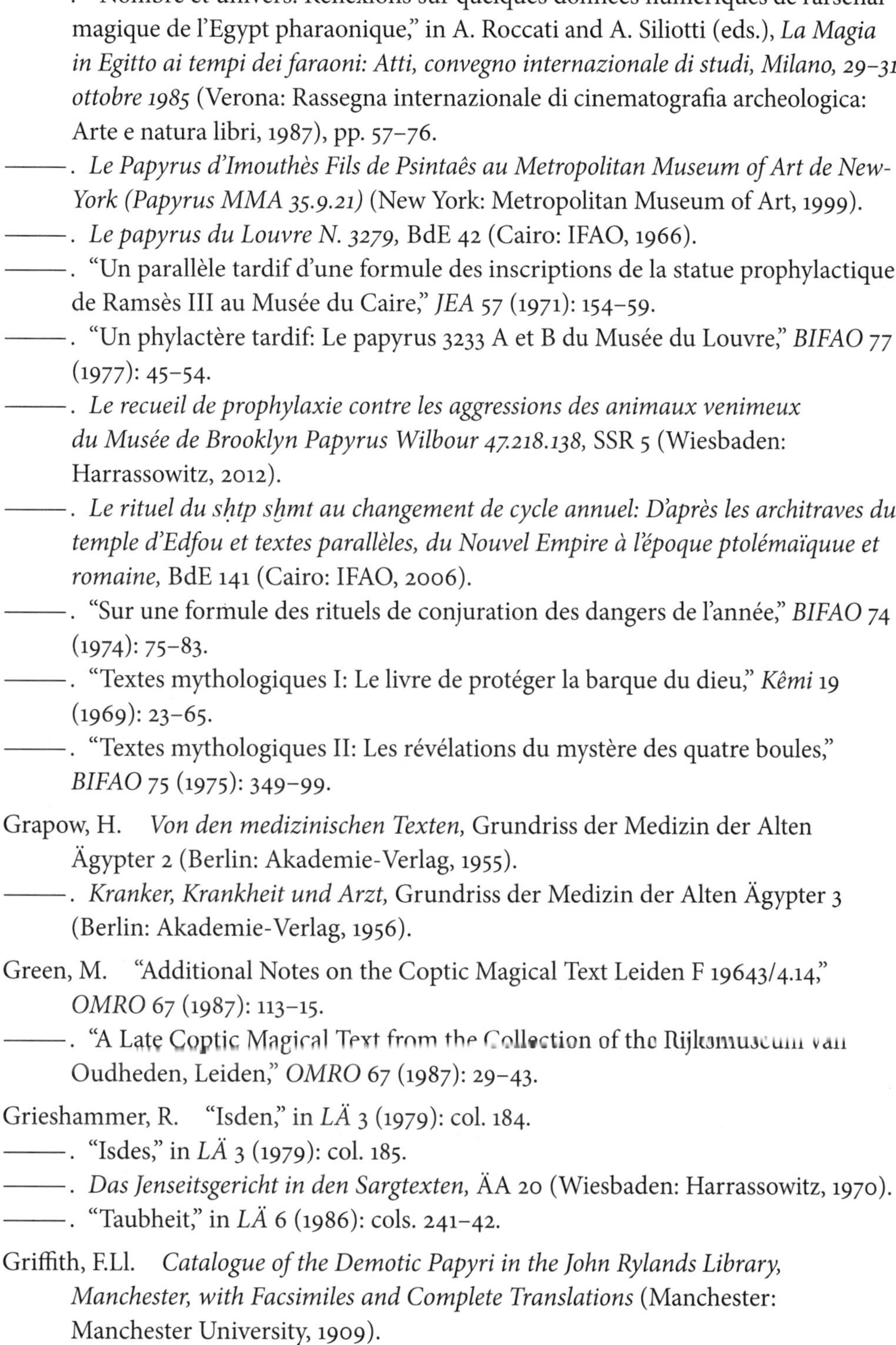

———. "Nombre et univers: Réflexions sur quelques données numériques de l'arsenal magique de l'Egypt pharaonique," in A. Roccati and A. Siliotti (eds.), *La Magia in Egitto ai tempi dei faraoni: Atti, convegno internazionale di studi, Milano, 29–31 ottobre 1985* (Verona: Rassegna internazionale di cinematografia archeologica: Arte e natura libri, 1987), pp. 57–76.

———. *Le Papyrus d'Imouthès Fils de Psintaês au Metropolitan Museum of Art de New-York (Papyrus MMA 35.9.21)* (New York: Metropolitan Museum of Art, 1999).

———. *Le papyrus du Louvre N. 3279,* BdE 42 (Cairo: IFAO, 1966).

———. "Un parallèle tardif d'une formule des inscriptions de la statue prophylactique de Ramsès III au Musée du Caire," *JEA* 57 (1971): 154–59.

———. "Un phylactère tardif: Le papyrus 3233 A et B du Musée du Louvre," *BIFAO* 77 (1977): 45–54.

———. *Le recueil de prophylaxie contre les aggressions des animaux venimeux du Musée de Brooklyn Papyrus Wilbour 47.218.138,* SSR 5 (Wiesbaden: Harrassowitz, 2012).

———. *Le rituel du sḥtp sḫmt au changement de cycle annuel: D'après les architraves du temple d'Edfou et textes parallèles, du Nouvel Empire à l'époque ptolémaïquue et romaine,* BdE 141 (Cairo: IFAO, 2006).

———. "Sur une formule des rituels de conjuration des dangers de l'année," *BIFAO* 74 (1974): 75–83.

———. "Textes mythologiques I: Le livre de protéger la barque du dieu," *Kêmi* 19 (1969): 23–65.

———. "Textes mythologiques II: Les révélations du mystère des quatre boules," *BIFAO* 75 (1975): 349–99.

Grapow, H. *Von den medizinischen Texten,* Grundriss der Medizin der Alten Ägypter 2 (Berlin: Akademie-Verlag, 1955).

———. *Kranker, Krankheit und Arzt,* Grundriss der Medizin der Alten Ägypter 3 (Berlin: Akademie-Verlag, 1956).

Green, M. "Additional Notes on the Coptic Magical Text Leiden F 19643/4.14," *OMRO* 67 (1987): 113–15.

———. "A Late Coptic Magical Text from the Collection of the Rijksmuseum van Oudheden, Leiden," *OMRO* 67 (1987): 29–43.

Grieshammer, R. "Isden," in *LÄ* 3 (1979): col. 184.

———. "Isdes," in *LÄ* 3 (1979): col. 185.

———. *Das Jenseitsgericht in den Sargtexten,* ÄA 20 (Wiesbaden: Harrassowitz, 1970).

———. "Taubheit," in *LÄ* 6 (1986): cols. 241–42.

Griffith, F.Ll. *Catalogue of the Demotic Papyri in the John Rylands Library, Manchester, with Facsimiles and Complete Translations* (Manchester: Manchester University, 1909).

Griffith, F.Ll. and H. Thompson *The Demotic Magical Papyrus of London and Leiden,* 3 vols. (London: Gevel, 1904–1909).

Griffiths, J.G. *The Conflict of Horus and Seth from Egyptian and Classical Sources* (Liverpool: Liverpool University, 1960).

——. *The Origins of Osiris* (Berlin: Hessling, 1966).
——. "The Horus-Seth Motif in the Daily Temple Liturgy," *Aeg* 38 (1958): 3–10.

Grimal, N.-C. *La stèle triomphale de Pi(ʿankh)y au Musée du Caire*, MIFAO 105 (Cairo: IFAO, 1981).

Guglielmi, W. "Die Funktion von Tempeleingang und Gegentempel als Gebetsort. Zur Deutung einiger Widder- und Gansstelen des Amun," in R. Gundlach and M. Rochholz (eds.), *Ägyptische Tempel-Struktur, Funktion und Programm. Akten der Ägyptologischen Tempeltagungen in Goren 1990 und Mainz 1992, HÄB* 37 (1994) (Hildesheim: Gerstenberg, 2001): 55–68.

Gunn, B. *Studies in Egyptian Syntax* (Paris: P. Geuthner, 1924).

Gutekunst, W. "Wie 'magisch' ist die 'Magie' im alten Ägypten? Einige theoretische Bemerkungen zur Magie-Problematik," in A. Roccati and A. Siliotti (eds.), *La Magia in Egitto ai tempi dei faraoni: Atti, convegno internazionale di studi, Milano, 29–31 ottobre 1985* (Verona: Rassegna internazionale di cinematografia archeologica: Arte e natura libri, 1987), pp. 77–98.

Gyóry, H. "Some Aspects of Magic in Ancient Egyptian Medicine," in P. Kousoulis (ed.), *Ancient Egyptian Demonology. Studies on the Boundaries between the Demonic and the Divine in Egyptian Magic*, OLA 175 (Leuven: Peeters, 2011), pp. 151–66.

Habachi, L. "Sais and its Monuments," *ASAE* 42 (1943): 369–407.

Haikal, F.M.H. *Two Funerary Papyri of Nesmin I–II*, Bibliotheca Aegyptiaca 14 and 15 (Brussels: Fondation Égyptologique Reine Élisabeth, 1970–72).

Hallo, W.W. (ed.) *The Context of Scripture. Canonical Compositions from the Biblical World*, 3 vols. (Leiden: Brill, 2003).

Hannig, R. *Großes Handwörterbuch Ägyptisch–Deutsch* (Mainz: von Zabern, 2001).

Harris, J.R. *Lexicographical Studies in Ancient Egyptian Minerals* (Berlin: Akademie-Verlag, 1961).

Hasel, M. *Domination and Resistance: Egyptian Military Activity in the Southern Levant, 1300–1185 BC*, Probleme der Ägyptologie 28 (Leiden: Brill, 1998).

Hayes, W.C. *A Papyrus of the Late Middle Kingdom in the Brooklyn Museum [Papyrus Brooklyn 35.1446]*, Wilbour Monographs 5 (Brooklyn: Brooklyn Museum, 1955).

Heerma van Voss, M. "Ein ägyptischer Papyrus in Houston," in M. Heerma van Voss (ed.), *Studies in Egyptian Religion: Dedicated to Professor Jan Zandee* (Leiden: Brill, 1982), pp. 56–60.
——. "Kontakt met teksten," *Phoenix* 30 (1984): 25–34.
——. "Ziegel (magische)," in *LÄ* 6 (1986): col. 1402.

Helck, W. *Altägyptische Aktenkunde des 3. und 2. Jahrtausends v. Chr.*, MÄS 31 (München: Deutscher Kunstverlag, 1974).
——. *Die Lehre für König Merikare*, KÄT (Wiesbaden: Harrassowitz, 1977).
——. *Der Text des 'Nilhymnus'*, KÄT (Wiesbaden: Harrassowitz, 1972).

Herbin, F. *Le livre de parcourir l'éternité*, OLA 58 (Leuven: Peeters, 1994).

——. "Une hymne à la lune croissante," *BIFAO* 82 (1982): 237–82 and pl. XLVII.

Hoffmann, F. and J.F. Quack *Anthologie der demotischen Literatur. Einführung und Quellentexte zur Ägyptologie,* Band 4 (Munich: LIT Verlag, 2007).

Hollis, S.T. *The Ancient Egyptian "Tale of Two Brothers:" A Mythological, Religious, Literary, and Historico-Political Study* (Oakville, CT: Bannerstone, 2008).

Hornung, E. *Altägyptische Höllenvorstellungen* (Berlin: Akademie-Verlag, 1968).

——. *Das Amduat. Die Schrift des verborgenen Raumes,* 2 vols. ÄA 7 (Wiesbaden: Harrassowitz, 1963).

——. *Das Buch der Anbetung des Re im Westen,* 2 vols. AH 2 (Geneva: Editions de Belles-Lettres, 1975).

——. "Chaotische Bereiche in der geordneten Welt," *ZÄS* 81 (1956): 28–32.

——. "Fisch und Vogel: Zur altägyptischen Sicht des Menschen," *Eranos Jahrbuch* 52 (1983): 455–96.

Jansen-Winckeln, K. *Ägyptische Biographien der 22. und 23. Dynastie,* 2 vols. ÄAT 8 (Wiesbaden: Harrassowitz, 1985).

——. "Diglossie und Zweisprachigkeit im alten Ägypten," *WZKM* 85 (1995): 85–115.

Jasnow, R. *A Late Period Wisdom Text (P. Brooklyn 47.218.135),* SAOC 52 (Chicago: University of Chicago, 1992).

Jasnow, R. and K.-H. Zauzich *The Ancient Egyptian Book of Thoth: A Demotic Discourse on Knowledge and Pendant to the Classical Hermetica* (Wiesbaden: Harrassowitz, 2005).

Jelínková-Reymond, E. *Les inscriptions de la statue guérisseuse de Djed-her-le-saveur,* BdE 23 (Cairo: IFAO, 1956).

Jéquier, G. "Matériaux pour servir à l'établissement d'un dictionnaire d'archéologie égyptienne," *BIFAO* 19 (1922): 1–249.

Johnson, J.H. "The Demotic Magical Spells of Leiden I 384," *OMRO* 56 (1975): 29–64.

——. "Louvre E. 3229: A Demotic Magical Text," *Enchoria* 7 (1977): 55–102.

Johnson, S. *The Cobra Goddess of Ancient Egypt: Predynastic, Early Dynastic, and Old Kingdom Periods* (London: Kegan Paul International, 1990).

Jonckheere, F. *Une maladie égyptienne, l'hématurie parasitaire* (Brussels: Fondation Égyptologique Reine Élisabeth, 1944).

——. *Les médecins de l'Égypte pharaonique* (Brussels: Fondation Égyptologique Reine Élisabeth, 1958).

——. *Le papyrus médical Chester Beatty* (Brussels: Fondation Égyptologique Reine Élisabeth, 1947).

——. "Prescriptions médicales sur ostraca hiératiques," *CdE* 29 (1954): 46–61.

Josephson, J.A., O'Rourke, P.F. and R. Fazzini "The Doha Head: A Late Period Egyptian Portrait," *MDAIK* 61 (2005): 219–41; pls. 37–41.

Junge, F. *Late Egyptian Grammar* (Oxford: Griffith Institute, 2005).

Junker, H. *Die Onurislegende,* DAWW 59 (Wien: A. Hölder, 1917).

——. *Der sehende und blinde Gott,* SAWW 7 (Munich: Bayerische Akademie der Wissenschaften, 1942).

Kadish, G. "The Scatophagous Egyptian," *JSSEA* 9 (1979): 203–17.

Känel, F. von *Les prêtres-ouâb de Sekhmet et les conjurateurs de Serket,* Bibliothèque de l'École des Hautes Études, Section des sciences religieuses 87 (Paris: Presses universitaires de France, 1984).

Kákosy, L. *Egyptian Healing Statues in Three Museums in Italy (Turin, Florence, Naples).* Catalogo del Museo Egizio di Torino, Seria prima: Monumenti e Testi 9 (Turin: Ministero per i beni e le attività culturali, Soprintendenza al Museo delle antichità egizie, 1999).

——. "Fragmente eines unpublizierten magischen Textes in Budapest," *ZÄS* 117 (1990): 140–57.

——. "Heka," in *LÄ* 3 (1979): cols. 60–62.

——. "Ein magischer Papyrus des Kunsthistorischen Museums in Budapest," *Acta Antiqua Academiae Scientiarum Hungaricae* 19:3–4 (1979): 159–77.

——. "Some Problems of the Magical Healing Statues," in A. Roccati and A. Siliotti (eds.), *La Magia in Egitto ai tempi dei faraoni: Atti, convegno internazionale di studi, Milano, 29–31 ottobre 1985* (Verona: Rassegna internazionale di cinematografia archeologica: Arte e natura libri, 1987), pp. 171–85.

——. "Vorläufiger Bericht über den Zauberpapyrus des Kunsthistorischen Museums in Budapest," *Trudy dvacat' pjatogo Meždunarodnogo Kongressa Vostokovedov Moskva, 9–16 Avgusta 1960* (Moscow 1962), pp. 96–99.

Kees, H. *Bemerkungen zum Tieropfer der Ägypter und seiner Symbolik* (Göttingen: Vandenhoeck & Ruprecht, 1942).

——. "Göttinger Totenbuchstudien. Ein Mythus vom Königtum des Osiris in Herakleopolis aus dem Totenbuch Kap. 175," *ZÄS* 65 (1930): 6–83 and 1*–10.*

——. "Kulttopographische und mythologische Beiträge," *ZÄS* 64 (1929): 99-112.

——. "*Nbd* als Dämon der Finsternis," *ZÄS* 59 (1924): 69–70.

Kessler, D. "Himmelsrichtungen," in *LÄ* 2 (1977): cols. 1213–15.

Kitchen, K.A. *Ramesside Inscriptions: Historical and Biographical,* 8 vols. (Oxford: Blackwell, 1969–1990).

——. *The Third Intermediate Period in Egypt: 1100–650 B.C.* (Warminster: Aris & Phillips, 1986).

Klasens, A. "An Amuletic Papyrus of the 25th Dynasty," *OMRO* 56 (1975), 20–28.

——. *A Magical Statue Base (Socle Behague) in the Museum of Antiquities at Leiden,* OMRO 33 (Leiden: Brill, 1952).

Klotz, D. *Adoration of the Ram: Five Hymns to Amun-Re from Hibis Temple,* YES 6 (New Haven: Yale Egyptological Seminar, 2006).

——. "Fish at Night and Birds by Day (Kemit VIII)," *ZÄS* 136 (2009): 136–40.

Koenig, Y. "Deux amulettes de Deir el-Médineh," *BIFAO* 79 (1979): 103–19.

——. "The Image of the Foreigner in the Magical Texts," in P. Koussoulis and K. Magliveras (eds.), *Moving Across Borders. Foreign Relations, Religion and*

Cultural Interactions in the Ancient Mediterranean, OLA 159 (Leuven: Peeters, 2007), pp. 223–38.

———. "Les effrois de Keniherkhepeshef (Papyrus Deir el-Médineh 40)," *RdE* 33 (1981): 29–37.

———. *Le papyrus Boulaq 6: Transcription, traduction et commentaire,* BdE 87 (Cairo: IFAO, 1981).

———. "Un revenant inconvenant? (Papyrus Deir el-Médineh 37)" *BIFAO* 79 (1979): 103–19.

Korostovtsev, M. "Egipetskiy ieraticheskiy papirus No. 167 iz gosudarstvennovo muzeya izobrazitel'nykh isskustv im A.S. Pushkina v Moskve," *Drevniy Egipet* (Moscow, 1960), pp. 119–32.

Kraeling, E.G. *The Brooklyn Museum Aramaic Papyri. New Documents of the Fifth Century B.C. from the Jewish Colony at Elephantine* (New Haven: The Brooklyn Museum, 1969, reprint ed.).

Kuhlmann, K. "Gottesepithet," in *LÄ* 2 (1977): col. 683.

Kurth, D. "Haroeris," in *LÄ* 2 (1977): cols. 999–1003.

Kurth, D., Thissen, H.J. and M. Weber *Kölner ägyptische Papyri (P. Köln ägypt.)* (Opladen: Westdeutscher Verlag, 1980).

Labrique, F. *Stylistique et théologie à Edfou,* OLA 51 (Leuven: Peeters, 1992).

Lacau, P. and H. Chevrier *Une chapelle d'Hatshepsout à Karnak,* vol. 1 (Cairo: IFAO, 1977).

Lange, H.O. *Der magische Papyrus Harris* (Copenhagen: Andr. Fred. Høst, 1927).

———. *Das Weisheitsbuch des Amenemope aus dem Papyrus 10474 des British Museum* (Copenhagen: Andr. Fred. Høst, 1925).

Leca, A-P. *La médecine égyptienne au temps des Pharaons* (Paris: Dacosta, 1971).

Leclant, J. "Les génies-gardiens de Montouemhat," *Drevniy Mir* (Moscow 1962), pp. 104–20.

———. "La 'Mascarade' des boeufs gras et la triomphe de l'Egypte," *MDAIK* 14 (1956): 128–45.

Ledrain, E. "Le papyrus de Luynes," *RT* 1 (1870): 89–95.

Lefebvre, G. *Essai sur la médecine égyptienne de l'époque pharaonique* (Paris: Presses universitaires de France, 1952).

———. *Tableau des parties du corps humain mentionnées par les Égyptiens,* SASAE 17 (Supplement) (Cairo: IFAO, 1952).

Leitz, C. *Magical and Medical Papyri of the New Kingdom,* HPBM 7th ser. (London: British Museum, 1999).

———. *Tagewählerei. Das Buch ḥ3t nḥḥ pḥ.wy ḏt und verwandte Texte,* 2 vols. ÄA 55 (Wiesbaden: Harrassowitz, 1994).

Leitz, C. et al. *Lexikon der ägyptischen Götter und Götterbezeichnungen,* 8 vols. OLA 110–116, 129 (Leuven: Peeters, 2002–2003).

Lesko, L. *A Dictionary of Late Egyptian,* 5 vols. (Providence: B.C. Scribe Publications, 1984–1990).

Lexa, F. *La Magie dans l'Égypte antique*, 3 vols. (Paris: P. Geuthner, 1925).

Lopez, J. "Naufragé, Col. 36–37 et 105–106," *RdE* 24 (1972): 111–15.

Lorton, D. "The Expression *šms-ib*," *JARCE* 7 (1968): 41–54.

Lucarelli, R. "Demons in the Book of the Dead," in B. Backes, I. Munro, and S. Stöhr, *Totenbuch-Forschungen. Gesammelte Beiträge des 2. Internationalen Totenbuch-Symposiums 2005*, SAT 11 (Wiesbaden: Harrassowitz, 2006), pp. 203–12.

———. "The Guardian-Demons of the Book of the Dead," *British Museum Studies in Ancient Egypt and Sudan* 15 (London, 2010), http://www.britishmuseum.org/research/publications/online_journals/bmsaes/issue_15.aspx.

———. "Popular Belief in Demons in the Libyan Period: The Evidence of the Oracular Amuletic Decrees," in G.P.F Broekman, R.J. Demarée, and O.E. Kaper (eds.), *The Libyan Period in Egypt. Historical and Cultural Studies into the 21th–24th Dynasties. Proceedings of a Conference at Leiden University, 25–27 October 2007.* EU 23 (Leuven: Peeters, 2009), pp. 231–40.

Lucas, A. *Ancient Egyptian Materials and Industries*, 4th edition, revised and enlarged by J.R. Harris (London: E. Arnold, 1989).

Lüscher, B. *Untersuchungen zu Tb 151*, SAT 2 (Wiesbaden: Harrassowitz, 1998).

Lustman, J. *Étude grammaticale du papyrus Bremner-Rhind* (Paris: Lustman, 1999).

Malaise, M. *Les scarabées de cœur dans l'Égypte ancienne*, MRE 4 (Brussels: Fondation Égyptologique Reine Élisabeth, 1978).

Malinine, M. "L'Hiératique anormal," in S. Sauneron (ed.), *Textes et langages de l'Égypte pharaonique. Cent cinquante années de recherche, 1822–1972. Hommage à Jean-Francois Champollion*, 3 vols. BdE 64 (Cairo: IFAO, 1973), pp. 31–35.

Manassa, C. *The Late Egyptian Underworld: Sarcophagi and Related Texts from the Nectanebid Period*, 2 vols., ÄAT 72 (Wiesbaden: Harrassowitz, 2007).

Manichee, L. *An Ancient Egyptian Herbal* (Austin: University of Texas, 1989).

Mariette, A. *Les papyrus égyptiens du Musée de Boulaq* 1 (Paris: A. Franck, 1871).

Massart, A. "The Egyptian Geneva Papyrus MAH 15274," *MDAIK* 15 (1957): 172–85.

———. *The Leiden Magical Papyrus I 343 + I 345*, OMRO 34 (Supplement) (Leiden: Brill, 1954).

———. "À Propos des 'Listes' dans les textes égyptiens funéraires et magiques," *AnBib* 12, Studia Biblica et Orientalia 3. Oriens Antiquus (1962): 227–46.

Massy, A. *Le Papyrus de Leiden I 347* (Ghent: H. Engelcke, 1885).

Maystre, C. and Piankoff, A. *Le livre des portes*, 3 vols. (Cairo: IFAO, 1939–62).

McDowell, A.G. *Hieratic Ostraca in the Hunterian Museum, Glasgow* (Oxford: Griffith Institute, 1993).

Meeks, D. *Année lexicographique* 1–3 (Paris: Impr. de la Margeride, 1980–1982).

———. *Génies, anges et démons en Egypte*, SO 8 (Paris: Éditions du Seuil, 1971), pp. 17–84.

———. *Mythes et légendes du Delta d'après le papyrus Brooklyn 47.218.84*, MIFAO 125 (Cairo: IFAO, 2006).

———. "Les quatre *ka* du démiurge memphite," *RdE* 15 (1963): 35–47.

Meeks. D. and Favard-Meeks, C. *Daily Life of the Egyptian Gods* (Ithaca: Cornell University, 1996).

Meltzer, E. "Horus," in D.B. Redford (ed.), *Oxford Encyclopedia of Ancient Egypt*, vol. 2 (New York: Oxford University, 2001), pp. 118–22.

Menu, B. "Le tombeau de Pétosiris. Nouvel examen," *BIFAO* 94 (1994): 311–27.

——. "Le tombeau de Pétosiris (2). Maat, Thot et la Droit," *BIFAO* 95 (1995): 281–95.

Meyer, M. and R. Smith (eds.) *Ancient Christian Magic. Coptic Texts of Ritual Power* (San Francisco: Harper, 1994).

Miller, R.L. " *Ḏaais*, Peganum harmala L.," *BIFAO* 94 (1994): 349–59.

Möller, G. *Hieratische Paläographie*, 3 vols. (Leipzig: J.C. Hinrichs, 1927–36).

Morenz, S. "Die Bedeutungsentwicklung von 'Das, was kommt' zu 'Unheil' und 'Unrecht,'" *Mélanges syriens offerts à M. René Dussaud, secrétaire perpétuel de l'Académie des Inscriptions et Belles-Lettres* (Paris: P. Geuthner, 1939), pp. 139–50.

Munro, I. "The Evolution of the Book of the Dead," in J. Taylor (ed.), *Journey Through the Afterlife. Ancient Egyptian Book of the Dead* (Cambridge: Harvard University Press, 2010), pp. 54–64.

——. *Das Totenbuch des Jah-mes (pLouvre E. 11085) aus der frühen 18. Dynastie*, HÄT 1 (Wiesbaden: Harrassowitz, 1995).

——. *Die Totenbuch-Papyri des Ehepaars Ta-scheret-en-Aset und Djed-chi aus der Bes-en-Mut-Familie (26. Dynastie, Zeit des Königs Amasis)*, HAT 12 (Wiesbaden: Harrassowitz, 2011).

Myśliwiec, K. *Studien zum Gott Atum*, 2 vols. HÄB 5, HÄB 8 (Hildesheim: Gerstenberg, 1978–79).

Nelson, H. "The Rite of 'Bringing the Foot' as Portrayed in Temple Reliefs," *JEA* 35 (1949): 82–86.

Niwinski, A. "The Solar-Osirian Unity as a Principle of the Theology of the 'State of Amun' in Thebes in the 21st Dynasty," *JEOL* 30 (1987–88): 89–106.

——. *Studies on the Illustrated Theban Funerary Papyri of the 11th and 10th Centuries B.C.*, OBO 86 (Fribourg: Universitätsverlag, 1989).

Nordh, K. *Aspects of Ancient Egyptian Curses and Blessings. Conceptual Background and Transmission*, Uppsala Studies in Ancient Mediterranean and Near Eastern Civilizations 26 (Uppsala: Uppsala Universitet, 1996).

O'Rourke, P.F. "The *ꜥmꜥt*-Woman," *ZÄS* 134 (2007): 165–71.

——. "Charles Edwin Wilbour and the Provenance of His Papyri," in V. Lepper, ed., *Essays on Elephantine* (forthcoming).

——. "La codification du savoir medical à l'époque saïte," *Égypte Afrique et Orient* 71 (2013): 33–40.

——. "The Old Kingdom Papyri from Elephantine Island in the Brooklyn Museum," in V. Lepper, ed., *Essays on Elephantine* (forthcoming).

——. *The Papyri in the Egyptian Collection of the Brooklyn Museum* (forthcoming).

O'Rourke, P.F. and J.F. Quack "New Fragments of the Late Hieratic Illustrated Magical Papyrus at the Brooklyn Museum (pBrooklyn 47.218.156) and Related Fragments at Berlin," in V. Lepper, ed., *Essays on Elephantine* (forthcoming).

Osing, J. *Der spätägyptische Papyrus BM 10808,* ÄA 33 (Wiesbaden: Harrassowitz, 1976).

Pardee, D. "The Bal'u Myth," in W.W. Hallo (ed.), *The Context of Scripture,* vol. 1 (Leiden: Brill, 2003), pp. 241–74.

Parker, R.A. *A Saite Oracle Papyrus from Thebes in The Brooklyn Museum [Papyrus Brooklyn Museum 47.218.3],* Brown Egyptological Studies 4 (Providence: Brown University, 1962).

Parker, R.A., Leclant, J. and J.-C. Goyon, *The Edifice of Taharqa by the Sacred Lake of Karnak,* Brown Egyptological Studies 8 (Providence: Brown University, 1979).

Perdu, O. *Recueil des inscriptions saïtes* (Paris: Cybèle, 2002).

Pestman, P.W. "The Diospolis Parva Documents: Chronological Problems Concerning Psammetichus III and IV," in H.-J. Thissen and K.-Th. Zauzich (eds.), *Grammata Demotika: Festschrift für Erich Lüddeckens, zum 15. Juni 1983* (Würzburg: Zauzich, 1984) 145–55.

Piankoff, A. Le "cœur" dans les textes Égyptiens depuis l'Ancien jusqu'à la fin du Nouvel Empire (Paris: P. Geuthner, 1930).

———. *The Litany of Re,* Bollingen Series 40: Egyptian Religious Texts and Representations 4 (New York: Bollingen Foundation, 1964).

———. *Le livre du jour et de la nuit* (Cairo: IFAO, 1942).

———. "Le livre des Quererts," *BIFAO* 41 (1942): 1–11; *BIFAO* 42 (1944): 13–74; *BIFAO* 43 (1945): 1–90; *BIFAO* 45 (1947): 1–42.

van der Plas, D. *L'Hymne à la crue du Nil,* EU 4 (Leiden: Nederlands Instituut voor het Nabije Oosten, 1986).

Pleyte, W. and Rossi, F. *Papyrus de Turin* (Leiden: Brill, 1869–1876).

Polotsky, H. J. "Egyptian Tenses," in H.J. Polotsky, *Collected Papers* (Jerusalem: Magnes Press, Hebrew University, 1971), pp. 71–96 = Israel Academy of Science and Humanities 2, No. 5 (1965), 1–25.

———. "The Emphatic *sḏm.n.f* Form," RdE 11 (1957): 109–17.

Posener, G. "La complainte de l'echanson Bay," in J. Assmann, E. Feucht, and R. Grieshammer (eds.), *Fragen an die altägyptische Literatur. Studien zum Gedenken an Eberhard Otto* (Wiesbaden: Reichert, 1977), pp. 385–97.

———. *De la divinité du pharaon,* Cahiers de la Société Asiatique 15 (Paris: Imprimerie Nationale, 1960).

———. "Les empreintes magiques de Gizeh et les morts dangereux," *MDAIK* 16 (1958): 252–70.

———. *Le Papyrus Vandier,* Bibliothèque générale 7 (Cairo: IFAO, 1985).

———. "Philologie et archéologie égyptiennes," *ACF* 75 (1975): 405-412

———. "Recherches sur le dieu Khonsu," *ACF* 65 (1965): 342–43; 66 (1966): 339–46; 67 (1967): 345–54; 68 (1968): 401–10; 69 (1969): 375–82; 70 (1970): 391–98.

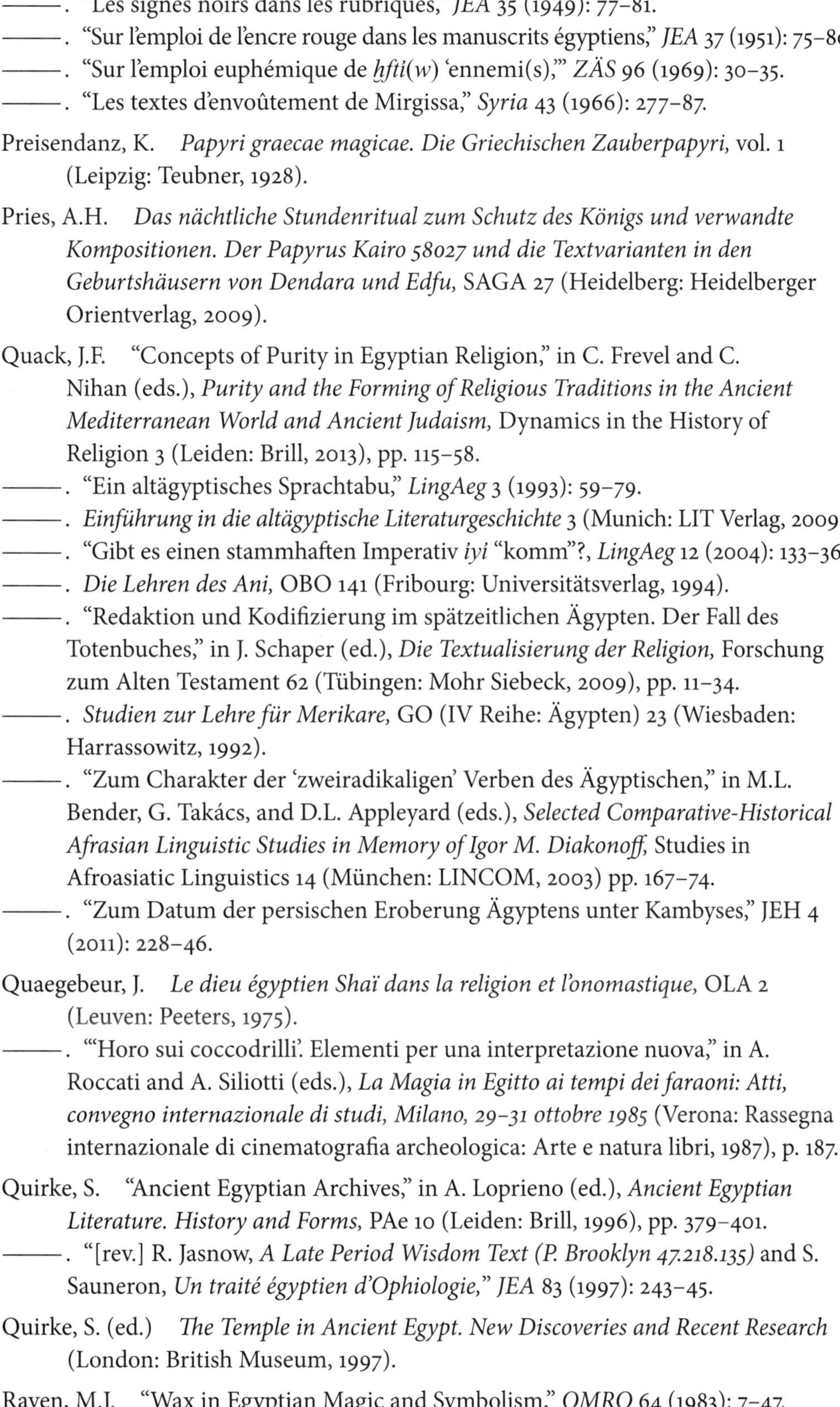

——. "Les signes noirs dans les rubriques," *JEA* 35 (1949): 77–81.
——. "Sur l'emploi de l'encre rouge dans les manuscrits égyptiens," *JEA* 37 (1951): 75–80.
——. "Sur l'emploi euphémique de *ḫfti(w)* 'ennemi(s),'" *ZÄS* 96 (1969): 30–35.
——. "Les textes d'envoûtement de Mirgissa," *Syria* 43 (1966): 277–87.

Preisendanz, K. *Papyri graecae magicae. Die Griechischen Zauberpapyri,* vol. 1 (Leipzig: Teubner, 1928).

Pries, A.H. *Das nächtliche Stundenritual zum Schutz des Königs und verwandte Kompositionen. Der Papyrus Kairo 58027 und die Textvarianten in den Geburtshäusern von Dendara und Edfu,* SAGA 27 (Heidelberg: Heidelberger Orientverlag, 2009).

Quack, J.F. "Concepts of Purity in Egyptian Religion," in C. Frevel and C. Nihan (eds.), *Purity and the Forming of Religious Traditions in the Ancient Mediterranean World and Ancient Judaism,* Dynamics in the History of Religion 3 (Leiden: Brill, 2013), pp. 115–58.
——. "Ein altägyptisches Sprachtabu," *LingAeg* 3 (1993): 59–79.
——. *Einführung in die altägyptische Literaturgeschichte* 3 (Munich: LIT Verlag, 2009)
——. "Gibt es einen stammhaften Imperativ *iyi* "komm"?, *LingAeg* 12 (2004): 133–36.
——. *Die Lehren des Ani,* OBO 141 (Fribourg: Universitätsverlag, 1994).
——. "Redaktion und Kodifizierung im spätzeitlichen Ägypten. Der Fall des Totenbuches," in J. Schaper (ed.), *Die Textualisierung der Religion,* Forschung zum Alten Testament 62 (Tübingen: Mohr Siebeck, 2009), pp. 11–34.
——. *Studien zur Lehre für Merikare,* GO (IV Reihe: Ägypten) 23 (Wiesbaden: Harrassowitz, 1992).
——. "Zum Charakter der 'zweiradikaligen' Verben des Ägyptischen," in M.L. Bender, G. Takács, and D.L. Appleyard (eds.), *Selected Comparative-Historical Afrasian Linguistic Studies in Memory of Igor M. Diakonoff,* Studies in Afroasiatic Linguistics 14 (München: LINCOM, 2003) pp. 167–74.
——. "Zum Datum der persischen Eroberung Ägyptens unter Kambyses," JEH 4 (2011): 228–46.

Quaegebeur, J. *Le dieu égyptien Shaï dans la religion et l'onomastique,* OLA 2 (Leuven: Peeters, 1975).
——. "'Horo sui coccodrilli'. Elementi per una interpretazione nuova," in A. Roccati and A. Siliotti (eds.), *La Magia in Egitto ai tempi dei faraoni: Atti, convegno internazionale di studi, Milano, 29–31 ottobre 1985* (Verona: Rassegna internazionale di cinematografia archeologica: Arte e natura libri, 1987), p. 187.

Quirke, S. "Ancient Egyptian Archives," in A. Loprieno (ed.), *Ancient Egyptian Literature. History and Forms,* PAe 10 (Leiden: Brill, 1996), pp. 379–401.
——. "[rev.] R. Jasnow, *A Late Period Wisdom Text (P. Brooklyn 47.218.135)* and S. Sauneron, *Un traité égyptien d'Ophiologie,*" *JEA* 83 (1997): 243–45.

Quirke, S. (ed.) *The Temple in Ancient Egypt. New Discoveries and Recent Research* (London: British Museum, 1997).

Raven, M.J. "Wax in Egyptian Magic and Symbolism," *OMRO* 64 (1983): 7–47.

Ray, J.D. *The Archive of Hor* (London: Egypt Exploration Society, 1976).

Redford, D.B. "An Interim Report on the Second Season of Work at the Temple of Osiris, Ruler of Eternity, Karnak," *JEA* 59 (1973): 16–30.

———. *Pharaonic King-Lists, Annals, and Daybooks: A Contribution to the Study of the Egyptian Sense of History,* SSEA Publication 4 (Mississauga: Benben Publications, 1986).

Reymond, E.A.E. *A Medical Book from Crocodilopolis. P. Vindob.D.6257* (Vienna: Brüder Hollinek, 1976).

Ritner, R.K. "An Eternal Curse upon the Reader of These Lines (with Apologies to M. Puig)," in P. Kousoulis (ed.), *Ancient Egyptian Demonology. Studies on the Boundaries between the Demonic and the Divine in Egyptian Magic,* OLA 175 (Leuven: Peeters, 2011), pp. 3–24.

———. "Medicine," in D.B. Redford (ed.), *Oxford Encyclopedia of Ancient Egypt* 2 (New York: Oxford University, 2001), pp. 353–56.

———. "Gleanings from Magical Texts," *Enchoria* 14 (1986): 95–106.

———. "Horus on the Crocodiles," in W.K. Simpson (ed.), *Religion and Philosophy in Ancient Egypt,* YES 3 (New Haven: Yale Egyptological Seminar, 1989), pp. 103–16.

———. *The Mechanics of Ancient Egyptian Magical Practice,* SAOC 54 (Chicago: University of Chicago, 1992).

———. "O. Gardiner 363: A Spell against Night Terrors," *JARCE* 27 (1990): 25–41.

———. "A Uterine Amulet in the Oriental Institute Collection," *JNES* 43 (1984): 219–20.

Roccati, A. "Magia e litteratura nell'Egitto del II millennio a.C.," *Mélanges Adolphe Gutbub* (Montpellier: Université de Montpellier, 1984), pp. 201–10.

———. "Magia e scienza nell'Egitto antico," in A. Roccati and A. Siliotti (eds.), *La Magia in Egitto ai tempi dei faraoni: Atti, convegno internazionale di studi, Milano, 29–31 ottobre 1985* (Verona: Rassegna internazionale di cinematografia archeologica: Arte e natura libri, 1987), pp. 111–20.

———. *Magica Taurinensia. Il grande papiro magico di Torino e i suoi duplicati,* AnOr 56 (Rome: Gregorian & Biblical Press, 2011).

———. "Nuovi paralleli torinesi di testi magici ramessidi," *Aeg* 44 (1969): 5–13.

———. "Un nuovo rotolo magico diviso tra le raccolte di Ginevra e Torino," *BSEG* 7 (1982): 91–94.

———. *Papiro Ieratico N. 54003: Estratti magici e rituali del Primo Medio Regno,* Catalogo del Museo egizio di Torino, Seria prima: Monumenti e testi 2 (Turin: Edizioni d'Arte F.lli Posso, 1970).

Rössler-Köhler, U. *Kapitel 17 des ägyptischen Totenbuches,* GO (IV. Reihe: Ägypten) 10 (Wiesbaden: Harrassowitz, 1979).

Roulin, G. *Le livre de la nuit,* OBO 147/1–2 (Fribourg: Universitätsverlag, 1996).

Ruffle, J. "A New Meaning of the Word ," *JEA* 50 (1964): 177–78.

Sadek, A.I. *Popular Religion in Egypt During the New Kingdom,* HÄB 27 (Hildesheim: Gerstenberg, 1987).

Sanchez, G.M. and E. Meltzer *The Edwin Smith Papyrus. Updated Translation of the Trauma Treatise and Modern Medical Commentaries* (Atlanta: Lockwood Press, 2012).

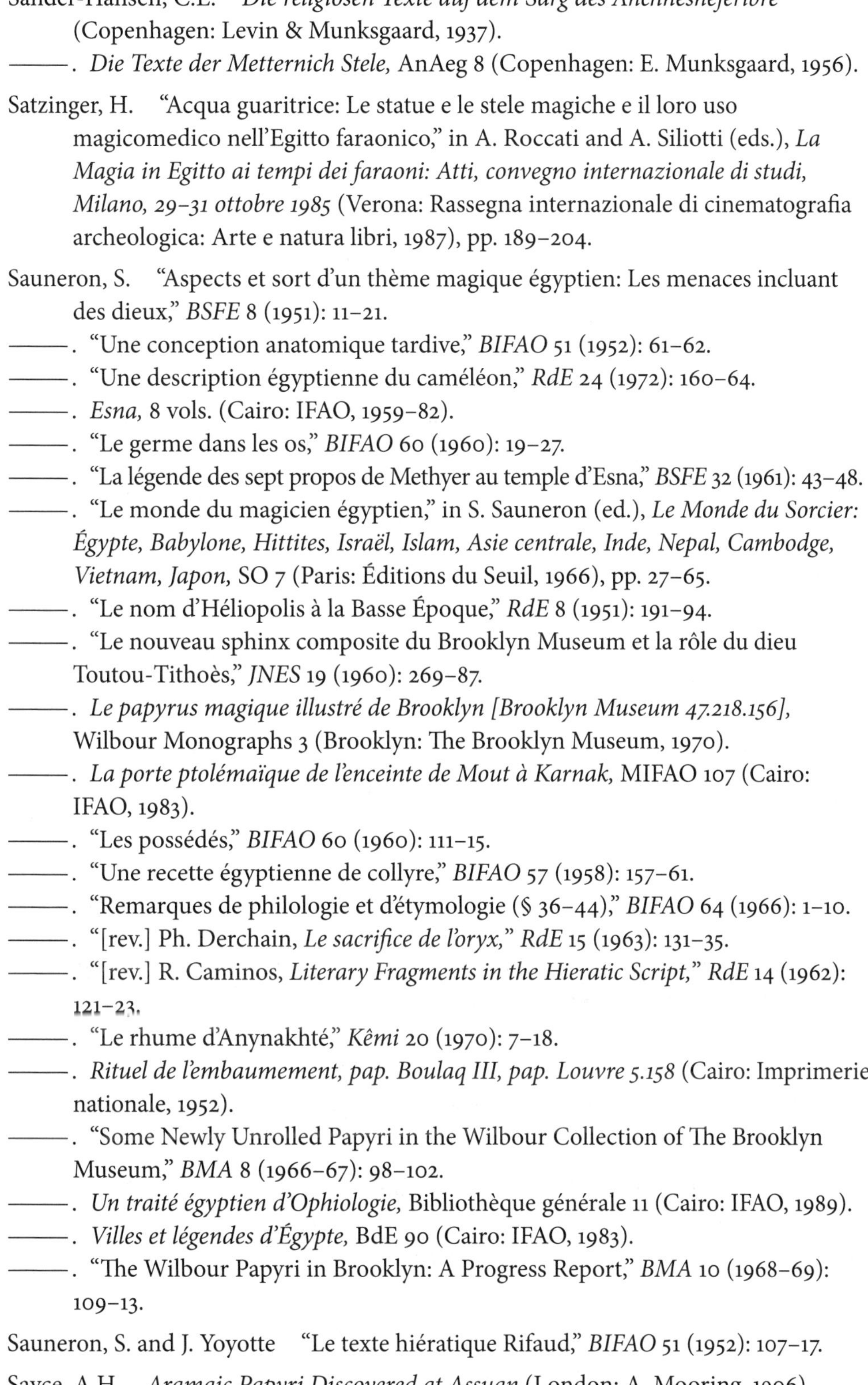

Sander-Hansen, C.E. *Die religiösen Texte auf dem Sarg des Anchnesneferibre* (Copenhagen: Levin & Munksgaard, 1937).

———. *Die Texte der Metternich Stele,* AnAeg 8 (Copenhagen: E. Munksgaard, 1956).

Satzinger, H. "Acqua guaritrice: Le statue e le stele magiche e il loro uso magicomedico nell'Egitto faraonico," in A. Roccati and A. Siliotti (eds.), *La Magia in Egitto ai tempi dei faraoni: Atti, convegno internazionale di studi, Milano, 29–31 ottobre 1985* (Verona: Rassegna internazionale di cinematografia archeologica: Arte e natura libri, 1987), pp. 189–204.

Sauneron, S. "Aspects et sort d'un thème magique égyptien: Les menaces incluant des dieux," *BSFE* 8 (1951): 11–21.

———. "Une conception anatomique tardive," *BIFAO* 51 (1952): 61–62.

———. "Une description égyptienne du caméléon," *RdE* 24 (1972): 160–64.

———. *Esna,* 8 vols. (Cairo: IFAO, 1959–82).

———. "Le germe dans les os," *BIFAO* 60 (1960): 19–27.

———. "La légende des sept propos de Methyer au temple d'Esna," *BSFE* 32 (1961): 43–48.

———. "Le monde du magicien égyptien," in S. Sauneron (ed.), *Le Monde du Sorcier: Égypte, Babylone, Hittites, Israël, Islam, Asie centrale, Inde, Nepal, Cambodge, Vietnam, Japon,* SO 7 (Paris: Éditions du Seuil, 1966), pp. 27–65.

———. "Le nom d'Héliopolis à la Basse Époque," *RdE* 8 (1951): 191–94.

———. "Le nouveau sphinx composite du Brooklyn Museum et la rôle du dieu Toutou-Tithoès," *JNES* 19 (1960): 269–87.

———. *Le papyrus magique illustré de Brooklyn [Brooklyn Museum 47.218.156],* Wilbour Monographs 3 (Brooklyn: The Brooklyn Museum, 1970).

———. *La porte ptolémaïque de l'enceinte de Mout à Karnak,* MIFAO 107 (Cairo: IFAO, 1983).

———. "Les possédés," *BIFAO* 60 (1960): 111–15.

———. "Une recette égyptienne de collyre," *BIFAO* 57 (1958): 157–61.

———. "Remarques de philologie et d'étymologie (§ 36–44)," *BIFAO* 64 (1966): 1–10.

———. "[rev.] Ph. Derchain, *Le sacrifice de l'oryx,*" *RdE* 15 (1963): 131–35.

———. "[rev.] R. Caminos, *Literary Fragments in the Hieratic Script,*" *RdE* 14 (1962): 121–23.

———. "Le rhume d'Anynakhté," *Kêmi* 20 (1970): 7–18.

———. *Rituel de l'embaumement, pap. Boulaq III, pap. Louvre 5.158* (Cairo: Imprimerie nationale, 1952).

———. "Some Newly Unrolled Papyri in the Wilbour Collection of The Brooklyn Museum," *BMA* 8 (1966–67): 98–102.

———. *Un traité égyptien d'Ophiologie,* Bibliothèque générale 11 (Cairo: IFAO, 1989).

———. *Villes et légendes d'Égypte,* BdE 90 (Cairo: IFAO, 1983).

———. "The Wilbour Papyri in Brooklyn: A Progress Report," *BMA* 10 (1968–69): 109–13.

Sauneron, S. and J. Yoyotte "Le texte hiératique Rifaud," *BIFAO* 51 (1952): 107–17.

Sayce, A.H. *Aramaic Papyri Discovered at Assuan* (London: A. Mooring, 1906).

el-Sayed, R. "Un document relatif au culte dans Kher-Aha (statue Caire CG 682)," *BIFAO* 82 (1982): 187–204.

Schenkel, W. "Kritisches zur Textkritik: Die sogenannten Hörfehler," *GM* 29 (1978): 119–26.

———. "Textradierung, -kritik," in *LÄ* 6 (1986): cols. 459–62.

Schmitz, F.J. "Zur Lesung und Deutung von [hieroglyphs] und [hieroglyph]," *GM* 27 (1978): 51–58.

Schott, S. *Bücher und Bibliotheken im alten Ägypten: Verzeichnis der Buch- und Spruchtitel und der Termini technici* (Wiesbaden: Harrassowitz, 1990).

———. "Drei Sprüche gegen Feinde," *ZÄS* 65 (1930): 35–42.

———. *Urkunden VI. Urkunden mythologischen Inhalts* I. *Bücher und Sprüche gegen den Gott Seth* (Leipzig: Hinrichs, 1929).

———. "'Zweimal' als Ausrufungszeichen," *ZÄS* 79 (1954): 54–56.

Schwann, H. "Die altägyptische Ohrenheilkunde aus medizinischer und otologischer Sicht," *AF* 10 (1983): 199–207.

———. "Der Beitrag der altägyptischen Medizin zur ärztlichen Ethik unter besonderer Berücksichtigung der Sterbebetreuung," *AF* 11 (1984): 3–9.

Serrano, J. "Origin and Basic Meaning of the Word *ḥnmmt* (the so-called 'Sun-folk'), *SAK* 27 (1999): 353–68.

Sethe, K. *Urkunden des ägyptischen Altertums* I: *Urkunden des Alten Reichs* (Leipzig: Hinrichs, 1903).

———. *Von Zahlen und Zahlworten bei den alten Ägyptern und was für andere Völker und Sprachen daraus zu lernen ist* (Strassburg: K. J. Trübner, 1916).

Shirun-Grumach, I. "Lehre des Amenemope," in *LÄ* 3 (1979): cols. 971–74.

Smith, H.S. and W.J. Tait *Saqqâra Demotic Papyri*, vol. 1 (London: Egypt Exploration Society, 1983).

Smith, M. "The Reign of Seth: Egyptian Perspectives from the First Millennium BCE," in L. Bareš, F. Coppens, and K. Smoláriková (eds.), *Egypt in Transition. Social and Religious Development of Egypt in the First Millennium* BCE (Prague: Charles University, 2010), pp. 396–430.

———. *Traversing Eternity: Texts for the Afterlife from Ptolemaic and Roman Egypt* (Oxford: Oxford University, 2009).

Smither, P.C. "An Old Kingdom Letter Concerning the Crimes of Count Sabni," *JEA* 28 (1942): 16–19.

Sørensen, J.P. "The Argument in Ancient Egyptian Magical Formulae," *Acta Orientalia* 45 (1984): 5–21.

Spalinger, A. "Psamtik I–III," in *LÄ* 4 (1982): cols. 1173–76.

Spiegelberg, W. "Horus als Arzt," *ZÄS* 57 (1922): 70–71.

———. "*nṯr.w*, Götter = Bilder," *ZÄS* 65 (1930): 119–21.

Spieser, C. *Les noms du Pharaon comme êtres autonomes au Nouvel Empire*, OBO 174 (Fribourg: Universitätsverlag, 2000).

Sternberg el-Hotabi, H. *Untersuchungen zur Überlieferungsgeschichte der Horusstelen: Ein Beitrag zur Religionsgeschichte Ägyptens im 1. Jahrtausend v. Chr,* ÄA 62 (Wiesbaden: Harrassowitz, 1999).

———. "The Excavation of Temple C: Appendix I. Magische Stele," *JSSEA* 18 (1988): 14–18.

Störk, L. "Aurispizien," *GM* 108 (1989): 65–74.

———. "Das Ohr in den altägyptischen Sexualvorstellungen," *GM* 5 (1973): 33–38.

———. "Das Ohr in den altägyptischen Sexualvorstellungen — Nachtrag," *GM* 8 (1973): 39–42.

Stricker, B.H. "De Egyptische Mysteriën: Pap. Leiden T 32 (Vervolg)," *OMRO* 34 (1953): 13–63.

———. "De Egyptische Mysteriën: Pap. Leiden T 32 (Slot)," *OMRO* 37 (1956): 49–67.

———. "The Enemies of Re I: The Doctrine of Ascesis," *DIE* 23 (1992): 45–76.

———. "The Enemies of Re II: The Textual Tradition," *DIE* 28 (1994): 95–122.

———. "Spreuken tot Beveiliging gedurende de Schrikkeldagen naar Pap. I 346," *OMRO* 29 (1948): 55–70.

———. "Teksten tegen Schorpioenen," *OMRO* 21 (1940): 53–62.

Suys, P. "Le papyrus magique du Vatican," *Or* 3 (1934): 63–87.

Sweeny, D. "What is a Rhetorical Question?," *LingAeg* 1 (1991): 315–31.

Szpakowska, K. "Demons in the Dark: Nightmares and Other Nocturnal Enemies in Ancient Egypt," in P. Kousoulis (ed.), *Ancient Egyptian Demonology. Studies on the Boundaries between the Demonic and the Divine in Egyptian Magic,* OLA 175 (Leuven: Peeters, 2011), pp. 63–76.

Tait, W.J. *Papyri from Tebtunis in Egyptian and Greek,* Egyptian Exploration Society: Texts from Excavations 3 (London: Egypt Exploration Society, 1977).

te Velde, H. *Seth, God of Confusion,* Probleme der Ägyptologie 6 (Leiden: Brill, 1977).

———. "Some Egyptian Deities and their Piggishness," in U. Luft (ed.), *The Intellectual Heritage of Egypt. Studies Presented to László Kákosy by Friends and Colleagues on the Occasion of his 60th Birthday.* Studia Agyptiaca 14 (Budapest : La chaire d'Egyptologie, 1992), pp. 571–78.

Thausig, G. "Über die Personifikation des Todes," *Archiv für ägyptische Archäologie* 1 (1938): 215–21.

Theis, C. "[hieroglyphs] Erdwolf oder Schwein? Ein Vergleich von Archäologie und schriftlichem Material," *ZÄS* 138 (2011): 79–86.

Thissen, H.J. "Ägyptologische Beiträge zu den griechischen magischen Papyri," in U. Verhoeven and E. Graefe (eds.), *Religion und Philosophie im alten Ägypten: Festgabe für Philippe Derchain zu seinem 65. Geburtstag am 24. Juli 1991* (Leuven: Peeters, 1991), pp. 293–302.

Thissen, H.-J. and K.-Th. Zauzich (eds.), *Grammata demotika: Festschrift für Erich Lüddeckens, zum 15. Juni 1983* (Würzburg: Zauzich, 1984).

Thomas, E., "Solar Barks Prow to Prow," *JEA* 42 (1956): 65–79.

Traunecker, C. *Coptos. Hommes et Dieux sur le parvis de Geb,* OLA 43 (Leuven: Peeters, 1992).

Vallogia, M. "Le papyrus Lausanne No. 3391," in J. Vercoutter (ed.), *Hommages à la Mémoire de Serge Sauneron, 1927–1976*, BdE 81 (Cairo: IFAO, 1979), pp. 285–304.

——. *Recherche sur les "Messagers" (WPWTYW) dans les sources égyptiennes profanes* (Paris: Librairie Droz, 1976).

van de Walle, B. "Une base de statue-guerisseuse avec une nouvelle mention de la déesse-scorpion Ta-Bithet," *JNES* 31 (1972): 68–73.

Vandier, J. *Mo'alla. La tombe d'Ankhtifi et la tombe de Sébekhotep*, BdE 18 (Cairo: IFAO, 1950).

——. *Le papyrus Jumilhac* (Paris: Centre National de la Recherche Scientifique, 1962).

Verhoeven, U. *Das saitische Totenbuch des Iatesnacht: P. Colon. Aeg. 10207* (Bonn: Habelt, 1993).

——. *Das Totenbuch des Monthpriesters Nespasefy aus der Zeit Psammetichs I: pKairo JE 95714 + pAlbany 1900.3.1, pKairo JE 95649, pMarseille 192*, HÄT 5 (Wiesbaden: Harrassowitz, 1999).

——. *Untersuchungen zur späthieratischen Buchschrift* (Leuven: Peeters, 2001).

——. "Von hieratischen Literaturwerken in der Spätzeit," in J. Assmann and E. Blumenthal (eds.), *Literatur und Politik im pharaonischen und ptolemäischen Ägypten*, BdE 127 (Cairo: IFAO, 1999), pp. 255–65.

Verhoeven, U. and P. Derchain *La déesse Libyque. Ein Text aus dem "Mutritual des Pap. Berlin 3053,"* Rites égyptiens 5 (Brussels: Fondation Égyptologique Reine Élisabeth, 1985).

Vernus, P. *Athribis*, BdE 74 (Cairo, IFAO, 1978).

——. "Un décret de Thoutmosis à la santé publique," *Or* 48 (1979): 176–84.

——. "Entre néo-égyptien et démotique: La langue utilisée dans la traduction du rituel de repousser l'agressif (Étude sur la diglossie I)," *RdE* 41 (1990): 153–208.

——. *Future at Issue. Tense, Mood and Aspect in Middle Egyptian: Studies in Syntax and Semantics*, YES 3 (New Haven, CT: Yale Egyptological Seminar, 1990)

Vittmann, G. "Ein Amulett aus der Spätzeit zum Schutz gegen Feinde," *ZÄS* 111 (1984): 164–70.

——. *Priester und Beamte im Theben der Spätzeit: Genealogische und prosopographische Untersuchungen zum Thebanischen Priester- und Beamtentum der 25 und 26 Dynastie* (Wien: Institute für Afrikanistik und Ägyptologie der Universität Wien, 1978).

——. "Papyri, kursivhieratische," in *LÄ* 4 (1982): cols. 748–50.

Vleeming, S. "La phase initiale du démotique ancien," *CdE* 56 (1981): 31–48.

——. *The Gooseherds of Hou: (Pap. Hou), A Dossier Relating to Various Agricultural Affairs from Provincial Egypt of the Early Fifth Century* B.C. (Leuven: Peeters, 1991).

Vogelsang, F. *Kommentar zu den Klagen des Bauern*, UGAÄ 6 (Leipzig: Hinrichs, 1913).

Vycichl, W. "Sur les noms des parties du corps en égyptien," *CdE* 47 (1972): 173–82.

Waddell, W.G. *Manetho*, Loeb Classical Library 350 (Cambridge: Harvard University, 1980).

Wainwright, G.A. "Letopolis," *JEA* 18 (1932): 159–72.

Walker, C. "Egyptian Medicine and the Gods," *BACE* 4 (1993): 83–101.

Walker, J.H. *Studies in Ancient Egyptian Anatomical Terminology* (Warminster, Aris and Phillips, 1996).

Ward, W. "The *hiw*-ass, the *hiw*-serpent and the God Seth," *JNES* 37 (1978): 23–34.

———. "Lexicographical Miscellanies," *SAK* 5 (1980): 265–92.

Weber, M. "Lebenshaus I," in *LÄ* 3 (1979): cols. 954–57.

Weeks, K.R. "Studies of P. Ebers," *BIE* 58–59 (1976–77; 1977–78): 292–99.

Wessetzky, W. "Die ägyptische Tempelbibliothek," *ZÄS* 100 (1973): 54–59.

———. "Bibliothek," in *LÄ* 1 (1975): cols. 783–85.

Westendorf, W. "Beiträge aus und zu den medizinischen Texten," *ZÄS* 92 (1966): 128–54.

———. "Beiträge aus und zu den medizinischen Texten," *ZÄS* 96 (1970): 145–51.

———. "Beiträge aus und zu den medizinischen Texten V. Der 'lastende' Nil und 'die Seuche des Jahres'," *GM* 49 (1981): 77–83.

———. "Eine auf die Maat anspielende Form des Osirisnamens," *MIO* 2 (1954): 165–82.

———. *Erwachen der Heilkunst. Die Medizin im Alten Ägypten* (Zürich: Artemis & Winkler, 1992).

———. *Handbuch der altägyptischen Medizin,* 2 vols. (Leiden: Brill, 1999).

———. "Magie in der altägyptischen Medizin," *Die Grünenthal Waage* 1, I/3 (1963): 15–22.

———. "Papyrus Berlin 10456. Ein Fragment des wiederentdeckten medizinischen Papyrus Rubensohn," in *Staatliche Museum zu Berlin. Festschrift zum 150-jährigen Bestehen des Berliner Ägyptischen Museums,* Mitteilungen aus der Ägyptischen Sammlung (Berlin: Akademie-Verlag, 1974), pp. 247–54.

———. *Papyrus Edwin Smith. Ein medizinisches Lehrbuch aus dem alten Ägypten* (Bern: Huber, 1966).

———. "Der Rezitationsvermerk *ṯs-pẖr,*" in O. Firchow (ed.), *Ägyptologische Studien: Hermann Grapow zum 70. Geburtstag gewidmet* (Berlin: Akademie-Verlag, 1955), pp. 383–402.

Wilson, P. *A Ptolemaic Lexicon,* OLA 78 (Leuven: Peeters 1997).

———. "Slaughtering the Crocodile at Edfu and Dendera" in S. Quirke (ed.), *The Temple in Ancient Egypt. New Discoveries and Recent Research* (London: British Museum, 1997), pp. 179–203.

Winand, J. *Études de néo-égyptien,* 1: *La morphologie verbale,* AL 2 (Liège: Centre Informatique de Philosophie et Lettres, 1992).

———. "La grammaire au secours de la datation des textes," *RdE* 46 (1995): 187–202.

———. "Une nouvelle sagesse hiératique de la Basse Époque (Papyrus Brooklyn Museum 47.218.135)," *CdE* 73 (1998): 42–53.

Wreszinski, W. *Die Medizin der alten Ägypter,* 3 vols. (Leipzig: Hinrichs, 1909–13).

Wüthrich, A. *Elements de théologie Thébaine: Les chapitres supplementaires du Livre des Morts,* SAT 16 (Wiesbaden: Harrassowitz, 2010).

Yoyotte, J. "Études géographiques II. Les localités méridionales de la région Memphite et le Pehou d'Héracléopolis," *RdE* 14 (1962): 101–10.

———. "Hera d'Héliopolis et le sacrifice humain," *ÉPHE* V[e] 89 (1980–81): 31–102.

———. "Une théorie étiologique des médecins égyptiens," *Kêmi* 18 (1968): 79–84.

Žabkar, L. *A Study of the Ba Concept in Ancient Egyptian Texts,* SAOC 34 (Chicago: University of Chicago, 1968).

Zandee, J. *Der Amunhymnus des Papyrus Leiden I 344, Verso,* 3 vols. Collections of the National Museum of Antiquities at Leiden 7 (Leiden: Rijksmuseum van Oudheden, 1992).

———. "The Birth-Giving Creator God in Ancient Egypt," in A.B. Lloyd (ed.), *Studies in Pharaonic Religion and Society in Honour of J. Gwyn Griffiths* (London: Egypt Exploration Society, 1992), pp. 169–85.

———. *Death as an Enemy According to Ancient Egyptian Conceptions,* Studies in the History of Religions 5 (Leiden: Brill, 1960).

———. *De Hymnen aan Amon van Papyrus Leiden I 350,* OMRO 28 (Leiden: Brill 1947).

Zibelius, K. "Zu 'Speier' und 'Speichel' in Ägypten," in F. Junge (ed.), *Studien zu Sprache und Religion Ägyptens zu Ehren von Wolfhart Westendorf, überreicht von seinen Freunden und Schülern,* 2 vols. (Göttingen: Hubert & Co., 1984), pp. 399–407.

Zivie, C.M. "Les rites d'érection de l'obélisque et du pilier *ioun,*" in J. Vercoutter (ed.), *Hommages à la Mémoire de Serge Sauneron, 1927–1976,* BdE 81 (Cairo: IFAO, 1979), pp. 477–98.

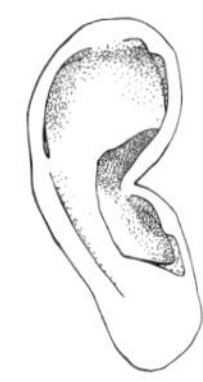

Index of Words Discussed

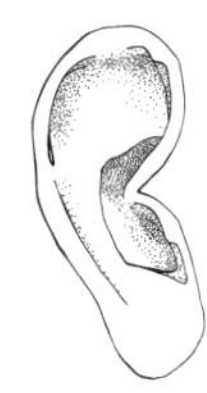

Index of Divine Names and Attributes

Index of Geographical Terms

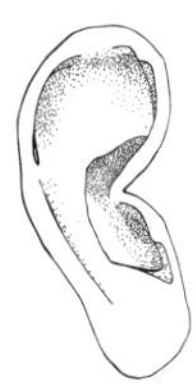

Index of Texts Cited

(numbers refer to page where the text is cited)

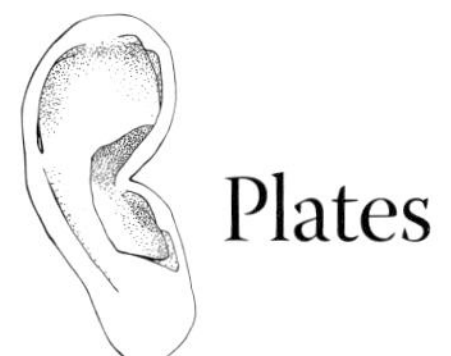

Plates

PLATE 1A *pBrooklyn 47.218.49* — COLUMN X + 1

PLATE 1B *pBrooklyn 47.218.49* — COLUMN X + 1

Plate 2a *pBrooklyn 47.218.49* — COLUMN X + 2

Plate 2b *pBrooklyn 47.218.49* — COLUMN X + 2

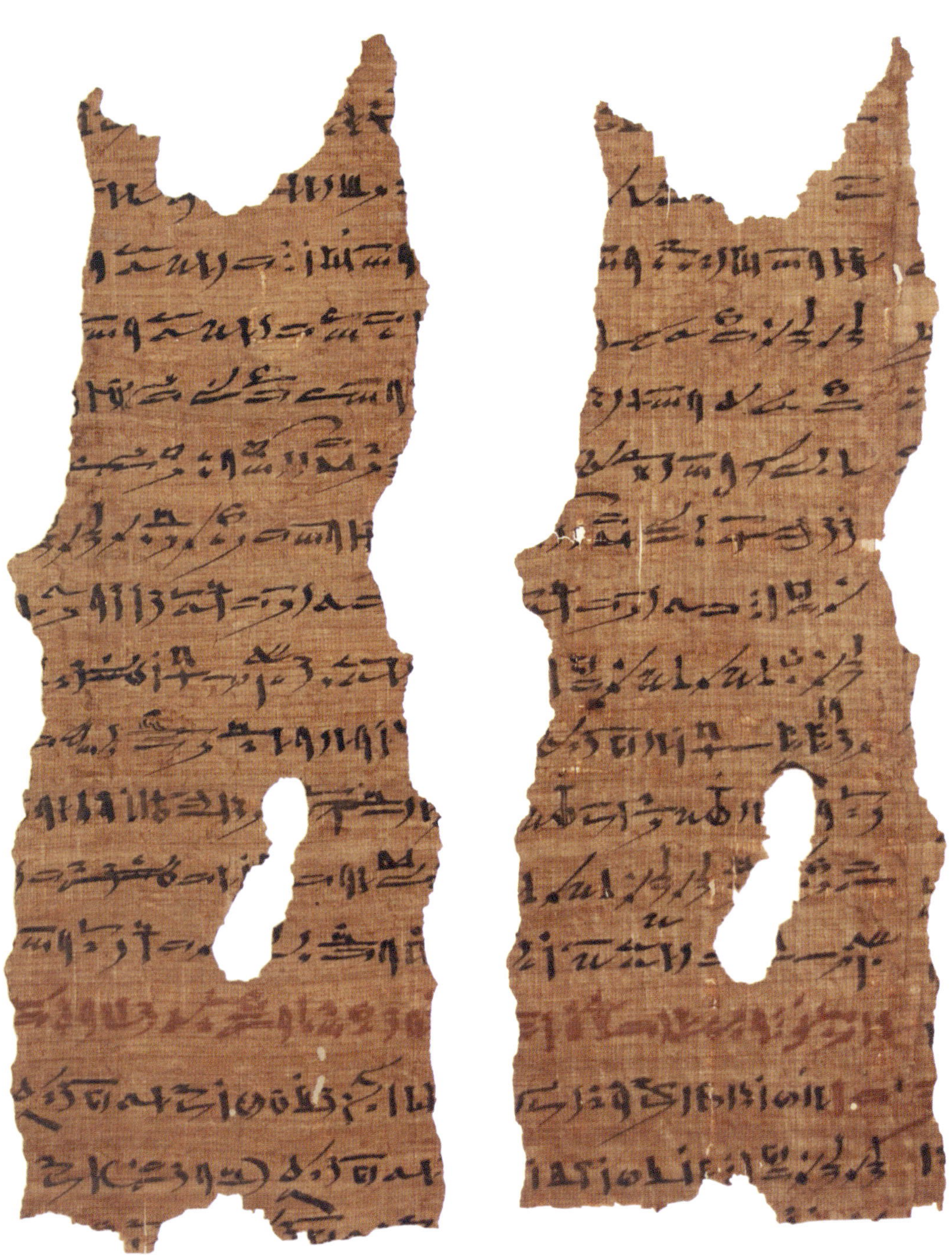

PLATE 3A *pBrooklyn 47.218.49* — COLUMN X + 3

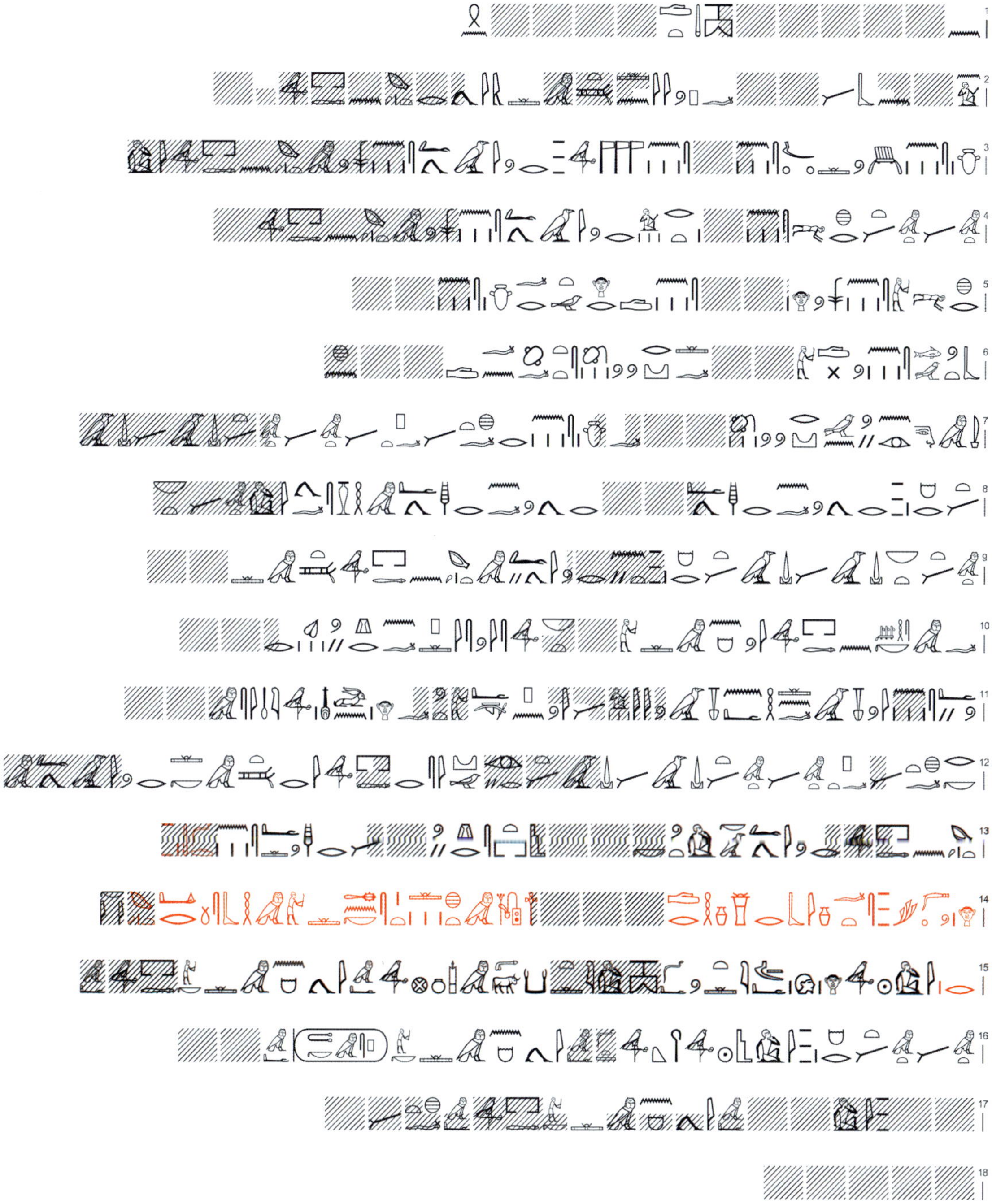

Plate 3b *pBrooklyn 47.218.49* — COLUMN X + 3

PLATE 4A *pBrooklyn 47.218.49* — COLUMN X + 4

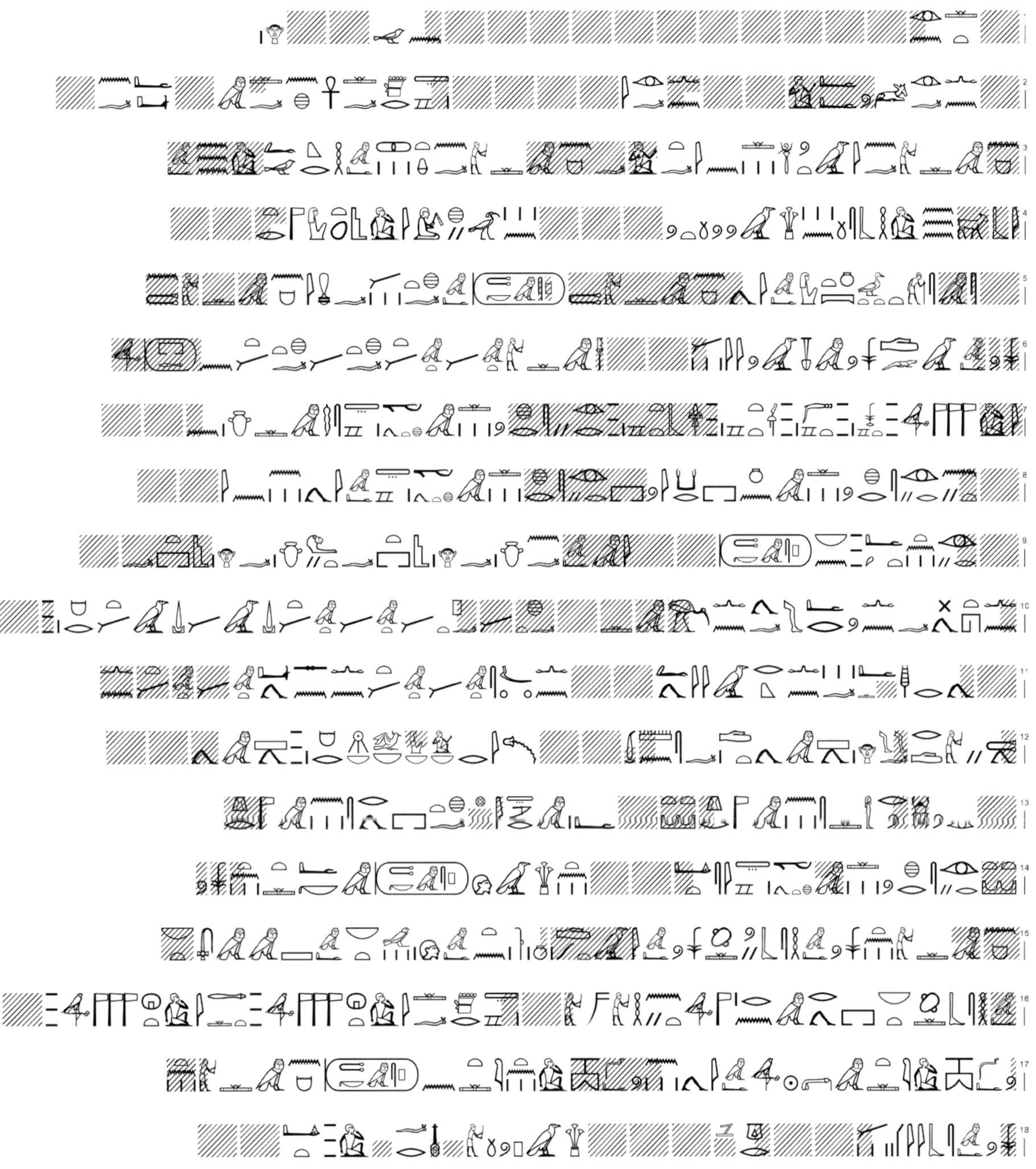

PLATE 4B *pBrooklyn 47.218.49* — COLUMN X + 4

PLATE 5A *pBrooklyn 47.218.49* — COLUMN X + 5

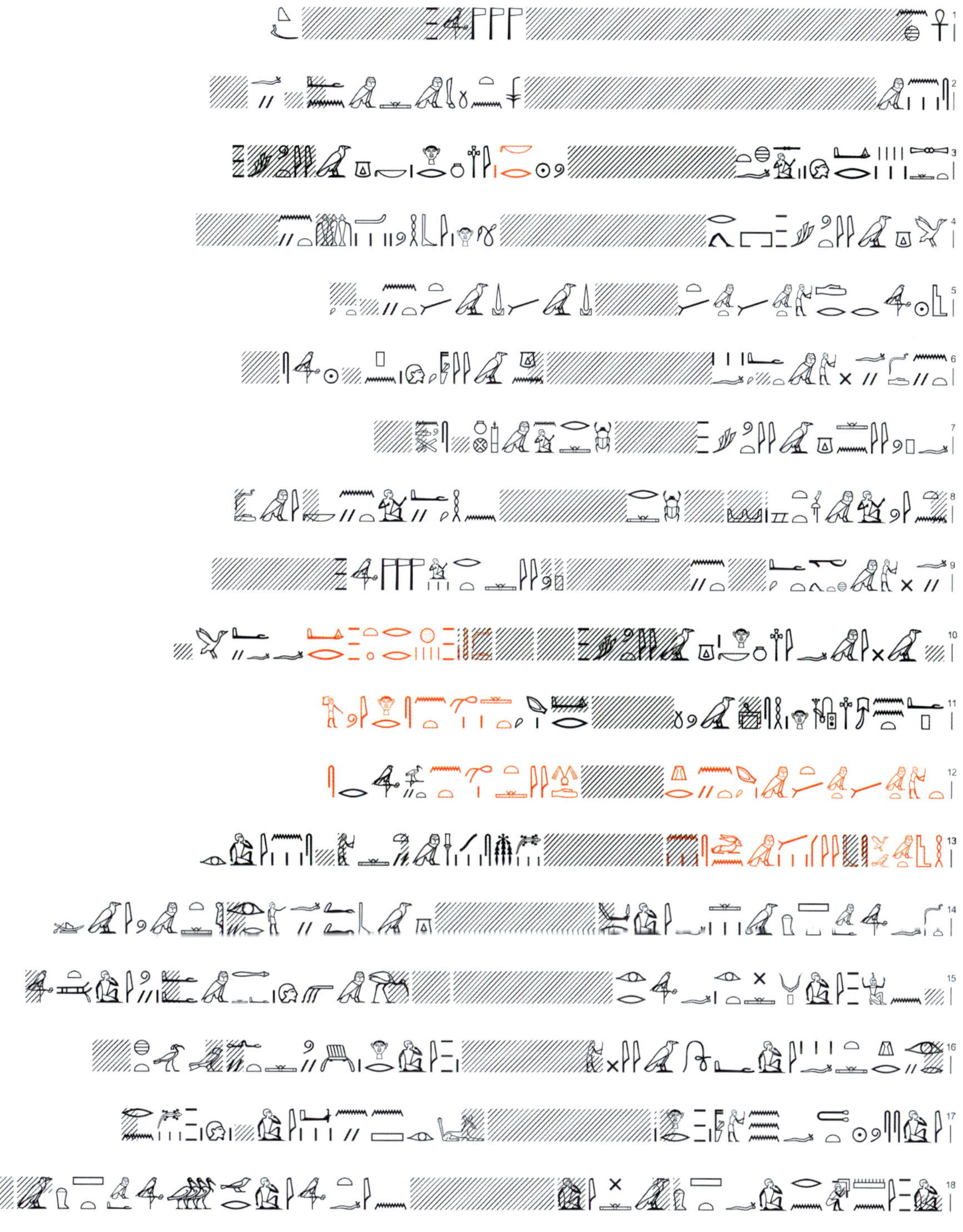

Plate 5b *pBrooklyn 47.218.49* — COLUMN X + 5

Plate 6a *pBrooklyn 47.218.49* — COLUMN X + 6

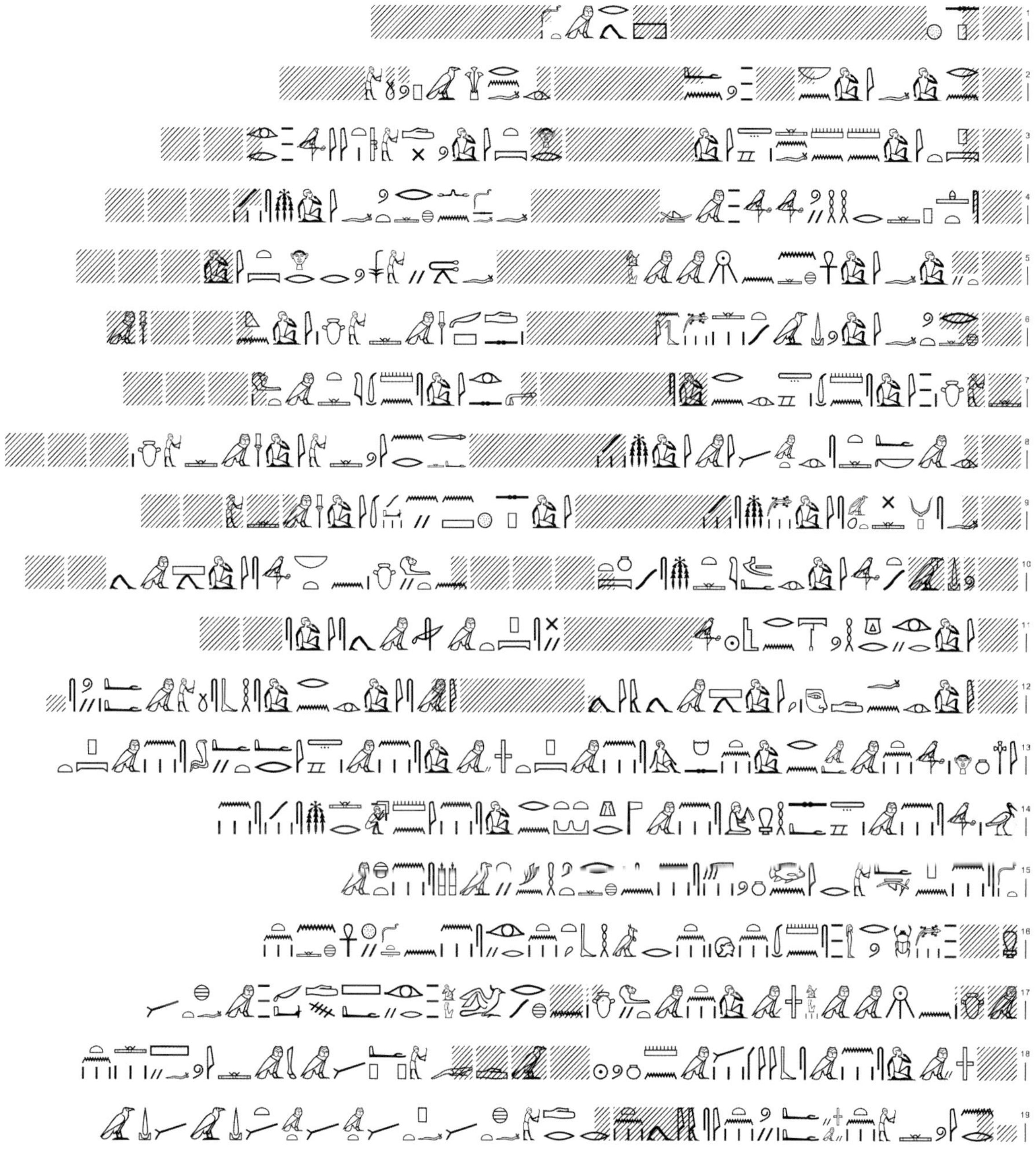

PLATE 6B *pBrooklyn 47.218.49* — COLUMN X + 6

Plate 7a *pBrooklyn 47.218.49* — COLUMN X + 7

Plate 7b *pBrooklyn 47.218.49* — COLUMN X + 7

PLATE 8A *pBrooklyn 47.218.49* — COLUMN X + 8

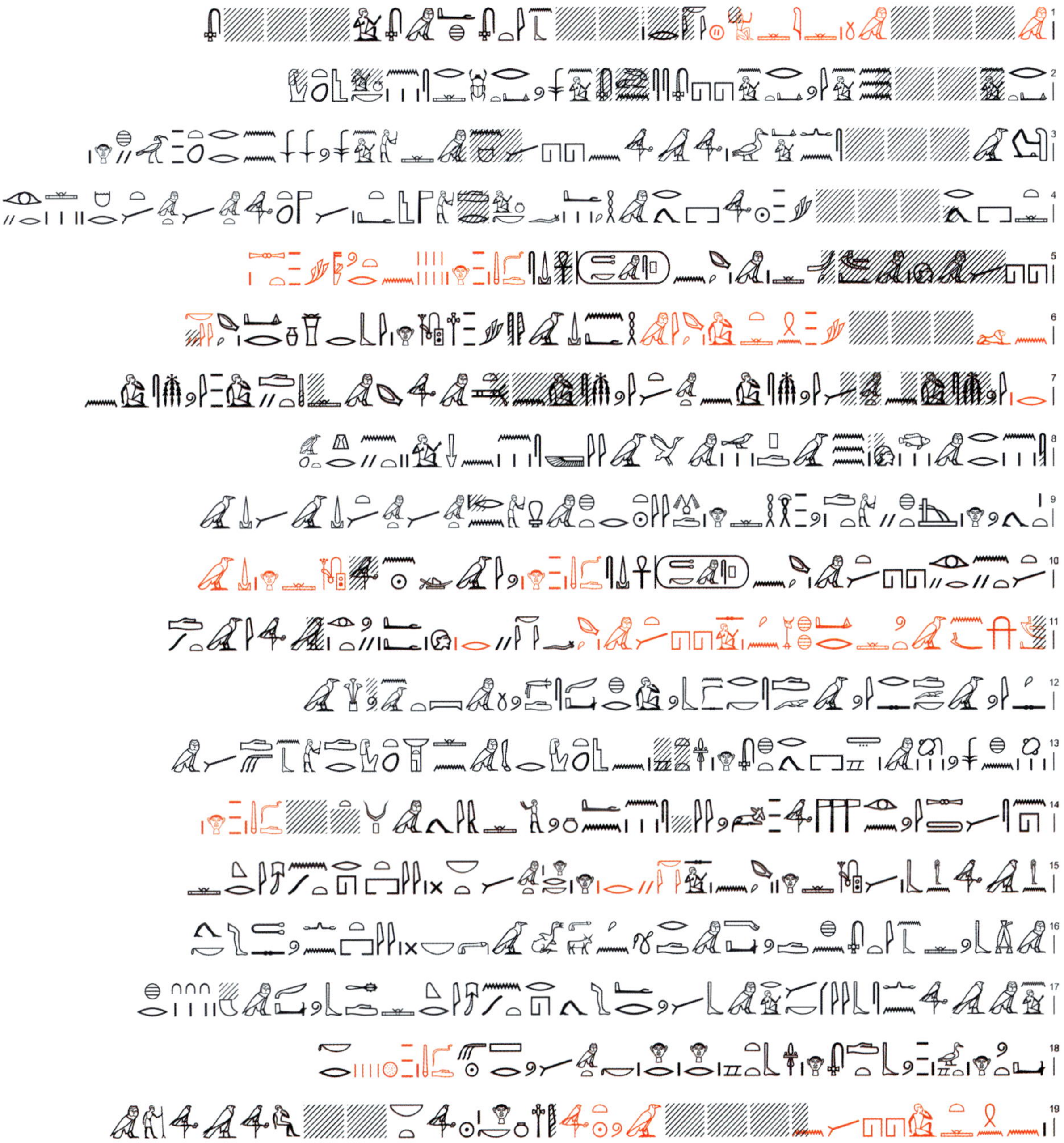

1
2
3
4
5
6
7
8
9
10
11
12
13
14
15
16
17
18
19

Plate 8b *pBrooklyn 47.218.49* — COLUMN X + 8

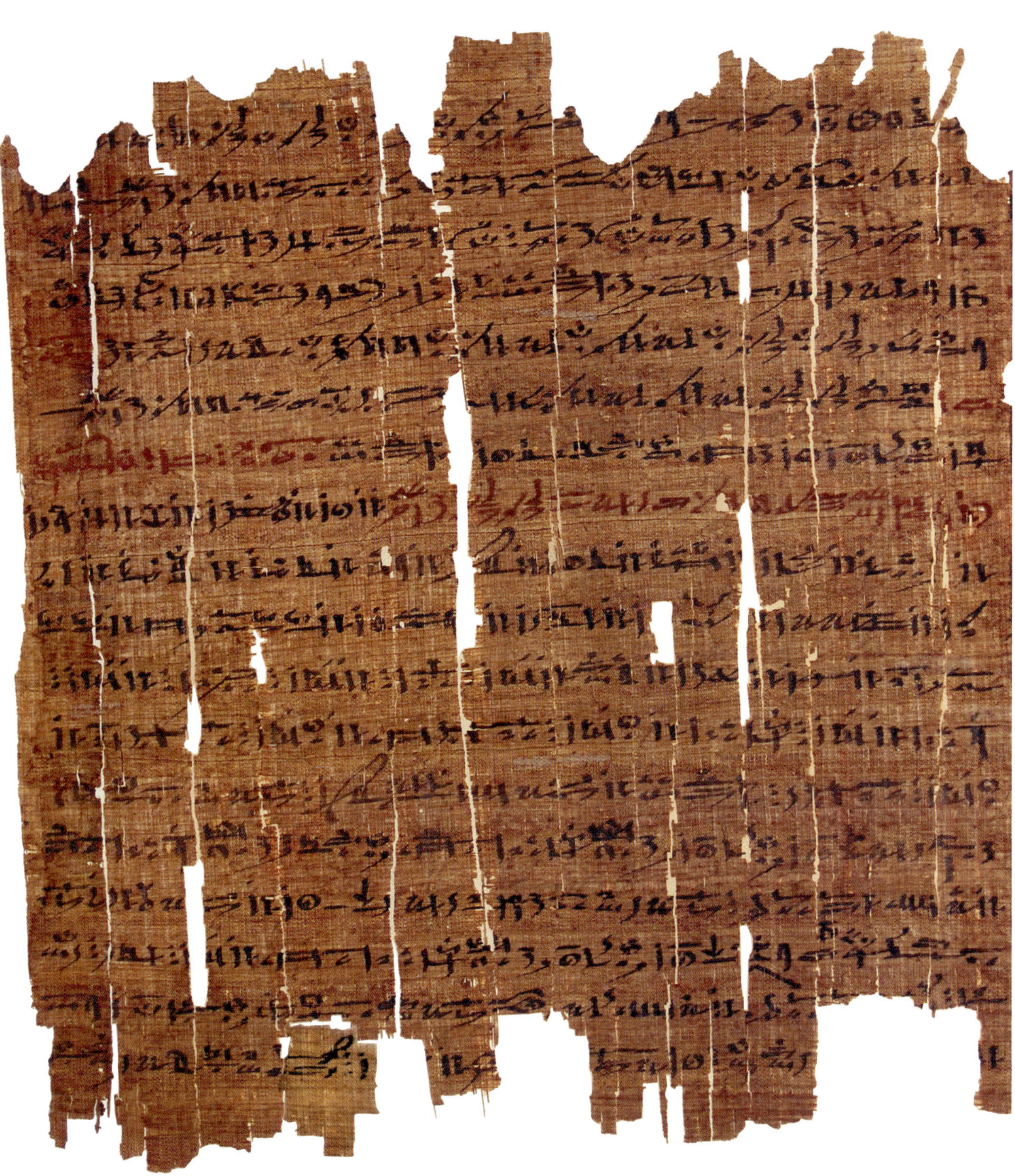

PLATE 9A *pBrooklyn 47.218.49* — COLUMN X + 9

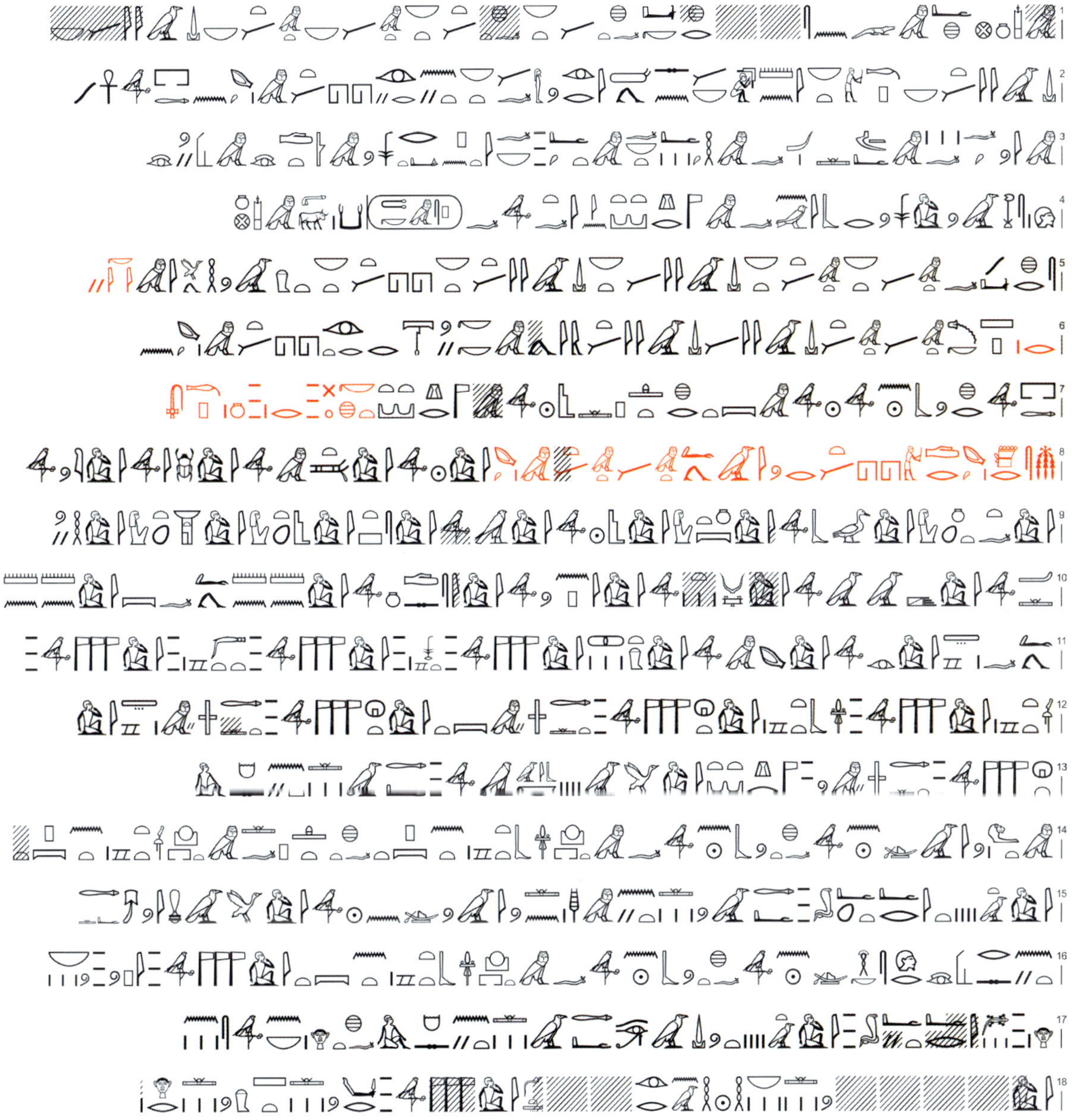

PLATE 9B *pBrooklyn 47.218.49* — COLUMN X + 9

PLATE 10A *pBrooklyn 47.218.49* — COLUMN X + 10

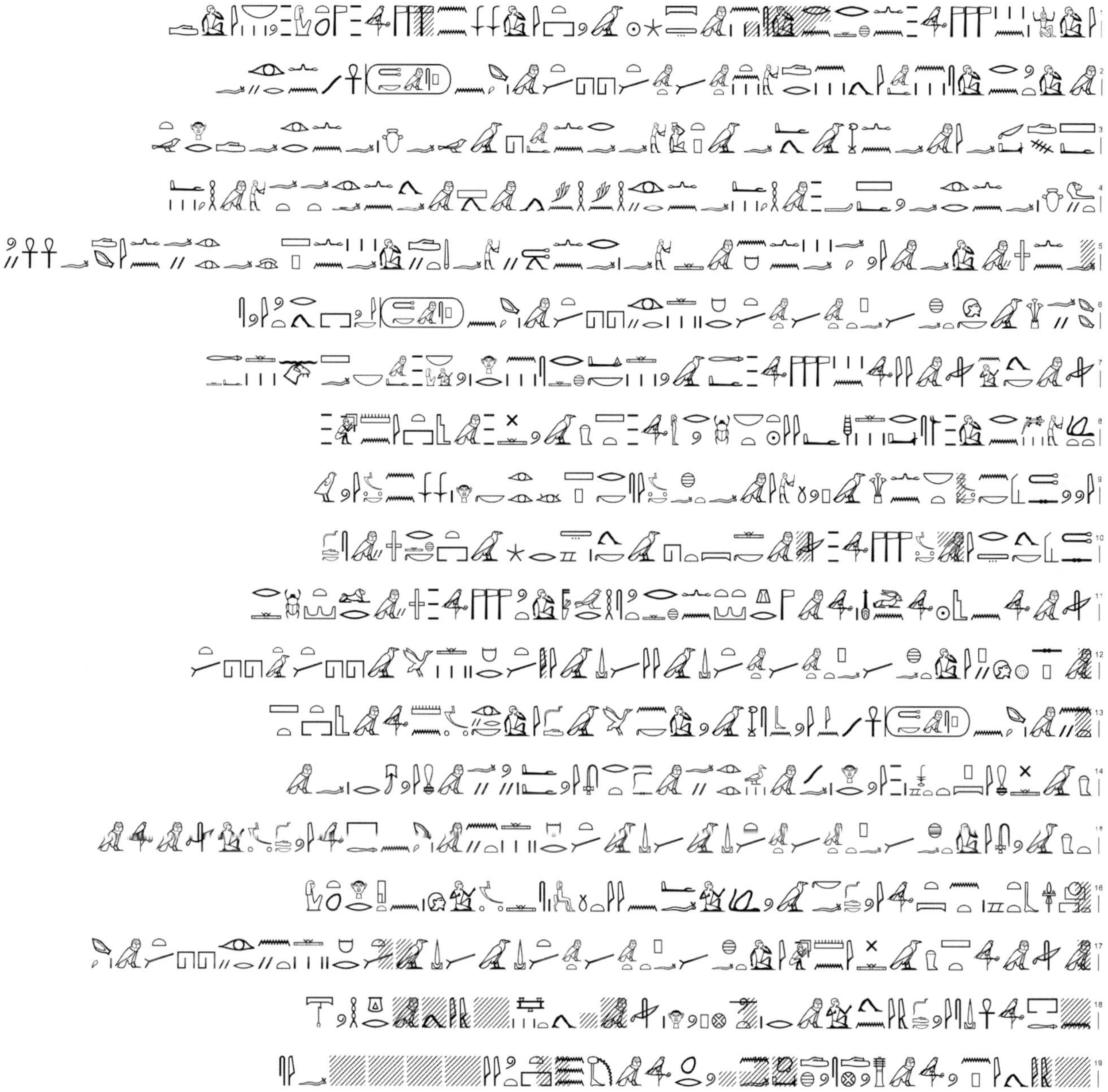

Plate 10b *pBrooklyn 47.218.49* — COLUMN X + 10

Plate 11a *pBrooklyn 47.218.49* — COLUMN X + 11

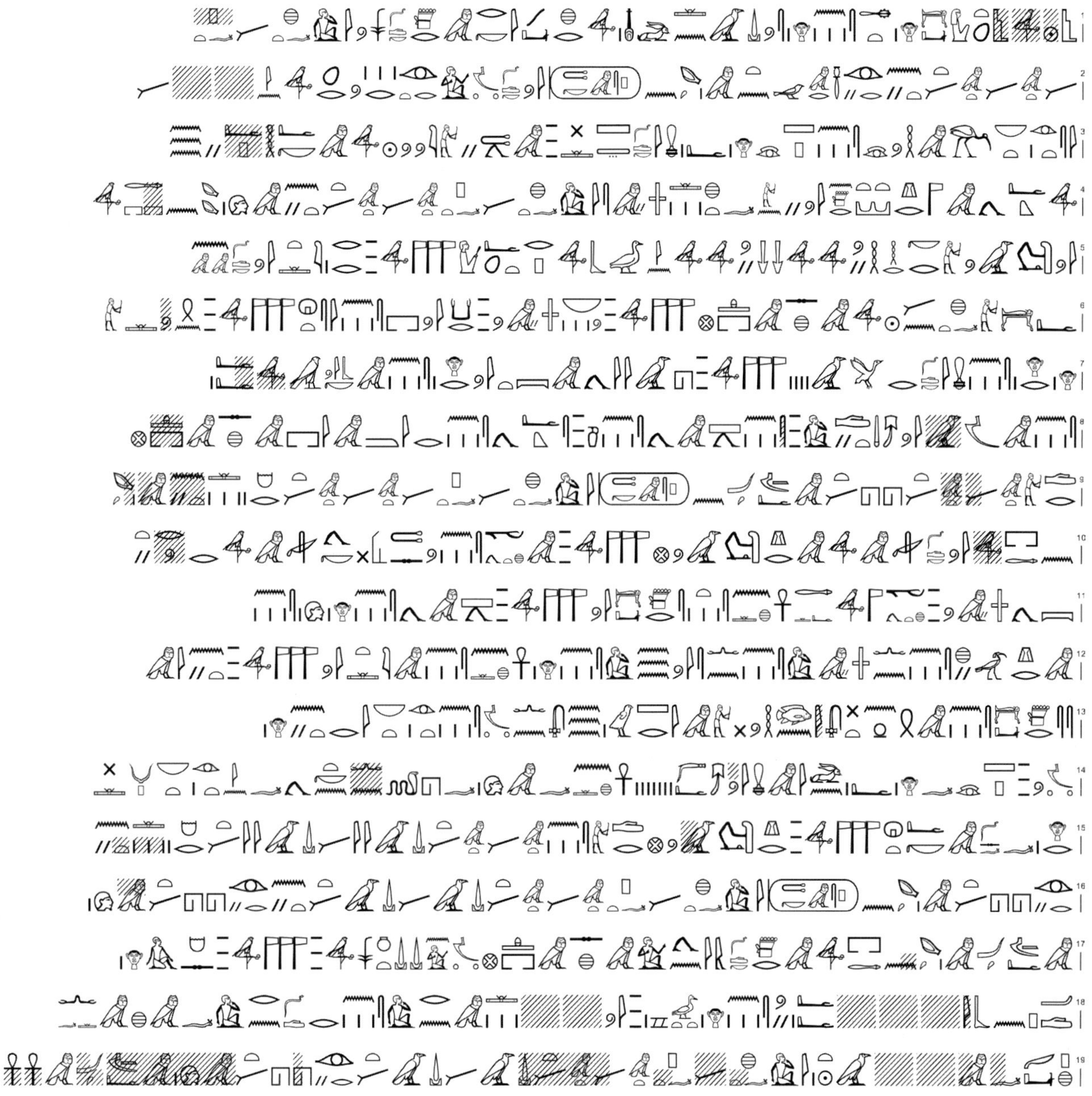

Plate 11b *pBrooklyn 47.218.49* — COLUMN X + 11

PLATE 12A *pBrooklyn 47.218.49* — COLUMN X + 12

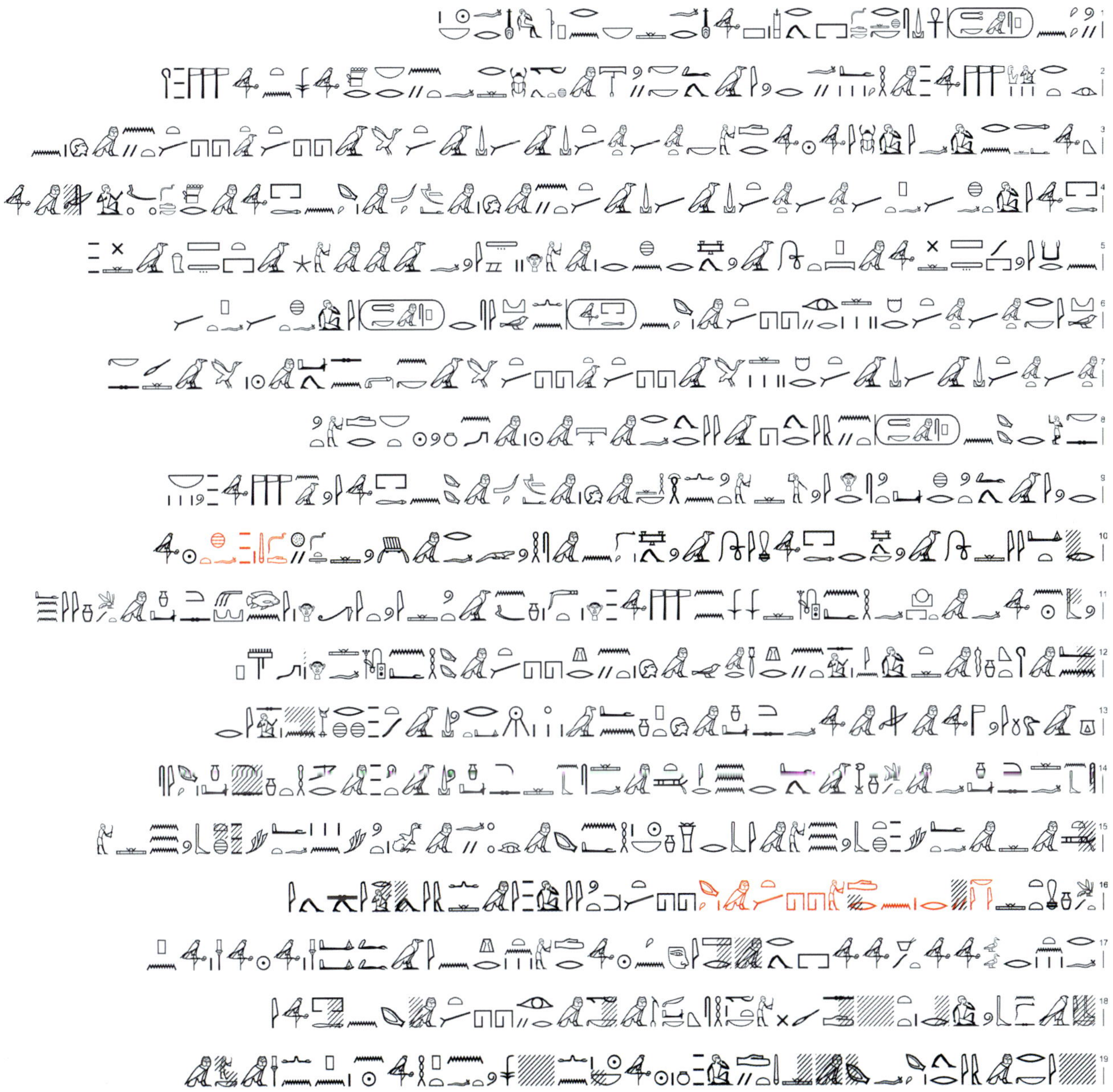

PLATE 12B *pBrooklyn 47.218.49* — COLUMN X + 12

Plate 13a *pBrooklyn 47.218.49* — COLUMN X + 13

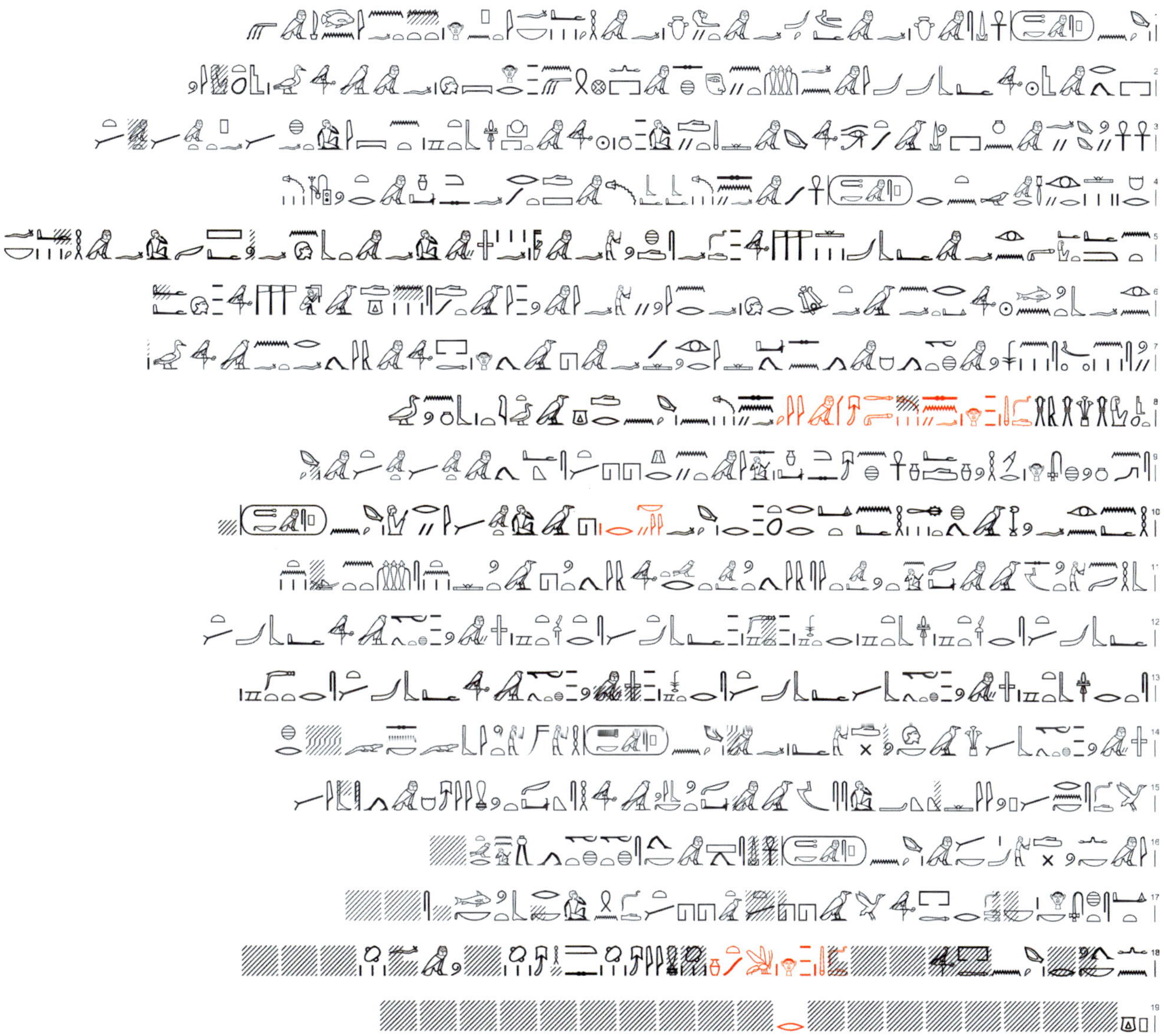

Plate 13b *pBrooklyn 47.218.49* — COLUMN X + 13

PLATE 14A *pBrooklyn 47.218.49* — COLUMN X + 14

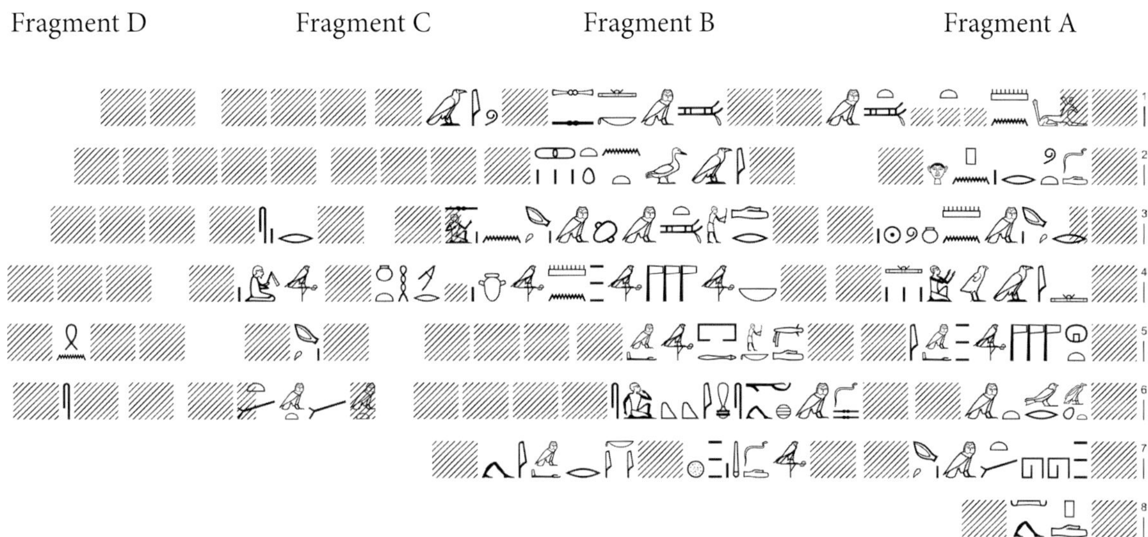

Plate 14b *pBrooklyn 47.218.49* — COLUMN X + 14

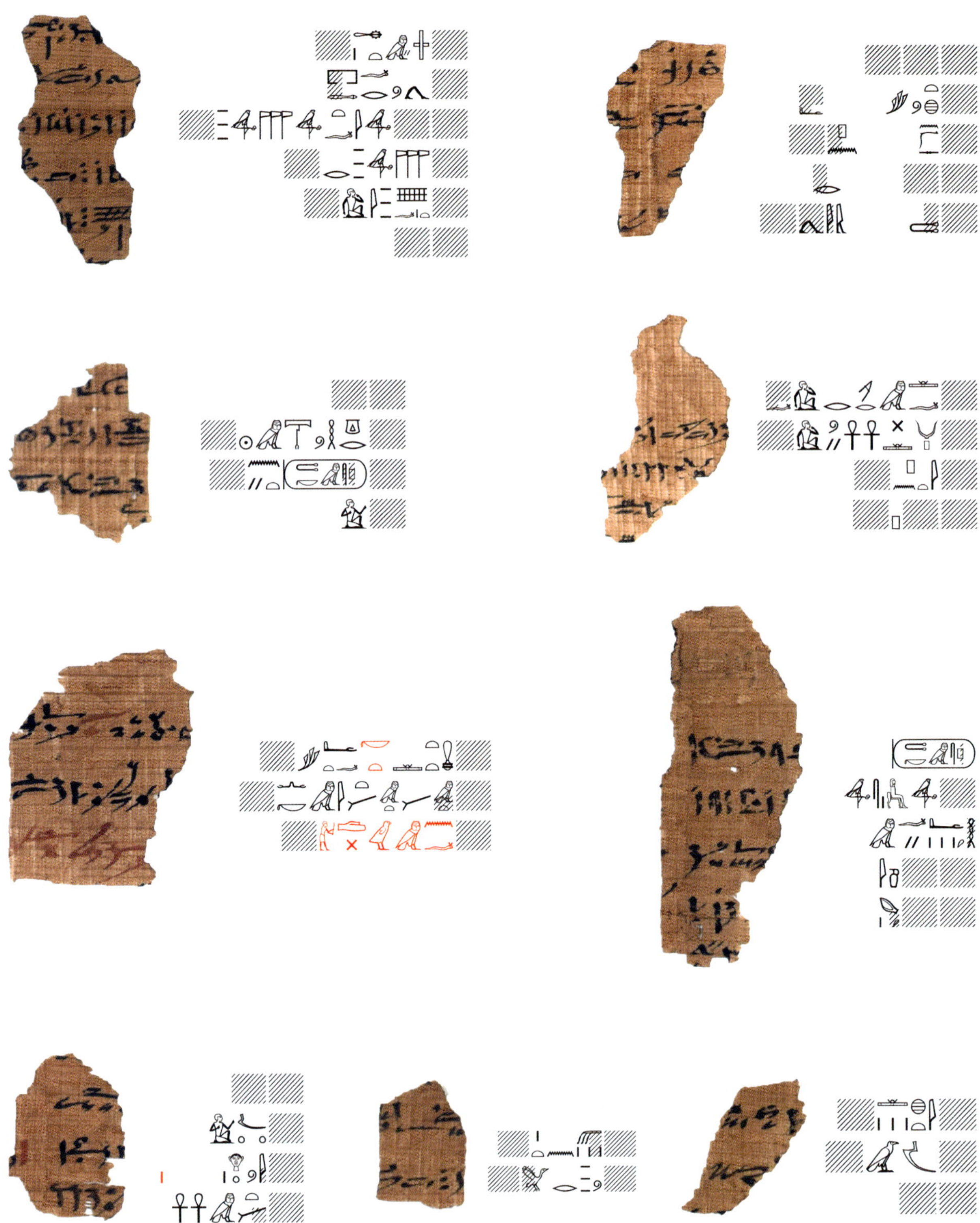

PLATE 15 Fragments from Column x + 1 or Lost Column(s) of *pBrooklyn 47.218.49*

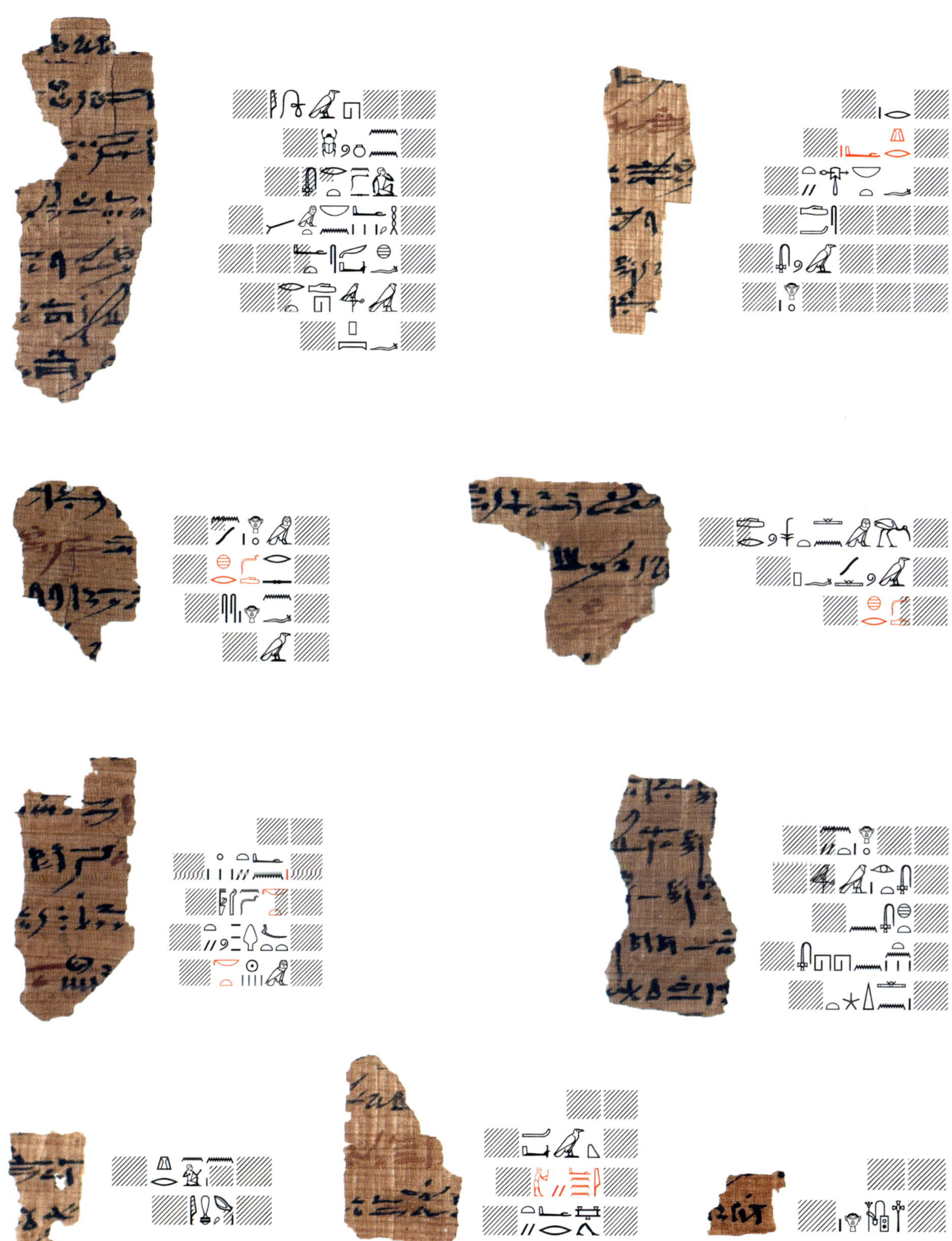

Plate 16 Fragments from Column x + 1 or Lost Column(s) of *pBrooklyn 47.218.49*

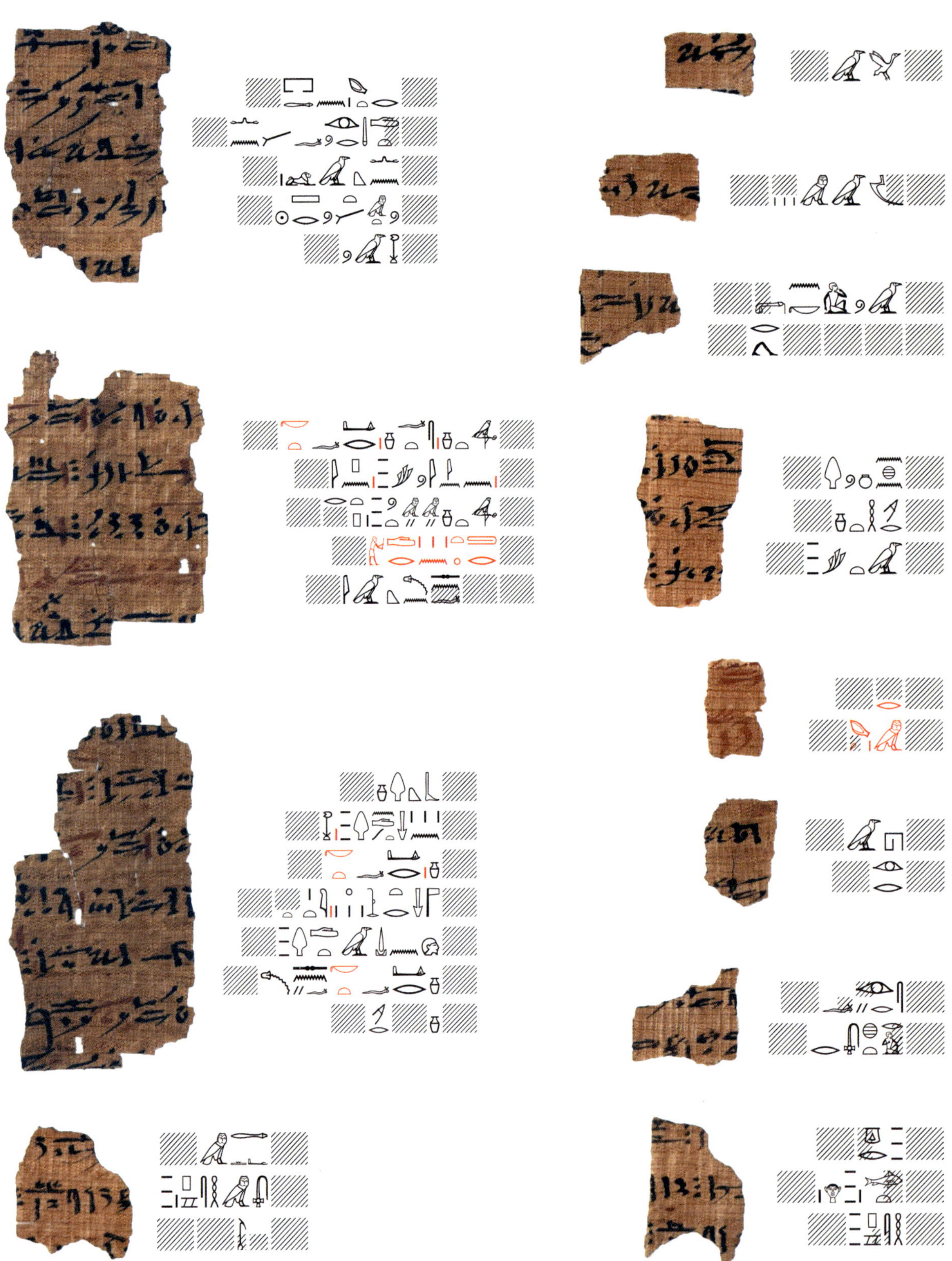

PLATE 17 Fragments from Column x + 1 or Lost Column(s) of *pBrooklyn 47.218.49*